NORTON's 2000.0

STAR ATLAS AND REFERENCE HANDBOOK

ARTHUR P. NORTON 1876–1955

NORTON's
2000.0

STAR ATLAS AND
REFERENCE HANDBOOK

EDITED BY
IAN RIDPATH

(Epoch 2000.0) Eighteenth Edition

Longman
Scientific &
Technical

Copublished in the United States with
John Wiley & Sons, Inc., New York

Longman Scientific & Technical
Longman Group UK Limited
Longman House, Burnt Mill, Harlow
Essex CM20 2JE, England
and Associated Companies throughout the world

Copublished in the United States with
John Wiley & Sons Inc., 605 Third Avenue, New York, NY 10158

© Longman Group UK Limited 1989

First published in 1989
Reprinted 1990, 1991

British Library Cataloguing in Publication Data
Norton, Arthur P. (Arthur Philip)
Norton's 2000.0 star atlas and reference
handbook. (Epoch 2000.0) – 18th ed.
1. Astronomy
I. Title   II. Ridpath, Ian
520

ISBN 0–582–03163–X

Library of Congress Cataloging-in-Publication Data
Norton, Arthur P. (Arthur Philip)
Star atlas and reference handbook (epoch 2000.0)
"Norton's 2000.0."
Includes index.
1. Astronomy—Observers' manuals   I. Ridpath, Ian.
II. Title.   III. Title: Norton's 2000.0.
QB65.N7   1989   523   89–12226
ISBN 0–470–21460–0

Set in 9/11 Linotron 202 Times Roman

CONTENTS

FOREWORD

Once in a blue moon a book appears that dramatically and forever changes its subject; in short, the work becomes an indispensable resource for generations. *Norton's Star Atlas* is such a work, the quintessential map of stars and fuzzy things that dot our nighttime sky. *Norton's* did for the heavens what Roger Tory Peterson's field guides did for nature study on Earth – both not only made recognizing objects fun and easy, they also created a paradigm for learning.

In 1956 the Los Angeles Astronomical Society held a prize draw among its junior members. The prize was, by the standards of those days and certainly by those of a 17 year old, a very nice mounting for a 6-inch telescope. Since only a winner would tell this story, I'll go on to say that my parents added a first-class mirror and a couple of eyepieces. Thus my career as a telescopic observer was launched.

What happened next, of course, was purchasing a copy of *Norton's* – famous even then and already in its 12th edition. It was not a big book, but it sure had a big impact on this budding amateur. Since then, I've referred to *Norton's* thousands upon thousands of times as I sought sights in the sky or checked facts at my editor's desk.

As I scan the maps in that ancient edition, I'm amazed at the history recorded upon them. There's a pencil line documenting the path of a fireball I saw in 1961 – one so bright that it made my dark-adapted eyes see a *negative* image of my surroundings. And there is a little 'x' in ballpoint, marking the position of what is now known as TT Coronae Borealis. As a youngster I proved this star varies in brightness, so now I feel very paternal toward it. On Map 9 another ballpoint 'x' identifies 3C 273. Undoubtedly I made that mark in 1963, the year quasars first staggered our imagination and the Universe became a less understandable place.

There is a clutter of other marks on my maps. Some mean nothing to me now, but their subjects must have once seemed very important. Oh yes . . . that dot must be Nova Cygni 1975, and the one below it Nova Delphini 1967 – now *that* was an interesting star, a so-called slow nova I observed every possible night for months. My old *Norton's* is truly an astronomical diary. Yours will surely turn into one too. In fact, it's the one book that has traveled with me throughout my career.

Looking back, *Norton's* had a two-fold influence. One, of course, was its collection of star charts, a pioneering presentation of six shield-shaped gores and two polar plots. All of them cover huge sweeps of sky, which greatly helped me recognize constellations and relate one to another. Yet, at the same time, the charts had enough detail to encourage me to seek countless new sights.

Norton's second influence was its text. It took some time for me to discover this handbook section – after all, observing is much more fun than reading! But after I began to explore it, I found a goldmine of observing tips, explanations of technical matters and snippets of history. The text also raised many 'how to' and 'what if' questions. These prompted more reading and led me to an ever greater appreciation of astronomy. I can trace a lot of what I know to inspirations from *Norton's*. It's no exaggeration to say it started me on a life-long love affair with astronomy. Heaven knows how many others would say the same – there must be an awful lot of us!

Now we have a new, expanded, and updated edition of *Norton's*. A superb tradition of excellence is carried forth once again. We will all benefit.

LEIF J. ROBINSON
Editor, *Sky & Telescope* magazine

PREFACE

Norton's Star Atlas first appeared in 1910. It achieved immediate success, due largely to its uniquely convenient arrangement of maps in slices, or gores, each covering approximately one-fifth of the sky, and its inclusion of stars down to sixth magnitude, the naked-eye limit. The Atlas was intended for owners of small telescopes, particularly those who wanted to find the objects of interest that were listed in two famous observing guides by nineteenth-century amateur astronomers: *Celestial Objects for Common Telescopes* by the Rev. T. W. Webb, and *Cycle of Celestial Objects* by W. H. Smyth. Over the years *Norton's Star Atlas* established an international reputation, becoming a standard reference work for amateur and professional astronomers alike.

The author of the Atlas, Arthur Philip Norton (1876–1955), was an amateur astronomer; his full-time occupation was as a schoolmaster. Had it not been for his Atlas he would have remained almost unknown in the world of astronomy.

Norton was born in Cardiff, Wales, the son of a clergyman. His interest in astronomy started as a small boy when he acquired a telescope that had belonged to his great-grandfather. After receiving his BA degree from Trinity College, Dublin, Norton taught at various schools in England. For 22 years he was geography master at the Judd School, Tonbridge, Kent, retiring in 1936. Norton seems to have published nothing other than the Atlas on which his fame rests, but during his lifetime it went through numerous editions and he updated the star maps twice.

Back in 1910 when *Norton's Star Atlas* first appeared there were no officially recognized boundaries to the constellations, a situation that the International Astronomical Union rectified in 1930. For the fifth edition of his Atlas, published in 1933, Arthur Norton redrew the maps to incorporate the newly defined IAU constellation boundaries, and he set the magnitude limit of the stars to 6.2, based on the *Harvard Revised Photometry* catalogue (the magnitude limit of the first edition was not precisely defined).

Celestial cartographers are faced with a problem that does not afflict their terrestrial counterparts – the coordinates of all stars are gradually changing with time, because of an effect called precession. This means that all star maps are bound to become progressively out of date. The epoch (i.e. the reference date for the star positions) of the original *Norton's* was 1920. For the ninth edition, published in 1943, Norton redrew his maps again, this time for the standard epoch of 1950.0, and further extended the magnitude limit of the stars to 6.35. That version of the maps remained in print long after Norton's death.

Inevitably, the passage of time has made another change of epoch necessary. For the 18th edition of *Norton's* the maps have been redrawn to the standard epoch of 2000.0, using modern technology that Norton could hardly have dreamed of.

The maps

An early decision in preparing this new edition was to retain the existing arrangement of the star maps, which has stood the test of time. In this edition, for the first time, both the polar charts and the equatorial gores use the same projection, known as Lambert's azimuthal equidistant projection, which allows large areas of sky to be represented with little distortion. (Norton never stated the projections that he used; the gores were apparently plotted on a modified globular projection of his own devising.)

In our maps, the plane of the projection surface touches the celestial sphere at the poles for the polar charts and at the celestial equator for the gores. Each gore has been projected from its central meridian at the equator to minimize distortion. All projections have been generated by computer for maximum accuracy.

The projection software was written at the cartographic company of John Bartholomew & Son in Edinburgh. Initial plots for checking were output at Bartholomews using Apricot microcomputers linked to a Calcomp pen plotter. The outlines of the Milky Way, the Magellanic Clouds, the galactic equator and the ecliptic were added at this stage by our cartographic consultant, Mike Swan. In addition to being a professional cartographer with the Ordnance Survey, he is a deep-sky observer with the Webb Society.

His expertise in both astronomy and cartography was a vital ingredient in the project.

With all the data converted into machine-readable form, the charts were generated on film at Bartholomews by a Scitex laser plotter. These films then went to Mike Swan for hand-labelling and final checking. Films combining the star charts and labelling were output at Bartholomews by the Scitex laser plotter, from which printing plates were produced.

The maps in *Norton's 2000.0* mark a new advance in the computerized production of star atlases. In its previous editions, *Norton's* earned the reputation of being the most famous and most widely used star atlas in the world. We believe that the quality and accuracy of the maps in this edition will successfully carry the tradition of *Norton's Star Atlas* well into the 21st century.

Data

For information on positions and magnitudes of stars we adopted the Yale *Bright Star Catalogue* (BS) and its Supplement. These are probably the most complete and reliable sources of data on naked-eye stars available. The BS contains the same stars as the *Harvard Revised Photometry* catalogue that Arthur Norton used for his maps, but with considerably improved magnitude measurements. We chose a magnitude limit of 6.49 (i.e. encompassing all stars of 6th magnitude and brighter), against the 6.35 used for the 1950.0 maps in *Norton's*.

We thank Dorrit Hoffleit of Yale University Observatory, senior author of the BS, and Wayne Warren of the National Space Science Data Center in Greenbelt, Maryland, for supplying magnetic tapes of the 5th edition of the *Bright Star Catalogue* ahead of publication, and for their interest in our project. They also supplied tapes of the 1983 Supplement to the BS, from which we extracted stars brighter than mag. 6.50 that were not included in the main BS (because they had been missed by the original *Harvard Revised Photometry*).

Data required for *Norton's 2000.0* were extracted from the BS tapes by the Royal Observatory, Edinburgh, and were supplied to John Bartholomew & Son with the constellation boundaries added. Data for the galactic charts were also supplied by the ROE.

Even in a computerized operation such as this, considerable manual intervention was still necessary. Since the BS does not include deep-sky objects, lists of star clusters, nebulae and galaxies were drawn up by Mike Swan for addition to the stellar database. He also spent many hours identifying variable stars and stars that are both variable and double for depiction by special symbols on the maps. Ordinary double stars were identified directly from the BS tapes.

In all, the maps in *Norton's 2000.0* show approximately 8700 stars, more than in any previous edition of *Norton's Star Atlas*. The star symbols are graduated in whole-magnitude steps, for ease of identification. The few stars of magnitude 0 and −1 are given the same size symbol as stars of magnitude +1. The percentage of stars in each magnitude range is as follows:

Magnitude range	Percentage of stars in *Norton's 2000.0*
−1.50 to +1.49	0.25
+1.50 to +2.49	0.9
+2.50 to +3.49	2.5
+3.50 to +4.49	7.2
+4.50 to +5.49	22.6
+5.50 to +6.49	66.5

Double and multiple stars

Stars that are listed in the BS as double or multiple are identified on the maps with a special symbol (a line bisecting the star dot) if their separation is at least 0.1 arcsec. The exceptions to this system are stars whose components are wide enough to be plotted separately; these do not carry the double-star symbol unless they have other, closer companions. Spectroscopic binaries and other exceptionally close doubles (for example, those found by occultation studies or speckle interferometry) are not denoted by the double-star symbol on the maps.

In the list of interesting objects that precedes each map in *Norton's 2000.0*, the double stars cited are restricted to those with a combined magnitude brighter than 6.5. All the double stars named in these lists are labelled on the maps.

Variable stars

Those variable stars with a range of at least 0.1 mag. and a maximum magnitude brighter than 6.5, as listed in the BS and other sources consulted by us, are identified with a variable-star symbol. This symbol consists of a ring surrounding a solid dot; the size of the outer ring indicates the maximum magnitude of the star. Those variables, including novae, whose minimum brightness takes them below our map limit of mag. 6.49 are denoted by an open circle only. More than 500 variable stars are identified on the maps, including over 40 that are not in the BS or its Supplement but for which we found evidence of maxima above mag. 6.5 (certain classes of variable, particularly those of long period, have ranges of variation that are not precisely bounded). A combined symbol is used to identify nearly 150 stars that are both variable and double.

The lists of variable stars that accompany the charts are believed to include all variables that have an amplitude of at least 0.4 mag. and a maximum brighter than approximately 6.5 mag. All variables contained in these lists are labelled on the maps.

Deep-sky objects

In a departure from previous editions of *Norton's*, we have used separate symbols to distinguish each class of deep-sky object: open star clusters, globular star clusters, diffuse nebulae, planetary nebulae and galaxies. This considerably increases the usefulness of the maps for observers (prior to *Norton's 2000.0* all deep-sky objects were denoted by one standard symbol, a group of dots). Additionally, *Norton's 2000.0* depicts the true shape and extent of those nebulae and galaxies that are larger than about 0°.5 in apparent diameter. In all, over 600 deep-sky objects are shown on the maps in this edition. The most interesting of them are briefly described in the notes preceding each map.

Reference handbook

Over the years the Reference Handbook section has become as valuable a part of *Norton's* as the Atlas itself. In the first edition the text amounted to only 18 pages, mostly written by James Gall Inglis. By the 5th edition in 1933 the text had grown to 51 pages, and by the 17th edition in 1978 it covered 116 pages.

For *Norton's 2000.0* we have rewritten the text almost entirely while attempting to retain the essential character of *Norton's*. The emphasis is on reference information and practical observing advice that is often difficult to obtain elsewhere.

As in previous editions we have decided against giving a bibliography, but mention must be made of *Burnham's Celestial Handbook* (in three volumes) by Robert Burnham Jr. (Dover Publications). This is an invaluable companion to *Norton's*, and even though it is based on epoch 1950.0 it remains a classic guide for observers. A more compact handbook, with individual constellation charts to epoch 2000.0 and notes on objects of interest, is *Guide to Stars and Planets* by Ian Ridpath and Wil Tirion (Collins/Universe).

ACKNOWLEDGEMENTS

The editor of *Norton's 2000.0* acknowledges with gratitude the following contributors and consultants who have applied their expertise to various sections of the text, as indicated: Margaret Penston (position), John Pilkington (time), Bernard Yallop (tables 3, 5, 6, 7, 8, 9), James Muirden (visual observing, telescopes and accessories), Robin Scagell (astrophotography), David Stickland (the Sun), Lionel Wilson (the Moon), Richard Baum (Mercury, Venus and the outer planets), John Murray (Mars), John Rogers (Jupiter), Alan Heath (Saturn), Daniel Green and Brian Marsden (minor planets and comets), George Spalding (meteors), Leslie Morrison and Norman Wright (eclipses and occultations), Neil Bone (aurorae), Russell Eberst (artificial satellites, John Isles (stars), Brian Jones (clusters, nebulae and galaxies) and Tony Jones (units and notation). The computer program for calculating the positions and separations of visual binaries was written by Ted Wood. John Isles prepared the lists of interesting double and variable stars that accompany the star maps.

The maps of the Moon are based on the US Air Force Lunar Reference Mosaic; the overlays of named features and the list of lunar formations were prepared by John Murray. John Murray also drew the map of Mars and prepared the list of Martian features.

Leif Robinson of *Sky & Telescope* reviewed the entire manuscript and made many useful suggestions. In addition, the following people reviewed specific parts of the manuscript: Denis Buczynski, Dennis di Cicco, David Graham, Andrew Hollis, Tony Jones, Graham Keitch, John Murray, Robin Scagell and John Smith. Bob Marriott's researches uncovered valuable biographical information on Arthur P. Norton. The photograph of Arthur P. Norton was supplied by G. M. Taylor, deputy headmaster of the Judd School.

The manuscript was painstakingly prepared for the printer by John Woodruff, who performed beyond the call of duty in assiduously weeding out remaining blemishes and helping to correct them. He also provided valuable assistance with the proofs. The final version of the text was materially improved by his skill.

A book of such complexity could not have been produced without the full support of the staff at Longman. In particular, I would like to thank Michael Rodgers and Sara Wilbourne for their personal interest and patient encouragement during the long journey from the inception of the project to its completion.

Ian Ridpath

LIST OF TABLES

I

STAR CHARTS

INDEX TO THE CONSTELLATIONS

NORTHERN INDEX MAP

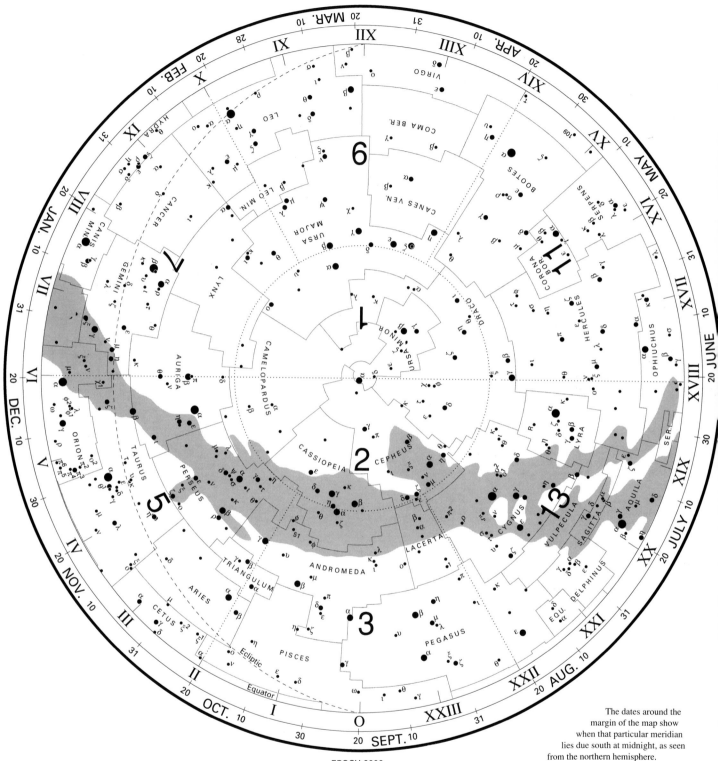

EPOCH 2000

The dates around the margin of the map show when that particular meridian lies due south at midnight, as seen from the northern hemisphere.

SOUTHERN INDEX MAP

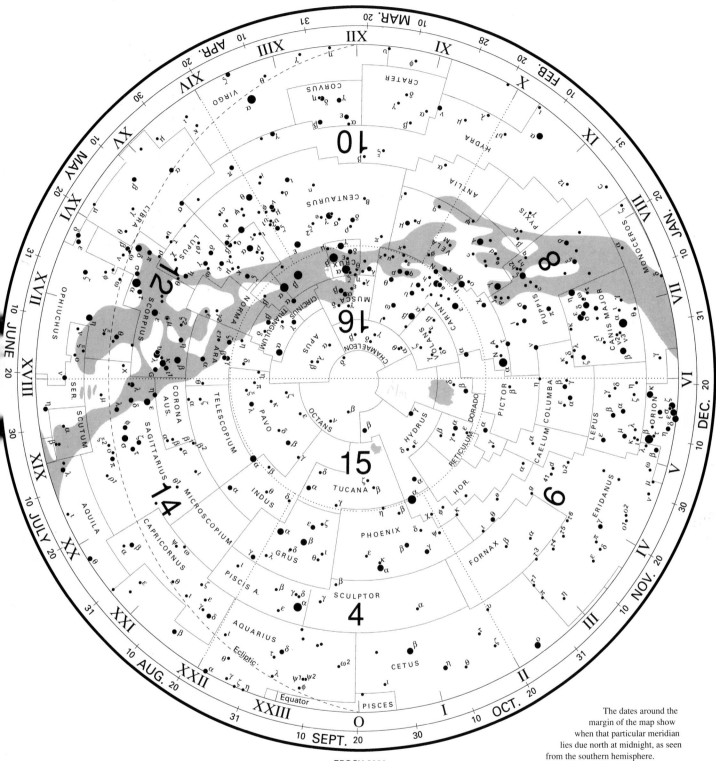

EPOCH 2000

The dates around the margin of the map show when that particular meridian lies due north at midnight, as seen from the southern hemisphere.

Interesting Objects, Maps 1 and 2

Dec. +60° to +90°

Double stars

ADS	Star	RA 2000.0 h m	Dec. ° ′	Magnitudes	PA °	Dist. ″	Notes
624	HN 122	00 45.7	+74 59	var. 9.4	160	36.1	Optical; fixed. A is YZ Cas
782	γ Cas	00 56.7	+60 43	var. 11.2	248	2.1	Little change
1129	ψ Cas	01 25.9	+68 08	4.7 8.9	113	25.0	Closing, PA increasing. B is double: 9.6, 9.7; 254°, 2″.9; fixed
1598	48 Cas	02 02.0	+70 54	4.7 6.4	263	0.9	Binary, 60 years[a]
1860	ι Cas	02 29.1	+67 24	4.6 6.9	230	2.5	AB binary, 840 years[a]. C slowly closing, PA
				8.4	114	7.2	increasing. Fine object in 100 mm
1477	α UMi	02 31.8	+89 16	2.0 9.0	218	18.4	Optical pair. Slow increase of PA
2867	OΣ67 Cam	03 57.1	+61 07	5.3 8.5	44	1.9	Fixed; yellowish, greenish (by contrast)
4177	19 Cam	05 37.3	+64 09	6.0 10.0	47	1.3	Fixed
6724	Σ1193 UMa	08 20.7	+72 24	6.1 9.1	87	43.1	Little change
7203	σ² UMa	09 10.4	+67 08	4.8 8.2	355	3.9	Binary, 1100 years[a]
7402	23 UMa	09 31.5	+63 04	3.7 8.9	270	22.7	Fixed
8197	OΣ235 UMa	11 32.3	+61 05	5.8 7.1	341	0.6	Binary, 73 years[a]
8682	Σ1694 Cam	12 49.2	+83 25	5.3 5.8	326	21.6	Fixed
10058	η Dra	16 24.0	+61 31	2.7 8.7	142	5.2	Slow binary
10279	20 Dra	16 56.4	+65 02	7.1 7.3	68	1.3	Binary, 580 years[a]
10660	26 Dra	17 35.0	+61 52	5.3 8.0	330	1.7	Binary, 76 years[a]
10759	ψ¹ Dra	17 41.9	+72 09	4.9 6.1	15	30.3	Fixed
11061	40/41 Dra	18 00.2	+80 00	5.7 6.1	232	19.3	Slow binary, but little change
12789	Σ2573 Dra	19 40.2	+60 30	6.2 9.5	27	18.2	Fixed
13007	ε Dra	19 48.2	+70 16	3.8 7.4	15	3.1	Slow binary; PA increasing
13371	Σ2640 Dra	20 04.7	+63 53	6.3 10.2	16	5.6	Opening slowly with decrease of PA
13524	κ Cep	20 08.9	+77 43	4.4 8.4	122	7.4	Fixed
15032	β Cep	21 28.7	+70 34	3.2 7.9	249	13.3	Fixed
15600	ξ Cep	22 03.8	+64 38	4.4 6.5	274	8.2	Binary, 4000 years[a]
15719	Σ2883 Cep	22 10.6	+70 08	5.6 7.6	254	14.6	Fixed
15764	Σ2893 Cep	22 12.0	+73 04	6.2 8.3	348	28.9	Fixed
16538	π Cep	23 07.9	+75 23	4.6 6.6	355	1.1	Binary, 150 years[a]
16666	ο Cep	23 18.6	+68 07	4.9 7.1	223	2.8	Binary, 800 years[a]. Test for 50 mm
17022	6 Cas	23 48.8	+62 13	5.5 8.0	193	1.6	Fixed

[a] Orbital elements for these binaries are given in Table 46. PA and Dist. are predictions for 2000.0.

Variable stars

Star	RA 2000.0		Dec.		Type	Range	Period	Spectral type	Notes
	h	m	°	′		(mags)	(d)		
YZ Cas	00	45.7	+74	59	EA/DM	5.7–6.1	4.47	A2+F2	See Double stars
γ Cas	00	56.7	+60	43	GCAS	1.6–3.0	—	B0	X-ray source. See Double stars
RZ Cas	02	48.9	+69	38	EA/SD	6.2–7.7	1.20	A3	
SU Cas	02	52.0	+68	53	DCEPS	5.7–6.2	1.95	F	
ST Cam	04	51.2	+68	10	SRB	6–8	300?	C	
Y Dra	09	42.4	+77	51	M	6.2–15.0	325.79	M	
R UMa	10	44.6	+68	47	M	6.5–13.7	301.62	M	Mean range 7.5–13.0
VY UMa	10	45.1	+67	25	LB	5.9–7.0	—	C	
RY Dra	12	56.4	+66	00	SRB?	6.0–8.0	200?	C	
AZ Dra	16	40.7	+72	40	LB	6.4–7.2	—	M	
VW Dra	17	16.5	+60	40	SRD?	6.0–7.0	170?	K	
UX Dra	19	21.6	+76	34	SRA?	5.9–7.1	168	C	Eclipsing?
T Cep	21	09.5	+68	29	M	5.2–11.3	388.14	M	Mean range 6.0–10.3
VV Cep	21	56.7	+63	38	EA/GS+SRC	4.8–5.4	7430	M+B8	Main oscillations with period of 118 d, also 25, 58 and 150 d. Eclipses too shallow for visual detection

Clusters, nebulae and galaxies

NGC	M	RA 2000.0		Dec.		Notes
		h	m	°	′	
225	—	00	43	+61	47	7th-mag. open cluster in Cassiopeia
581	103	01	33	+60	42	Open cluster in Cassiopeia; 7th mag., consists of faint stars
663	—	01	46	+61	15	Open cluster in Cassiopeia; good binocular object
1502	—	04	08	+62	20	6th-mag. open cluster in Camelopardalis
2403	—	07	37	+65	36	Spiral galaxy in Camelopardalis; 8th mag.
3031	81	09	56	+69	04	Spiral galaxy in Ursa Major; 7th mag.
3034	82	09	56	+69	41	Peculiar galaxy in Ursa Major seen edge-on; 8th mag.; forms a pair with M81
6543	—	17	59	+66	38	Planetary nebula in Draco; 9th mag., one of the brightest of its kind
7654	52	23	24	+61	35	Open cluster in Cassiopeia; 7th mag.

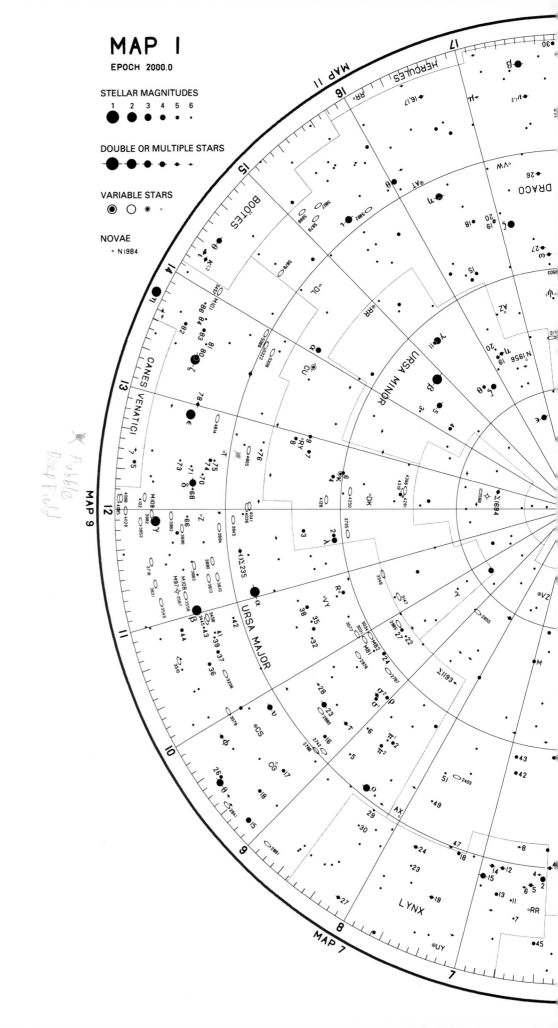

MAP I

EPOCH 2000.0

STELLAR MAGNITUDES

1 2 3 4 5 6

DOUBLE OR MULTIPLE STARS

VARIABLE STARS

NOVAE

° N 1984

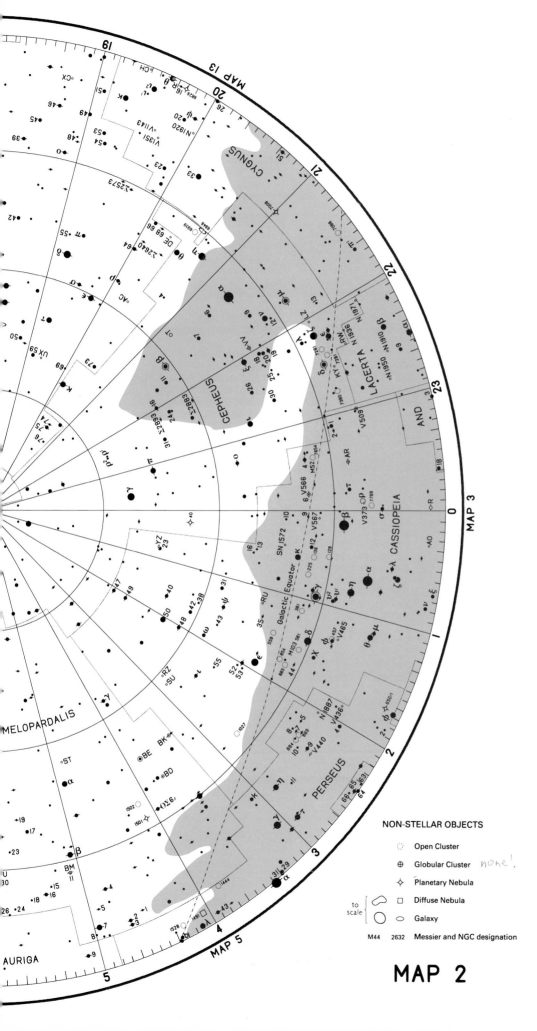

NON-STELLAR OBJECTS

- ⊙ Open Cluster
- ⊕ Globular Cluster   none!
- ✦ Planetary Nebula
- ▢ Diffuse Nebula
- ⬭ Galaxy

to scale

M44 2632   Messier and NGC designation

MAP 2

Interesting Objects, Maps 3 and 4

RA 22h to 02h, Dec. +60° to −60°

Double stars

ADS	Star	RA		Dec.		Magnitudes		PA	Dist.	Notes
			2000.0							
		h	m	°	′			°	″	
15536	η PsA	22	00.8	−28	27	5.8	6.8	115	1.7	Fixed
15753	41 Aqr	22	14.3	−21	04	5.6	7.1	114	5.0	Slow binary, little change
15828	Σ2894 Lac	22	18.9	+37	46	6.1	8.3	194	15.6	Fixed
15934	53 Aqr	22	26.6	−16	45	6.4	6.6	334	3.1	Closing, slow increase of PA; binary
15971	ζ Aqr	22	28.8	−00	01	4.3	4.5	192	2.1	Binary, 850 years[a]. Opening with decrease of PA. Test for 50 mm
15987	δ Cep	22	29.2	+58	25	var.	7.5	191	41.0	C.p.m.; yellow, bluish
	β PsA	22	31.5	−32	21	4.4	7.9	172	30.3	Fixed; optical
16095	8 Lac	22	35.9	+39	38	5.7	6.5	186	22.4	C.p.m.; distant stars, mags. 9.3 and 10.5
16261	ξ Peg	22	46.7	+12	10	4.2	12.2	100	11.5	Slow binary; PA decreasing
16268	τ¹ Aqr	22	47.7	−14	03	5.8	9.0	121	23.7	Optical; closing, PA increasing
	γ PsA	22	52.5	−32	53	4.5	8.0	262	4.2	PA slowly decreasing; slow binary
	θ Gru	23	06.9	−43	31	4.5	7.0	75	1.1	Slow binary; PA increasing
16633	ψ¹ Aqr	23	15.9	−09	05	4.5	10.3	312	49.6	C.p.m.; B is very close double
16672	94 Aqr	23	19.1	−13	28	5.3	7.3	350	12.7	Slow binary; yellowish, bluish
16836	72 Peg	23	34.0	+31	20	5.7	5.8	97	0.5	Binary, 240 years[a]
	θ Phe	23	39.5	−46	38	6.6	7.2	275	4.0	Slow binary, little change
16957	78 Peg	23	44.0	+29	22	5.0	8.1	235	1.0	Binary, PA increasing
16979	107 Aqr	23	46.0	−18	41	5.7	6.7	136	6.6	Opening; slow binary
17140	σ Cas	23	59.0	+55	45	5.0	7.1	326	3.0	Fixed. Fine field in low power
17175	85 Peg	00	02.2	+27	05	5.8	8.9	184	0.7	Binary, 26 years[a]
111	κ¹ Scl	00	09.3	−27	59	6.1	6.2	265	1.4	Slow binary
191	35 Psc	00	15.0	+08	49	6.0	7.6	148	11.6	Fixed
434	λ Cas	00	31.8	+54	31	5.5	5.8	191	0.6	Binary, 600 years[a]
513	π And	00	36.9	+33	43	4.4	8.6	173	35.9	C.p.m.
520	β395 Cet	00	37.3	−24	46	6.3	6.4	289	0.5	Binary, 25 years[a]
558	55 Psc	00	39.9	+21	26	5.4	8.7	194	6.5	Fixed; orange, bluish
671	η Cas	00	49.1	+57	49	3.5	7.5	317	12.9	Binary, 500 years[a]
683	65 Psc	00	49.9	+27	43	6.3	6.3	297	4.4	Fixed
755	36 And	00	55.0	+23	38	6.0	6.4	313	0.9	Binary, 165 years[a]
899	ψ¹ Psc	01	05.6	+21	28	5.6	5.8	159	30.0	Fixed
	β Phe	01	06.1	−46	43	4.0	4.2	346	1.4	Slow binary, PA decreasing
996	ζ Psc	01	13.7	+07	35	5.6	6.5	63	23.0	C.p.m.
1003	37 Cet	01	14.4	−07	55	5.2	8.7	331	49.7	Fixed
1081	42 Cet	01	19.8	−00	31	6.5	6.8	11	1.6	Slow binary, PA increasing. B is very close binary
	p Eri	01	39.8	−56	12	5.8	5.8	191	11.5	Binary, 500 years[a]
1394	ε Scl	01	45.6	−25	03	5.4	8.6	23	4.7	Slow binary, 1200 years[a]
1457	1 Ari	01	50.1	+22	17	6.2	7.4	166	2.8	Slow binary. Test for 50 mm
1507	γ Ari	01	53.5	+19	18	4.8	4.8	0	7.8	Slowly closing. Beautiful, very easy pair
1538	Σ186 Cet	01	55.9	+01	51	6.8	6.8	60	1.1	Binary, 170 years[a]
1563	λ Ari	01	57.9	+23	36	4.9	7.7	46	37.4	Fixed

[a] Orbital elements for these binaries are given in Table 46. PA and Dist. are predictions for 2000.0.

Variable stars

Star	RA 2000.0 h m	Dec. ° '	Type	Range (mags)	Period (d)	Spectral type	Notes
DX Aqr	22 02.4	−16 58	EA/KE?	6.4–6.8	0.95	A2	Secondary minimum 6.7
AR Lac	22 08.7	+45 44	EA/AR/RS	6.1–6.8	1.98	G2+K0	Secondary minimum 6.4
π^1 Gru	22 22.7	−45 57	SRB	5.4–6.7	150?	S	
RW Cep	22 23.1	+55 58	SRD	6.2–7.6	346?	K	
S Gru	22 26.1	−48 26	M	6.0–15.0	401.51	M	Mean range 7.7–14.4
δ Cep	22 29.2	+58 25	DCEP	3.5–4.4	5.37	G	See Double stars
KY Cep	22 32.3	+57 40	★	4?–13?	—	Pec	Flare of 65 seconds
V509 Cas	23 00.1	+56 57	SRD	4.8–5.5	—	G+B1	Pulsations with period 3 years; shell ejected 1975
β Peg	23 03.8	+28 05	LB	2.3–2.7	—	M	
R Aqr	23 43.8	−15 17	M	5.8–12.4	386.96	M+Pec	Range varies; possible cycle of 24 years
TX Psc	23 46.4	+03 29	LB	4.8–5.2	—	C	
ρ Cas	23 54.4	+57 30	SRD	4.1–6.2	—	G	Usually 4.4–5.2, but peculiar fade to deep minimum in 1945–47
V373 Cas	23 55.6	+57 25	E?/GS	5.9–6.3	13.42	B0+B0	Unique binary with possible eclipses and physical variation of components. Normally range is only 0.1 mag.
R Cas	23 58.4	+51 24	M	4.7–13.5	430.46	M	Mean range 7.0–12.6
S Scl	00 15.4	−32 03	M	5.5–13.6	362.57	M	Mean range 6.7–12.9
T Cet	00 21.8	−20 03	SRC	5.0–6.9	158.9	M	
R And	00 24.0	+38 35	M	5.8–14.9	409.33	S	Mean range 6.9–14.3
TV Psc	00 28.0	+17 54	SR	4.7–5.4	49.1	M	
ζ Phe	01 08.4	−55 15	EA/DM	3.9–4.4	1.67	B6+B9	Secondary minimum 4.2
V465 Cas	01 18.2	+57 48	SRB	6.2–7.2	60	M	
RR Ari	01 55.9	+23 35	EA?	5.5–5.9?	47.9?	K0	Constant?
AA Cet	01 59.0	−22 55	EW/KE	6–6.5	0.54	F2	Secondary minimum 6.5

Clusters, nebulae and galaxies

NGC	M	RA 2000.0 h m	Dec. ° '	Notes
7293	—	22 30	−20 48	Planetary nebula, the Helix, in Aquarius; the largest planetary, 0°.2 across, best seen with binoculars in a dark sky
7662	—	23 26	+42 33	Planetary nebula in Andromeda, 9th mag.; one of the easiest planetaries for small telescopes, appears star-like at low powers
55	—	00 15	−39 11	Spiral galaxy in Sculptor, edge-on; 8th mag.
205	110	00 40	+41 41	Elliptical galaxy, larger of the two companions of the Andromeda Galaxy but less easy to see; 8th mag.
221	32	00 43	+40 52	8th-mag. elliptical companion to the Andromeda Galaxy
224	31	00 43	+41 16	The Andromeda Galaxy, naked-eye spiral 2.2 million l.y. away; ideal for binoculars and telescopes with low powers
253	—	00 48	−25 17	7th-mag. spiral galaxy in Sculptor, seen edge-on
457	—	01 19	+58 20	Open cluster in Cassiopeia, including 5th-mag. ϕ Cas
598	33	01 34	+30 39	Spiral galaxy in Triangulum, large but with low surface brightness; best in binoculars
628	74	01 37	+15 47	Spiral galaxy in Pisces; 9th mag., but one of the most difficult Messier objects to observe
650–1	76	01 42	+51 34	Planetary nebula in Perseus, the Little Dumbbell; 12th mag., the faintest Messier object, given as a double nebula in the NGC
752	—	01 58	+37 41	Large open cluster in Andromeda

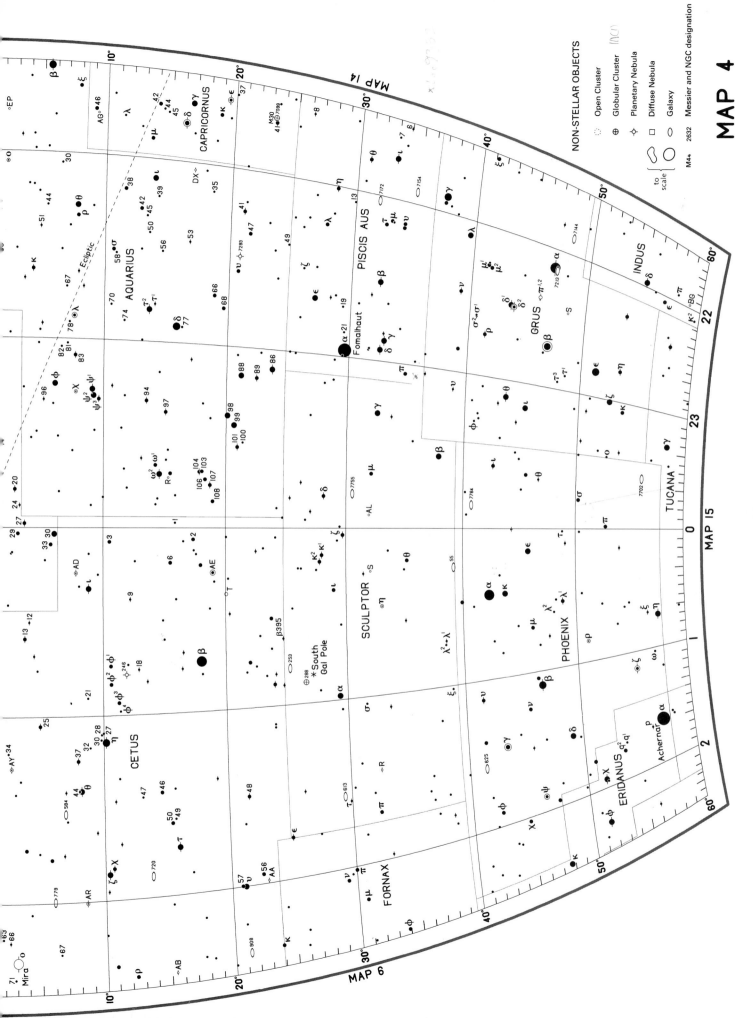

MAP 4

NON-STELLAR OBJECTS

- ⊙ Open Cluster
- ⊕ Globular Cluster
- ✧ Planetary Nebula
- □ Diffuse Nebula
- ◯ Galaxy

M44 2632 Messier and NGC designation

⬤◯ to scale

Constellations and objects labelled on map:

CAPRICORNUS, AQUARIUS, PISCIS AUS, GRUS, INDUS, TUCANA, SCULPTOR, PHOENIX, FORNAX, CETUS, ERIDANUS

Fomalhaut, Achernar, Mira, South Gal Pole

Ecliptic

MAP 14, MAP 15, MAP 6

Interesting Objects, Maps 5 and 6

RA 02h to 06h, Dec. +60° to −60°

Double stars

ADS	Star	RA h m	Dec. ° ′	Magnitudes	PA °	Dist. ″	Notes
			2000.0				
1615	α Psc	02 02.0	+02 46	4.2 5.2	272	1.8	Binary, 900 years[a]
1631	10 Ari	02 03.7	+25 56	5.9 7.3	346	1.1	Binary, 300 years[a]
1630	γ And	02 03.9	+42 20	2.3 5.1	63	9.8	Little change. Superb pair; orange, bluish
1630	γ² And	02 03.9	+42 20	5.5 6.3	103	0.4	Companion of γ And. Binary, 61 years[a]
1683	59 And	02 10.9	+39 02	6.1 6.8	35	16.6	Fixed
1697	6 Tri	02 12.4	+30 18	5.3 6.9	71	3.9	Slow binary; yellowish, bluish
1703	66 Cet	02 12.8	−02 24	5.7 7.5	234	16.5	Slow binary; yellow, blue; fine pair
1778	o Cet	02 19.3	−02 59	var. 9.5	9	0.1	Binary, 400 years[a]. B (VZ Cet) is variable, 9.5–12
1954	ω For	02 33.8	−28 14	5.0 7.7	244	10.8	Slow binary
2080	γ Cet	02 43.3	+03 14	3.5 7.3	294	2.8	Slow binary; little change
2157	η Per	02 50.7	+55 54	3.8 8.5	300	28.3	Fixed; yellowish, bluish
2200	20 Per	02 53.7	+38 20	5.3 10.1	237	14.1	Fixed. Test for 75 mm. A is very close binary, 62 years
	θ Eri	02 58.3	−40 18	3.4 4.5	88	4.5	Slow increase of PA; fine pair
2257	ε Ari	02 59.2	+21 20	5.2 5.5	203	1.4	Slow binary. Test for 75 mm
2312	ρ² Eri	03 02.7	−07 41	5.3 9.5	75	1.8	PA and distance decreasing
2362	β Per	03 08.2	+40 57	var. 10.5	192	81.9	Optical; fixed
2402	α For	03 12.1	−28 59	4.0 6.6	299	5.1	Binary, 300 years[a]
2616	7 Tau	03 34.4	+24 28	6.6 6.7	360	0.8	Binary, 600 years[a]
2799	OΣ65 Tau	03 50.3	+25 35	5.8 6.2	25	0.2	Binary, 62 years[a]
2843	ζ Per	03 54.1	+31 53	2.9 9.5	208	12.9	Little change
2888	ε Per	03 57.9	+40 01	2.9 8.1	10	8.8	Fixed
3079	39 Eri	04 14.4	−10 15	5.0 8.0	146	6.4	Slow binary; little change
3093	o² Eri	04 15.2	−07 39	4.4 9.3	104	83.4	Little change. B is itself double; 9.5, 11.2; 336°, 9″.2
3137	φ Tau	04 20.4	+27 21	5.0 8.4	250	52.1	Optical; closing, PA increasing
3161	χ Tau	04 22.6	+25 38	5.5 7.6	24	19.4	Fixed
3321	α Tau	04 35.9	+16 31	0.9 13.4	34	121.7	Opening
	ι Pic	04 50.9	−53 28	5.6 6.4	58	12.3	Fixed
3572	ω Aur	04 59.3	+37 53	5.0 8.0	359	5.4	Slow binary; PA increasing
	γ¹ Cae	05 04.4	−35 29	4.6 8.1	308	2.9	Slow binary; PA decreasing
3800	κ Lep	05 13.2	−12 56	4.5 7.4	358	2.6	Fixed
3797	ρ Ori	05 13.3	+02 52	4.5 8.3	64	7.0	Fixed; other stars in the field
3823	β Ori	05 14.5	−08 12	0.1 6.8	202	9.5	Fixed. Test for 50 mm
4002	η Ori	05 24.5	−02 24	3.8 4.8	80	1.5	PA slowly decreasing. Test for 100 mm
	θ Pic	05 24.8	−52 19	6.3 6.8	287	38.2	Little change; optical. θ¹ is very close double
4066	β Lep	05 28.2	−20 46	2.8 7.3	330	2.5	PA increasing; slow binary
4134	δ Ori	05 32.0	−00 18	2.2 6.3	359	52.6	Fixed
4179	λ Ori	05 35.1	+09 56	3.6 5.5	43	4.4	Fixed. Very fine region
4186	θ¹ Ori	05 35.3	−05 23	5.1 6.7 / 6.7 (var.) 8.0 (var.)			The Trapezium; two components are eclipsing binaries. Two other faint stars (mags. 11.1, 11.5) are test for 100 mm. Fine fixed multiple group
4241	σ Ori	05 38.7	−02 36	4.0 6.0	115	0.2	Binary, 170 years[a]
4263	ζ Ori	05 40.8	−01 57	1.9 4.0	165	2.3	Binary, 1500 years[a]. Test for 75 mm
4334	γ Lep	05 44.5	−22 27	3.7 6.3	350	96.3	Little change
4566	θ Aur	05 59.7	+37 13	2.6 7.1	313	3.6	Slow binary. Test for 100 mm

[a] Orbital elements for these binaries are given in Table 46. PA and Dist. are predictions for 2000.0.

Variable stars

Star	RA 2000.0 h m	Dec. ° ′	Type	Range (mags)	Period (d)	Spectral type	Notes
o Cet	02 19.3	−02 59	M	2.0–10.1	331.96	M	Mean range 3.5–9.1. See Double stars
R Tri	02 37.0	+34 16	M	5.4–12.6	266.9	M	Mean range 6.2–11.7
Z Eri	02 47.9	−12 28	SRB	5.6–7.2	80	M	Secondary period 746.4 d
RR Eri	02 52.2	−08 16	SRB	6.3–8.1	97	M	
R Hor	02 53.9	−49 53	M	4.7–14.3	407.6	M	Mean range 6.0–13.0
ρ Per	03 05.2	+38 50	SRB	3.3–4.0	50?	M	Mean mag. varies?
β Per	03 08.2	+40 57	EA/SD	2.1–3.4	2.87	B8	Weak X-ray source
TW Hor	03 12.6	−57 19	SRB	5.5–6.0	158?	C	
S For	03 46.2	−24 24	CST?	5.6–8.5	—	F8	Reported unusually bright on one night only, 1899 Mar. 6
BU Tau	03 49.2	+24 08	GCAS	4.8–5.5	—	B8	Pleione, in the Pleiades
X Per	03 55.4	+31 03	GCAS+XP	6.0–7.0	—	O	
λ Tau	04 00.7	+12 29	EA/DM	3.4–3.9	3.95	B3+A4	
SZ Tau	04 37.2	+18 33	DCEPS	6.3–6.8	3.15	F	In halo of open cluster NGC 1647
HU Tau	04 38.3	+20 41	EA/SD?	5.9–6.7	2.06	B8	
R Pic	04 46.2	−49 15	SR	6.4–10.1	170.9	M	
R Lep	04 59.6	−14 48	M	5.5–11.7	427.07	C	Amplitude varies, period over 40 years? Maxima can be as faint as 9.5
ε Aur	05 02.0	+43 49	EA/GS	2.9–3.8	9892	F+B	Fluctuations of 0.2 mag. in cycle of about 110 d
W Ori	05 05.4	+01 11	SRB	5.9–7.7	212	C	Secondary period of 2450 d
S Pic	05 11.0	−48 30	M	6.5–14.0	428.0	M	Mean range 8.1–13.8
RX Lep	05 11.4	−11 51	SRB	5.0–7.4	60?	M	
μ Lep	05 12.9	−16 12	ACV	3.0–3.4	2?	B9	
AR Aur	05 18.3	+33 46	EA/DM	6.2–6.8	4.13	Ap+B9	Secondary minimum 6.7
CK Ori	05 30.3	+04 12	SR?	5.9–7.1	120?	K	
TU Tau	05 45.2	+24 25	SRB	5.9–9.2	190?	C+A2	
Y Tau	05 45.7	+20 42	SRB	6.5–9.2	241.5	C	
V1031 Ori	05 47.4	−10 32	ACV	6.0–6.4	3.41	A4	
α Ori	05 55.2	+07 24	SRC	0.0–1.3	2335	M	Also waves of 200–400 d
U Ori	05 55.8	+20 10	M	4.8–13.0	368.3	M	Mean range 6.3–12.0
V474 Mon	05 59.0	−09 23	DSCT	5.9–6.4	0.14	F2	

Clusters, nebulae and galaxies

NGC	M	RA 2000.0 h m	Dec. ° ′	Notes
869	—	02 19	+57 09	Double cluster in Perseus, also known as h and χ Persei, each cluster covering 0°.5;
884	—	02 22	+57 07	NGC 869 is the richer. Naked-eye and binocular object
1039	34	02 42	+42 47	5th-mag. open cluster in Perseus, 0°.5 wide
1068	77	02 43	−00 01	Spiral galaxy of Seyfert variety (bright nucleus) in Cetus; 9th mag.
—	45	03 47	+24 07	Pleiades open cluster in Taurus; at least five stars visible to naked eye; covers nearly 2°; ideal binocular object
1904	79	05 25	−24 33	Globular cluster in Lepus; 8th mag. In same field as multiple star h 3752
1912	38	05 29	+35 50	6th-mag. open cluster in Auriga; one of a chain with M36 and M37
1952	1	05 35	+22 01	The Crab Nebula in Taurus, mag. 8.4; remnant of a supernova; covers 6′×4′
1976	42	05 35	−05 30	Orion Nebula, covering over 1°; superb in all apertures. At its centre is the multiple star θ¹ Orionis
1981	—	05 35	−04 26	Open cluster north of the Orion Nebula
1977	—	05 36	−04 52	Nebula surrounding 42 Orionis
1982	43	05 36	−05 16	Part of the Orion Nebula, just to the north of the main cloud
1960	36	05 36	+34 08	Smallest of the three open clusters in Auriga; the most prominent in binoculars
2068	78	05 47	+00 03	Nebulosity in Orion
2099	37	05 52	+32 33	Largest and richest of the three open clusters in Auriga; 0°.4 across

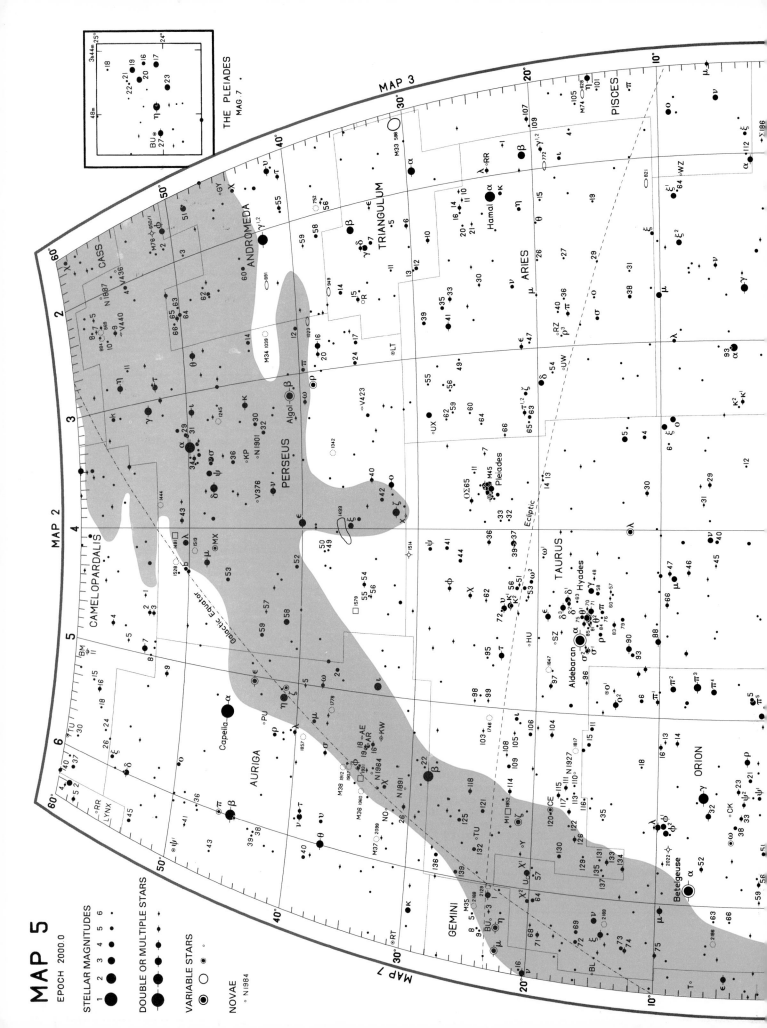

MAP 5

EPOCH 2000.0

STELLAR MAGNITUDES

1 2 3 4 5 6

DOUBLE OR MULTIPLE STARS

VARIABLE STARS

NOVAE
○ N1984

THE PLEIADES
MAG .7

MAP 3

MAP 2

MAP 7

CASS

ANDROMEDA

TRIANGULUM

ARIES

PISCES

PERSEUS

CAMELOPARDALIS

AURIGA

TAURUS

ORION

GEMINI

LYNX

Algol

Capella

Aldebaran

Hamal

Betelgeuse

Pleiades

Hyades

Galactic Equator

Ecliptic

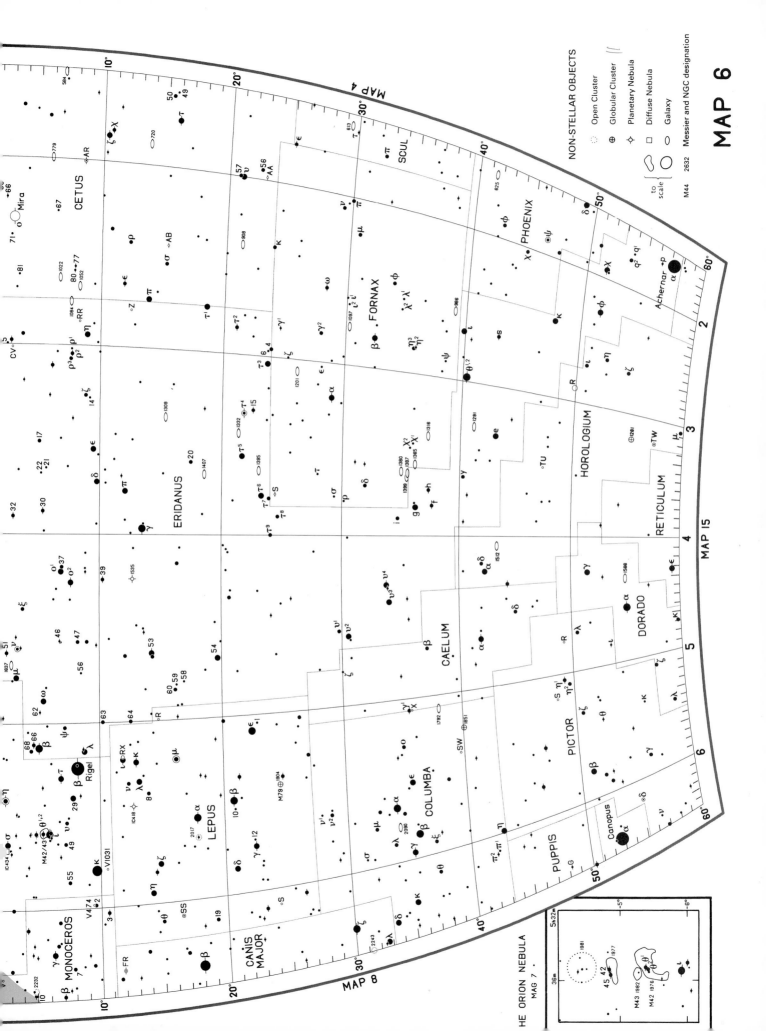

MAP 6

NON-STELLAR OBJECTS

Open Cluster
Globular Cluster
Planetary Nebula
Diffuse Nebula
Galaxy

Messier and NGC designation

to scale

M44   2632

THE ORION NEBULA
MAG 7

Interesting Objects, Maps 7 & 8

RA 06h to 10h, Dec. +60° to −60°

Double stars

ADS	Star	RA 2000.0 h m	Dec. 2000.0 ° ′	Magnitudes	PA °	Dist. ″	Notes
4773	41 Aur	06 11.6	+48 43	6.6 7.0	356	7.7	Little change; very slow binary
4841	η Gem	06 14.9	+22 30	var. 8.8	257	1.6	Binary, 500 years[a]
4990	μ Gem	06 22.9	+22 31	3.2 9.4	141	121.7	Wide optical pair, fixed. B is double: 9.8, 10.7; 260°, 0″.8; PA slowly decreasing
5012	ε Mon	06 23.8	+04 36	4.5 6.5	27	13.4	Fixed. Fine field with low power
5107	β Mon	06 28.8	−07 02	4.7 4.8	132	7.3	Fainter component is itself double: 5.2, 6.1; 106°, 2″.8. Fine fixed triple
	μ Pic	06 32.0	−58 45	5.8 9.0	231	2.4	Fixed
5166	20 Gem	06 32.3	+17 47	6.3 6.9	210	20.0	Fixed; yellowish, bluish
5253	ν¹ CMa	06 36.4	−18 40	5.8 8.5	262	17.5	Fixed
	Δ31 Pup	06 38.6	−48 13	5.0 8.3	321	13.0	Fixed
5423	α CMa	06 45.1	−16 43	−1.5 8.3	150	4.6	Binary, 50 years[a]
5400	12 Lyn	06 46.2	+59 27	5.4 6.0 7.3	69 308	1.7 8.7	Brighter components make a binary, 700 years[a]. C is a test for 75 mm
5514	14 Lyn	06 53.1	+59 27	5.6 6.8	270	0.4	Binary, 500 years[a]
5559	38 Gem	06 54.6	+13 11	4.7 7.7	350	5.2	Binary, 2000 years[a]
5605	μ CMa	06 56.1	−14 03	5.3 8.6	340	3.0	Fixed; yellowish, bluish
5654	ε CMa	06 58.6	−28 58	1.5 7.4	161	7.5	Fixed
5961	λ Gem	07 18.1	+16 32	3.6 10.7	33	9.6	Fixed. Easy test for 75 mm
5983	δ Gem	07 20.1	+21 59	3.5 8.2	226	5.8	Binary, 1200 years[a]
6101	η CMi	07 28.0	+06 57	5.3 11.1	25	4.0	Fixed
	σ Pup	07 29.2	−43 18	3.3 9.4	74	22.3	Fixed
6190	n Pup	07 34.3	−23 28	5.8 5.9	114	9.6	Slow binary
6175	α Gem	07 34.6	+31 53	1.9 2.9	65	3.9	Binary, 500 years[a]. Castor C (YY Gem), mag. 8.9–9.6, lies at 163°, 70″; fixed
6255	k Pup	07 38.8	−26 48	4.5 4.7	318	9.9	Fixed
6321	κ Gem	07 44.4	+24 24	3.6 8.1	240	7.1	Very slow binary; little change
6420	9 Pup	07 51.8	−13 54	5.6 6.2	335	0.2	Binary, 23 years[a]
	γ Vel	08 09.5	−47 20	1.9 4.2	220	41.2	Fixed
6650	ζ Cnc	08 12.2	+17 39	5.1 6.2	72	6.0	Binary, 1200 years[a]. Brighter component is itself binary: 5.6, 6.0; 86°, 0″.8; 60 years[a]
	h² Pup	08 14.0	−40 21	4.4 9.5	341	51.1	Fixed
6815	φ² Cnc	08 26.8	+26 56	6.3 6.3	218	5.1	Slow binary; little change
6914	β208 Pyx	08 39.1	−22 40	5.3 6.7	30	1.6	Binary, 140 years[a]
	I314 Pyx	08 39.4	−36 36	6.5 7.6	249	0.4	Binary, 66 years[a]
6988	ι Cnc	08 46.7	+28 46	4.2 6.6	307	30.5	Fixed
6993	ε Hya	08 46.8	+06 25	3.4 6.8	302	2.7	Binary, 900 years[a]. A is a close binary, 15 years
	H Vel	08 56.3	−52 43	4.8 7.4	339	2.7	Little change
7114	ι UMa	08 59.2	+48 02	3.1 10.2	177	2.0	Binary, 800 years[a]. B is itself binary
7292	38 Lyn	09 18.8	+36 48	3.9 6.6	229	2.7	Slow binary; PA decreasing
7307	Σ1338 Lyn	09 21.0	+38 11	6.8 7.0	290	1.0	Binary, 400 years[a]
7351	κ Leo	09 24.7	+26 11	2.1 4.5	208	2.1	Slow binary
7390	ω Leo	09 28.5	+09 03	5.9 6.5	84	0.6	Binary, 118 years[a]
	ψ Vel	09 30.7	−40 28	4.1 4.6	264	0.5	Binary, 34 years[a]
	ζ¹ Ant	09 30.8	−31 53	6.2 7.1	212	8.0	Little change
	I Hya	09 41.3	−23 36	4.8 10.0	292	54.7	Optical pair; fixed
7545	φ UMa	09 52.1	+54 04	5.3 5.4	264	0.3	Binary, 106 years[a]
7555	γ Sex	09 52.5	−08 06	5.6 6.1	56	0.6	Binary, 76 years[a]

[a] Orbital elements for these binaries are given in Table 46. PA and Dist. are predictions for 2000.0.

Variable stars

Star	RA 2000.0 h m	Dec. 2000.0 ° ′	Type	Range (mags)	Period (d)	Spectral type	Notes
S Lep	06 05.8	−24 11	SRB	6.0–7.6	89.0	M	Secondary period 890 d
BU Gem	06 12.3	+22 54	LC	5.7–8.1	—	M	
η Gem	06 14.9	+22 30	SRA+EA	3.2–3.9	232.9	M	Deep minima (eclipses?) every 8.2 years. See Double stars
V Mon	06 22.7	−02 12	M	6.0–13.9	340.5	M	Mean range 7.0–13.1
ψ¹ Aur	06 24.9	+49 17	LC	4.8–5.7	—	M	
T Mon	06 25.2	+07 05	DCEP	5.6–6.6	27.02	G	
BL Ori	06 25.5	+14 43	LB	6.3–6.9	—	C	
RR Lyn	06 26.4	+56 17	EA/DM	5.5–6.0	9.95	A7+F3	Secondary minimum 5.9
RT Aur	06 28.6	+30 30	DCEP	5.0–5.8	3.73	G	

Variable stars (*continued*)

Star	RA 2000.0 h m	Dec. ° '	Type	Range (mags)	Period (d)	Spectral type	Notes
WW Aur	06 32.5	+32 27	EA/DM	5.8–6.5	2.53	A3+A3	Secondary minimum 6.4
W Gem	06 35.0	+15 20	DCEP	6.5–7.4	7.91	G	
UU Aur	06 36.5	+38 27	SRB	5.1–6.8	234	C	
IS Gem	06 49.7	+32 36	SRC	5.3–6.0	47?	K	
ζ Gem	07 04.1	+20 34	DCEP	3.6–4.2	10.15	G	
R Gem	07 07.4	+22 42	M	6.0–14.0	369.91	S	Mean range 7.1–13.5
W CMa	07 08.1	−11 55	LB	6.4–7.9	—	C	
BQ Gem	07 13.4	+16 10	SRB	5.1–5.5	50?	M	
L² Pup	07 13.5	−44 39	SRB	2.6–6.2	140.6	M	
EW CMa	07 14.3	−26 21	GCAS	4.4–4.8	—	B3	
ω CMa	07 14.8	−26 46	GCAS	3.6–4.2	—	B2	
UW CMa	07 18.7	−24 34	EB/KE?	4.8–5.3	4.39	O7+OB	Secondary minimum 5.3
R CMa	07 19.5	−16 24	EA/SD	5.7–6.3	1.14	F1	
VY CMa	07 23.0	−25 46	★	6.5–9.6	—	M	Unique variable in reflection nebula near young open cluster NGC 2362. Cyclic variations and slow fade since 1801
FW CMa	07 24.7	−16 12	GCAS	5.0–5.5	—	B3	
U Mon	07 30.8	−09 47	RVB	5.9–7.8	91.32	G	Secondary period 2320 d
QY Pup	07 47.6	−15 59	SRD	6.2–6.7	—	G	
PX Pup	07 56.4	−30 17	LB?	6.0–6.5	—	M	
V341 Car	07 56.8	−59 08	L	6.2–7.1	—	M	In variable reflection nebula IC 2220, and near open cluster NGC 2516
V Pup	07 58.2	−49 15	EB/SD	4.4–4.9	1.45	B1+B3	Secondary minimum 4.8
RS Pup	08 13.1	−34 35	DCEP	6.5–7.7	41.39	G	
AI Vel	08 14.1	−44 34	DSCT	6.2–6.8	0.11	F	
R Cnc	08 16.6	+11 44	M	6.1–11.8	361.60	M	Mean range 6.8–11.2
NO Pup	08 26.3	−39 04	EA/KE?	6.5–7.0	1.26	B8	
RZ Vel	08 37.0	−44 07	DCEP	6.4–7.6	20.40	G	
AK Hya	08 39.9	−17 18	SRB	6.3–6.9	75?	M	
BO Cnc	08 52.5	+28 16	LB?	5.9–6.4	—	M	
X Cnc	08 55.4	+17 14	SRB	5.6–7.5	195?	C	
T Pyx	09 04.7	−32 23	NR	6.5–15.3	(7000)	Pec	Outbursts in 1890, 1902, 1920, 1944, 1966
RS Cnc	09 10.6	+30 58	SRC?	5.1–7.0	120?	M	Secondary period 700 d
KW Hya	09 12.4	−07 07	EA/DM	6.1–6.6	7.75	A3+A0	Secondary minimum 6.4
IN Hya	09 20.6	+00 11	SRB	6.3–6.9	65?	M	
CG UMa	09 21.7	+56 42	LB	5.5–6.0	—	M	
S Ant	09 32.3	−28 38	EW/KE?	6.4–6.9	0.65	A9	Secondary minimum 6.9
R LMi	09 45.6	+34 31	M	6.3–13.2	372.19	M	Mean range 7.1–12.6
R Leo	09 47.6	+11 26	M	4.4–11.3	309.95	M	Mean range 5.8–10.0
Y Hya	09 51.1	−23 01	SRB	5–8	302.8	C	Mean mag. varies

Clusters, nebulae and galaxies

NGC	M	RA 2000.0 h m	Dec. ° '	Notes
2168	35	06 09	+24 20	Open cluster in Gemini; large and rich, good binocular object
2232	—	06 27	−04 45	Large, scattered cluster in Monoceros including 5th-mag. star 10 Mon
2244	—	06 32	+04 52	Large, elongated open cluster in Monoceros; surrounded by the faint Rosette Nebula, NGC 2237, 1° across, visible in binoculars under dark skies
2264	—	06 41	+09 53	Arrow-shaped open cluster in Monoceros including the 5th-mag. star 15 Mon. The surrounding nebulosity, including the dark Cone Nebula, shows up well only on photographs
2287	41	06 46	−20 44	Naked-eye open cluster in Canis Major, 0°.6 wide, good in binoculars
2323	50	07 03	−08 20	Open cluster in Monoceros; 6th mag.
2392	—	07 29	+20 55	Planetary nebula in Gemini, called the Eskimo; reported mags. vary from 8 to 10
2422	47	07 37	−14 30	Large naked-eye cluster in Puppis, brightest stars of 6th mag.
2437	46	07 42	−14 49	Open cluster in Puppis, makes a contrasting binocular pair with M47
2447	93	07 45	−23 52	Open cluster in Puppis
2451	—	07 45	−37 58	Large, scattered open cluster in Puppis containing the 4th-mag. star c Pup
2477	—	07 52	−38 33	Open cluster in Puppis, like a large globular through binoculars
2547	—	08 11	−49 16	Open cluster in Vela
2548	48	08 14	−05 48	Large open cluster in Hydra
2632	44	08 40	+20 00	Praesepe, the Beehive Cluster, in Cancer; covers 1°.5; visible to the naked eye as a misty patch; best seen in binoculars
IC 2391	—	08 40	−53 04	Large, scattered cluster in Vela containing the 4th-mag. star o Vel
IC 2395	—	08 41	−48 12	Open cluster in Vela; 5th mag.
2682	67	08 50	+11 49	Rich open cluster in Cancer

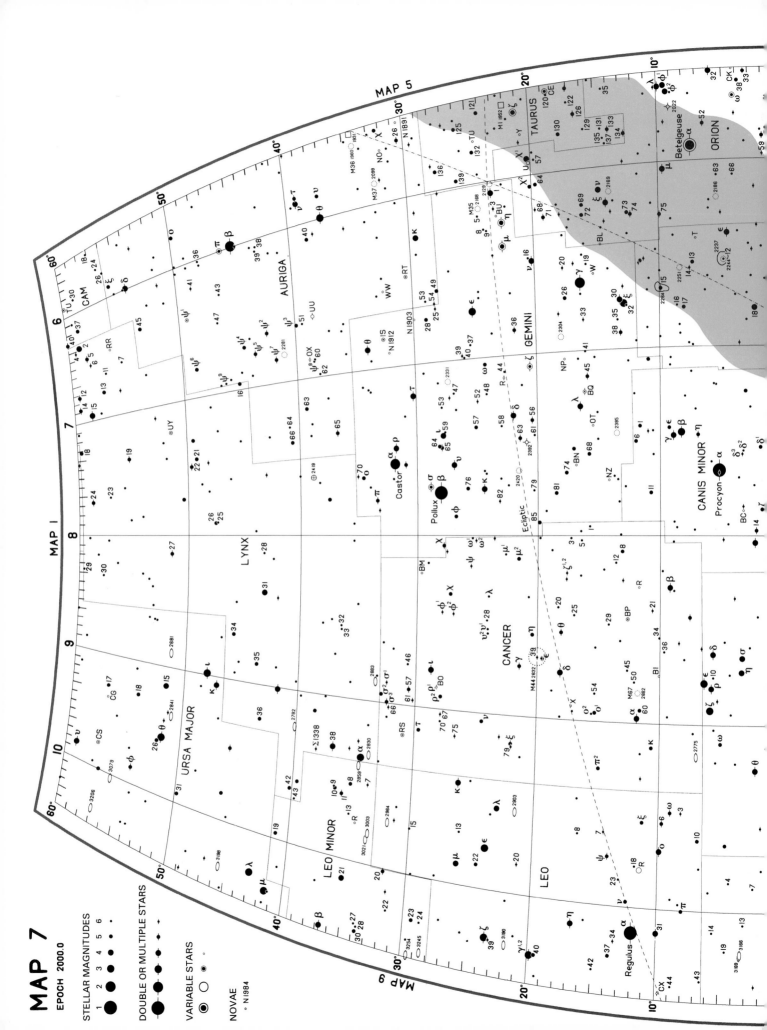

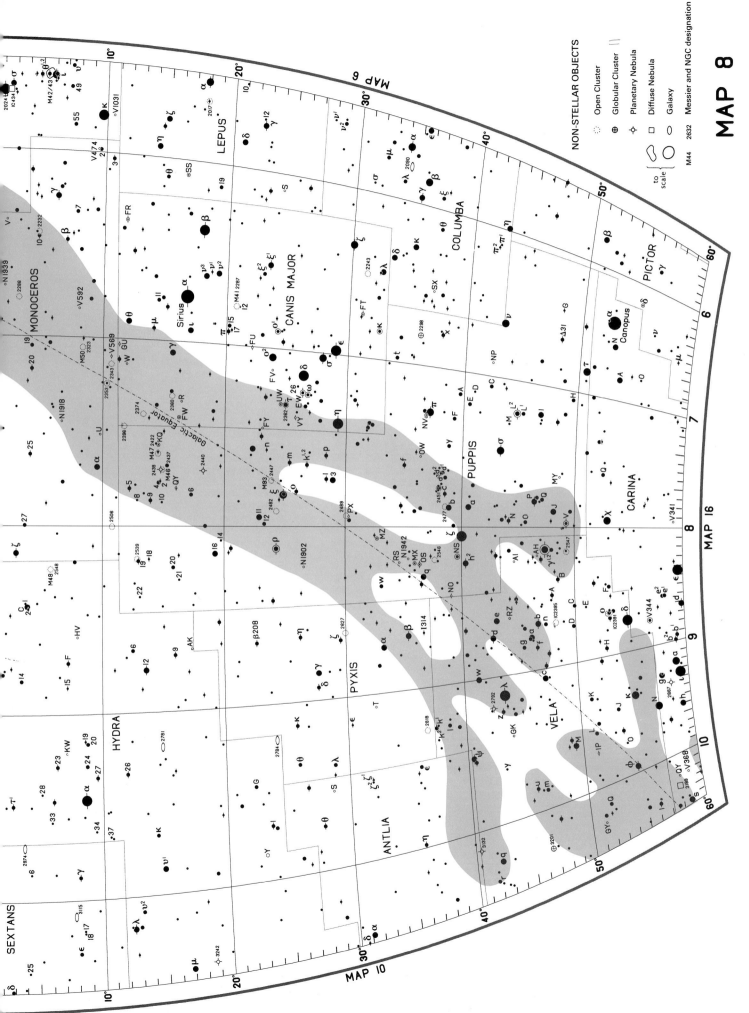

MAP 8

MAP 6

MAP 16

MAP 10

SEXTANS

HYDRA

MONOCEROS

LEPUS

CANIS MAJOR

COLUMBA

PICTOR

Canopus

PUPPIS

CARINA

VELA

PYXIS

ANTLIA

Sirius

Galactic Equator

Interesting Objects, Maps 9 and 10
RA 10h to 14h, Dec. +60° to −60°

Double stars

ADS	Star	RA 2000.0 h m	Dec. ° ′	Magnitudes		PA °	Dist. ″	Notes
7654	α Leo	10 08.4	+11 58	1.4	7.7	307	176.9	Fixed
7724	γ Leo	10 20.0	+19 51	2.2	3.5	125	4.4	Binary, 620 years[a]. Fine pair
	I Vel	10 20.9	−56 03	4.7	8.4	102	7.2	Little change
	δ Ant	10 29.6	−30 36	5.6	9.6	226	11.0	Fixed
7846	β411 Hya	10 36.1	−26 40	6.7	7.5	315	1.4	Binary, 210 years[a]
8119	ξ UMa	11 18.2	+31 32	4.3	4.8	273	1.8	Binary, 60 years[a]
8123	ν UMa	11 18.5	+33 06	3.5	9.9	147	7.2	Fixed
8148	ι Leo	11 23.9	+10 32	4.0	6.7	116	1.7	Binary, 192 years[a]
8153	γ Crt	11 24.9	−17 41	4.1	9.6	96	5.2	Fixed
8175	57 UMa	11 29.1	+39 20	5.4	5.4	359	5.4	PA slowly decreasing
8196	88 Leo	11 31.7	+14 22	6.4	8.4	328	8.4	Little change; yellow, bluish
	β Hya	11 52.9	−33 54	4.7	5.5	8	0.9	Closing, PA increasing
8406	2 Com	12 04.3	+21 28	5.9	7.4	237	3.7	Fixed
	D Cen	12 14.0	−45 43	5.6	6.8	244	2.9	Fixed
8539	Σ1639 Com	12 24.4	+25 35	6.8	7.8	324	1.7	Binary, 700 years[a]
8572	δ Crv	12 29.9	−16 31	3.0	9.2	214	24.2	Fixed
8573	β28 Crv	12 30.1	−13 24	6.5	8.6	336	2.2	Binary, 162 years[a]
	γ Cru	12 31.2	−57 07	1.6	6.7	31	110.6	Optical; widening, PA decreasing
8600	24 Com	12 35.1	+18 23	5.2	6.7	271	20.3	Fixed; yellow, bluish
	γ Cen	12 41.5	−48 58	2.9	2.9	347	1.0	Binary, 84 years[a]
8630	γ Vir	12 41.7	−01 27	3.5	3.5	267	1.8	Binary, 171 years[a]
8695	35 Com	12 53.3	+21 14	5.1	7.2	182	1.2	Binary, 500 years[a]
8706	α CVn	12 56.0	+38 19	2.9	5.5	229	19.4	Little change
8801	θ Vir	13 09.9	−05 32	4.4	9.4	343	7.1	Fixed. Test for 75 mm. Mag. 10.4 star at 298°, 69″.6; fixed
8891	ζ UMa	13 23.9	+54 56	2.3	4.0	152	14.4	Little change. Naked-eye pair with Alcor (80 UMa), mag. 4.0: 71°, 708″.7; fixed
8974	25 CVn	13 37.5	+36 18	5.0	6.9	99	1.8	Binary, 240 years[a]
	Q Cen	13 41.7	−54 34	5.3	6.7	163	5.3	Fixed
9000	84 Vir	13 43.1	+03 32	5.5	7.9	229	2.9	Slow binary. Test for 75 mm
9025	τ Boo	13 47.3	+17 27	4.5	11.1	11	4.8	Optical; closing, PA increasing
	3 Cen	13 51.8	−33 00	4.5	6.0	108	7.9	Little change
	4 Cen	13 53.2	−31 56	4.7	8.4	185	14.9	Fixed

[a] Orbital elements for these binaries are given in Table 46. PA and Dist. are predictions for 2000.0.

Variable stars

Star	RA 2000.0 h m	Dec. ° ′	Type	Range (mags)	Period (d)	Spectral type	Notes
U Ant	10 35.2	−39 34	LB	5–6	—	C	
U Hya	10 37.6	−13 23	SRB	4.3–6.5	450?	C	
η Car	10 45.1	−59 41	SDOR	−0.8–7.9	—	Pec	Very massive young star in emission nebula NGC 3372 and cluster Tr 16. Maximum brightness 1843. Since 1880 range has been 5.9–7.9
U Car	10 57.8	−59 44	DCEP	5.7–7.0	38.77	G	
ST UMa	11 27.8	+45 11	SRB	6.0–7.6	110?	M	
o¹ Cen	11 31.8	−59 27	SRD	4.7–5.5	200?	G	
Z UMa	11 56.5	+57 52	SRB	6.2–9.4	195.5	M	Usually double maxima and minima
SS Vir	12 25.3	+00 48	SRA	6.0–9.6	364.14	C	
R Vir	12 38.5	+06 59	M	6.1–12.1	145.63	M	Mean range 6.9–11.5
Y CVn	12 45.1	+45 26	SRB	5.2–6.6	157	C	Secondary period 2000 d

Variable stars (*continued*)

Star	RA 2000.0 h m	Dec. ° ′	Type	Range (mags)	Period (d)	Spectral type	Notes
S Cru	12 54.4	−58 26	DCEP	6.2–6.9	4.69	G	
TU CVn	12 54.9	+47 12	SRB	5.6–6.6	50	M	
FS Com	13 06.4	+22 37	SRB	5.3–6.1	58?	M	
SW Vir	13 14.1	−02 48	SRB	6.4–7.9	150?	M	
V CVn	13 19.5	+45 32	SRA	6.5–8.6	191.89	M	
R Hya	13 29.7	−23 17	M	3.5–10.9	388.87	M	Mean range 4.5–9.5; period shortening from about 500 d in 17th century
S Vir	13 33.0	−07 12	M	6.3–13.2	375.10	M	Mean range 7.0–12.7
V744 Cen	13 40.0	−49 57	SRB	5.1–6.6	90?	M	
T Cen	13 41.8	−33 36	SRA	5.5–9.0	90.44	K	
R CVn	13 49.0	+39 33	M	6.5–12.9	328.53	M	Mean range 7.7–11.9
W Hya	13 49.0	−28 22	SRA	6–9	361	M	Amplitude and shape of light curve vary strongly
μ Cen	13 49.6	−42 28	GCAS	2.9–3.5	—	B2	
V767 Cen	13 53.9	−47 08	GCAS	5.9–6.3	—	B2	
V412 Cen	13 57.5	−57 43	LB	6.5–8.5	—	M	

Clusters, nebulae and galaxies

NGC	M	RA 2000.0 h m	Dec. ° ′	Notes
3132	—	10 08	−40 26	Planetary nebula on Vela–Antlia border; 8th mag.
3242	—	10 25	−18 38	Planetary nebula in Hydra called the 'ghost of Jupiter'; 9th mag.
3351	95	10 44	+11 42	} Pair of spiral galaxies in Leo, 10th and 9th mags. respectively
3368	96	10 47	+11 49	
3379	105	10 48	+12 35	9th-mag. elliptical galaxy in Leo
3532	—	11 06	−58 40	Naked-eye cluster in Carina covering 0°.9
3587	97	11 15	+55 01	Planetary nebula in Ursa Major, the Owl; large (3′) and faint (12th mag.), probably needs at least 150 mm aperture
3623	65	11 19	+13 05	} Pair of 9th-mag. spiral galaxies in Leo tilted at an angle to us
3627	66	11 20	+12 59	
3918	—	11 50	−57 11	Planetary nebula in Centaurus, known as the Blue Planetary; 8th mag.
4258	106	12 19	+47 18	Spiral galaxy in Canes Venatici; 8th mag., 17′×10′
4374	84	12 25	+12 53	Elliptical galaxy in Virgo; 9th mag.
4382	85	12 25	+18 11	9th-mag. elliptical galaxy in Coma
4406	86	12 26	+12 57	9th-mag. elliptical galaxy in Virgo
4472	49	12 30	+08 00	8th-mag. elliptical galaxy in Virgo
4486	87	12 31	+12 24	9th-mag. elliptical galaxy, centre of the Virgo Cluster of galaxies
4501	88	12 32	+14 25	10th-mag. spiral galaxy in Coma
4552	89	12 36	+12 33	10th-mag. elliptical galaxy in Virgo
4565	—	12 36	+25 59	10th-mag. spiral galaxy in Coma, seen edge-on
4569	90	12 37	+13 10	9th-mag. spiral galaxy in Virgo
4579	58	12 38	+11 49	10th-mag. spiral galaxy in Virgo
4590	68	12 40	−26 45	Globular cluster in Hydra; 8th mag.
4594	104	12 40	−11 37	Spiral galaxy in Virgo, the Sombrero, seen edge-on; 8th mag.
4621	59	12 42	+11 39	10th-mag. elliptical galaxy in Virgo
4649	60	12 44	+11 33	9th-mag. elliptical galaxy in Virgo
4736	94	12 51	+41 07	8th-mag. spiral galaxy in Canes Venatici
4826	64	12 57	+21 41	The Black Eye spiral galaxy in Coma; 9th mag.; the 'black eye' feature probably needs 150 mm aperture to be seen
5024	53	13 13	+18 10	Globular cluster in Coma; 8th mag.
5055	63	13 16	+42 02	9th-mag. spiral galaxy in Canes Venatici
5128	—	13 26	−43 01	Centaurus A, a large 7th-mag. elliptical galaxy; a strong radio source
5139	—	13 27	−47 29	ω Centauri, the largest and brightest globular cluster in the sky, mag. 3.7, diameter 0°.6
5194	51	13 30	+47 12	The Whirlpool Galaxy in Canes Venatici, an 8th-mag. spiral with a small satellite galaxy, NGC 5195, at the end of one arm
5236	83	13 37	−29 52	Face-on spiral galaxy in Hydra; 8th mag.
5272	3	13 42	+28 23	Globular cluster in Canes Venatici; 6th mag.

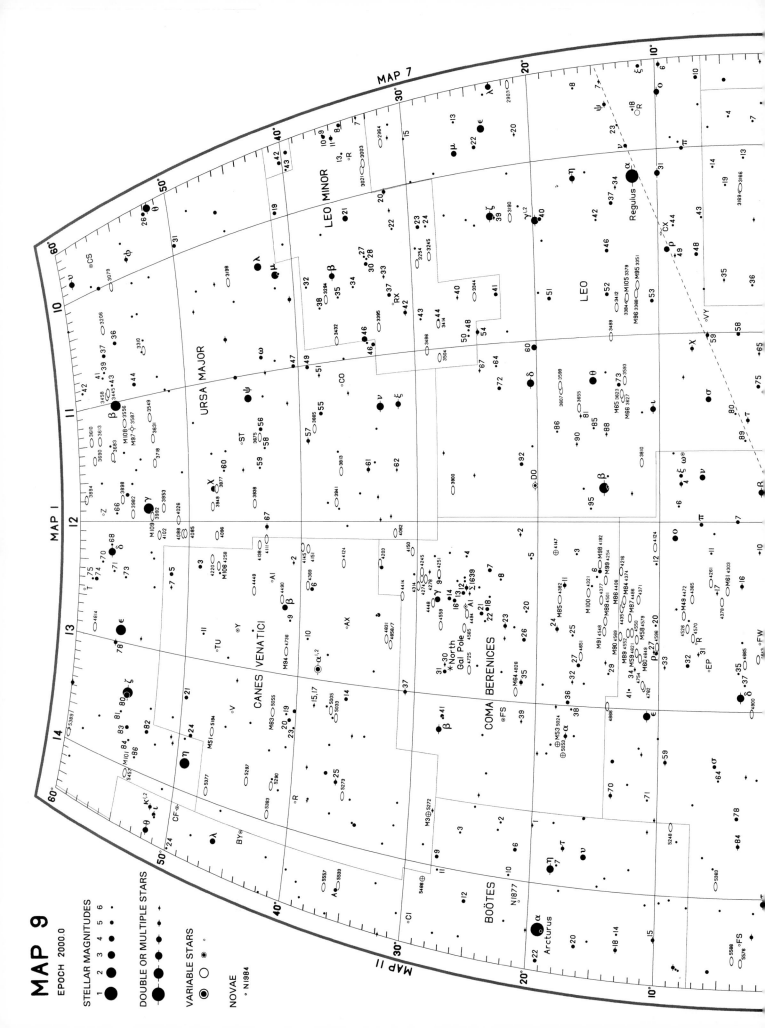

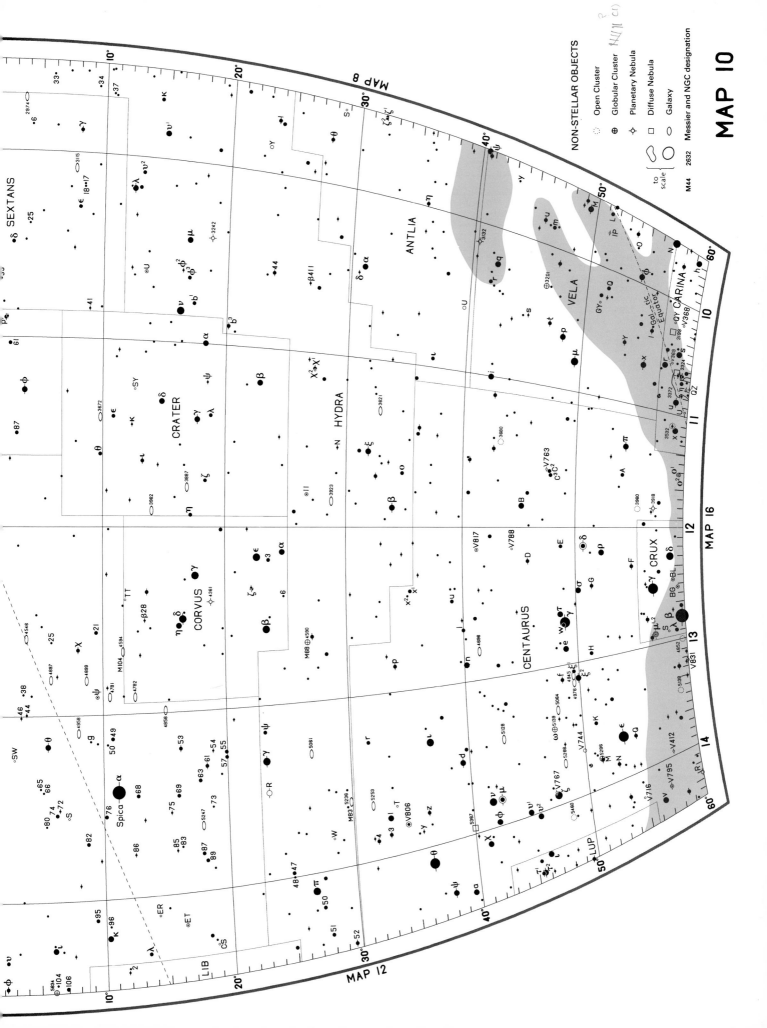

MAP 10

Interesting Objects, Maps 11 and 12
RA 14h to 18h, Dec. +60° to −60°

Double stars

ADS	Star	RA 2000.0 h m	Dec. ° ′	Magnitudes	PA °	Dist. ″	Notes
9085	τ Vir	14 01.6	+01 33	4.3 9.6	290	80.0	Optical
9173	κ Boo	14 13.5	+51 47	4.6 6.6	236	13.4	Little change
9198	ι Boo	14 16.2	+51 22	4.9 7.5	33	38.5	Fixed
9273	φ Vir	14 28.2	−02 14	4.8 9.3	110	4.8	Fixed. Test for 75 mm
9338	π Boo	14 40.7	+16 25	4.9 5.8	108	5.6	PA slowly increasing
9343	ζ Boo	14 41.1	+13 44	4.5 4.6	299	0.8	Binary, 123 years[a]
9372	ε Boo	14 45.0	+27 04	2.5 4.9	339	2.8	PA increasing; yellowish, bluish. Test for 50 mm
9396	μ Lib	14 49.3	−14 09	5.8 6.7	355	1.8	Slow binary. Easy test for 75 mm
9406	39 Boo	14 49.7	+48 43	6.2 6.9	45	2.9	Slowly closing
9413	ξ Boo	14 51.4	+19 06	4.7 6.9	318	6.6	Binary, 152 years[a]
9425	OΣ288 Boo	14 53.4	+15 42	6.8 7.5	159	0.8	Binary, 215 years[a]
9494	44,i Boo	15 03.8	+47 39	5.3 var.	53	2.2	Binary, 225 years[a]
	π Lup	15 05.1	−47 03	4.6 4.7	73	1.4	Opening, PA decreasing
	κ Lup	15 11.9	−48 44	3.9 5.8	144	26.8	Fixed
9532	ι¹ Lib	15 12.2	−19 47	4.5 9.4	111	57.8	Fixed. A is very close binary, 22 years
	μ Lup	15 18.5	−47 53	5.1 5.2	142	1.2	PA and distance decreasing. Mag. 7.2 star at 130°, 23″.7; fixed
9584	5 Ser	15 19.3	+01 46	5.1 10.1	36	11.2	Little change. Near cluster M5
9617	η CrB	15 23.2	+30 17	5.6 5.9	63	0.8	Binary, 42 years[a]
	γ Cir	15 23.4	−59 19	5.1 5.5	20	0.7	Binary, 180 years[a]
9626	μ Boo	15 24.5	+37 23	4.3 6.5	171	108.3	μ² is binary, 260 years[a]: 7.0, 7.6; 8°, 2″.3
9701	δ Ser	15 34.8	+10 32	4.2 5.2	176	4.4	Binary, 3000 years[a]
	γ Lup	15 35.1	−41 10	3.5 3.6	274	0.7	Binary, 147 years[a]
9737	ζ CrB	15 39.4	+36 38	5.1 6.0	305	6.3	Little change
	η Lup	16 00.1	−38 24	3.6 7.8	20	15.0	Fixed
9909	ξ Sco	16 04.4	−11 22	4.9 4.9	308	0.4	Binary, 46 years[a]. Mag. 7.3 star at 51°, 7″.6; opening with decrease of PA
9913	β Sco	16 05.4	−19 48	2.6 4.9	21	13.6	Little change. β¹ has a companion, mag. 10.3, at 132°, 0″.5; PA increasing
9951	ν Sco	16 12.0	−19 28	4.2 6.1	337	41.1	Fixed. Both components are close doubles. ν¹: 4.3, 6.8; 3°, 0″.9; fixed. ν²: 6.4, 7.8; 51°, 2″.3; widening, PA increasing
9979	σ CrB	16 14.7	+33 52	5.6 6.6	236	7.1	Binary, 1000 years[a]
10049	ρ Oph	16 25.6	−23 27	5.3 6.0	344	3.1	Slow binary
10074	α Sco	16 29.4	−26 26	var. 5.4	273	2.6	Binary, 900 years[a]. Red, green (by contrast)
10087	λ Oph	16 30.9	+01 59	4.2 5.3	30	1.5	Binary, 130 years[a]
10157	ζ Her	16 41.3	+31 36	2.9 5.5	12	0.8	Binary, 34 years[a]
10345	μ Dra	17 05.3	+54 28	5.7 5.7	8	1.9	Binary, 500 years[a]
10418	α Her	17 14.6	+14 23	var. 5.4	104	4.6	Binary, 3600 years[a]. Reddish, greenish (by contrast)
10424	δ Her	17 15.0	+24 50	3.1 8.2	236	8.9	Optical; closing, PA increasing
	MlbO 4 Sco	17 19.0	−34 59	6.1 7.6	244	1.8	Binary, 42 years[a]. C mag. 10.0 at 136°, 30″.8; PA slowly increasing
	BrsO 13 Ara	17 19.1	−46 38	5.5 8.7	252	9.6	Binary, 2000 years[a]
10526	ρ Her	17 23.7	+37 09	4.6 5.6	316	4.1	Slow binary; PA and distance slowly increasing
10628	ν Dra	17 32.2	+55 11	4.9 4.9	312	61.9	Fixed. Physical pair; very wide and easy
10786	μ Her	17 46.5	+27 43	3.4 10.1	247	33.8	Slow binary
10875	90 Her	17 53.3	+40 00	5.2 8.5	116	1.6	Slow increase of PA; yellowish, bluish

[a] Orbital elements for these binaries are given in Table 46. PA and Dist. are predictions for 2000.0.

Variable stars

Star	RA 2000.0 h m	Dec. °	Type	Range (mags)	Period (d)	Spectral type	Notes
V716 Cen	14 13.7	−54 38	EB/KE	6.0–6.5	1.49	B5	
R Cen	14 16.6	−59 55	M	5.3–11.8	546.2	M	Double maxima (mean 5.8 and 6.0) and minima (11.1 and 8.3)
V Cen	14 32.5	−56 53	DCEP	6.4–7.2	5.49	G	Near open cluster NGC 5662
R Boo	14 37.2	+26 44	M	6.2–13.1	223.40	M	Mean range 7.2–12.3
RV Boo	14 39.3	+32 32	SRB	6.3–8.0	137	M	
RW Boo	14 41.2	+31 34	SRB	6.4–7.9	209	M	
W Boo	14 43.4	+26 32	SRB?	4.7–5.4	—	M	Periods of 30 and 450 d have been reported
δ Lib	15 01.0	−08 31	EA/SD	4.9–5.9	2.33	A0	
44,i Boo B	15 03.8	+47 39	EW/KW	5.8–6.4	0.27	G2+G2	Secondary minimum 6.3. See Double stars

Variable stars (continued)

Star	RA 2000.0 h m	Dec. ° '	Type	Range (mags)	Period (d)	Spectral type	Notes
GG Lup	15 18.9	−40 47	EB/DM	5.5–6.0	2.16	B7	Secondary minimum 5.8
S CrB	15 21.4	+31 22	M	5.8–14.1	360.26	M	Mean range 7.3–12.9
R Nor	15 36.0	−49 30	M	5–12	507.50	M	Double maxima and minima
τ⁴ Ser	15 36.5	+15 06	SRB	5.9–7.1	100?	M	
T Nor	15 44.1	−54 59	M	6.2–13.6	240.7	M	Mean range 7.4–13.2
R CrB	15 48.6	+28 09	RCB	5.7–14.8	—	C	
R Ser	15 50.7	+15 08	M	5.2–14.4	356.41	M	Mean range 6.9–13.4
T CrB	15 59.5	+25 55	NR	2.0–10.8	—	M3+Pec	Outbursts 1866, 1946
X Her	16 02.7	+47 14	SRB	6.3–7.4	95.0	M	Secondary period 746 d
RR Her	16 04.2	+50 30	SRB	6–10	239.7	C	
AT Dra	16 17.3	+59 45	LB	5.3–6.0	—	M	
S Nor	16 18.9	−57 54	DCEP	6.1–6.8	9.75	G	In centre of open cluster NGC 6087
U Her	16 25.8	+18 54	M	6.4–13.4	406.1	M	Mean range 7.5–12.5
χ Oph	16 27.0	−18 27	GCAS	4.2–5.0	—	B2	
30,g Her	16 28.6	+41 53	SRB	4.3–6.3	89.2	M	Also slow pulsations (period about 2.4 years) and irregular variations
α Sco	16 29.4	−26 26	LC	0.9–1.2	—	M	See Double stars
R Ara	16 39.7	−57 00	EA/DM?	6.0–6.9	4.43	B9	
V1010 Oph	16 49.5	−15 40	EB/KE	6.1–7.0	0.66	A5	
S Her	16 51.9	+14 56	M	6.4–13.8	307.28	M	Mean range 7.6–12.6
RS Sco	16 55.6	−45 06	M	6.2–13.0	319.91	M	Mean range 7.0–12.2
RR Sco	16 56.6	−30 35	M	5.0–12.4	281.45	M	Mean range 5.9–11.8
κ Oph	16 57.7	+09 22	LB?	2.8–3.6	—	K	
V915 Sco	17 14.5	−36 03	?	6.2–6.6	—	G5	Faded between 1978 and 1979
α Her	17 14.6	+14 23	SRC	2.7–4.0	—	M	Slow variations (period about 6 years) and quicker changes (over about 100 d). See Double stars
U Oph	17 16.5	+01 13	EA/DM	5.8–6.6	1.68	B5+B5	Secondary minimum 6.5
68, u Her	17 17.3	+33 06	EA/SD	4.7–5.4	2.05	B2+B5	
V636 Sco	17 22.8	−45 37	DCEP	6.4–6.9	6.80	G	
V862 Sco	17 40.0	−32 12	GCAS?	2–8.5	—	B	In open cluster M6. Flare of 40 min on 1965 July 3
BM Sco	17 41.0	−32 13	SRD	5.0–6.9	815?	K	Brightest star in open cluster M6
V Pav	17 43.3	−57 43	SRB	6.3–8.2	225.4	C	Secondary period 3735 d
X Sgr	17 47.6	−27 50	DCEP	4.2–4.9	7.01	G	
RS Oph	17 50.2	−06 43	NR	4.3–12.5	—	OB+M	Outbursts 1898, 1933, 1958, 1967, 1985
V539 Ara	17 50.5	−53 37	EA/DM	5.7–6.2	3.17	B2+B3	
Y Oph	17 52.6	−06 09	DCEPS	5.9–6.5	17.12	G	
OP Her	17 56.8	+45 21	SRB	5.9–6.7	120.5	M	

Clusters, nebulae and galaxies

NGC	M	RA 2000.0 h m	Dec. ° '	Notes
5457	101	14 03	+54 21	Spiral galaxy in Ursa Major, seen face-on; 8th mag.
5460	—	14 08	−48 19	Open cluster in Centaurus; 6th mag.
5822	—	15 05	−54 21	Open cluster in Lupus; rich, with faint stars; 0°.6 across
5904	5	15 19	+02 05	Globular cluster in Serpens; 6th mag.
6067	—	16 13	−54 13	Open cluster in Norma; 6th mag.
6093	80	16 17	−22 59	Globular cluster in Scorpius; 7th mag.
6121	4	16 24	−26 32	Globular cluster in Scorpius; large (0°.4) but low surface brightness
6193	—	16 41	−48 46	Open cluster in Ara; 5th mag.
6205	13	16 42	+36 28	Globular cluster in Hercules, the finest of its class in northern skies, easy in binoculars; 6th mag., 0°.25 across
6210	—	16 45	+23 49	Planetary nebula in Hercules; 9th mag.
6218	12	16 47	−01 57	} Pair of 7th-mag. globular clusters in Ophiuchus, each covering 0°.25
6254	10	16 57	−04 06	
6231	—	16 54	−41 48	Outstanding cluster in Scorpius for small telescopes, brightest stars of 5th mag.
6266	62	17 01	−30 07	} Pair of 7th-mag. globular clusters in Ophiuchus
6273	19	17 03	−26 16	
6341	92	17 17	+43 08	Globular cluster in Hercules, smaller and fainter than M13
6333	9	17 19	−18 31	Globular cluster in Ophiuchus; 8th mag.
6402	14	17 38	−03 15	Globular cluster in Ophiuchus; 8th mag.
6405	6	17 40	−32 13	Open cluster in Scorpius, 4th mag., 0°.25, good binocular object
6397	—	17 41	−53 40	6th-mag. globular cluster in Ara, 0°.4 diameter, scattered stars
IC 4665	—	17 46	+05 43	Loose binocular cluster in Ophiuchus
6475	7	17 54	−34 49	Outstanding naked-eye cluster in Scorpius covering over 1°; forms an excellent binocular pair with M6
6494	23	17 57	−19 01	6th-mag. cluster of faint stars in Sagittarius covering nearly 0°.5

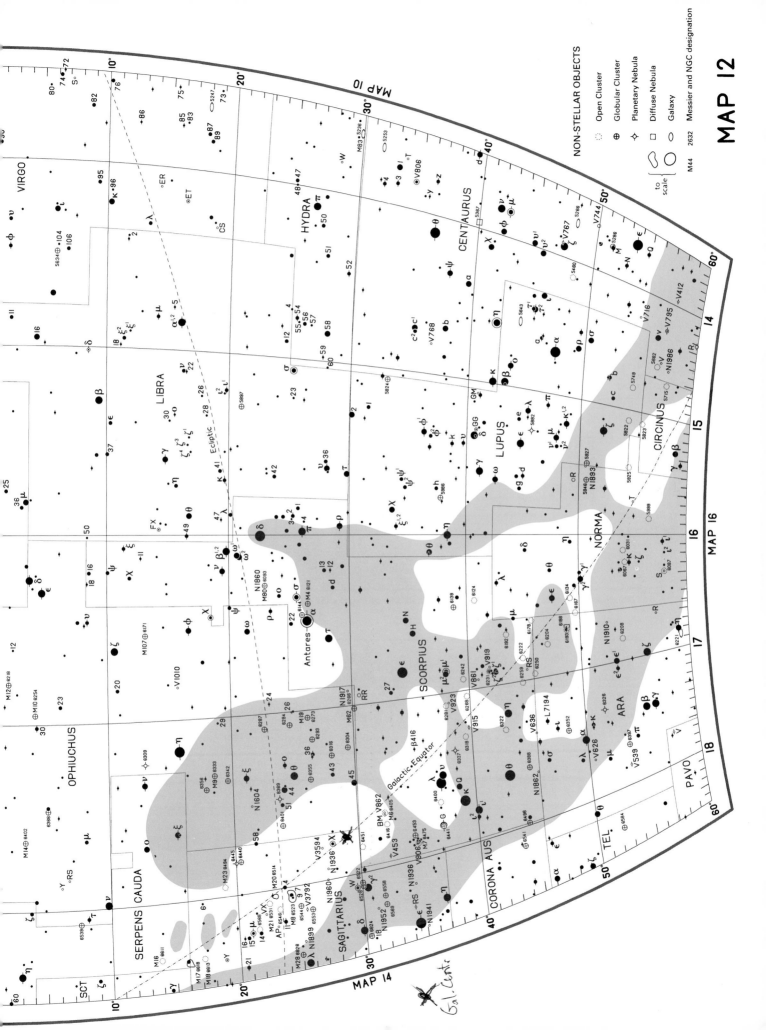

MAP 12

NON-STELLAR OBJECTS

- ⬡ Open Cluster
- ⊕ Globular Cluster
- ✦ Planetary Nebula
- ☐ Diffuse Nebula
- ⬭ Galaxy

to scale

M44   2632   Messier and NGC designation

Interesting Objects, Maps 13 and 14

RA 18h to 22h, Dec. +60° to −60°

Double stars

ADS	Star	RA 2000.0 h m	Dec. ° ′	Magnitudes	PA °	Dist. ″	Notes
11005	τ Oph	18 03.1	−08 11	5.2 5.9	283	1.7	Binary, 280 years[a]
11046	70 Oph	18 05.5	+02 30	4.2 6.0	164	4.5	Binary, 88 years[a]
	h 5014 CrA	18 06.8	−43 25	5.7 5.7	345	0.9	Binary, 191 years[a]
	κ CrA	18 33.4	−38 44	5.9 6.6	359	21.4	Fixed
11483	OΣ358 Her	18 35.9	+16 59	6.8 7.0	147	1.3	Binary, 290 years[a]
11635	ε Lyr	18 44.3	+39 40	4.7 4.6	173	207.7	Fixed naked-eye pair. Both binary: ε¹ 5.0, 6.1; 350°, 2″.6; 1200 years[a]. ε² 5.2, 5.5; 82°, 2″.3; 600 years[a]
11639	ζ Lyr	18 44.8	+37 36	4.3 5.9	150	43.7	Fixed. Very easy pair
11745	β Lyr	18 50.1	+33 22	3.4 8.6	149	45.7	Fixed
11853	θ Ser	18 56.2	+04 12	4.5 5.4	104	22.3	Fixed. Fine, easy pair
	γ CrA	19 06.4	−37 04	4.8 5.1	55	1.3	Binary, 120 years[a]
12197	η Lyr	19 13.8	+39 09	4.4 9.1	82	28.1	Fixed. Fine low-power field
12540	β Cyg	19 30.7	+27 58	3.1 5.1	54	34.4	Fixed. Glorious pair: yellow, greenish (by contrast)
12880	δ Cyg	19 45.0	+45 08	2.9 6.3	221	2.5	Binary, 800 years[a]. Test for 100 mm
12962	π Aql	19 48.7	+11 49	6.1 6.9	110	1.4	Slow decrease of PA. Test for 75 mm
13148	ψ Cyg	19 55.6	+52 26	4.9 7.4	178	3.2	Slow decrease of PA
13442	θ Sge	20 09.9	+20 55	6.5 9.0	325	11.9	Little change
13632	α¹ Cap	20 17.6	−12 30	4.2 9.2	221	45.4	Optical; little change
13645	α² Cap	20 18.1	−12 33	3.6 10.4	172	6.6	Binary. Fainter component is itself double: 11.0, 11.3; 240°, 1″.2; fixed. Naked-eye pair with α¹ at 29°, 377″.7; little change
13765	γ Cyg	20 22.2	+40 15	2.2 9.5	196	41.2	Optical; fixed. B is itself double: 9.9, 10.9; 302°, 1″.8; fixed
	κ² Sgr	20 23.9	−42 25	6.0 6.9	234	0.8	Closing; PA increasing slowly
13887	ρ Cap	20 28.9	−17 49	5.0 10.0	158	0.5	Closing; PA decreasing
14158	49 Cyg	20 41.0	+32 18	5.7 7.8	47	2.7	Fixed; yellowish, bluish
14259	52 Cyg	20 45.7	+30 43	4.2 9.4	67	6.0	Slow binary. In nebula NGC 6960
14279	γ Del	20 46.7	+16 07	4.5 5.5	268	9.6	Slow decrease of distance and PA; yellow, greenish (by contrast)
14296	λ Cyg	20 47.4	+36 29	4.9 6.1	6	0.9	Binary, 400 years[a]
14360	4 Aqr	20 51.4	−05 38	6.4 7.2	22	0.8	Binary, 187 years[a]
14499	ε Equ	20 59.1	+04 18	5.8 6.1 7.1	284 70	0.8 10.7	AB binary, 101 years[a]. PA of C slowly decreasing
14636	61 Cyg	21 06.9	+38 45	5.2 6.0	150	30.3	Binary, 650 years[a]. Large p.m.
14787	τ Cyg	21 14.8	+38 03	3.8 6.4	306	0.8	Binary, 50 years[a]
15270	μ Cyg	21 44.1	+28 45	4.8 6.1	320	1.2	Binary, 500 years[a]
15281	κ Peg	21 44.6	+25 39	4.7 5.0	103	0.2	Very close binary, 12 years[a]. Mag. 10.6 star at 292°, 13″.8; widening, PA decreasing

[a] Orbital elements for these binaries are given in Table 46. PA and Dist. are predictions for 2000.0.

Variable stars

Star	RA 2000.0 h m	Dec. ° ′	Type	Range (mags)	Period (d)	Spectral type	Notes
W Sgr	18 05.0	−29 35	DCEP	4.3–5.1	7.60	G	
VX Sgr	18 08.1	−22 13	SRC	6.5–14.0	732	M	
V3792 Sgr	18 08.9	−25 28	EB/DM	6.4–6.9	2.25	B5	
AP Sgr	18 13.0	−23 07	DCEP	6.5–7.4	5.06	G	
RS Sgr	18 17.6	−34 06	EA/SD	6.0–7.0	2.42	B3+A	Secondary minimum 6.3
Y Sgr	18 21.4	−18 52	DCEP	5.3–6.2	5.77	G	
U Sgr	18 31.9	−19 07	DCEP	6.3–7.2	6.75	G	In open cluster M25
XY Lyr	18 38.1	+39 40	LC	5.8–6.4	—	M	
X Oph	18 38.3	+08 50	M	5.9–9.2	328.85	M	Mean range 6.8–8.8
V3879 Sgr	18 42.9	−19 16	SRB	6.1–6.6	50?	M	
R Sct	18 47.5	−05 42	RVA	4.2–8.6	146.5	K	
β Lyr	18 50.1	+33 22	EB	3.3–4.4	12.94	B8	Period increasing. See Double stars
R Lyr	18 55.3	+43 57	SRB	3.9–5.0	46?	M	
FF Aql	18 58.2	+17 22	DCEPS	5.2–5.7	4.47	F	
R Aql	19 06.4	+08 14	M	5.5–12.0	284.2	M	Mean range 6.1–11.5; period shortening
TT Aql	19 08.2	+01 18	DCEP	6.5–7.7	13.75	G	
RY Sgr	19 16.5	−33 31	RCB	5.8–14.0	—	G	Pulsations up to 1.5 mag. in period 38 d
U Sge	19 18.8	+19 37	EA/SD	6.5–9.3	3.38	B8+G2	
CH Cyg	19 24.5	+50 14	ZAND+SR	5.6–9.0	—	M+B	Pulsations with period 97 d, secondary period 4700 d; also cycle of 725 d, flares, and possible eclipses
U Aql	19 29.4	−07 03	DCEP	6.1–6.9	7.02	F	
AF Cyg	19 30.2	+46 09	SRB	6.4–8.4	92.5	M	Secondary periods 175.8 and 941.2 d
AQ Sgr	19 34.3	−16 22	SRB	6–8	199.6	C	

Variable stars (continued)

Star	RA	Dec. 2000.0	Type	Range (mags)	Period (d)	Spectral type	Notes
	h m	° ′					
R Cyg	19 36.8	+50 12	M	6.1–14.4	426.45	S	Mean range 7.5–13.9
V1143 Cyg	19 38.7	+54 58	EA/DM	5.9–6.4	7.64	F5+F5	
RT Cyg	19 43.6	+48 47	M	6.0–13.1	190.28	M	Mean range 7.3–11.8
V973 Cyg	19 44.8	+40 43	SRB	6.2–7.0	40?	M	
SU Cyg	19 44.8	+29 16	DCEP	6.4–7.2	3.85	G+B7	
χ Cyg	19 50.6	+32 55	M	3.3–14.2	408.05	S	Mean range 5.2–13.4
η Aql	19 52.5	+01 00	DCEP	3.5–4.4	7.18	G	
V505 Sgr	19 53.1	−14 36	EA/SD	6.5–7.5	1.18	A2+F6	
RR Sgr	19 55.9	−29 11	M	5.4–14.0	336.33	M	Mean range 6.8–13.2
S Sge	19 56.0	+16 38	DCEP	5.2–6.0	8.38	G	
RU Sgr	19 58.7	−41 51	M	6.0–13.8	240.49	M	Mean range 7.2–12.8
HU Sge	20 03.7	+21 30	LB	6.3–7.3	—	M	
RS Cyg	20 13.4	+38 44	SRA	6.5–9.5	417.39	C	Shape of light curve varies strongly; maxima sometimes double
RT Cap	20 17.2	−21 20	SRB	6–9	393	C	
RT Sgr	20 17.7	−39 07	M	6.0–14.1	306.46	M	Mean range 7.0–13.3
P Cyg	20 17.8	+38 02	SDOR	3–6	—	B1	'Nova' of 1600. Since 18th century range has been 4.6–5.6
U Cyg	20 19.6	+47 54	M	5.9–12.1	463.24	C	Mean range 7.2–10.7
EU Del	20 37.9	+18 16	SRB	5.8–6.9	59.7	M	
X Cyg	20 43.4	+35 35	DCEP	5.9–6.9	16.39	G	
U Del	20 45.5	+18 05	SRB	5.6–7.5	110?	M	Period 160–180 d?
T Vul	20 51.5	+28 15	DCEP	5.4–6.1	4.44	G	
T Ind	21 20.2	−45 01	SRB	5–6.5	320?	C	
V1070 Cyg	21 22.8	+40 56	SRB	6.5–8.5	73.5	M	
W Cyg	21 36.0	+45 22	SRB	5.0–7.6	131.1	M	Secondary period 235.3 d
V460 Cyg	21 42.0	+35 31	SRB	5.6–7.0	180?	C	
V1339 Cyg	21 42.1	+45 46	SRB	5.9–7.1	35?	M	
μ Cep	21 43.5	+58 47	SRC	3.4–5.1	730	M	Secondary period 4400 d
ε Peg	21 44.2	+09 52	LC	0.7–3.5	—	K	Normally 2.3–2.4; unconfirmed flare 1972 Sept. 26/27
EP Aqr	21 46.5	−02 13	SRB	6.4–6.8	55?	M	
AG Peg	21 51.0	+12 38	NC	6.0–9.4	—	W+M3	Maximum in 1870. In recent years range has been 8.0–8.6 in period of about 800 d

Clusters, nebulae and galaxies

NGC	M	RA	Dec. 2000.0	Notes
		h m	° ′	
6514	20	18 02	−23 02	Trifid Nebula in Sagittarius, with embedded stars; 9th mag.
6523	8	18 04	−24 23	Lagoon Nebula in Sagittarius, 1°.5×0°.6, containing star cluster NGC 6530
6531	21	18 05	−22 30	6th-mag. open cluster in Sagittarius, in same field as M20
6572	—	18 12	+06 51	Planetary nebula in Ophiuchus; 9th mag.
6603	24	18 18	−18 30	Small, faint star cluster in a rich Milky Way star field in Sagittarius
6611	16	18 19	−13 47	Open cluster in Serpens; appears hazy since it is embedded in the Eagle Nebula, which shows up well in photographs
6613	18	18 20	−17 08	7th-mag. cluster in Sagittarius, in same binocular field as M17
6618	17	18 21	−16 11	Omega Nebula in Sagittarius, noticeably elongated, containing a star cluster
6633	—	18 28	+06 34	5th-mag. star cluster in Ophiuchus
IC 4725	25	18 32	−19 15	5th-mag. open cluster in Sagittarius, containing U Sgr
6656	22	18 36	−23 54	Globular cluster in Sagittarius, large (0°.4) and bright (5th mag.); excellent binocular object
6705	11	18 51	−06 16	Wild Duck Cluster in Scutum; 5th mag., fan-shaped; superb in all apertures
6720	57	18 54	+33 02	Ring Nebula in Lyra, elliptical 9th-mag. planetary nebula, 1′ across
6715	54	18 55	−30 29	8th-mag. globular cluster in Sagittarius
6779	56	19 17	+30 11	8th-mag. globular cluster in Lyra
—	—	19 25	+20 11	Collinder 399 in Vulpecula, also known as Brocchi's Cluster, consisting of ten stars in the shape of a coathanger
6809	55	19 40	−30 58	7th-mag. globular cluster in Sagittarius
6826	—	19 45	+50 31	Planetary nebula in Cygnus, called the 'blinking planetary' because it seems to wink in and out of view; 9th mag.
6838	71	19 54	+18 47	8th-mag. globular cluster in Sagitta
6853	27	20 00	+22 43	The Dumbbell Nebula, planetary nebula in Vulpecula; visible in binoculars as a rounded haze; telescopes show its twin lobes; 8th mag., 6′ long
6864	75	20 06	−21 55	9th-mag. globular cluster in Sagittarius
6992	—	20 56	+31 43	Brightest part of the Veil Nebula in Cygnus, a supernova remnant, visible in binoculars under dark skies
7000	—	21 00	+44 20	North America Nebula in Cygnus; 2° long, but with low surface brightness; visible in binoculars under dark skies
7009	—	21 04	−11 22	Saturn Nebula, 8th-mag. planetary nebula in Aquarius; large telescopes are needed to show the Saturn-like shape
7078	15	21 30	+12 10	Globular cluster in Pegasus; 6th mag.
7092	39	21 32	+48 26	Open cluster in Cygnus; 5th mag.; stars thinly scattered over 0°.5
7089	2	21 34	−00 49	Globular cluster in Aquarius; stars densely packed; mag. 6.5
7099	30	21 40	−23 11	8th-mag. globular cluster in Capricornus

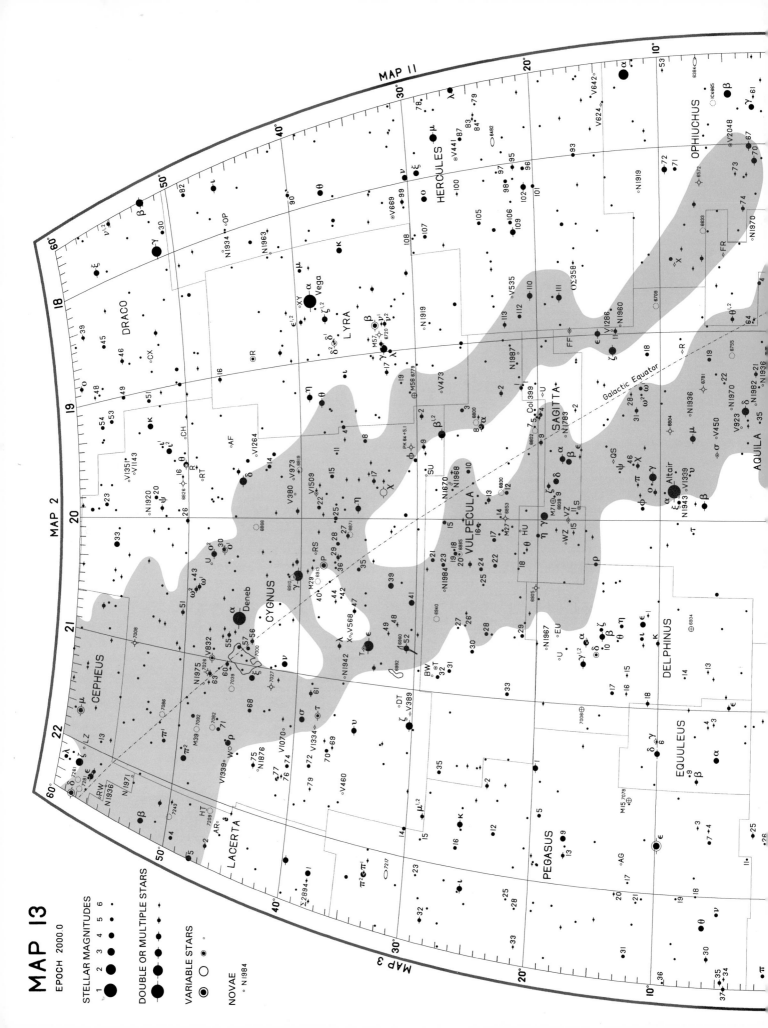

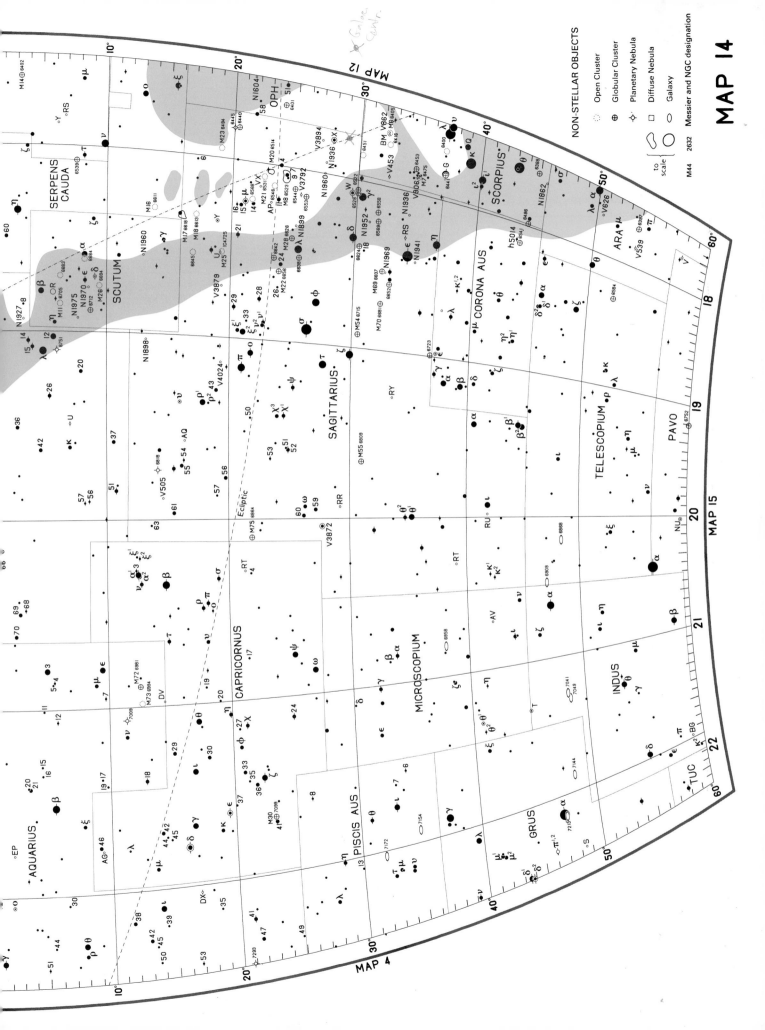

MAP 14

NON-STELLAR OBJECTS

⊕ Open Cluster
⊕ Globular Cluster
✧ Planetary Nebula
☐ Diffuse Nebula
○ Galaxy

to scale { ⬭ ○ }

M44   2632   Messier and NGC designation

Interesting Objects, Maps 15 and 16

Dec. −60° to −90°

Double stars

Star	RA 2000.0 h m	Dec. ° ′	Magnitudes	PA °	Dist. ″	Notes
β[1,2] Tuc	00 31.5	−62 58	4.4 4.5	169	27.1	Fixed. Both double. β[1]: 4.4, 13.5; 151°, 2″.4; fixed. β[2]: 4.8, 6.0; 276°, 0″.5; binary, 44 years
λ[1] Tuc	00 52.4	−69 30	6.5 7.9	81	20.7	Optical; little change
κ Tuc	01 15.8	−68 53	5.1 7.3	336	5.4	Slow binary
h3568 Hyi	03 07.5	−78 59	5.6 9.3	224	15.2	Fixed
θ Ret	04 17.7	−63 15	6.2 8.2	4	4.1	Little change
h3670 Ret	04 33.6	−62 49	5.9 9.2	99	31.9	Optical; fixed
I 5 Pic	06 38.0	−61 32	6.4 8.4	270	2.4	Little change
γ Vol	07 08.8	−70 30	4.0 5.9	300	13.6	Physical pair, but fixed
ε Vol	08 07.9	−68 37	4.4 8.0	24	6.1	Fixed
C Car	08 14.5	−62 46	5.3 8.0	66	3.9	Little change
θ Vol	08 39.1	−70 23	5.3 10.3	108	45.0	Optical; fixed
h4128 Car	08 39.2	−60 19	6.9 7.5	210	1.4	Slowly closing; PA decreasing
υ Car	09 47.1	−65 04	3.1 6.1	127	5.0	Fixed
h4306 Car	10 19.1	−64 41	7.0 7.0	134	2.1	Little change
h4432 Mus	11 23.4	−64 57	5.4 6.6	303	2.3	Binary; PA increasing slowly
ε Cha	11 59.6	−78 13	5.4 6.0	188	0.9	Binary; PA increasing slowly
α Cru	12 26.6	−63 06	1.3 1.7	115	4.4	Little change. Very easy
ι Cru	12 45.6	−60 59	4.7 9.5	22	26.9	Optical pair; PA decreasing
β Mus	12 46.3	−68 06	3.7 4.0	43	1.3	Binary, 400 years[a]
θ Mus	13 08.1	−65 18	5.7 7.3	187	5.3	Fixed
J Cen	13 22.6	−60 59	4.7 6.5	343	60.0	Fixed. Wide, easy pair. A is very close double: 5.4, 5.4; 168°, 0″.1
β Cen	14 03.8	−60 22	0.7 3.9	251	1.3	PA slowly decreasing
α Cen	14 39.6	−60 50	0.0 1.3	222	14.1	Superb binary, 80 years[a]
α Cir	14 42.5	−64 59	3.2 8.6	232	15.7	PA slowly decreasing
ι TrA	16 28.0	−64 03	5.3 10.3	16	19.6	Optical pair; PA and distance slowly decreasing
ξ Pav	18 23.2	−61 30	4.4 8.6	154	3.3	Very slow binary
λ Oct	21 50.9	−82 43	5.4 7.7	70	3.1	Slow binary; PA decreasing
δ Tuc	22 27.3	−64 58	4.5 9.0	282	6.9	Fixed

[a] Orbital elements for these binaries are given in Table 46. PA and Dist. are predictions for 2000.0.

Variable stars

Star	RA 2000.0 h m	Dec. ° ′	Type	Range (mags)	Period (d)	Spectral type	Notes
R Ret	04 33.5	−63 02	M	6.5–14.2	278.46	M	Mean range 7.6–13.3
R Dor	04 36.8	−62 05	SRB	4.8–6.6	338?	M	
R Oct	05 26.1	−86 23	M	6.3–13.2	405.39	M	Mean range 7.9–12.4
TZ Men	05 30.2	−84 47	EA/D	6.2–6.9	8.57	A1+B9	
β Dor	05 33.6	−62 29	DCEP	3.5–4.1	9.84	G	
RS Cha	08 43.2	−79 04	EA+DSCT	6.0–6.7	1.67	A5+A7	Secondary minimum 6.5
R Car	09 32.2	−62 47	M	3.9–10.5	308.71	M	Mean range 4.6–9.6
l Car	09 45.2	−62 30	DCEP	3.3–4.2	35.54	G	
S Car	10 09.4	−61 33	M	4.5–9.9	149.49	M	Mean range 5.7–8.5
S Mus	12 12.8	−70 09	DCEP	5.9–6.5	9.66	G	
T Cru	12 21.4	−62 17	DCEP	6.3–6.8	6.73	G	Near open cluster NGC 4349
R Cru	12 23.6	−61 38	DCEP	6.4–7.2	5.83	G	Near open cluster NGC 4349
BO Mus	12 34.9	−67 45	LB	5.9–6.6	—	M	
R Mus	12 42.1	−69 24	DCEP	5.9–6.7	7.51	G	
V766 Cen	13 47.2	−62 35	SDOR?	6.2–7.5	—	G8	
θ Aps	14 05.3	−76 48	SRB	5–7	119	M	
AX Cir	14 52.6	−63 49	DCEP	5.7–6.1	5.27	G+B4	
θ Cir	14 56.7	−62 47	GCAS	5.0–5.4	—	B3	
X TrA	15 14.3	−70 05	LB	5.0–6.4	—	C	
R TrA	15 19.8	−66 30	DCEP	6.3–7.0	3.39	G	
S TrA	16 01.2	−63 47	DCEP	6.0–6.8	6.32	G	
VZ Aps	16 16.3	−74 02	M	6–15	385	M	
κ Pav	18 56.9	−67 14	CEP	3.9–4.8	9.09	G	
Y Pav	21 24.3	−69 44	SRB	5.6–7.3	233.3	C	
SX Pav	21 28.7	−69 30	SRB	5.3–6.0	50?	M	
ε Oct	22 20.0	−80 26	SRB	4.6–5.3	55?	M	

Clusters, nebulae and galaxies

NGC	RA 2000.0 h m	Dec. ° ′	Notes
104	00 24	−72 05	Globular cluster 47 Tucanae; 4th mag., diameter 0°.5, the second most prominent globular, after ω Centauri
362	01 03	−70 51	7th-mag. globular cluster in Tucana, near the Small Magellanic Cloud but not part of it
2070	05 39	−69 06	Tarantula Nebula, also called 30 Doradus, in the Large Magellanic Cloud, with embedded stars; 0°.5 across, visible to the naked eye
2516	07 58	−60 52	Rich naked-eye cluster in Carina, 0°.5 across; brightest star 5th mag.
2808	09 12	−64 52	6th-mag. globular cluster in Carina; large, with bright centre
3114	10 03	−60 07	4th-mag. open cluster in Carina
IC 2602	10 43	−64 24	Naked-eye cluster nearly 1° across centred on 3rd-mag. θ Carinae
3372	10 45	−59 50	Naked-eye nebula around the star η Carinae; 2° wide with embedded stars; contains dark nebula called the Keyhole
3766	11 36	−61 37	5th-mag. open cluster in Centaurus
—	12 50	−63 00	The Coalsack, a dark nebula in front of the Milky Way in Crux, 6°.5×5°
4755	12 54	−60 20	The Jewel Box cluster, a collection of glittering coloured stars including the 6th-mag. κ Crucis
4833	13 00	−70 53	7th-mag. globular cluster in Musca
6025	16 04	−60 30	5th-mag. open cluster in Triangulum Australe
6752	19 11	−59 59	Large 5th-mag. globular cluster in Pavo

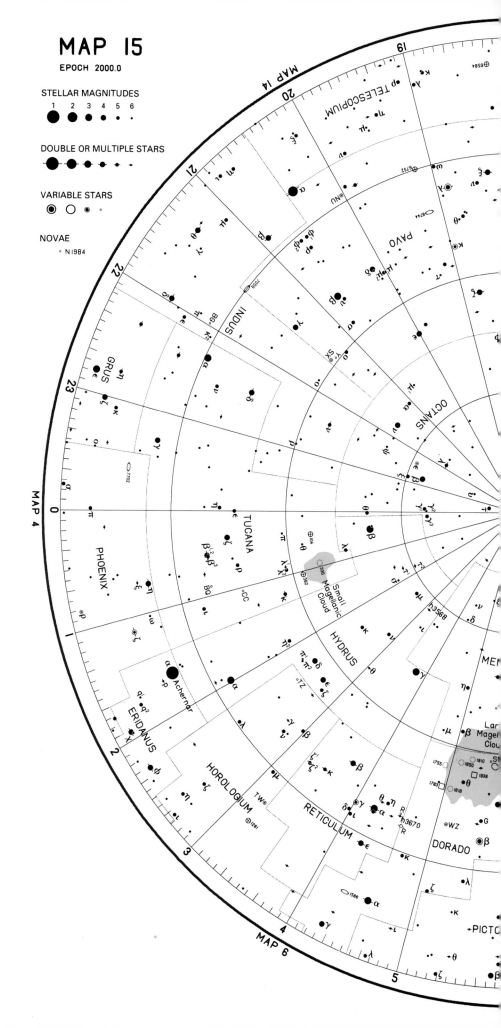

MAP 15

EPOCH 2000.0

STELLAR MAGNITUDES

1 2 3 4 5 6

DOUBLE OR MULTIPLE STARS

VARIABLE STARS

NOVAE

∘ N 1984

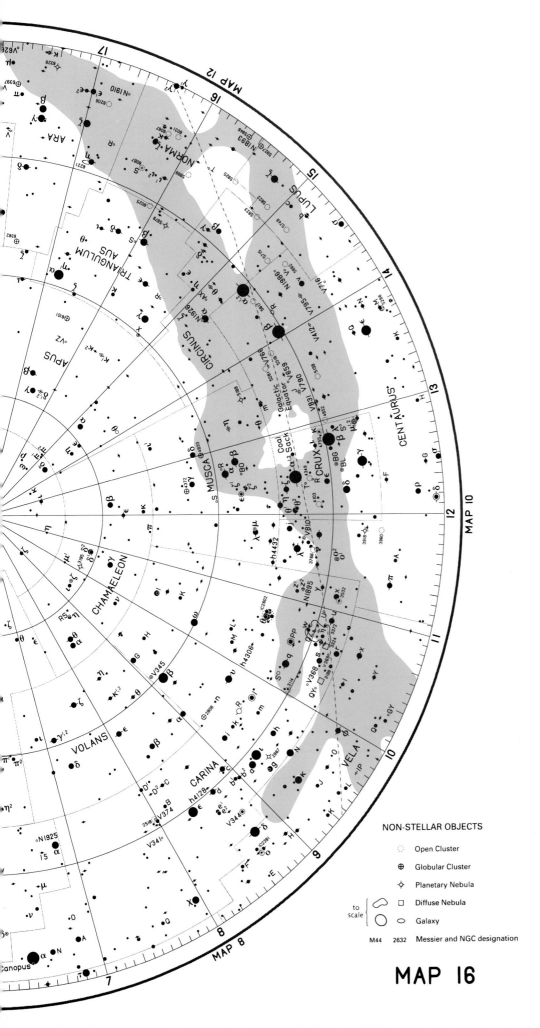

NON-STELLAR OBJECTS

⬚ Open Cluster

⊕ Globular Cluster

✧ Planetary Nebula

◻ Diffuse Nebula

⬭ Galaxy

to scale

M44 2632 Messier and NGC designation

MAP 16

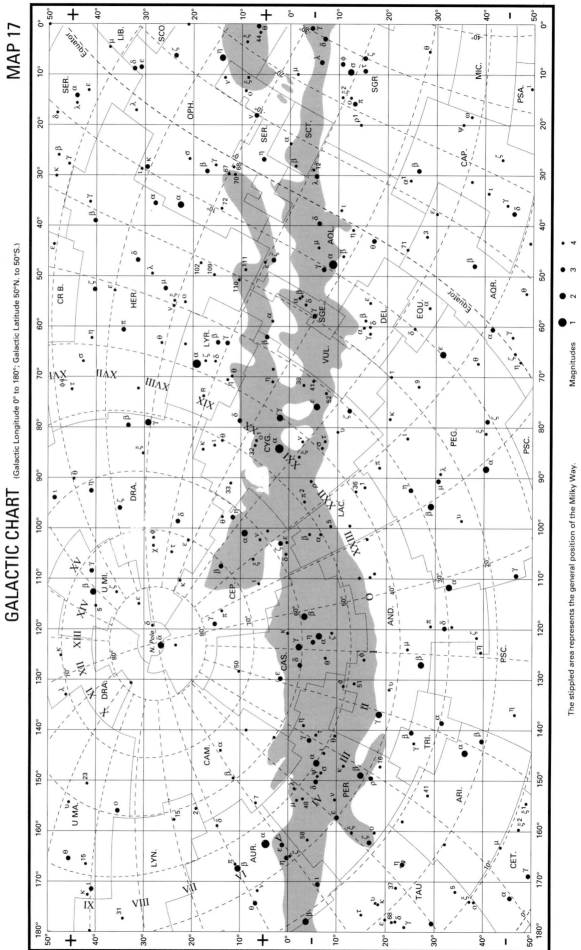

GALACTIC CHART (Galactic Longitude 0° to 180°; Galactic Latitude 50°N. to 50°S.)

MAP 17

Magnitudes

● 1
● 2
● 3
• 4

The stippled area represents the general position of the Milky Way.

MAP 18

GALACTIC CHART (Galactic Longitude 180° to 360°; Galactic Latitude 50°N. to 50°S.)

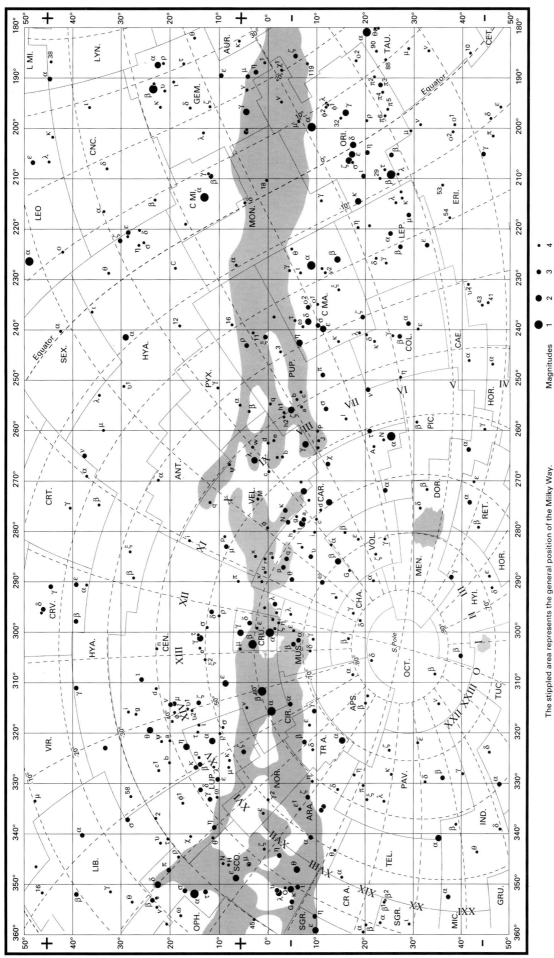

The stippled area represents the general position of the Milky Way.

Magnitudes

1 2 3 4

II

POSITION AND TIME

THE HEAVENS ABOVE

The celestial sphere

All astronomical objects can be considered as lying on an imaginary sphere surrounding the Earth, called the celestial sphere (Figure 1). Like any sphere, the celestial sphere has

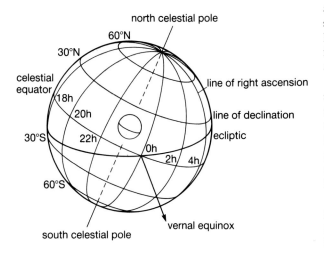

Figure 1. The celestial sphere, with the Earth at its centre, showing lines of right ascension and declination, and the ecliptic.

two poles and an equator. The *celestial poles* lie directly above the poles of the Earth, while the *celestial equator* lies directly above the Earth's equator. The celestial sphere appears to rotate once a day around the celestial poles, actually as a result of the rotation of the Earth on its axis.

An observer standing on the surface of the Earth sees only half the celestial sphere at any one time. The visible half of the celestial sphere is bounded by the observer's *horizon*, a plane that cuts the celestial sphere 90° from the observer's *zenith*. The zenith is the point on the celestial sphere directly above the observer. Directly beneath the observer is the point called the *nadir*.

For the coordinate systems used to measure the positions of objects on the celestial sphere, see the section on Position (p. 41).

Daily rotation

Every day the celestial sphere appears to turn as the Earth rotates, causing the daily rising and setting of the Sun, stars and other celestial bodies. As seen from the equator, all stars rise at right angles to the horizon and remain above the horizon for 12 hours. But as seen from the poles, stars move in circles parallel to the horizon and remain permanently above the horizon, never rising or setting.

At intermediate latitudes, the apparent motion of the stars lies between these two extremes. Some stars rise and set, but others circle around the pole without setting; these are known as circumpolar stars (see below). At any latitude, the stars that rise and set always do so at the same points on the horizon. This is not the case for the Sun, Moon and planets, which move against the celestial sphere and hence rise and set at different points from day to day.

The length of time an object spends above the horizon as seen from a particular location depends on its declination (angular distance north or south of the celestial equator). Stars on the celestial equator rise due east and set due west, and are above the horizon for 12 hours as seen from anywhere on Earth (except at the poles). Stars nearer the visible pole are above the horizon for longer than 12 hours, whereas stars more than 90° from the pole set in less than 12 hours.

Table 1 gives the length of time that objects at various declinations take to reach the meridian (see p. 40) after rising; the total time for which the object is above the horizon from rising to setting is twice the time given in this table.

Circumpolar stars are stars that never set as seen from a given location. The area of sky that is circumpolar depends on the observer's latitude on Earth, since the altitude of the celestial pole equals the observer's latitude. For example, from latitude 40° the celestial pole has an altitude above the

Table 1. Semi-diurnal arcs. For stars of particular declination, the time interval between rising or setting of the star and its transit over the observer's meridian (i.e. its culmination) is given for different latitudes. The total time for which the star is visible, from rising to setting, is twice this interval. The figures are calculated from the formula:

$$\cos(\text{semi-diurnal arc}) = -\tan(\text{dec.}) \times \tan(\text{lat.})$$

To convert degrees to hours, divide by 15. Atmospheric refraction is ignored.

Latitude of observer	Declination of star (north declination for northern observers, south declination for southern observers)							Declination of star (south declination for northern observers, north declination for southern observers)					
	30°	25°	20°	15°	10°	05°	00°	05°	10°	15°	20°	25°	30°
°	h m	h m	h m	h m	h m	h m	h m	h m	h m	h m	h m	h m	h m
5	06 12	06 09	06 07	06 05	06 04	06 02	06 00	05 58	05 56	05 55	05 53	05 51	05 48
10	06 23	06 19	06 15	06 11	06 07	06 04	06 00	05 56	05 53	05 49	05 45	05 41	05 37
15	06 36	06 29	06 22	06 16	06 11	06 05	06 00	05 55	05 49	05 44	05 38	05 31	05 24
20	06 49	06 39	06 30	06 22	06 15	06 07	06 00	05 53	05 45	05 38	05 30	05 21	05 11
25	07 02	06 50	06 39	06 29	06 19	06 09	06 00	05 51	05 41	05 31	05 21	05 10	04 58
30	07 18	07 02	06 49	06 36	06 23	06 12	06 00	05 48	05 37	05 24	05 11	04 58	04 42
35	07 35	07 16	06 59	06 43	06 28	06 14	06 00	05 46	05 32	05 17	05 01	04 44	04 25
40	07 56	07 32	07 11	06 52	06 34	06 17	06 00	05 43	05 26	05 08	04 49	04 28	04 04
45	08 21	07 51	07 25	07 02	06 41	06 20	06 00	05 40	05 19	04 58	04 35	04 09	03 39
50	08 54	08 15	07 43	07 14	06 49	06 24	06 00	05 36	05 11	04 46	04 17	03 45	03 06
55	09 42	08 47	08 05	07 30	06 58	06 29	06 00	05 31	05 02	04 30	03 55	03 13	02 18
60	—	09 35	08 36	07 51	07 11	06 35	06 00	05 25	04 49	04 09	03 24	02 25	—

horizon of 40°, and all objects within 40° of the pole are circumpolar. Equally, there is a corresponding area within 40° of the opposite pole that is never visible. At the poles, all stars visible are circumpolar. From the equator, none are circumpolar.

The meridian

An observer's meridian is the imaginary line that runs from north to south in the sky, passing through both celestial poles and through the zenith. When an object lies on the meridian it is said to be *at culmination* or *in transit* (both phrases mean the same thing).

A circumpolar object culminates twice. *Upper culmination* refers to its highest altitude as it passes from east to west across the meridian. *Lower culmination* refers to its lowest altitude as it passes across the meridian between the pole and the horizon. When used without qualification, 'culmination' refers to the moment when a celestial body reaches its greatest altitude above the horizon, i.e. upper culmination.

The ecliptic

During the year the Sun appears to move once around the celestial sphere, as a result of the Earth's orbital motion. The Sun's yearly path on the celestial sphere is called the ecliptic. It is inclined to the celestial equator by about $23\frac{1}{2}°$, an angle known as the *obliquity of the ecliptic* (see below), which results from the axial tilt of the Earth. During the year the Sun's declination ranges from $23\frac{1}{2}°$ north to $23\frac{1}{2}°$ south, reaching its greatest values north and south at the summer and winter solstices respectively. If the Earth's axis

were not tilted, the Sun would appear to move along the celestial equator and there would be no seasons on Earth.

When the Sun crosses the celestial equator at the spring equinox around March 21 every year its position is right ascension 0h, declination 0°. Six months later, around September 23 (the autumnal equinox), it is at right ascension 12h, declination 0°. Between these dates it has been north of the celestial equator; for the following six months of the year, between September 23 and March 21, the Sun lies south of the celestial equator. Table 7 on page 54 gives the right ascension and declination of the Sun at various times of the year.

The *ecliptic poles* lie 90° north and south of the ecliptic. They are at right ascension 18h, declination $66\frac{1}{2}°$ north; and right ascension 6h, declination $66\frac{1}{2}°$ south.

Obliquity of the ecliptic (symbol ϵ) is the angle at which the celestial equator is tilted with respect to the ecliptic; it is equal to the tilt of the Earth's axis from the perpendicular to the plane of its orbit. The obliquity of the ecliptic varies slightly with time due to the effects of nutation and the gravitational pulls of the planets on the Earth. Nutation causes a variation of up to $9''.2$ from the mean value every 18.6 years, while planetary precession is currently causing the mean value of the obliquity to decrease by $0''.47$ per year. On 1950 January 1 the obliquity was 23° 26′ 45″, and on 2000 January 1 it will be 23° 26′ 21″.

The equinoxes

These two points mark where the ecliptic intersects the celestial equator. The Sun reaches these points around March 21 and September 23 each year. At an equinox the centre of the Sun lies exactly on the celestial equator but, although the word 'equinox' means 'equal night', day and night are not exactly equal at the equinoxes. There are two reasons for this. Firstly, sunrise and sunset are calculated for the upper limb of the Sun, not its centre; secondly, the effect of refraction in the Earth's atmosphere lifts the image of the Sun by about half a degree at the horizon. These both have the effect of slightly lengthening the day.

Vernal equinox (symbol Υ). This is the point where the Sun crosses the celestial equator moving northwards, about March 21 each year, and is hence the ascending node of the ecliptic. The vernal (or spring) equinox is also known as the *first point of Aries*, since it lay in the constellation Aries 2000 years ago when its position was determined by the Greeks. Since then it has moved into the neighbouring constellation of Pisces as a result of the effect of precession (p. 44).

The vernal equinox is the zero point for the measurement of right ascension. Precession moves the vernal equinox westwards on the celestial sphere by about 0.14 arcsec per day.

Autumnal equinox (symbol $\triangleq$). This is the point where the Sun crosses the celestial equator moving southwards, about September 23 each year, and is hence the descending node of the ecliptic. It is also known as the *first point of Libra*, although precession has moved it into Virgo.

Colures. The *equinoctial colure* is the hour circle (see below) that passes through the vernal and autumnal equinoxes, and is therefore the hour circle of right ascension 0h and 12h. The *solstitial colure* is the hour circle that passes through the summer and winter solstices, i.e. the hour circle of right ascension 6h and 18h.

The solstices

The two points on the ecliptic at which the Sun reaches its greatest declination of $23\frac{1}{2}°$ north or south of the celestial equator, around June 21 (the summer solstice) and December 22 (the winter solstice) each year. At the *summer solstice* the Sun lies directly overhead at noon on the Tropic of Cancer, and the northern hemisphere then has its longest day and shortest night (vice versa in the southern hemisphere). At the *winter solstice* the Sun lies overhead on the Tropic of Capricorn so that the northern hemisphere has its shortest day and longest night (vice versa in the southern hemisphere).

Paradoxically, the dates of latest sunrise and earliest sunset do not coincide with the shortest day; neither do the dates of earliest sunrise and latest sunset coincide with the longest day. The reason is to be found in the changing value of the equation of time (p. 57), as a result of which sunrise and sunset are both getting later each day at the solstices, although by different amounts. The net result is that the latest sunrise actually occurs after the shortest day, and the earliest sunset before it, while the earliest sunrise occurs before the longest day, and the latest sunset after it. In each case the exact date depends on the observer's latitude, but the offset from the solstices is greater at lower latitudes. The effect is more pronounced at the December solstice than the June solstice because the day-to-day increase in the equation of time is greater in December.

POSITION

Celestial coordinate systems

Astronomical positions can be measured on the celestial sphere by using one of five different systems of coordinates, each of which suits a particular requirement. Four systems give positions as seen from the Earth; each uses a different reference plane (see Table 2). A fifth system, heliocentric coordinates, gives positions as seen from the Sun.

In catalogues, equatorial and ecliptic coordinates are listed for *geocentric* positions, i.e. as the object would be seen from the centre of the Earth. With distant objects such as stars and galaxies the observer's specific location on the Earth makes no difference to the object's observed position, but for objects in the Solar System slight corrections are needed to give the *topocentric* coordinates, i.e. as observed from a given place on the surface of the Earth.

Equatorial coordinates are the ones most usually encountered in astronomical work. Their reference plane is the celestial equator, and the coordinates used are right ascension and declination, although hour angle and polar distance are sometimes used instead.

Right ascension (RA, symbol α) and *declination* (dec., symbol δ) are the celestial equivalents of longitude and latitude on the Earth. Declination is measured in degrees, from 0° at the celestial equator to 90° at the celestial poles.

The zero line of right ascension is the equivalent of the Greenwich meridian on the Earth. It passes through the point where the Sun crosses the celestial equator from the southern into the northern hemisphere each year; this happens around March 21, at the vernal equinox. Right ascension is measured eastwards from the vernal equinox along the celestial equator in hours, minutes and seconds, from 0 to 24 hours, although sometimes degrees are used. Each hour of right ascension is equivalent to 15° (and thus 1° is equivalent to 4 minutes).

An *hour circle* is the circle passing through a body on the celestial sphere and through the celestial poles; it is perpendicular to the celestial equator. *Hour angle* is the angle between the meridian and the hour circle through a celestial body, measured westwards along the celestial equator. An object on the meridian has an hour angle of 0h; an object that crossed the meridian one hour ago has an hour angle of 1h, and so on. Hence the hour angle is the time that has elapsed since the object last crossed the meridian.

Polar distance is the angular distance of an object from the celestial pole, measured along the hour circle. It is equal to 90° minus the object's declination.

Horizontal coordinates, also called *azimuthal coordinates*, are the simplest positional system. Their reference plane is the observer's horizon, and the object's position is given in terms of altitude and azimuth (or zenith distance).

Altitude (symbol h or a) is the angle of elevation of a celestial object above the observer's horizon, measured perpendicular to the horizon. When the object is on the horizon, it has an altitude of 0°; an object at the zenith has an altitude of 90°. The *zenith distance* (symbol z) is sometimes used in place of altitude. This is the angular distance of an object from the zenith, and is equal to 90° minus the altitude. *Azimuth* (symbol A) is the angular distance measured clockwise around the horizon from due north, through east, to the point where a circle through the zenith and an object intersects the horizon. An object due north has an azimuth of 0°, an object due east has an azimuth of 90°, and so on.

The altitude and azimuth of an object at a particular time depend on the point on the Earth's surface from which they are measured, i.e. they are purely topocentric. Hence horizontal coordinates must be worked out for the observer's location and the required time from the right ascension and declination of the object.

Ecliptic coordinates take the ecliptic as their reference plane. Although they are less commonly met with than equatorial coordinates, they are sometimes used to give the positions of bodies in the Solar System, as seen from the Earth's centre. Their coordinates are celestial longitude and celestial latitude.

Celestial (or *ecliptic*) *longitude* (symbol λ) is measured along the ecliptic from 0° to 360° east of the vernal equinox. *Celestial* (or *ecliptic*) *latitude* (symbol β) is measured from 0° to 90° at right angles to the ecliptic, along a circle passing through the object and the ecliptic poles.

Galactic coordinates are used for studies of the positions of objects within our Galaxy. The reference plane is the galactic equator, which is inclined at about 63° to the celestial equator. The coordinates are *galactic latitude* (symbol b), which is measured perpendicular to the galactic equator from 0° to 90°, and *galactic longitude* (symbol l), which is measured in degrees eastwards along the galactic equator. The zero point of galactic longitude lies in the direction of the galactic centre; its position as adopted by the

International Astronomical Union in 1959 is RA 17h 45.6m, dec. −28° 56′.3 (2000.0 coordinates). The north galactic pole, which lies in Coma Berenices, is at RA 12h 51.4m, dec. 27° 7′.7 (2000.0 coordinates); the south galactic pole lies in Sculptor, at RA 00h 51.4m, dec. −27° 7′.7.

Heliocentric coordinates give the positions of objects as viewed from the centre of the Sun, and are used in particular for bodies in the Solar System. The reference plane of the heliocentric system is the ecliptic, and the coordinates are *heliocentric latitude* (symbol b) and *heliocentric longitude* (symbol l); the zero point of heliocentric longitude is the vernal equinox. The Earth's heliocentric longitude at a given instant is equal to the Sun's geocentric longitude plus 180°. More rigorous would be to use *barycentric* positions. These refer to the centre of mass of the Solar System, which is offset from the centre of the Sun because of the presence of the planets, in particular Jupiter, the most massive.

Planes of reference

The planes of reference used for the various position systems, with the coordinates and their points of origin, are summarized in Table 2.

The *invariable plane* of the Solar System is defined by its total angular momentum (i.e. by the rotational spins and orbital motions of all the planets and moons), and passes through the centre of mass of the Solar System. It forms an unvarying reference plane since its position in space is not changed by planetary perturbations, unlike the ecliptic. It is inclined at 1°.58 to the ecliptic.

Star places

The positions of the 'fixed' stars are usually given in terms of their right ascension and declination. But precession (see below) is constantly changing the positions of the equator and equinox on the celestial sphere, with consequent changes in the right ascensions and declinations of the stars. In addition, there are other effects (described below), such as nutation, aberration, parallax, proper motion and refraction, that affect the observed place of a star. In precise work it is therefore necessary to apply corrections for these various effects.

Three forms of a star's place are commonly used: the apparent place, the true place and the mean place.

Table 2. Planes of reference for coordinate systems, and points of origin.

Plane of reference	Coordinates
Celestial equator	Declination; right ascension from the vernal equinox
Ecliptic (from Earth's centre)	Celestial (geocentric) latitude; celestial (geocentric) longitude from the vernal equinox
Ecliptic (from Sun's centre)	Heliocentric latitude; heliocentric longitude from the vernal equinox
Horizon of the observer	Altitude; azimuth from north
Meridian	Declination from the celestial equator; hour angle from the meridian
Galactic plane	Galactic latitude; galactic longitude from the centre of the Galaxy
Sun's equator	Heliographic latitude; heliographic longitude from arbitrary zero
Equator of the Moon or a planet	Planetographic latitude and longitude from an agreed prime meridian
Limb of the Sun, Moon or a planet	Distance from either the north point or the vertex (the uppermost point)

Table 3. Precession.

Precession in RA over 10.0 years

Dec.	\multicolumn{13}{Hours of RA for objects with northerly declination}

Dec.	0, 12	1, 11	2, 10	3, 9	4, 8	5, 7	6	18	19, 17	20, 16	21, 15	22, 14	23, 13
(southerly)	0, 12	23, 13	22, 14	21, 15	20, 16	19, 17	18	6	5, 7	4, 8	3, 9	2, 10	1, 11
°	m	m	m	m	m	m	m	m	m	m	m	m	m
80	+0.51	+0.84	+1.15	+1.41	+1.61	+1.73	+1.78	−0.75	−0.71	−0.58	−0.38	−0.12	+0.19
70	+0.51	+0.67	+0.82	+0.95	+1.04	+1.10	+1.12	−0.10	−0.08	−0.02	+0.08	+0.21	+0.35
60	+0.51	+0.61	+0.71	+0.79	+0.85	+0.89	+0.90	+0.13	+0.14	+0.18	+0.24	+0.32	+0.41
50	+0.51	+0.58	+0.65	+0.70	+0.74	+0.77	+0.78	+0.25	+0.26	+0.28	+0.32	+0.38	+0.44
40	+0.51	+0.56	+0.61	+0.64	+0.67	+0.69	+0.70	+0.33	+0.33	+0.35	+0.38	+0.42	+0.46
30	+0.51	+0.55	+0.58	+0.60	+0.62	+0.64	+0.64	+0.38	+0.39	+0.40	+0.42	+0.45	+0.48
20	+0.51	+0.53	+0.55	+0.57	+0.58	+0.59	+0.59	+0.43	+0.43	+0.44	+0.46	+0.47	+0.49
10	+0.51	+0.52	+0.53	+0.54	+0.55	+0.55	+0.55	+0.47	+0.47	+0.48	+0.48	+0.49	+0.50
0	+0.51	+0.51	+0.51	+0.51	+0.51	+0.51	+0.51	+0.51	+0.51	+0.51	+0.51	+0.51	+0.51

Precession in declination over 10.0 years

Hours of RA for northern and southern objects

0	1, 23	2, 22	3, 21	4, 20	5, 19	6, 18	7, 17	8, 16	9, 15	10, 14	11, 13	12
′	′	′	′	′	′	′	′	′	′	′	′	′
+3.3	+3.2	+2.9	+2.4	+1.7	+0.9	+0.0	−0.9	−1.7	−2.4	−2.9	−3.2	−3.3

How to use the table

To estimate precession in RA, look at the column for the RA hour nearest to that being precessed. Note whether declination is north (positive) or south (negative) and choose the correct column. Read off the tabulated value against the declination; interpolate as necessary for greater accuracy. The table gives the correction for 10 years of precession, so multiply the figure as necessary for the required interval. Then apply the resulting correction to the object's RA.

For declination, read off the correction, interpolating as necessary, and multiply the figure for the required time interval. Apply the resulting correction to the object's declination.

Example. The 1950 coordinates of the star Beta (β) Capricorni are RA 20h 18.2m, dec. −14° 56′.5. What is the star's approximate position in 2000 coordinates?

From the table, the correction for 10 years is +0.56m. Multiply by 5 to obtain the correction for 50 years, and add to the 1950 RA, thus:

RA 1950	20h 18.2m
5 × (+0.56m)	+2.8m
RA 2000	20h 21.0m

The approximate correction for 10 years in declination is +1′.9, so the change over 50 years is

dec. 1950	−14° 56′.5
5 × (+1′.9)	+9′.5
dec. 2000	−14° 47′.0

Take care to add the correction algebraically: for like signs, add; for unlike signs (as here), subtract.

The actual 2000 coordinates for Beta (β) Capricorni are RA 20h 21.0m, dec. −14°46′.9. Inaccuracies will occur when estimating precession over long periods of time for stars with large proper motions.

Coordinates may be estimated for a previous epoch by reversing the sign of each correction factor.

The *apparent place* of a star is its position on the celestial sphere as would actually be observed from the centre of the Earth (i.e. in geocentric coordinates) at a given time. It is referred to the true equator and equinox at the instant of observation.

The *true place* of a star is given by the heliocentric (barycentric) coordinates of the star on the celestial sphere at the instant of observation, i.e. with the effects of annual parallax and aberration resulting from the movement of the Earth removed, and is referred to the true equator and equinox at that instant.

The *mean place* of a star is its heliocentric (barycentric) position on the celestial sphere with the effects of refraction, parallax and aberration removed, and is reduced to the mean equator and equinox for a stated epoch. The mean place varies with time, but only as a result of proper motion and precession, and is the position given in star catalogues.

True equator and equinox. These are the actual positions of the equator and equinox as observed at any given time. They are constantly shifting because of the progressive effect of precession and the cyclical effect of nutation.

Mean equator and equinox. These are the positions of the equator and equinox, corrected for the effect of nutation, and hence affected only by precession. Positions in star catalogues are referred to a stated mean equator and equinox, usually for the start or the middle of a given year.

Standard epoch is a set date and time used for comparing star coordinates and other data. Since 1984, the standard epoch for coordinates has been 2000 January 1.5, denoted by J2000.0. The prefix J signifies the Julian epoch, which is based on the Julian year of exactly 365.25 days. The current standard epoch is exactly one Julian century (36 525 days) removed from the standard epoch of 1900 January 0.5. It is usual for a standard epoch to be retained for half a century or so. Future epochs will be based on multiples of the Julian year.

Precession is a westward movement of the equinoxes on the celestial sphere. Its main component, caused by the gravitational pulls of the Sun and Moon on the Earth's equatorial bulge, is known as *lunisolar precession*, and there is a small additional effect due to the pulls of the planets called *planetary precession*. The sum of these two components, called *general precession*, amounts to about 50″.3 per year, or 1° every 71.6 years. Precession causes all stars to move parallel to the ecliptic, so that the stars visible from a given place or at a given time of night gradually change throughout one cycle of precession.

Because of precession the right ascension and declination of stars are continually changing. Catalogues and atlases such as this one give the star positions for a standard epoch, which by international agreement is currently the start of the year 2000. To find the approximate position of a star for another date, Table 3 can be used.

One complete cycle of precession lasts 25 800 years, during which time the Earth's axis, inclined at $23\frac{1}{2}°$ to the perpendicular of its orbit, traces out a circle on the celestial sphere with a radius of $23\frac{1}{2}°$. Hence Polaris (Alpha (α) Ursae Minoris) is only temporarily the closest bright star to the north celestial pole. About 4500 years ago the pole star was Thuban (Alpha (α) Draconis). Deneb (Alpha (α) Cygni) will be the brightest star near the pole in 8000 years' time, and in 12 000 years' time Vega (Alpha (α) Lyrae) will be at its closest to the pole, although still about 12° away.

Nutation. The circular path of precession that the celestial pole traces out on the celestial sphere is not perfectly smooth, but slightly wavy. This irregularity is called nutation, the result of a regular 'nodding' of the Earth's poles towards and away from the ecliptic poles; it perceptibly modifies the changes in star positions caused by precession. As a result of the varying distances and relative positions of the Moon and Sun, their gravitational pulls on the Earth vary in both strength and direction. The net effect is a combination of three components: *lunar nutation* (which causes the pole to wander from its mean position by $\pm9″$ in a period of 18.6 y), *solar nutation* ($\pm1″.2$ in 0.5 y) and *fortnightly nutation* ($\pm0″.1$ in 15 d). As the 18.6 year lunar nutation has the greatest effect, the Earth's axis passes the mean position about 2750 times during one precessional cycle of 25 800 years. Nutation causes a slight variation in the obliquity of the ecliptic, and this component is called *nutation in obliquity*. The component of nutation measured along the ecliptic is termed *nutation in longitude*, or the *equation of the equinoxes*.

Aberration. The finite velocity of light combines with the Earth's orbital velocity of about $30\,\mathrm{km\,s^{-1}}$ to produce a small displacement of celestial objects from their true positions known as *annual aberration*. During the year a star seems to move in a small ellipse around its true position, the eccentricity of the ellipse varying from a circle

Table 4. Refraction. For altitudes of 15° or more, the refraction R, in degrees, can be calculated from the following formula:

$$R = \frac{0.004\,52\,p}{(273 + T)\tan a}$$

where p is the atmospheric pressure in millibars, T is the temperature in degrees Celsius, and a is the altitude in degrees. For altitudes below 15° this simple formula becomes increasingly inaccurate, and the following more precise formula must be used:

$$R = \frac{p(0.1594 + 0.0196\,a + 0.000\,02\,a^2)}{(273 + T)(1 + 0.505\,a + 0.0845\,a^2)}$$

The values given below for the amount of refraction (in arc minutes) for various altitudes have been calculated from the above formulae for a pressure of 1013.25 millibar (1 atmosphere) and a temperature of 10°C.

Altitude (a)	Refraction (R)	Altitude (a)	Refraction (R)
°	′	°	′
90	0.0	14	3.8
80	0.2	13	4.1
70	0.4	12	4.4
65	0.5	11	4.8
60	0.6	10	5.3
55	0.7	9	5.9
50	0.8	8	6.5
45	1.0	7	7.4
40	1.2	6	8.4
35	1.4	5	9.8
30	1.7	4	11.7
25	2.1	3	14.3
20	2.7	2	18.2
18	3.0	1	24.2
16	3.4	0.5	28.5
15	3.6	0	34.2

for a star at the ecliptic pole to a straight line for a star on the ecliptic. The maximum amount by which a star is displaced from its true position is 20″.5, known as the *constant of aberration*; it is the angle whose tangent is obtained by dividing the Earth's mean orbital speed by the speed of light. There is also a small additional effect due to the Earth's speed of rotation, called *diurnal aberration*.

Annual parallax (symbol π) is the difference between the geocentric and heliocentric positions of a star. The apparent position of nearby stars varies slightly throughout the year because the Earth is constantly changing its position as it orbits the Sun. Annual parallax is defined as the angle subtended at the star by the semi-major axis of the Earth's orbit. Measurement of parallax is the only direct way of determining the distances of individual stars.

Proper motion (symbol μ) is the motion of a star relative to the Sun as projected onto the celestial sphere. Proper motion is tabulated in star catalogues as changes in right ascension (μ_α) and declination (μ_δ) per year or per century. The largest proper motion known is for Barnard's Star, 10″.3 per year.

Refraction. Light paths are bent as they pass through the Earth's atmosphere, so the observed altitude of an object is greater than its true altitude. The amount of refraction ranges from just over half a degree at the horizon to zero at the zenith, and it changes with atmospheric conditions. Table 4 gives refraction for selected altitudes.

Latitude variation (polar motion). The measured declinations of stars show minute, irregular cyclic changes up to a maximum value of $0''.04$, as a result of the Earth's poles of rotation wandering around a mean position in a counterclockwise direction. The variation consists of two components. The principal component arises from the Earth's axis of rotation being slightly inclined to its axis of symmetry; this causes a polar wandering of maximum amplitude $\pm 0''.3$ in latitude (equivalent to a circle with a radius of about 9 metres on the ground) in a period of 428 days. The origin of the second component is seasonal movements of air masses, and it has an amplitude of $\pm 0''.18$ (± 5 metres) in a period of one year.

DATE AND TIME

The main time-scales used in astronomy are based on natural divisions: the rotation of the Earth (the day) and its orbital motion around the Sun (the year). The day is subdivided into artificial units of hours, minutes and seconds; the second, originally defined as a fraction of the day, is now defined in terms of atomic properties (specifically, the duration of 9 192 631 770 cycles of radiation corresponding to the transition between two hyperfine levels of the ground state of the caesium-133 atom).

In practice, the Earth's rotation is affected by precession, nutation and tidal friction, and also by the slight, unpredictable effects of winds, ocean currents and motions of material inside the planet. The Earth's orbital motion also departs from the perfect ellipse of Kepler's laws because of the gravitational effects of the Moon and the planets, and consequently there are many variants of the day and year. The most important of these variants are defined below, but few of the numerical values quoted are truly constant.

Writing the date

In astronomical work, the date is usually written in order of successively smaller units of increasing precision, i.e. year, month, day and either fractions of a day or hours, minutes and seconds, thus:

2001 January 1d 2h 34m 4.8s

or

2001 January 1.107

Julian date (JD). Astronomers use a system of dates that counts the number of days that have elapsed since a given starting date; it is useful for comparing dates separated by long intervals since it is unaffected by changes in the calendar. The Julian day is reckoned from Greenwich noon and is given in decimal form, not hours and minutes. For example, 2000 January 1 at Greenwich noon is JD

245 1545.0. The starting point for the Julian day system is Greenwich noon on 4713 BC January 1, sufficiently long ago for all past astronomical events which we might wish to consider to have positive Julian day numbers. Any time less than 12 h (0.5 d) belongs to the Julian day preceding the civil date. The Julian date at midnight may be calculated for the years from 1901 to 2099 as follows:

The Gregorian calendar date is Y, M, D, where Y is the year, M the month and D the day.

If $M > 2$, set $y = Y$ and $m = M - 3$; otherwise set $y = Y - 1$ and $m = M + 9$.

Then

$$JD = 172\,1103.5 + INT(365.25y) + INT(30.6m + 0.5) + D$$

where INT means 'take the whole-number part inside the brackets'.

To find the Julian date at H hours past Greenwich midnight, add $H/24$ to the JD already calculated for 0h UT.

Example: Find the Julian date of 1989 June 7 at 18h UT.

$Y = 1989$, $M = 6$, $D = 7$, $H = 18$
Since $M > 2$, $y = 1989$, $m = 3$
JD at 0h UT = 172 1103.5 + INT(72 6482.5)
           + INT(92.3) + 7
        = 172 1103.5 + 72 6482 + 92 + 7
JD at 18h UT = 244 7684.5 + 18/24 = 244 7685.25

Modified Julian date (MJD). When dealing with dates close to the present, the modified Julian date is more convenient to use: it is JD − 240 0000.5. Hence, for example, the MJD of 1989 June 7.75 is 47684.75. Note that the MJD begins at Greenwich midnight.

The day

The unit of time called the day is based on the rotation of the Earth upon its axis. The day relative to the Sun (the solar day) is about 4 minutes longer than the day relative to the stars (the sidereal day) because of the Earth's orbital motion around the Sun, which causes the apparent position of the Sun against the star background to change each day.

There are two types of solar day: the apparent solar day and the mean solar day.

Apparent solar day. The interval between two successive meridian transits of the centre of the Sun. This time interval is not constant, since the Earth's orbit around the Sun is not circular but elliptical, and the Sun moves along the ecliptic, not the celestial equator.

Mean Sun. An imaginary body that moves along the celestial equator at a constant speed, on which a uniform time-scale can be based.

Mean solar day. The interval between two successive meridian transits of the mean Sun, equal to the mean value of the apparent solar day. The mean solar day is the one used for civil time-keeping purposes.

Continued on p. 54

Table 5. Times of sunrise and sunset at various latitudes.

January

Sunrise

	50°S	45°S	40°S	30°S	20°S	10°S	0	10°N	20°N	30°N	40°N	45°N	50°N	55°N	60°N	65°N	70°N
	h	h	h	h	h	h	h	h	h	h	h	h	h	h	h	h	h
1	3.9	4.3	4.6	5.0	5.4	5.7	6.0	6.3	6.6	6.9	7.4	7.6	8.0	8.4	9.0	10.1	—
6	4.0	4.4	4.7	5.1	5.5	5.8	6.0	6.3	6.6	6.9	7.4	7.6	8.0	8.4	9.0	10.0	—
11	4.1	4.5	4.7	5.2	5.5	5.8	6.1	6.3	6.6	7.0	7.4	7.6	7.9	8.3	8.9	9.8	—
16	4.2	4.6	4.8	5.2	5.6	5.8	6.1	6.4	6.6	6.9	7.3	7.6	7.9	8.2	8.8	9.6	—
21	4.4	4.7	4.9	5.3	5.6	5.9	6.1	6.4	6.6	6.9	7.3	7.5	7.8	8.1	8.6	9.4	11.0
26	4.5	4.8	5.0	5.4	5.7	5.9	6.1	6.4	6.6	6.9	7.2	7.4	7.7	8.0	8.5	9.1	10.4
31	4.7	4.9	5.1	5.5	5.7	6.0	6.2	6.4	6.6	6.9	7.2	7.4	7.6	7.9	8.3	8.9	9.9

Sunset

	50°S	45°S	40°S	30°S	20°S	10°S	0	10°N	20°N	30°N	40°N	45°N	50°N	55°N	60°N	65°N	70°N
	h	h	h	h	h	h	h	h	h	h	h	h	h	h	h	h	h
1	20.2	19.8	19.5	19.1	18.7	18.4	18.1	17.8	17.5	17.2	16.8	16.5	16.1	15.7	15.1	14.0	—
6	20.2	19.8	19.5	19.1	18.7	18.4	18.2	17.9	17.6	17.2	16.8	16.6	16.2	15.8	15.2	14.2	—
11	20.1	19.8	19.5	19.1	18.8	18.5	18.2	17.9	17.6	17.3	16.9	16.7	16.3	15.9	15.4	14.5	—
16	20.1	19.7	19.5	19.1	18.8	18.5	18.2	18.0	17.7	17.4	17.0	16.8	16.5	16.1	15.6	14.7	—
21	20.0	19.7	19.4	19.1	18.8	18.5	18.2	18.0	17.8	17.5	17.1	16.9	16.6	16.2	15.8	15.0	13.4
26	19.9	19.6	19.4	19.0	18.7	18.5	18.3	18.0	17.8	17.5	17.2	17.0	16.7	16.4	16.0	15.3	14.1
31	19.8	19.5	19.3	19.0	18.7	18.5	18.3	18.1	17.9	17.6	17.3	17.1	16.9	16.6	16.2	15.6	14.6

February

Sunrise

	50°S	45°S	40°S	30°S	20°S	10°S	0	10°N	20°N	30°N	40°N	45°N	50°N	55°N	60°N	65°N	70°N
	h	h	h	h	h	h	h	h	h	h	h	h	h	h	h	h	h
1	4.7	4.9	5.1	5.5	5.7	6.0	6.2	6.4	6.6	6.8	7.1	7.3	7.6	7.9	8.2	8.8	9.8
6	4.8	5.1	5.2	5.5	5.8	6.0	6.2	6.4	6.6	6.8	7.1	7.2	7.4	7.7	8.0	8.5	9.3
11	5.0	5.2	5.4	5.6	5.8	6.0	6.2	6.3	6.5	6.7	7.0	7.1	7.3	7.5	7.8	8.2	8.9
16	5.1	5.3	5.5	5.7	5.9	6.0	6.2	6.3	6.5	6.7	6.9	7.0	7.2	7.3	7.6	8.0	8.5
21	5.3	5.4	5.5	5.7	5.9	6.0	6.2	6.3	6.4	6.6	6.8	6.9	7.0	7.2	7.4	7.7	8.1
26	5.4	5.5	5.6	5.8	5.9	6.1	6.2	6.3	6.4	6.5	6.6	6.7	6.8	7.0	7.1	7.4	7.7

Sunset

	50°S	45°S	40°S	30°S	20°S	10°S	0	10°N	20°N	30°N	40°N	45°N	50°N	55°N	60°N	65°N	70°N
	h	h	h	h	h	h	h	h	h	h	h	h	h	h	h	h	h
1	19.7	19.5	19.3	19.0	18.7	18.5	18.3	18.1	17.9	17.6	17.3	17.1	16.9	16.6	16.2	15.7	14.7
6	19.6	19.4	19.2	18.9	18.7	18.5	18.3	18.1	17.9	17.7	17.4	17.2	17.0	16.8	16.4	16.0	15.2
11	19.5	19.3	19.1	18.9	18.6	18.5	18.3	18.1	18.0	17.8	17.5	17.4	17.2	17.0	16.7	16.3	15.6
16	19.3	19.1	19.0	18.8	18.6	18.4	18.3	18.1	18.0	17.8	17.6	17.5	17.3	17.1	16.9	16.5	16.0
21	19.2	19.0	18.9	18.7	18.5	18.4	18.3	18.2	18.0	17.9	17.7	17.6	17.5	17.3	17.1	16.8	16.4
26	19.0	18.9	18.8	18.6	18.5	18.4	18.3	18.2	18.1	17.9	17.8	17.7	17.6	17.5	17.3	17.1	16.8

March

Sunrise

	50°S	45°S	40°S	30°S	20°S	10°S	0	10°N	20°N	30°N	40°N	45°N	50°N	55°N	60°N	65°N	70°N
	h	h	h	h	h	h	h	h	h	h	h	h	h	h	h	h	h
1	5.5	5.6	5.7	5.8	6.0	6.1	6.2	6.2	6.3	6.4	6.6	6.6	6.7	6.8	7.0	7.2	7.5
6	5.6	5.7	5.8	5.9	6.0	6.1	6.1	6.2	6.3	6.3	6.4	6.5	6.6	6.6	6.7	6.9	7.1
11	5.8	5.8	5.9	6.0	6.0	6.1	6.1	6.2	6.2	6.2	6.3	6.3	6.4	6.4	6.5	6.6	6.7
16	5.9	5.9	6.0	6.0	6.0	6.1	6.1	6.1	6.1	6.2	6.2	6.2	6.2	6.2	6.2	6.3	6.3
21	6.0	6.1	6.1	6.1	6.1	6.1	6.1	6.1	6.1	6.1	6.0	6.0	6.0	6.0	6.0	6.0	5.9
26	6.2	6.2	6.1	6.1	6.1	6.1	6.0	6.0	6.0	5.9	5.9	5.9	5.8	5.8	5.7	5.7	5.5
31	6.3	6.3	6.2	6.2	6.1	6.1	6.0	6.0	5.9	5.8	5.8	5.7	5.7	5.6	5.5	5.3	5.2

Sunset

	50°S	45°S	40°S	30°S	20°S	10°S	0	10°N	20°N	30°N	40°N	45°N	50°N	55°N	60°N	65°N	70°N
	h	h	h	h	h	h	h	h	h	h	h	h	h	h	h	h	h
1	18.9	18.8	18.7	18.6	18.4	18.4	18.3	18.2	18.1	18.0	17.9	17.8	17.7	17.6	17.4	17.3	17.0
6	18.7	18.6	18.6	18.5	18.4	18.3	18.2	18.2	18.1	18.0	18.0	17.9	17.8	17.8	17.7	17.5	17.3
11	18.5	18.5	18.4	18.4	18.3	18.3	18.2	18.2	18.1	18.1	18.0	18.0	18.0	17.9	17.9	17.8	17.7
16	18.4	18.3	18.3	18.3	18.2	18.2	18.2	18.2	18.2	18.1	18.1	18.1	18.1	18.1	18.1	18.0	18.0
21	18.2	18.2	18.2	18.2	18.2	18.2	18.2	18.2	18.2	18.2	18.2	18.2	18.2	18.3	18.3	18.3	18.4
26	18.0	18.0	18.0	18.1	18.1	18.1	18.1	18.2	18.2	18.2	18.3	18.3	18.4	18.4	18.5	18.6	18.7
31	17.8	17.9	17.9	18.0	18.0	18.1	18.1	18.2	18.2	18.3	18.4	18.4	18.5	18.6	18.7	18.8	19.0

Table 5 (*continued*). Times of sunrise and sunset at various latitudes.

April

	50°S	45°S	40°S	30°S	20°S	10°S	0	Sunrise 10°N	20°N	30°N	40°N	45°N	50°N	55°N	60°N	65°N	70°N
	h	h	h	h	h	h	h	h	h	h	h	h	h	h	h	h	h
1	6.3	6.3	6.2	6.2	6.1	6.1	6.0	6.0	5.9	5.8	5.7	5.7	5.6	5.5	5.4	5.3	5.1
6	6.5	6.4	6.3	6.2	6.1	6.1	6.0	5.9	5.8	5.7	5.6	5.5	5.4	5.3	5.2	5.0	4.7
11	6.6	6.5	6.4	6.3	6.2	6.1	6.0	5.9	5.8	5.6	5.5	5.4	5.3	5.1	4.9	4.7	4.3
16	6.7	6.6	6.5	6.3	6.2	6.1	5.9	5.8	5.7	5.5	5.4	5.2	5.1	4.9	4.7	4.4	3.9
21	6.9	6.7	6.6	6.4	6.2	6.1	5.9	5.8	5.6	5.5	5.2	5.1	4.9	4.7	4.4	4.1	3.4
26	7.0	6.8	6.7	6.4	6.2	6.1	5.9	5.7	5.6	5.4	5.1	5.0	4.8	4.5	4.2	3.7	3.0

	50°S	45°S	40°S	30°S	20°S	10°S	0	Sunset 10°N	20°N	30°N	40°N	45°N	50°N	55°N	60°N	65°N	70°N
	h	h	h	h	h	h	h	h	h	h	h	h	h	h	h	h	h
1	17.8	17.8	17.9	17.9	18.0	18.1	18.1	18.2	18.2	18.3	18.4	18.5	18.5	18.6	18.7	18.9	19.1
6	17.6	17.7	17.7	17.8	17.9	18.0	18.1	18.2	18.3	18.4	18.5	18.6	18.7	18.8	18.9	19.1	19.5
11	17.4	17.5	17.6	17.8	17.9	18.0	18.1	18.2	18.3	18.4	18.6	18.7	18.8	18.9	19.1	19.4	19.8
16	17.3	17.4	17.5	17.7	17.8	17.9	18.1	18.2	18.3	18.5	18.7	18.8	18.9	19.1	19.3	19.7	20.2
21	17.1	17.2	17.4	17.6	17.7	17.9	18.0	18.2	18.3	18.5	18.7	18.9	19.0	19.3	19.5	19.9	20.6
26	16.9	17.1	17.3	17.5	17.7	17.9	18.0	18.2	18.4	18.6	18.8	19.0	19.2	19.4	19.7	20.2	21.0

May

	50°S	45°S	40°S	30°S	20°S	10°S	0	Sunrise 10°N	20°N	30°N	40°N	45°N	50°N	55°N	60°N	65°N	70°N
	h	h	h	h	h	h	h	h	h	h	h	h	h	h	h	h	h
1	7.1	6.9	6.7	6.5	6.3	6.1	5.9	5.7	5.5	5.3	5.0	4.8	4.6	4.3	4.0	3.4	2.5
6	7.2	7.0	6.8	6.5	6.3	6.1	5.9	5.7	5.5	5.2	4.9	4.7	4.5	4.2	3.8	3.1	2.0
11	7.3	7.1	6.9	6.6	6.3	6.1	5.9	5.7	5.4	5.2	4.8	4.6	4.3	4.0	3.5	2.8	1.4
16	7.5	7.2	7.0	6.6	6.4	6.1	5.9	5.6	5.4	5.1	4.7	4.5	4.2	3.9	3.3	2.5	0.4
21	7.6	7.3	7.1	6.7	6.4	6.1	5.9	5.6	5.4	5.1	4.7	4.4	4.1	3.7	3.2	2.3	—
26	7.7	7.4	7.1	6.7	6.4	6.1	5.9	5.6	5.3	5.0	4.6	4.3	4.0	3.6	3.0	2.0	—
31	7.8	7.4	7.2	6.8	6.5	6.2	5.9	5.6	5.3	5.0	4.6	4.3	3.9	3.5	2.9	1.7	—

	50°S	45°S	40°S	30°S	20°S	10°S	0	Sunset 10°N	20°N	30°N	40°N	45°N	50°N	55°N	60°N	65°N	70°N
	h	h	h	h	h	h	h	h	h	h	h	h	h	h	h	h	h
1	16.8	17.0	17.2	17.4	17.6	17.8	18.0	18.2	18.4	18.6	18.9	19.1	19.3	19.6	20.0	20.5	21.4
6	16.6	16.9	17.1	17.3	17.6	17.8	18.0	18.2	18.4	18.7	19.0	19.2	19.4	19.7	20.2	20.8	22.0
11	16.5	16.8	17.0	17.3	17.5	17.8	18.0	18.2	18.5	18.7	19.1	19.3	19.6	19.9	20.4	21.1	22.6
16	16.4	16.7	16.9	17.2	17.5	17.8	18.0	18.2	18.5	18.8	19.2	19.4	19.7	20.0	20.6	21.4	—
21	16.3	16.6	16.8	17.2	17.5	17.8	18.0	18.3	18.5	18.8	19.2	19.5	19.8	20.2	20.8	21.7	—
26	16.2	16.5	16.8	17.2	17.5	17.7	18.0	18.3	18.6	18.9	19.3	19.6	19.9	20.3	20.9	22.0	—
31	16.2	16.5	16.7	17.1	17.5	17.8	18.0	18.3	18.6	18.9	19.4	19.6	20.0	20.4	21.1	22.3	—

June

	50°S	45°S	40°S	30°S	20°S	10°S	0	Sunrise 10°N	20°N	30°N	40°N	45°N	50°N	55°N	60°N	65°N	70°N
	h	h	h	h	h	h	h	h	h	h	h	h	h	h	h	h	h
1	7.8	7.5	7.2	6.8	6.5	6.2	5.9	5.6	5.3	5.0	4.6	4.3	3.9	3.5	2.8	1.6	—
6	7.9	7.5	7.3	6.8	6.5	6.2	5.9	5.6	5.3	5.0	4.5	4.2	3.9	3.4	2.7	1.4	—
11	7.9	7.6	7.3	6.9	6.5	6.2	5.9	5.6	5.3	5.0	4.5	4.2	3.8	3.4	2.6	1.2	—
16	8.0	7.6	7.3	6.9	6.5	6.2	5.9	5.7	5.3	5.0	4.5	4.2	3.8	3.3	2.6	1.1	—
21	8.0	7.6	7.4	6.9	6.6	6.3	6.0	5.7	5.4	5.0	4.5	4.2	3.8	3.3	2.6	1.0	—
26	8.0	7.7	7.4	6.9	6.6	6.3	6.0	5.7	5.4	5.0	4.5	4.2	3.9	3.4	2.6	1.1	—

	50°S	45°S	40°S	30°S	20°S	10°S	0	Sunset 10°N	20°N	30°N	40°N	45°N	50°N	55°N	60°N	65°N	70°N
	h	h	h	h	h	h	h	h	h	h	h	h	h	h	h	h	h
1	16.1	16.5	16.7	17.1	17.5	17.8	18.0	18.3	18.6	18.9	19.4	19.7	20.0	20.5	21.1	22.3	—
6	16.1	16.4	16.7	17.1	17.5	17.8	18.0	18.3	18.6	19.0	19.4	19.7	20.1	20.6	21.3	22.6	—
11	16.1	16.4	16.7	17.1	17.5	17.8	18.1	18.3	18.7	19.0	19.5	19.8	20.1	20.6	21.4	22.8	—
16	16.1	16.4	16.7	17.1	17.5	17.8	18.1	18.4	18.7	19.0	19.5	19.8	20.2	20.7	21.4	23.0	—
21	16.1	16.4	16.7	17.1	17.5	17.8	18.1	18.4	18.7	19.1	19.5	19.8	20.2	20.7	21.5	23.1	—
26	16.1	16.4	16.7	17.2	17.5	17.8	18.1	18.4	18.7	19.1	19.5	19.8	20.2	20.7	21.5	23.0	—

Table 5 (*continued*). Times of sunrise and sunset at various latitudes.

July

	50°S	45°S	40°S	30°S	20°S	10°S	0	Sunrise 10°N	20°N	30°N	40°N	45°N	50°N	55°N	60°N	65°N	70°N
	h	h	h	h	h	h	h	h	h	h	h	h	h	h	h	h	h
1	8.0	7.7	7.4	6.9	6.6	6.3	6.0	5.7	5.4	5.0	4.6	4.3	3.9	3.4	2.7	1.2	—
6	8.0	7.6	7.4	6.9	6.6	6.3	6.0	5.7	5.4	5.1	4.6	4.3	4.0	3.5	2.8	1.5	—
11	7.9	7.6	7.3	6.9	6.6	6.3	6.0	5.8	5.5	5.1	4.7	4.4	4.0	3.6	2.9	1.7	—
16	7.8	7.5	7.3	6.9	6.6	6.3	6.0	5.8	5.5	5.2	4.7	4.5	4.1	3.7	3.1	2.0	—
21	7.8	7.5	7.2	6.9	6.6	6.3	6.0	5.8	5.5	5.2	4.8	4.6	4.2	3.8	3.3	2.3	—
26	7.7	7.4	7.2	6.8	6.5	6.3	6.0	5.8	5.6	5.3	4.9	4.6	4.3	4.0	3.4	2.6	—
31	7.6	7.3	7.1	6.8	6.5	6.3	6.0	5.8	5.6	5.3	5.0	4.7	4.5	4.1	3.6	2.9	1.2

	50°S	45°S	40°S	30°S	20°S	10°S	0	Sunset 10°N	20°N	30°N	40°N	45°N	50°N	55°N	60°N	65°N	70°N
	h	h	h	h	h	h	h	h	h	h	h	h	h	h	h	h	h
1	16.1	16.5	16.8	17.2	17.5	17.8	18.1	18.4	18.7	19.1	19.5	19.8	20.2	20.7	21.4	22.9	—
6	16.2	16.5	16.8	17.2	17.6	17.9	18.1	18.4	18.7	19.1	19.5	19.8	20.2	20.6	21.3	22.7	—
11	16.3	16.6	16.8	17.3	17.6	17.9	18.2	18.4	18.7	19.1	19.5	19.8	20.1	20.6	21.2	22.4	—
16	16.4	16.7	16.9	17.3	17.6	17.9	18.2	18.4	18.7	19.0	19.5	19.7	20.1	20.5	21.1	22.1	—
21	16.5	16.7	17.0	17.3	17.7	17.9	18.2	18.4	18.7	19.0	19.4	19.7	20.0	20.4	20.9	21.9	—
26	16.6	16.8	17.0	17.4	17.7	17.9	18.2	18.4	18.7	19.0	19.3	19.6	19.9	20.2	20.8	21.6	—
31	16.7	16.9	17.1	17.4	17.7	17.9	18.2	18.4	18.6	18.9	19.3	19.5	19.7	20.1	20.6	21.3	22.8

August

	50°S	45°S	40°S	30°S	20°S	10°S	0	Sunrise 10°N	20°N	30°N	40°N	45°N	50°N	55°N	60°N	65°N	70°N
	h	h	h	h	h	h	h	h	h	h	h	h	h	h	h	h	h
1	7.5	7.3	7.1	6.8	6.5	6.3	6.0	5.8	5.6	5.3	5.0	4.7	4.5	4.1	3.7	2.9	1.4
6	7.4	7.2	7.0	6.7	6.5	6.2	6.0	5.8	5.6	5.4	5.0	4.8	4.6	4.3	3.9	3.2	2.0
11	7.3	7.1	6.9	6.6	6.4	6.2	6.0	5.8	5.6	5.4	5.1	4.9	4.7	4.4	4.1	3.5	2.6
16	7.1	6.9	6.8	6.5	6.4	6.2	6.0	5.8	5.7	5.5	5.2	5.0	4.8	4.6	4.3	3.8	3.0
21	7.0	6.8	6.7	6.5	6.3	6.1	6.0	5.9	5.7	5.5	5.3	5.1	5.0	4.8	4.5	4.1	3.4
26	6.8	6.7	6.6	6.4	6.2	6.1	6.0	5.9	5.7	5.6	5.4	5.2	5.1	4.9	4.7	4.3	3.8
31	6.6	6.5	6.4	6.3	6.2	6.1	6.0	5.8	5.7	5.6	5.4	5.3	5.2	5.1	4.9	4.6	4.2

	50°S	45°S	40°S	30°S	20°S	10°S	0	Sunset 10°N	20°N	30°N	40°N	45°N	50°N	55°N	60°N	65°N	70°N
	h	h	h	h	h	h	h	h	h	h	h	h	h	h	h	h	h
1	16.7	16.9	17.1	17.5	17.7	17.9	18.2	18.4	18.6	18.9	19.2	19.4	19.7	20.1	20.5	21.2	22.7
6	16.8	17.0	17.2	17.5	17.7	18.0	18.2	18.4	18.6	18.8	19.1	19.3	19.6	19.9	20.3	20.9	22.1
11	16.9	17.1	17.3	17.6	17.8	18.0	18.1	18.3	18.5	18.8	19.0	19.2	19.4	19.7	20.1	20.6	21.5
16	17.0	17.2	17.4	17.6	17.8	18.0	18.1	18.3	18.5	18.7	18.9	19.1	19.3	19.5	19.8	20.3	21.1
21	17.2	17.3	17.4	17.6	17.8	18.0	18.1	18.3	18.4	18.6	18.8	19.0	19.1	19.3	19.6	20.0	20.6
26	17.3	17.4	17.5	17.7	17.8	18.0	18.1	18.2	18.3	18.5	18.7	18.8	19.0	19.1	19.4	19.7	20.2
31	17.4	17.5	17.6	17.7	17.9	18.0	18.1	18.2	18.3	18.4	18.6	18.7	18.8	18.9	19.1	19.4	19.8

September

	50°S	45°S	40°S	30°S	20°S	10°S	0	Sunrise 10°N	20°N	30°N	40°N	45°N	50°N	55°N	60°N	65°N	70°N
	h	h	h	h	h	h	h	h	h	h	h	h	h	h	h	h	h
1	6.6	6.5	6.4	6.3	6.1	6.0	5.9	5.8	5.7	5.6	5.5	5.4	5.2	5.1	4.9	4.6	4.2
6	6.4	6.3	6.3	6.2	6.1	6.0	5.9	5.8	5.8	5.7	5.5	5.5	5.4	5.3	5.1	4.9	4.6
11	6.2	6.2	6.1	6.1	6.0	5.9	5.9	5.8	5.8	5.7	5.6	5.6	5.5	5.4	5.3	5.1	4.9
16	6.0	6.0	6.0	6.0	5.9	5.9	5.9	5.8	5.8	5.7	5.7	5.7	5.6	5.6	5.5	5.4	5.3
21	5.9	5.9	5.9	5.9	5.8	5.8	5.8	5.8	5.8	5.8	5.8	5.8	5.7	5.7	5.7	5.6	5.6
26	5.7	5.7	5.7	5.7	5.8	5.8	5.8	5.8	5.8	5.8	5.9	5.9	5.9	5.9	5.9	5.9	5.9

	50°S	45°S	40°S	30°S	20°S	10°S	0	Sunset 10°N	20°N	30°N	40°N	45°N	50°N	55°N	60°N	65°N	70°N
	h	h	h	h	h	h	h	h	h	h	h	h	h	h	h	h	h
1	17.4	17.5	17.6	17.7	17.9	18.0	18.1	18.2	18.3	18.4	18.5	18.6	18.7	18.9	19.1	19.3	19.7
6	17.6	17.6	17.7	17.8	17.9	18.0	18.0	18.1	18.2	18.3	18.4	18.5	18.6	18.7	18.8	19.0	19.3
11	17.7	17.7	17.8	17.8	17.9	17.9	18.0	18.1	18.1	18.2	18.3	18.3	18.4	18.5	18.6	18.7	18.9
16	17.8	17.8	17.8	17.9	17.9	17.9	18.0	18.0	18.0	18.1	18.1	18.2	18.2	18.2	18.3	18.4	18.5
21	17.9	17.9	17.9	17.9	17.9	17.9	17.9	17.9	18.0	18.0	18.0	18.0	18.0	18.0	18.1	18.1	18.1
26	18.1	18.0	18.0	18.0	17.9	17.9	17.9	17.9	17.9	17.9	17.9	17.8	17.8	17.8	17.8	17.8	17.8

Table 5 (*continued*). Times of sunrise and sunset at various latitudes.

October

	50°S	45°S	40°S	30°S	20°S	10°S	0	Sunrise 10°N	20°N	30°N	40°N	45°N	50°N	55°N	60°N	65°N	70°N
	h	h	h	h	h	h	h	h	h	h	h	h	h	h	h	h	h
1	5.5	5.5	5.6	5.6	5.7	5.7	5.8	5.8	5.8	5.9	5.9	6.0	6.0	6.0	6.1	6.1	6.2
6	5.3	5.4	5.4	5.5	5.6	5.7	5.7	5.8	5.9	5.9	6.0	6.1	6.1	6.2	6.3	6.4	6.6
11	5.1	5.2	5.3	5.4	5.6	5.6	5.7	5.8	5.9	6.0	6.1	6.2	6.3	6.4	6.5	6.7	6.9
16	5.0	5.1	5.2	5.4	5.5	5.6	5.7	5.8	5.9	6.0	6.2	6.3	6.4	6.5	6.7	6.9	7.3
21	4.8	4.9	5.1	5.3	5.4	5.6	5.7	5.8	5.9	6.1	6.3	6.4	6.5	6.7	6.9	7.2	7.6
26	4.6	4.8	5.0	5.2	5.4	5.5	5.7	5.8	6.0	6.2	6.4	6.5	6.7	6.9	7.1	7.5	8.0
31	4.5	4.7	4.8	5.1	5.3	5.5	5.7	5.8	6.0	6.2	6.5	6.6	6.8	7.0	7.3	7.7	8.4

	50°S	45°S	40°S	30°S	20°S	10°S	0	Sunset 10°N	20°N	30°N	40°N	45°N	50°N	55°N	60°N	65°N	70°N
	h	h	h	h	h	h	h	h	h	h	h	h	h	h	h	h	h
1	18.2	18.1	18.1	18.0	18.0	17.9	17.9	17.8	17.8	17.8	17.7	17.7	17.6	17.6	17.6	17.5	17.4
6	18.3	18.2	18.2	18.1	18.0	17.9	17.9	17.8	17.7	17.7	17.6	17.5	17.5	17.4	17.3	17.2	17.0
11	18.4	18.3	18.3	18.1	18.0	17.9	17.8	17.8	17.7	17.6	17.4	17.4	17.3	17.2	17.1	16.9	16.6
16	18.6	18.4	18.3	18.2	18.0	17.9	17.8	17.7	17.6	17.5	17.3	17.2	17.1	17.0	16.8	16.6	16.2
21	18.7	18.6	18.4	18.2	18.1	17.9	17.8	17.7	17.5	17.4	17.2	17.1	17.0	16.8	16.6	16.3	15.8
26	18.9	18.7	18.5	18.3	18.1	17.9	17.8	17.6	17.5	17.3	17.1	17.0	16.8	16.6	16.3	16.0	15.4
31	19.0	18.8	18.6	18.4	18.1	18.0	17.8	17.6	17.4	17.2	17.0	16.8	16.6	16.4	16.1	15.7	15.0

November

	50°S	45°S	40°S	30°S	20°S	10°S	0	Sunrise 10°N	20°N	30°N	40°N	45°N	50°N	55°N	60°N	65°N	70°N
	h	h	h	h	h	h	h	h	h	h	h	h	h	h	h	h	h
1	4.4	4.7	4.8	5.1	5.3	5.5	5.7	5.8	6.0	6.2	6.5	6.6	6.8	7.1	7.4	7.8	8.5
6	4.3	4.5	4.7	5.0	5.3	5.5	5.7	5.8	6.1	6.3	6.6	6.7	7.0	7.2	7.6	8.1	8.9
11	4.2	4.4	4.6	5.0	5.2	5.5	5.7	5.9	6.1	6.4	6.7	6.9	7.1	7.4	7.8	8.4	9.4
16	4.1	4.3	4.6	4.9	5.2	5.5	5.7	5.9	6.2	6.4	6.8	7.0	7.2	7.6	8.0	8.7	9.9
21	4.0	4.3	4.5	4.9	5.2	5.5	5.7	5.9	6.2	6.5	6.9	7.1	7.4	7.7	8.2	8.9	10.6
26	3.9	4.2	4.5	4.9	5.2	5.5	5.7	6.0	6.3	6.6	7.0	7.2	7.5	7.9	8.4	9.2	—

	50°S	45°S	40°S	30°S	20°S	10°S	0	Sunset 10°N	20°N	30°N	40°N	45°N	50°N	55°N	60°N	65°N	70°N
	h	h	h	h	h	h	h	h	h	h	h	h	h	h	h	h	h
1	19.0	18.8	18.6	18.4	18.1	18.0	17.8	17.6	17.4	17.2	17.0	16.8	16.6	16.4	16.1	15.6	14.9
6	19.2	18.9	18.7	18.4	18.2	18.0	17.8	17.6	17.4	17.2	16.9	16.7	16.5	16.2	15.9	15.4	14.5
11	19.3	19.0	18.8	18.5	18.2	18.0	17.8	17.6	17.4	17.1	16.8	16.6	16.4	16.1	15.7	15.1	14.1
16	19.4	19.2	18.9	18.6	18.3	18.0	17.8	17.6	17.3	17.1	16.7	16.5	16.2	15.9	15.5	14.8	13.6
21	19.6	19.3	19.0	18.6	18.3	18.1	17.8	17.6	17.3	17.0	16.7	16.4	16.2	15.8	15.3	14.6	13.0
26	19.7	19.4	19.1	18.7	18.4	18.1	17.8	17.6	17.3	17.0	16.6	16.4	16.1	15.7	15.2	14.3	—

December

	50°S	45°S	40°S	30°S	20°S	10°S	0	Sunrise 10°N	20°N	30°N	40°N	45°N	50°N	55°N	60°N	65°N	70°N
	h	h	h	h	h	h	h	h	h	h	h	h	h	h	h	h	h
1	3.8	4.2	4.4	4.9	5.2	5.5	5.8	6.0	6.3	6.6	7.0	7.3	7.6	8.0	8.6	9.5	—
6	3.8	4.1	4.4	4.9	5.2	5.5	5.8	6.1	6.4	6.7	7.1	7.4	7.7	8.1	8.7	9.7	—
11	3.8	4.1	4.4	4.9	5.2	5.5	5.8	6.1	6.4	6.8	7.2	7.5	7.8	8.2	8.9	9.9	—
16	3.8	4.1	4.4	4.9	5.3	5.6	5.9	6.2	6.5	6.8	7.3	7.5	7.9	8.3	9.0	10.1	—
21	3.8	4.2	4.5	4.9	5.3	5.6	5.9	6.2	6.5	6.9	7.3	7.6	7.9	8.4	9.0	10.2	—
26	3.8	4.2	4.5	5.0	5.3	5.7	5.9	6.2	6.5	6.9	7.3	7.6	8.0	8.4	9.1	10.2	—
31	3.9	4.3	4.6	5.0	5.4	5.7	6.0	6.3	6.6	6.9	7.4	7.6	8.0	8.4	9.0	10.1	—

	50°S	45°S	40°S	30°S	20°S	10°S	0	Sunset 10°N	20°N	30°N	40°N	45°N	50°N	55°N	60°N	65°N	70°N
	h	h	h	h	h	h	h	h	h	h	h	h	h	h	h	h	h
1	19.8	19.5	19.2	18.8	18.4	18.1	17.9	17.6	17.3	17.0	16.6	16.3	16.0	15.6	15.0	14.1	—
6	19.9	19.6	19.3	18.8	18.5	18.2	17.9	17.6	17.3	17.0	16.6	16.3	16.0	15.6	15.0	14.0	—
11	20.0	19.7	19.4	18.9	18.5	18.2	17.9	17.7	17.4	17.0	16.6	16.3	16.0	15.5	14.9	13.8	—
16	20.1	19.7	19.4	19.0	18.6	18.3	18.0	17.7	17.4	17.0	16.6	16.3	16.0	15.5	14.9	13.8	—
21	20.2	19.8	19.5	19.0	18.6	18.3	18.0	17.7	17.4	17.1	16.6	16.4	16.0	15.6	14.9	13.8	—
26	20.2	19.8	19.5	19.0	18.7	18.4	18.1	17.8	17.5	17.1	16.7	16.4	16.1	15.6	15.0	13.8	—
31	20.2	19.8	19.5	19.1	18.7	18.4	18.1	17.8	17.5	17.2	16.7	16.5	16.1	15.7	15.1	14.0	—

Table 6. Times at which astronomical twilight begins and ends at various latitudes.

January

Beginning

	50°S	45°S	40°S	30°S	20°S	10°S	0	10°N	20°N	30°N	40°N	45°N	50°N	55°N	60°N	65°N	70°N
	h	h	h	h	h	h	h	h	h	h	h	h	h	h	h	h	h
1	—	1.8	2.5	3.4	4.0	4.4	4.7	5.0	5.3	5.5	5.7	5.9	6.0	6.1	6.3	6.5	6.8
6	—	1.9	2.6	3.5	4.1	4.5	4.8	5.1	5.3	5.5	5.8	5.9	6.0	6.1	6.3	6.5	6.7
11	0.5	2.1	2.8	3.6	4.1	4.5	4.8	5.1	5.3	5.5	5.8	5.9	6.0	6.1	6.2	6.4	6.6
16	1.1	2.3	2.9	3.7	4.2	4.6	4.9	5.1	5.3	5.5	5.7	5.8	5.9	6.0	6.2	6.3	6.5
21	1.5	2.5	3.0	3.8	4.3	4.6	4.9	5.1	5.3	5.5	5.7	5.8	5.9	6.0	6.1	6.2	6.3
26	1.8	2.7	3.2	3.9	4.3	4.7	4.9	5.2	5.3	5.5	5.7	5.7	5.8	5.9	6.0	6.0	6.1
31	2.1	2.9	3.3	4.0	4.4	4.7	5.0	5.2	5.3	5.5	5.6	5.7	5.7	5.8	5.8	5.9	5.9

Ending

	50°S	45°S	40°S	30°S	20°S	10°S	0	10°N	20°N	30°N	40°N	45°N	50°N	55°N	60°N	65°N	70°N
	h	h	h	h	h	h	h	h	h	h	h	h	h	h	h	h	h
1	—	22.3	21.6	20.7	20.1	19.7	19.4	19.1	18.8	18.6	18.4	18.3	18.1	18.0	17.8	17.6	17.4
6	—	22.3	21.5	20.7	20.1	19.7	19.4	19.1	18.9	18.7	18.4	18.3	18.2	18.1	17.9	17.7	17.5
11	23.6	22.2	21.5	20.7	20.1	19.7	19.4	19.2	18.9	18.7	18.5	18.4	18.3	18.2	18.0	17.9	17.7
16	23.2	22.0	21.4	20.6	20.1	19.7	19.5	19.2	19.0	18.8	18.6	18.5	18.4	18.3	18.2	18.0	17.9
21	22.9	21.9	21.3	20.6	20.1	19.7	19.5	19.2	19.0	18.8	18.7	18.6	18.5	18.4	18.3	18.2	18.1
26	22.6	21.7	21.2	20.5	20.1	19.7	19.5	19.3	19.1	18.9	18.8	18.7	18.6	18.5	18.5	18.4	18.3
31	22.3	21.6	21.1	20.5	20.0	19.7	19.5	19.3	19.1	19.0	18.8	18.8	18.7	18.7	18.6	18.6	18.6

February

Beginning

	50°S	45°S	40°S	30°S	20°S	10°S	0	10°N	20°N	30°N	40°N	45°N	50°N	55°N	60°N	65°N	70°N
	h	h	h	h	h	h	h	h	h	h	h	h	h	h	h	h	h
1	2.2	2.9	3.4	4.0	4.4	4.7	5.0	5.2	5.3	5.5	5.6	5.7	5.7	5.8	5.8	5.8	5.9
6	2.5	3.1	3.5	4.1	4.5	4.8	5.0	5.2	5.3	5.4	5.5	5.6	5.6	5.6	5.6	5.6	5.6
11	2.7	3.3	3.7	4.2	4.5	4.8	5.0	5.2	5.3	5.4	5.4	5.5	5.5	5.5	5.5	5.4	5.3
16	3.0	3.4	3.8	4.3	4.6	4.8	5.0	5.1	5.2	5.3	5.4	5.4	5.3	5.3	5.3	5.2	5.0
21	3.2	3.6	3.9	4.4	4.6	4.9	5.0	5.1	5.2	5.2	5.3	5.2	5.2	5.1	5.0	4.9	4.6
26	3.4	3.8	4.0	4.4	4.7	4.9	5.0	5.1	5.1	5.2	5.1	5.1	5.0	5.0	4.8	4.6	4.3

Ending

	50°S	45°S	40°S	30°S	20°S	10°S	0	10°N	20°N	30°N	40°N	45°N	50°N	55°N	60°N	65°N	70°N
	h	h	h	h	h	h	h	h	h	h	h	h	h	h	h	h	h
1	22.2	21.5	21.1	20.4	20.0	19.7	19.5	19.3	19.1	19.0	18.9	18.8	18.8	18.7	18.7	18.6	18.6
6	22.0	21.4	20.9	20.4	20.0	19.7	19.5	19.3	19.2	19.0	18.9	18.9	18.9	18.9	18.9	18.9	18.9
11	21.7	21.2	20.8	20.3	19.9	19.7	19.5	19.3	19.2	19.1	19.0	19.0	19.0	19.0	19.1	19.1	19.2
16	21.5	21.0	20.7	20.2	19.9	19.6	19.5	19.3	19.2	19.2	19.1	19.1	19.1	19.2	19.2	19.3	19.5
21	21.2	20.8	20.5	20.1	19.8	19.6	19.4	19.3	19.3	19.2	19.2	19.2	19.3	19.3	19.4	19.6	19.9
26	21.0	20.6	20.4	20.0	19.7	19.6	19.4	19.3	19.3	19.3	19.3	19.3	19.4	19.5	19.6	19.9	20.2

March

Beginning

	50°S	45°S	40°S	30°S	20°S	10°S	0	10°N	20°N	30°N	40°N	45°N	50°N	55°N	60°N	65°N	70°N
	h	h	h	h	h	h	h	h	h	h	h	h	h	h	h	h	h
1	3.5	3.9	4.1	4.5	4.7	4.9	5.0	5.1	5.1	5.1	5.1	5.0	4.9	4.8	4.7	4.4	4.0
6	3.7	4.0	4.2	4.5	4.8	4.9	5.0	5.0	5.0	5.0	4.9	4.9	4.8	4.6	4.4	4.1	3.6
11	3.9	4.1	4.3	4.6	4.8	4.9	5.0	5.0	5.0	4.9	4.8	4.7	4.6	4.4	4.1	3.8	3.1
16	4.1	4.3	4.4	4.7	4.8	4.9	4.9	4.9	4.9	4.8	4.7	4.6	4.4	4.2	3.9	3.4	2.5
21	4.2	4.4	4.5	4.7	4.8	4.9	4.9	4.9	4.8	4.7	4.5	4.4	4.2	3.9	3.6	3.0	1.8
26	4.4	4.5	4.6	4.8	4.9	4.9	4.9	4.9	4.8	4.6	4.4	4.2	4.0	3.7	3.2	2.5	—
31	4.5	4.6	4.7	4.8	4.9	4.9	4.9	4.8	4.7	4.5	4.2	4.0	3.8	3.4	2.9	1.9	—

Ending

	50°S	45°S	40°S	30°S	20°S	10°S	0	10°N	20°N	30°N	40°N	45°N	50°N	55°N	60°N	65°N	70°N
	h	h	h	h	h	h	h	h	h	h	h	h	h	h	h	h	h
1	20.9	20.5	20.3	19.9	19.7	19.5	19.4	19.3	19.3	19.3	19.4	19.4	19.5	19.6	19.8	20.0	20.4
6	20.6	20.3	20.1	19.8	19.6	19.5	19.4	19.3	19.3	19.4	19.4	19.5	19.6	19.8	20.0	20.3	20.9
11	20.4	20.2	20.0	19.7	19.5	19.4	19.4	19.3	19.4	19.4	19.5	19.6	19.8	20.0	20.2	20.6	21.3
16	20.2	20.0	19.8	19.6	19.5	19.4	19.3	19.3	19.4	19.5	19.6	19.8	19.9	20.1	20.5	21.0	21.9
21	20.0	19.8	19.7	19.5	19.4	19.3	19.3	19.3	19.4	19.5	19.7	19.9	20.1	20.3	20.7	21.3	22.6
26	19.8	19.6	19.5	19.4	19.3	19.3	19.3	19.3	19.4	19.6	19.8	20.0	20.2	20.5	21.0	21.8	—
31	19.6	19.5	19.4	19.3	19.2	19.2	19.3	19.3	19.5	19.6	19.9	20.1	20.4	20.8	21.3	22.3	—

Table 6 (*continued*). Times at which astronomical twilight begins and ends at various latitudes.

April — Beginning

	50°S	45°S	40°S	30°S	20°S	10°S	0	10°N	20°N	30°N	40°N	45°N	50°N	55°N	60°N	65°N	70°N
	h	h	h	h	h	h	h	h	h	h	h	h	h	h	h	h	h
1	4.5	4.7	4.7	4.9	4.9	4.9	4.9	4.8	4.7	4.5	4.2	4.0	3.7	3.4	2.8	1.8	—
6	4.7	4.8	4.8	4.9	4.9	4.9	4.8	4.7	4.6	4.4	4.0	3.8	3.5	3.1	2.4	0.9	—
11	4.8	4.9	4.9	4.9	4.9	4.9	4.8	4.7	4.5	4.3	3.9	3.6	3.3	2.8	2.0	—	—
16	4.9	5.0	5.0	5.0	5.0	4.9	4.8	4.6	4.4	4.2	3.7	3.4	3.0	2.5	1.4	—	—
21	5.0	5.1	5.1	5.0	5.0	4.9	4.8	4.6	4.4	4.0	3.6	3.3	2.8	2.1	0.5	—	—
26	5.2	5.2	5.1	5.1	5.0	4.9	4.7	4.5	4.3	3.9	3.4	3.1	2.6	1.7	—	—	—

April — Ending

	50°S	45°S	40°S	30°S	20°S	10°S	0	10°N	20°N	30°N	40°N	45°N	50°N	55°N	60°N	65°N	70°N
	h	h	h	h	h	h	h	h	h	h	h	h	h	h	h	h	h
1	19.6	19.5	19.4	19.3	19.2	19.2	19.3	19.3	19.5	19.7	19.9	20.2	20.4	20.8	21.4	22.4	—
6	19.4	19.3	19.2	19.2	19.2	19.2	19.2	19.3	19.5	19.7	20.1	20.3	20.6	21.0	21.7	23.4	—
11	19.2	19.2	19.1	19.1	19.1	19.1	19.2	19.4	19.5	19.8	20.2	20.4	20.8	21.3	22.2	—	—
16	19.1	19.0	19.0	19.0	19.0	19.1	19.2	19.4	19.6	19.9	20.3	20.6	21.0	21.6	22.7	—	—
21	18.9	18.9	18.9	18.9	19.0	19.1	19.2	19.4	19.6	19.9	20.4	20.7	21.2	21.9	—	—	—
26	18.8	18.8	18.8	18.8	18.9	19.0	19.2	19.4	19.6	20.0	20.5	20.9	21.4	22.3	—	—	—

May — Beginning

	50°S	45°S	40°S	30°S	20°S	10°S	0	10°N	20°N	30°N	40°N	45°N	50°N	55°N	60°N	65°N	70°N
	h	h	h	h	h	h	h	h	h	h	h	h	h	h	h	h	h
1	5.3	5.2	5.2	5.1	5.0	4.9	4.7	4.5	4.2	3.8	3.3	2.9	2.3	1.3	—	—	—
6	5.4	5.3	5.3	5.2	5.0	4.9	4.7	4.5	4.2	3.8	3.1	2.7	2.0	0.6	—	—	—
11	5.5	5.4	5.3	5.2	5.1	4.9	4.7	4.4	4.1	3.7	3.0	2.5	1.8	—	—	—	—
16	5.6	5.5	5.4	5.3	5.1	4.9	4.7	4.4	4.1	3.6	2.9	2.4	1.5	—	—	—	—
21	5.7	5.6	5.5	5.3	5.1	4.9	4.7	4.4	4.0	3.5	2.8	2.2	1.2	—	—	—	—
26	5.7	5.6	5.5	5.3	5.1	4.9	4.7	4.4	4.0	3.5	2.7	2.0	0.8	—	—	—	—
31	5.8	5.7	5.6	5.4	5.2	4.9	4.7	4.4	4.0	3.4	2.6	1.9	0.3	—	—	—	—

May — Ending

	50°S	45°S	40°S	30°S	20°S	10°S	0	10°N	20°N	30°N	40°N	45°N	50°N	55°N	60°N	65°N	70°N
	h	h	h	h	h	h	h	h	h	h	h	h	h	h	h	h	h
1	18.6	18.6	18.7	18.8	18.9	19.0	19.2	19.4	19.7	20.1	20.6	21.0	21.6	22.7	—	—	—
6	18.5	18.5	18.6	18.7	18.8	19.0	19.2	19.4	19.7	20.1	20.8	21.2	21.9	23.4	—	—	—
11	18.4	18.5	18.5	18.7	18.8	19.0	19.2	19.5	19.8	20.2	20.9	21.4	22.2	—	—	—	—
16	18.3	18.4	18.5	18.6	18.8	19.0	19.2	19.5	19.8	20.3	21.0	21.6	22.4	—	—	—	—
21	18.2	18.3	18.4	18.6	18.8	19.0	19.2	19.5	19.9	20.4	21.1	21.7	22.8	—	—	—	—
26	18.2	18.3	18.4	18.6	18.8	19.0	19.2	19.5	19.9	20.4	21.2	21.9	23.2	—	—	—	—
31	18.1	18.2	18.3	18.5	18.8	19.0	19.3	19.6	20.0	20.5	21.3	22.0	—	—	—	—	—

June — Beginning

	50°S	45°S	40°S	30°S	20°S	10°S	0	10°N	20°N	30°N	40°N	45°N	50°N	55°N	60°N	65°N	70°N
	h	h	h	h	h	h	h	h	h	h	h	h	h	h	h	h	h
1	5.8	5.7	5.6	5.4	5.2	4.9	4.7	4.3	4.0	3.4	2.6	1.9	—	—	—	—	—
6	5.9	5.8	5.6	5.4	5.2	4.9	4.7	4.3	3.9	3.4	2.5	1.8	—	—	—	—	—
11	5.9	5.8	5.7	5.4	5.2	5.0	4.7	4.4	3.9	3.4	2.5	1.7	—	—	—	—	—
16	6.0	5.8	5.7	5.5	5.2	5.0	4.7	4.4	3.9	3.4	2.5	1.7	—	—	—	—	—
21	6.0	5.9	5.7	5.5	5.3	5.0	4.7	4.4	4.0	3.4	2.5	1.7	—	—	—	—	—
26	6.0	5.9	5.8	5.5	5.3	5.0	4.7	4.4	4.0	3.4	2.5	1.7	—	—	—	—	—

June — Ending

	50°S	45°S	40°S	30°S	20°S	10°S	0	10°N	20°N	30°N	40°N	45°N	50°N	55°N	60°N	65°N	70°N
	h	h	h	h	h	h	h	h	h	h	h	h	h	h	h	h	h
1	18.1	18.2	18.3	18.5	18.8	19.0	19.3	19.6	20.0	20.5	21.4	22.1	—	—	—	—	—
6	18.1	18.2	18.3	18.5	18.8	19.0	19.3	19.6	20.0	20.6	21.4	22.2	—	—	—	—	—
11	18.0	18.2	18.3	18.5	18.8	19.0	19.3	19.6	20.1	20.6	21.5	22.3	—	—	—	—	—
16	18.0	18.2	18.3	18.5	18.8	19.0	19.3	19.7	20.1	20.7	21.6	22.4	—	—	—	—	—
21	18.1	18.2	18.3	18.6	18.8	19.1	19.3	19.7	20.1	20.7	21.6	22.4	—	—	—	—	—
26	18.1	18.2	18.3	18.6	18.8	19.1	19.4	19.7	20.1	20.7	21.6	22.4	—	—	—	—	—

Table 6 (*continued*). Times at which astronomical twilight begins and ends at various latitudes.

July

								Beginning										
	50°S	45°S	40°S	30°S	20°S	10°S	0	10°N	20°N	30°N	40°N	45°N	50°N	55°N	60°N	65°N	70°N
	h	h	h	h	h	h	h	h	h	h	h	h	h	h	h	h	h
1	6.0	5.9	5.8	5.5	5.3	5.0	4.8	4.4	4.0	3.4	2.5	1.8	—	—	—	—	—
6	6.0	5.9	5.7	5.5	5.3	5.0	4.8	4.4	4.0	3.5	2.6	1.9	—	—	—	—	—
11	6.0	5.8	5.7	5.5	5.3	5.1	4.8	4.5	4.1	3.5	2.7	2.0	—	—	—	—	—
16	5.9	5.8	5.7	5.5	5.3	5.1	4.8	4.5	4.1	3.6	2.8	2.1	0.8	—	—	—	—
21	5.8	5.8	5.7	5.5	5.3	5.1	4.8	4.5	4.2	3.7	2.9	2.3	1.2	—	—	—	—
26	5.8	5.7	5.6	5.4	5.3	5.1	4.8	4.6	4.2	3.7	3.0	2.5	1.5	—	—	—	—
31	5.7	5.6	5.5	5.4	5.2	5.1	4.8	4.6	4.3	3.8	3.1	2.6	1.8	—	—	—	—

								Ending										
	50°S	45°S	40°S	30°S	20°S	10°S	0	10°N	20°N	30°N	40°N	45°N	50°N	55°N	60°N	65°N	70°N
	h	h	h	h	h	h	h	h	h	h	h	h	h	h	h	h	h
1	18.1	18.3	18.4	18.6	18.8	19.1	19.4	19.7	20.1	20.7	21.6	22.4	—	—	—	—	—
6	18.2	18.3	18.4	18.6	18.9	19.1	19.4	19.7	20.1	20.7	21.5	22.3	—	—	—	—	—
11	18.2	18.3	18.5	18.7	18.9	19.1	19.4	19.7	20.1	20.6	21.5	22.2	—	—	—	—	—
16	18.3	18.4	18.5	18.7	18.9	19.1	19.4	19.7	20.1	20.6	21.4	22.0	23.3	—	—	—	—
21	18.4	18.5	18.6	18.7	18.9	19.1	19.4	19.7	20.0	20.5	21.3	21.9	23.0	—	—	—	—
26	18.5	18.5	18.6	18.8	19.0	19.2	19.4	19.7	20.0	20.5	21.2	21.7	22.6	—	—	—	—
31	18.5	18.6	18.7	18.8	19.0	19.2	19.4	19.6	20.0	20.4	21.1	21.6	22.3	—	—	—	—

August

								Beginning										
	50°S	45°S	40°S	30°S	20°S	10°S	0	10°N	20°N	30°N	40°N	45°N	50°N	55°N	60°N	65°N	70°N
	h	h	h	h	h	h	h	h	h	h	h	h	h	h	h	h	h
1	5.7	5.6	5.5	5.4	5.2	5.1	4.8	4.6	4.3	3.8	3.2	2.6	1.9	—	—	—	—
6	5.5	5.5	5.5	5.3	5.2	5.0	4.8	4.6	4.3	3.9	3.3	2.8	2.1	0.5	—	—	—
11	5.4	5.4	5.4	5.3	5.2	5.0	4.8	4.6	4.3	4.0	3.4	3.0	2.4	1.3	—	—	—
16	5.3	5.3	5.3	5.2	5.1	5.0	4.8	4.6	4.4	4.0	3.5	3.1	2.6	1.7	—	—	—
21	5.1	5.2	5.2	5.1	5.1	5.0	4.8	4.7	4.4	4.1	3.6	3.3	2.8	2.1	—	—	—
26	5.0	5.0	5.0	5.0	5.0	4.9	4.8	4.7	4.5	4.2	3.7	3.4	3.0	2.4	1.2	—	—
31	4.8	4.9	4.9	5.0	4.9	4.9	4.8	4.7	4.5	4.2	3.8	3.6	3.2	2.7	1.8	—	—

								Ending										
	50°S	45°S	40°S	30°S	20°S	10°S	0	10°N	20°N	30°N	40°N	45°N	50°N	55°N	60°N	65°N	70°N
	h	h	h	h	h	h	h	h	h	h	h	h	h	h	h	h	h
1	18.6	18.6	18.7	18.8	19.0	19.2	19.4	19.6	19.9	20.4	21.0	21.5	22.3	—	—	—	—
6	18.7	18.7	18.8	18.9	19.0	19.2	19.4	19.6	19.9	20.3	20.9	21.4	22.0	23.5	—	—	—
11	18.8	18.8	18.8	18.9	19.0	19.2	19.3	19.5	19.8	20.2	20.8	21.2	21.8	22.8	—	—	—
16	18.9	18.9	18.9	18.9	19.0	19.2	19.3	19.5	19.8	20.1	20.6	21.0	21.5	22.3	—	—	—
21	19.0	19.0	19.0	19.0	19.1	19.1	19.3	19.5	19.7	20.0	20.5	20.8	21.3	22.0	23.8	—	—
26	19.1	19.0	19.0	19.0	19.1	19.1	19.2	19.4	19.6	19.9	20.3	20.6	21.0	21.6	22.7	—	—
31	19.2	19.1	19.1	19.1	19.1	19.1	19.2	19.3	19.5	19.8	20.2	20.4	20.8	21.3	22.1	—	—

September

								Beginning										
	50°S	45°S	40°S	30°S	20°S	10°S	0	10°N	20°N	30°N	40°N	45°N	50°N	55°N	60°N	65°N	70°N
	h	h	h	h	h	h	h	h	h	h	h	h	h	h	h	h	h
1	4.8	4.9	4.9	4.9	4.9	4.9	4.8	4.7	4.5	4.2	3.9	3.6	3.2	2.7	1.9	—	—
6	4.6	4.7	4.8	4.8	4.9	4.8	4.8	4.7	4.5	4.3	4.0	3.7	3.4	3.0	2.3	0.7	—
11	4.4	4.6	4.6	4.7	4.8	4.8	4.7	4.7	4.5	4.4	4.1	3.9	3.6	3.2	2.6	1.6	—
16	4.2	4.4	4.5	4.6	4.7	4.7	4.7	4.7	4.6	4.4	4.2	4.0	3.7	3.4	2.9	2.1	—
21	4.0	4.2	4.3	4.5	4.6	4.7	4.7	4.7	4.6	4.5	4.3	4.1	3.9	3.6	3.2	2.6	1.2
26	3.8	4.0	4.2	4.4	4.5	4.6	4.7	4.7	4.6	4.5	4.3	4.2	4.0	3.8	3.5	3.0	2.0

								Ending										
	50°S	45°S	40°S	30°S	20°S	10°S	0	10°N	20°N	30°N	40°N	45°N	50°N	55°N	60°N	65°N	70°N
	h	h	h	h	h	h	h	h	h	h	h	h	h	h	h	h	h
1	19.2	19.2	19.1	19.1	19.1	19.1	19.2	19.3	19.5	19.8	20.1	20.4	20.7	21.2	22.0	—	—
6	19.3	19.3	19.2	19.1	19.1	19.1	19.2	19.3	19.4	19.6	20.0	20.2	20.5	20.9	21.6	23.0	—
11	19.5	19.4	19.3	19.2	19.1	19.1	19.1	19.2	19.3	19.5	19.8	20.0	20.3	20.6	21.2	22.2	—
16	19.6	19.5	19.4	19.2	19.1	19.1	19.1	19.2	19.3	19.4	19.7	19.8	20.1	20.4	20.8	21.6	—
21	19.8	19.6	19.4	19.3	19.1	19.1	19.1	19.1	19.2	19.3	19.5	19.7	19.8	20.1	20.5	21.1	22.4
26	19.9	19.7	19.5	19.3	19.2	19.1	19.1	19.1	19.1	19.2	19.4	19.5	19.6	19.9	20.2	20.7	21.6

Table 6 (*continued*). Times at which astronomical twilight begins and ends at various latitudes.

October

Beginning

	50°S	45°S	40°S	30°S	20°S	10°S	0	10°N	20°N	30°N	40°N	45°N	50°N	55°N	60°N	65°N	70°N
	h	h	h	h	h	h	h	h	h	h	h	h	h	h	h	h	h
1	3.6	3.9	4.0	4.3	4.5	4.6	4.6	4.6	4.6	4.6	4.4	4.3	4.2	4.0	3.7	3.3	2.5
6	3.4	3.7	3.9	4.2	4.4	4.5	4.6	4.6	4.6	4.6	4.5	4.4	4.3	4.2	3.9	3.6	3.0
11	3.2	3.5	3.7	4.1	4.3	4.5	4.6	4.6	4.7	4.7	4.6	4.5	4.5	4.3	4.2	3.9	3.4
16	3.0	3.3	3.6	4.0	4.2	4.4	4.5	4.6	4.7	4.7	4.7	4.6	4.6	4.5	4.4	4.2	3.8
21	2.7	3.1	3.4	3.9	4.2	4.4	4.5	4.6	4.7	4.8	4.8	4.8	4.7	4.7	4.6	4.4	4.2
26	2.5	2.9	3.3	3.8	4.1	4.3	4.5	4.6	4.7	4.8	4.9	4.9	4.8	4.8	4.8	4.7	4.5
31	2.2	2.8	3.1	3.7	4.0	4.3	4.5	4.6	4.8	4.9	4.9	5.0	5.0	5.0	4.9	4.9	4.8

Ending

	50°S	45°S	40°S	30°S	20°S	10°S	0	10°N	20°N	30°N	40°N	45°N	50°N	55°N	60°N	65°N	70°N
	h	h	h	h	h	h	h	h	h	h	h	h	h	h	h	h	h
1	20.1	19.8	19.6	19.4	19.2	19.1	19.0	19.0	19.0	19.1	19.2	19.3	19.4	19.6	19.9	20.3	21.0
6	20.2	19.9	19.7	19.4	19.2	19.1	19.0	19.0	19.0	19.0	19.1	19.2	19.3	19.4	19.6	20.0	20.5
11	20.4	20.1	19.8	19.5	19.3	19.1	19.0	18.9	18.9	18.9	18.9	19.0	19.1	19.2	19.4	19.6	20.1
16	20.6	20.2	19.9	19.6	19.3	19.1	19.0	18.9	18.8	18.8	18.8	18.9	18.9	19.0	19.1	19.3	19.7
21	20.8	20.4	20.1	19.6	19.3	19.1	19.0	18.9	18.8	18.7	18.7	18.7	18.8	18.8	18.9	19.0	19.3
26	21.0	20.5	20.2	19.7	19.4	19.1	19.0	18.8	18.7	18.6	18.6	18.6	18.6	18.6	18.7	18.8	18.9
31	21.3	20.7	20.3	19.8	19.4	19.2	19.0	18.8	18.7	18.6	18.5	18.5	18.5	18.5	18.5	18.5	18.6

November

Beginning

	50°S	45°S	40°S	30°S	20°S	10°S	0	10°N	20°N	30°N	40°N	45°N	50°N	55°N	60°N	65°N	70°N
	h	h	h	h	h	h	h	h	h	h	h	h	h	h	h	h	h
1	2.2	2.7	3.1	3.7	4.0	4.3	4.5	4.6	4.8	4.9	5.0	5.0	5.0	5.0	5.0	4.9	4.8
6	1.9	2.5	3.0	3.6	4.0	4.3	4.5	4.7	4.8	4.9	5.0	5.1	5.1	5.1	5.2	5.2	5.1
11	1.7	2.4	2.9	3.5	3.9	4.2	4.5	4.7	4.8	5.0	5.1	5.2	5.2	5.3	5.3	5.4	5.4
16	1.4	2.2	2.7	3.4	3.9	4.2	4.5	4.7	4.9	5.0	5.2	5.3	5.3	5.4	5.5	5.6	5.7
21	1.1	2.1	2.6	3.4	3.8	4.2	4.5	4.7	4.9	5.1	5.3	5.4	5.5	5.5	5.6	5.8	5.9
26	0.7	1.9	2.5	3.3	3.8	4.2	4.5	4.7	5.0	5.2	5.4	5.5	5.6	5.7	5.8	5.9	6.1

Ending

	50°S	45°S	40°S	30°S	20°S	10°S	0	10°N	20°N	30°N	40°N	45°N	50°N	55°N	60°N	65°N	70°N
	h	h	h	h	h	h	h	h	h	h	h	h	h	h	h	h	h
1	21.3	20.8	20.4	19.8	19.4	19.2	19.0	18.8	18.7	18.6	18.5	18.5	18.4	18.4	18.5	18.5	18.6
6	21.6	20.9	20.5	19.9	19.5	19.2	19.0	18.8	18.6	18.5	18.4	18.4	18.3	18.3	18.3	18.3	18.3
11	21.9	21.1	20.6	20.0	19.6	19.2	19.0	18.8	18.6	18.5	18.3	18.3	18.2	18.2	18.1	18.1	18.0
16	22.2	21.3	20.8	20.1	19.6	19.3	19.0	18.8	18.6	18.4	18.3	18.2	18.1	18.1	18.0	17.9	17.8
21	22.5	21.5	20.9	20.2	19.7	19.3	19.0	18.8	18.6	18.4	18.2	18.2	18.1	18.0	17.9	17.8	17.6
26	22.9	21.7	21.1	20.3	19.8	19.4	19.1	18.8	18.6	18.4	18.2	18.1	18.0	17.9	17.8	17.6	17.5

December

Beginning

	50°S	45°S	40°S	30°S	20°S	10°S	0	10°N	20°N	30°N	40°N	45°N	50°N	55°N	60°N	65°N	70°N
	h	h	h	h	h	h	h	h	h	h	h	h	h	h	h	h	h
1	0.3	1.8	2.5	3.3	3.8	4.2	4.5	4.8	5.0	5.2	5.4	5.5	5.7	5.8	5.9	6.1	6.3
6	—	1.7	2.4	3.3	3.8	4.2	4.5	4.8	5.1	5.3	5.5	5.6	5.7	5.9	6.0	6.2	6.5
11	—	1.6	2.4	3.3	3.8	4.2	4.6	4.9	5.1	5.3	5.6	5.7	5.8	6.0	6.1	6.3	6.6
16	—	1.6	2.4	3.3	3.9	4.3	4.6	4.9	5.1	5.4	5.6	5.8	5.9	6.0	6.2	6.4	6.7
21	—	1.6	2.4	3.3	3.9	4.3	4.7	4.9	5.2	5.4	5.7	5.8	5.9	6.1	6.3	6.5	6.8
26	—	1.7	2.4	3.4	3.9	4.4	4.7	5.0	5.2	5.5	5.7	5.8	6.0	6.1	6.3	6.5	6.8
31	—	1.7	2.5	3.4	4.0	4.4	4.7	5.0	5.3	5.5	5.7	5.9	6.0	6.1	6.3	6.5	6.8

Ending

	50°S	45°S	40°S	30°S	20°S	10°S	0	10°N	20°N	30°N	40°N	45°N	50°N	55°N	60°N	65°N	70°N
	h	h	h	h	h	h	h	h	h	h	h	h	h	h	h	h	h
1	23.5	21.9	21.2	20.4	19.8	19.4	19.1	18.9	18.6	18.4	18.2	18.1	18.0	17.8	17.7	17.5	17.3
6	—	22.0	21.3	20.4	19.9	19.5	19.2	18.9	18.6	18.4	18.2	18.1	18.0	17.8	17.7	17.5	17.2
11	—	22.2	21.4	20.5	19.9	19.5	19.2	18.9	18.7	18.4	18.2	18.1	17.9	17.8	17.6	17.4	17.2
16	—	22.3	21.5	20.6	20.0	19.6	19.2	19.0	18.7	18.5	18.2	18.1	18.0	17.8	17.6	17.4	17.2
21	—	22.3	21.5	20.6	20.0	19.6	19.3	19.0	18.7	18.5	18.3	18.1	18.0	17.8	17.7	17.5	17.2
26	—	22.4	21.6	20.7	20.1	19.7	19.3	19.0	18.8	18.5	18.3	18.2	18.0	17.9	17.7	17.5	17.2
31	—	22.3	21.6	20.7	20.1	19.7	19.4	19.1	18.8	18.6	18.4	18.2	18.1	18.0	17.8	17.6	17.3

Table 7. The equation of time and the Sun's longitude, RA and declination at 0h UT for various dates throughout the year.
The longitude of the Sun is given to the nearest degree, and the equation of time (Eqn) to the nearest minute; the RA is given in whole hours at the nearest date; and the declination is given to the nearest degree. For the RA on intermediate dates, add 4 minutes per day, and for longitude add 1° per day. The equation of time and declination can be interpolated by inspection. The dates have been chosen so that the apparent longitude of the Sun is an exact multiple of 5°.
The intervals between dates in the table vary between 4 and 6 days because the longitude has been rounded to the nearest degree, and also because the elliptical orbit of the Earth means that the change of the Sun's longitude during the year is not uniform.

Date	Long.	Eqn	RA	Dec.	Date	Long.	Eqn	RA	Dec.
	°	m	h	°		°	m	h	°
Dec. 27	275	−1		−23	June 27	95	−3		+23
Jan. 1	280	−3		−23	July 2	100	−4		+23
6	285	−6	19	−23	7	105	−5	7	+23
10	290	−7		−22	13	110	−6		+22
15	295	−9		−21	18	115	−6		+21
20	300	−11	20	−20	23	120	−6	8	+20
25	305	−12		−19	28	125	−6		+19
30	310	−13		−18	Aug. 2	130	−6		+18
Feb. 4	315	−14	21	−16	8	135	−6	9	+16
9	320	−14		−15	13	140	−5		+15
14	325	−14		−13	18	145	−4		+13
19	330	−14	22	−11	23	150	−3	10	+12
24	335	−13		−10	28	155	−1		+10
Mar. 1	340	−12		−8	Sept. 3	160	0		+8
6	345	−11	23	−6	8	165	+2	11	+6
11	350	−10		−4	13	170	+4		+4
16	355	−9		−2	18	175	+6		+2
21	0	−7	0	0	23	180	+7	12	0
26	5	−6		+2	28	185	+9		−2
31	10	−4		+4	Oct. 3	190	+11		−4
Apr. 5	15	−3	1	+6	8	195	+12	13	−6
10	20	−1		+8	14	200	+14		−8
15	25	0		+10	19	205	+15		−10
20	30	+1	2	+11	24	210	+16	14	−12
25	35	+2		+13	29	215	+16		−13
May 1	40	+3		+15	Nov. 3	220	+16		−15
6	45	+3	3	+16	8	225	+16	15	−16
11	50	+4		+18	13	230	+16		−18
16	55	+4		+19	18	235	+15		−19
21	60	+3	4	+20	22	240	+14	16	−20
26	65	+3		+21	27	245	+13		−21
June 1	70	+2		+22	Dec. 2	250	+11		−22
6	75	+1	5	+23	7	255	+9	17	−23
11	80	+1		+23	12	260	+7		−23
16	85	−1		+23	17	265	+4		−23
22	90	−2	6	+23.4	22	270	+2	18	−23.4

Sidereal day. The time interval between two successive transits of the vernal equinox. The sidereal day is 3m 55.91s shorter than the mean solar day.

Sunrise and sunset are the times at which the upper limb of the Sun lies on the horizon, the effect of refraction by the Earth's atmosphere being taken into account. The times of sunrise and sunset would differ noticeably from the observed times if calculated for the centre of the Sun. At sunrise and sunset the Sun's centre is 50' below the horizon, based on adopted values of 34' for refraction at the horizon and 16' for the semi-diameter of the Sun. Table 5 gives the approximate times of sunrise and sunset at various latitudes on the Earth in any year.

Twilight is the period in the evening after sunset or in the morning before sunrise when the sky is not completely dark because of scattering of sunlight in the atmosphere. Three types of twilight are defined:

Civil twilight begins and ends when the centre of the Sun is 6° below the horizon.

Nautical twilight begins and ends when the centre of the Sun is 12° below the horizon. During nautical twilight the brightest stars are visible and the sea horizon can be seen.

Astronomical twilight begins and ends when the centre of the Sun is 18° below the horizon, so that in a clear sky 6th magnitude stars are just visible at the zenith.

Twilight lengthens with the distance of the observer from the equator, and is shortest as seen from anywhere on the Earth at the equinoxes. Table 6 gives times for the beginning and ending of astronomical twilight at various latitudes on the Earth throughout the year. Note that at high latitudes astronomical twilight is perpetual during the summer.

Continued on p. 57

Table 8. Greenwich sidereal time. The RA on the Greenwich meridian is given for the dates and times indicated. For times after midnight, add 1 day to the date at the side.

Intermediate dates: Add to the RA for the previous date the number of minutes from the 7 or 8 day interval table below.

7 days interval:	1d	2d	3d	4d	5d	6d		8 days interval:	1d	2d	3d	4d	5d	6d	7d
Add minutes:	4m	9m	13m	17m	21m	26m		Add minutes:	4m	8m	12m	15m	19m	23m	26m

Intermediate minutes of mean time: Add the same number of RA minutes to the previous RA hour. Thus Apr. 6 at 1709h=RA 6h 09m.

Date	1700	1800	1900	2000	2100	2200	UT 2300	0000	0100	0200	0300	0400	0500	0600
	h	h	h	h	h	h	h	h	h	h	h	h	h	h
Jan. 5	0	1	2	3	4	5	6	7	8	9	10	11	12	13
13	0½	1½	2½	3½	4½	5½	6½	7½	8½	9½	10½	11½	12½	13½
21	1	2	3	4	5	6	7	8	9	10	11	12	13	14
28	1½	2½	3½	4½	5½	6½	7½	8½	9½	10½	11½	12½	13½	14½
Feb. 5	2	3	4	5	6	7	8	9	10	11	12	13	14	15
13	2½	3½	4½	5½	6½	7½	8½	9½	10½	11½	12½	13½	14½	15½
20	3	4	5	6	7	8	9	10	11	12	13	14	15	16
28	3½	4½	5½	6½	7½	8½	9½	10½	11½	12½	13½	14½	15½	16½
Mar. 7	4	5	6	7	8	9	10	11	12	13	14	15	16	17
15	4½	5½	6½	7½	8½	9½	10½	11½	12½	13½	14½	15½	16½	17½
22	5	6	7	8	9	10	11	12	13	14	15	16	17	18
29	5½	6½	7½	8½	9½	10½	11½	12½	13½	14½	15½	16½	17½	18½
Apr. 6	6	7	8	9	10	11	12	13	14	15	16	17	18	19
14	6½	7½	8½	9½	10½	11½	12½	13½	14½	15½	16½	17½	18½	19½
22	7	8	9	10	11	12	13	14	15	16	17	18	19	20
29	7½	8½	9½	10½	11½	12½	13½	14½	15½	16½	17½	18½	19½	20½
May 7	8	9	10	11	12	13	14	15	16	17	18	19	20	21
15	8½	9½	10½	11½	12½	13½	14½	15½	16½	17½	18½	19½	20½	21½
22	9	10	11	12	13	14	15	16	17	18	19	20	21	22
30	9½	10½	11½	12½	13½	14½	15½	16½	17½	18½	19½	20½	21½	22½
June 6	10	11	12	13	14	15	16	17	18	19	20	21	22	23
14	10½	11½	12½	13½	14½	15½	16½	17½	18½	19½	20½	21½	22½	23½
22	11	12	13	14	15	16	17	18	19	20	21	22	23	0
29	11½	12½	13½	14½	15½	16½	17½	18½	19½	20½	21½	22½	23½	0½
July 7	12	13	14	15	16	17	18	19	20	21	22	23	0	1
15	12½	13½	14½	15½	16½	17½	18½	19½	20½	21½	22½	23½	0½	1½
22	13	14	15	16	17	18	19	20	21	22	23	0	1	2
30	13½	14½	15½	16½	17½	18½	19½	20½	21½	22½	23½	0½	1½	2½
Aug. 6	14	15	16	17	18	19	20	21	22	23	0	1	2	3
14	14½	15½	16½	17½	18½	19½	20½	21½	22½	23½	0½	1½	2½	3½
22	15	16	17	18	19	20	21	22	23	0	1	2	3	4
29	15½	16½	17½	18½	19½	20½	21½	22½	23½	0½	1½	2½	3½	4½
Sept. 6	16	17	18	19	20	21	22	23	0	1	2	3	4	5
13	16½	17½	18½	19½	20½	21½	22½	23½	0½	1½	2½	3½	4½	5½
21	17	18	19	20	21	22	23	0	1	2	3	4	5	6
29	17½	18½	19½	20½	21½	22½	23½	0½	1½	2½	3½	4½	5½	6½
Oct. 6	18	19	20	21	22	23	0	1	2	3	4	5	6	7
14	18½	19½	20½	21½	22½	23½	0½	1½	2½	3½	4½	5½	6½	7½
21	19	20	21	22	23	0	1	2	3	4	5	6	7	8
29	19½	20½	21½	22½	23½	0½	1½	2½	3½	4½	5½	6½	7½	8½
Nov. 6	20	21	22	23	0	1	2	3	4	5	6	7	8	9
13	20½	21½	22½	23½	0½	1½	2½	3½	4½	5½	6½	7½	8½	9½
21	21	22	23	0	1	2	3	4	5	6	7	8	9	10
28	21½	22½	23½	0½	1½	2½	3½	4½	5½	6½	7½	8½	9½	10½
Dec. 6	22	23	0	1	2	3	4	5	6	7	8	9	10	11
14	22½	23½	0½	1½	2½	3½	4½	5½	6½	7½	8½	9½	10½	11½
21	23	0	1	2	3	4	5	6	7	8	9	10	11	12
29	23½	0½	1½	2½	3½	4½	5½	6½	7½	8½	9½	10½	11½	12½

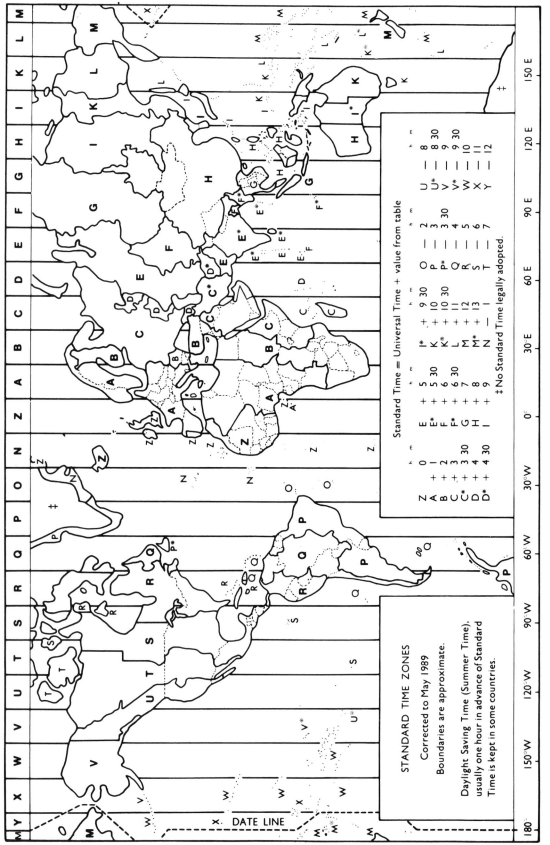

Figure 2. World map of time zones. Courtesy HM Nautical Almanac Office, Science and Engineering Research Council.

The measurement of time

Apparent solar time is the time shown on a sundial, which records the motion of the real Sun across the sky. But apparent solar time is not uniform because the motion of the real Sun varies throughout the year (see Apparent solar day, p. 45). For more uniform time-keeping, mean solar time is used.

Mean solar time is the time as shown on a clock, with the irregularities of apparent solar time smoothed out. Mean solar time is based on the movement of the imaginary mean Sun (see p. 45), although it is still affected by slight variations in the rotation of the Earth. The difference between mean solar time and apparent solar time is given by the equation of time (see below).

Greenwich Mean Time (GMT) is the mean solar time at the longitude of Greenwich, counted from midnight. In 1928, on the recommendation of the International Astronomical Union, GMT became known as Universal Time (UT). Before 1925, astronomers reckoned GMT from Greenwich noon, which avoided the need to change the date during a night's observing; this is now called Greenwich Mean Astronomical Time (GMAT).

Equation of time. The correction to be applied to apparent solar time to obtain mean solar time:

mean solar time = apparent solar time − equation of time

The equation of time is greatest in early November, when apparent solar time is over 16 minutes ahead of mean solar time, which is shown by giving it a positive value. In mid-February apparent solar time is over 14 minutes behind mean solar time, shown by a negative value. The difference is zero four times a year: on April 15, June 14, September 1 and December 25. Table 7 gives the values of the equation of time to the nearest minute for various dates throughout the year.

Sidereal time is the time that has elapsed since the vernal equinox last crossed the meridian, i.e. it is the local hour angle of the vernal equinox. At any place, the sidereal time is equal to the right ascension of a star that is on the meridian.

Greenwich sidereal time (GST) is the time that has elapsed since the vernal equinox last crossed the meridian at Greenwich. Table 8 gives approximate values of Greenwich sidereal time throughout the year. This table is intended for use with the star charts to find which part of the sky is near the meridian at a given date and time. Precise values for Greenwich sidereal time at 0h UT for every date are given in the *Astronomical Almanac* and, to a lower precision suitable for most purposes, in the *Handbook* of the British Astronomical Association.

Local sidereal time (LST). To obtain local sidereal time, the longitude of the observer relative to Greenwich must be taken into account. For each degree of longitude east of Greenwich, add 4 minutes to GST to obtain LST (1h for every 15°). For each degree west of Greenwich, subtract 4 minutes from GST (1h for every 15°).

Greenwich hour angle (GHA). To find the Greenwich hour angle of a star, subtract the star's right ascension from the Greenwich sidereal time.

Local hour angle (LHA). To find the local hour angle of a star, subtract the star's right ascension from the local sidereal time; alternatively, add the longitude east to the GHA.

Time zones. Figure 2 shows how the Earth is divided into 24 time zones, each 15° broad, with the prime zone centred on the Greenwich meridian. Countries in each zone keep time that is usually an exact number of hours (or in some cases half-hours) different from GMT. Time in the zones to the east of Greenwich is ahead of GMT, while times to the west of Greenwich are behind GMT. The date changes at the International Date Line, on the opposite side of the Earth from the Greenwich meridian.

Universal Time (UT) is the name by which Greenwich Mean Time became known for scientific purposes in 1928. However, precise observations have shown that the daily rotation of the Earth, on which UT is based, has various irregularities and hence can no longer be used as the basis of a uniform system of time. Several versions of UT are now defined:

UT0 is mean solar time determined directly from observations of the stars; because of the motion of the Earth's poles its value depends on the location of the observatory.

UT1 is UT0 corrected for the slight wandering of the Earth's geographical poles. UT1 is the time-scale used by astronomers and navigators, and is what is usually meant when the term UT is used without further qualification.

UT2 is UT1 corrected for seasonal variations in the Earth's rate of spin. It was used as the basis of time signals between 1956 and 1972, but its role as a quickly established, nearly uniform time-scale is now filled by International Atomic Time (see below).

UTC, Coordinated Universal Time, is the time given by broadcast time signals since 1972. It is derived from atomic clocks, so that one second of UTC is exactly the same length as one second of International Atomic Time. UTC is kept within 0.9 second of UT1 by introducing or deleting one second, known as a leap second, at the end of December, June, March or September, as necessary. This time-scale is widely known as GMT, although that term is no longer used in astronomy.

International Atomic Time (TAI) is the time given by atomic clocks that maintain a continuous count of seconds. TAI differs from UTC by an exact number of seconds, as a result of the introduction of leap seconds in the UTC time-scale to take account of changes in the rotation rate of the Earth. TAI and UTC are the recommended time-scales for the precise dating of obervations.

Terrestrial Dynamical Time (TDT) is a smooth and regular time-scale without the irregularities caused by variations of the Earth's rotation. It is used in calculating the orbits of bodies in the Solar System for observations made from the Earth. It was introduced in 1984, replacing Ephemeris Time (ET), which had previously served the same purpose. One second of TDT equals one second of atomic time. Because of the slowing of the Earth's rotation by tidal friction and other forces, Universal Time (UT1) is falling behind TDT by about one second per year. The difference between TDT and UT1 is given by a correction factor ΔT. Table 9 gives the observed and predicted values of ΔT, but note that ΔT cannot be precisely predicted far into the future.

Table 9. Values of ΔT, the amount by which Universal Time (UT1) lags behind Terrestrial Dynamical Time (TDT), from 1900 to 2010. Values for 1990.5 onwards are predicted using a rate of +0.0013 s per day, but this rate may change.

Year	$\Delta T(s)$	Year	$\Delta T(s)$	Year	$\Delta T(s)$
1900.5	-2	1955.5	$+31$	1985.5	$+55$
1910.5	$+11$	1960.5	$+33$	1990.5	$+57$
1920.5	$+22$	1965.5	$+36$	1995.5	$+59$
1930.5	$+24$	1970.5	$+41$	2000.5	$+62$
1940.5	$+25$	1975.5	$+46$	2005.5	$+64$
1950.5	$+29$	1980.5	$+51$	2010.5	$+67$

The year

Tropical year. The time taken by the Sun to complete one circuit of the celestial sphere from one vernal equinox to the next. Because of precession, the vernal equinox has an annual retrograde motion of 50″.29 against the celestial sphere, so during the tropical year the Sun covers an angular distance of 360° − 50″.29. The tropical year lasts 365.242 19 d, and is the year on which the calendar is based, since the declination of the Sun determines the occurrence of the seasons.

Sidereal year. The time taken by the Earth to orbit the Sun once with respect to the celestial sphere. In a sidereal year the Sun covers an angular distance of exactly 360° relative to the star background, taking 365.256 36 d.

Anomalistic year. The interval between one perihelion of the Earth and the next. The anomalistic year is slightly longer than the sidereal year because of a gradual advance of the Earth's perihelion caused by the gravitational pulls of the planets. During an anomalistic year the Sun covers an angular distance of 360° + 11″.64, taking 365.259 64 d.

Eclipse year. The time taken for the Sun to return to the same node of the Moon's orbit; it lasts 346.620 03 d. This is considerably shorter than a sidereal year, because the nodes of the Moon's orbit regress by about 19° per year. The eclipse year is responsible for the regular recurrence of both solar and lunar eclipses, which can take place only when these bodies are within a small distance of the node. Nineteen eclipse years are 6585.78 d, almost exactly the same as the Saros cycle of 223 synodic months, or 6585.32 d.

The month

Synodic month. The interval between successive new moons. It is also known as a *lunation*. Its mean length is 29.530 59 d, but the actual value can vary between $29\frac{1}{4}$ and $29\frac{3}{4}$ d.

Sidereal month. The period taken by the Moon to make one complete circuit of the celestial sphere as seen from the Earth. Its mean value is 27.321 66 d.

Tropical month. The time taken for the Moon to orbit the Earth once with respect to the vernal equinox. Its mean value is 27.321 58 d.

Anomalistic month. The interval between successive perigees of the Moon. Its mean value is 27.554 55 d.

Draconic month. The interval between successive passages of the Moon through its ascending node. Its mean value is 27. 212 22 d.

III

PRACTICAL ASTRONOMY

OBSERVING

Notes on the observation of specific objects are included in the relevant sections; this section deals with general aspects of observation.

The human eye

The eye consists of a hollow sphere filled with a transparent substance through which light rays are focused by a crystalline lens. The image is formed on a screen (the *retina*) which is covered with a large number of nerve endings. Some of these nerves (the *cones*) give the sensation of colour, while the *rods*, which can respond to much lower levels of illumination, interpret the image only in shades of grey.

Defects of the eye include an inability to focus on nearby or distant objects (long sight and short sight, respectively), and *astigmatism*, which results from the lens being distorted. An astigmatic eye focuses a point object such as a star as an oval or a short line. All these defects may be compensated by wearing suitable spectacles or contact lenses, although long or short sight is of no importance in telescopic astronomy since the instrument may be focused to suit the individual. Astigmatism is more of a problem, particularly at low magnifications, as the telescope's *exit pupil* is then large, and most or all of the defective lens is being used. At high magnifications, when the exit pupil is narrow, only the centre of the eye's lens is used, and the effect of any astigmatism is minimized. In particular, astigmatic users of binoculars may be forced to wear their spectacles while observing, which has the result of forcing the eyes back from the eyepieces, with the consequent loss of part of the field of view (except in binoculars with extra-large eye relief). The convenience of wearing contact lenses to counteract serious astigmatism is obvious.

The eye is not perfectly *achromatic* (free from false colour), but this is rarely if ever noticeable in practice. The defect of *spherical aberration* (in which the edge and the centre of the eye's lens bring light to different foci, producing a blurred image) is, like astigmatism, most noticeable at very low magnifications when the whole of the lens is being used. Since fine image detail is not being sought at these times, the defect is of little practical importance.

With age, the eye loses its ability to focus on objects over a wide range of distance. More importantly, the lens may become opaque. This can be corrected by a cataract operation, which has the effect of improving the eye's sensitivity to violet and near-ultraviolet wavelengths, which are absorbed both by glass in the telescope and by the eye's own lens.

Observing techniques

The observing eye should always be in its most relaxed state – in other words, focused at infinity. When straining to make out elusive details, it is easy for the eye to change its focus involuntarily. At intervals, therefore, particularly when observing planetary surfaces, it pays to pause, relax, and then refocus carefully on a nearby star.

Resolving power. The resolving power of the normal eye on naked-eye stars is about 4 arcmin – in other words, two stars separated by this amount can be made out individually (although some observers can better this). It follows that a magnification of about ×240 will permit two stars 1 arcsec apart to be distinguished. This is the limit of resolution, or resolving power, of a telescope with an aperture of 110 mm, from which it may be deduced that a magnification of about $2.2D$ (where D is the aperture in millimetres) will permit all the detail in any telescope's image to be made out (although particular circumstances may modify this rule). In any case, sheer resolution is not always the most important factor when selecting the best magnification.

Observing faint objects. The retina achieves maximum sensitivity through the secretion of a hormone (rhodopsin) which stimulates the rods. This happens only under conditions of poor illumination, and sensitivity can continue to improve noticeably for several minutes, and detectably for perhaps half an hour. Such *dark-adaptation* is rapidly destroyed upon exposure to bright light.

Continued on p. 62

59

NORTH POLAR LIMITING MAGNITUDE CHART

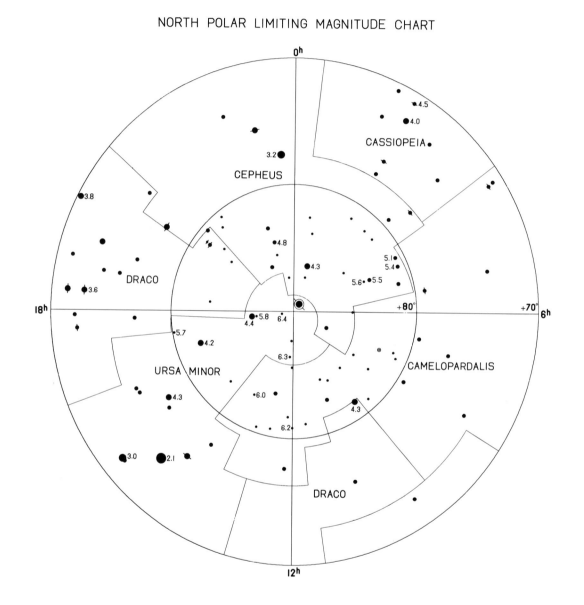

Figure 3(b). Polar limiting magnitudes. This chart shows stars within 20° of the south celestial pole. The magnitudes and positions of all stars down to mag. 5.5 are shown in the outer 10° circle; in the inner circle all stars plotted in the Atlas are shown, with sample magnitudes down to 6.5.

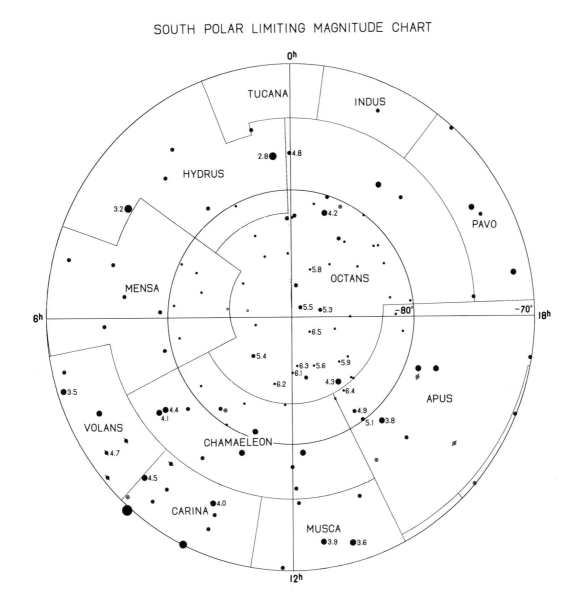

SOUTH POLAR LIMITING MAGNITUDE CHART

Figure 3(a). Polar limiting magnitudes. This chart shows stars within 20° of the north celestial pole. The magnitudes and positions of all stars down to mag. 5.5 are shown in the outer 10° circle; in the inner circle all stars plotted in the Atlas are shown, with sample magnitudes down to 6.5.

The dark-adapted eye loses sensitivity at the long-wavelength (red) end of the visible spectrum. In daylight, a normal eye has a visual range of approximately 400–750 nm, with a peak sensitivity in the yellow–green region of the spectrum, around 555 nm. For a dark-adapted eye the visual range is approximately 400–620 nm, and the peak sensitivity moves into the green region of the spectrum, around 510 nm. This shift of sensitivity is known as the *Purkinje effect*, and explains why moonlight appears bluer than direct sunlight.

Since the most sensitive part of the retina is an annular region around its centre, very faint objects may be detectable only by *averted vision*, in which the observer looks slightly to one side of the object being observed.

Atmospheric conditions

A celestial object should be observed when it is as far as possible above the haze and mist of the horizon; *culmination*, or maximum altitude, occurs when it crosses the meridian.

Nights when the air is most transparent, and the stars appear most brilliant, are not necessarily ideal for astronomical work since such conditions are often accompanied by flickering air currents, which cause the stars to twinkle to the naked eye and 'boil' when viewed through a telescope. Very transparent nights may, however, be ideal for observing faint, extended objects such as comets and large nebulae.

Slight haze is often a sign of steady air, and good views of the Moon, planets and bright stars may be obtained under such conditions.

Transparency is a measure of the clarity of the atmosphere. It always depends on altitude: even under perfect conditions a star will appear about three magnitudes fainter just above the horizon than at the zenith, and in practice horizon haze will usually increase this difference considerably. However, by selecting stars at a constant altitude (i.e. around the celestial pole) it is possible to classify the transparency of any night by noting the faintest star visible with the naked eye. Figure 3, on pages 60 and 61, indicates stars of suitable magnitudes for this purpose.

In practice, transparency as measured in this way is not always determined simply by the absorption of light by water or dirt in the atmosphere. Unless the observer is situated far from any built-up area, sky-brightening caused by artificial lighting reflected off airborne particles can also make the stars appear dim by contrast. Faint auroral glows in the upper atmosphere can have a similar effect.

Seeing is a term used to indicate the steadiness of the air, as judged by the appearance of the telescopic image. The two are connected by the fact that air currents are caused by masses of air at different temperatures, and the refractive index of air changes with temperature: therefore the currents cause the image to flicker. There are two basic components, often called 'high' and 'low' seeing. High seeing is affected by currents at altitudes of between about a thousand metres and several kilometres; the quality of low seeing, over which the observer has some control, depends on conditions near the ground and even inside the telescope itself. For example, after a summer's day the night air in contact with the ground around the telescope is warmed and rises, creating turbulence; similarly, warm air trapped inside an observatory, or in a telescope tube, can cause unsteadiness. Bad high-level seeing causes a star's image to move irregularly, or sharp undulations to cross a planet's disk; bad low-level seeing takes the form of sudden loss of focus. Seeing conditions also affect telescopes of different aperture in different ways. At first sight Jupiter may appear less distinct in a 300 mm telescope than in a 100 mm, since the larger aperture is affected by turbulent air across nine times the cross-sectional area of atmosphere.

Since seeing conditions can have a considerable influence on what is visible, they must always be recorded. The classification of seeing is likely to be more subjective than that of transparency, and expressions such as 'good' or 'poor' have little general meaning. More precise descriptions, such as 'boiling with steady moments' or 'image unsteady and rather diffuse', should be used. Several numerical scales have also been devised. For lunar and planetary work the Antoniadi scale is widely used:

   I perfect seeing, without a quiver
  II slight undulations, with moments of calm lasting several seconds
 III moderate seeing, with larger air tremors
 IV poor seeing, with constant troublesome undulations
  V very bad seeing, scarcely allowing a rough sketch to be made.

Recording observations

All observations should be written down at the time they are made. The notes should be clearly worded, and should have entered on them the year, month, day, hour and minute (UT) of the observation, together with the aperture and magnification used and the seeing conditions.

Observational records should be copied up from the notes made at the telescope as soon as possible, while they are still fresh in the mind. Many observers keep a separate book for each type of object being observed. Each observation should be given a serial number to permit later indexing.

Illumination of the notebook, star atlas or reference work used at the telescope is often provided by a torch (flashlight) with its bulb painted red, or a red filter over the glass. Removing the reflector behind the bulb lessens the intensity and gives a more even light. It is important to use only the minimum light necessary, so that dark-adaptation is affected as little as possible.

It is inconvenient to hold a torch as well as manipulate eyepieces, refer to sources, adjust the telescope, and hold the notebook and write in it. The observing light is best secured to the telescope tube or stand, with a readily accessible switch.

Timing observations

With the wide availability of reliable and accurate watches, the need for the observatory clock has diminished. A quartz-controlled watch checked against a radio time-signal or the telephone time service earlier in the evening will remain accurate to within a fraction of a second throughout the night, which is sufficient for general observational purposes.

For setting an equatorial telescope with circles, however, a clock showing sidereal time is necessary. An ordinary alarm clock, adjusted to gain at a rate of 4 minutes a day, may be set to the sidereal time as derived from Table 8 before the observing session begins. Alternatively, electronic sidereal clocks are available.

Precise timing of astronomical phenomena (such as eclipses of Jupiter's satellites, occultations of stars by the Moon or fixes on artificial satellites) requires a stopwatch. The stopwatch may either be started against a time-signal and stopped at the observed phenomenon, or vice versa. If a series of phenomena are to be observed, a split-action stopwatch will allow successive timings to be made and noted.

Directions in an inverting telescope

The north–south and east–west orientations of the telescopic field of view depend on its position in the sky. North can be at the top, bottom, right or left of the field, or any position in between; the same is true of the other cardinal points. The fact that most astronomical telescopes invert the image adds further to the initial confusion.

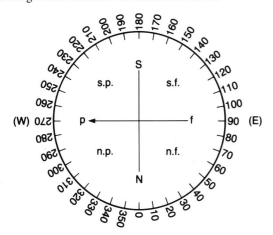

Figure 4. Inverted field of view, and position angle. The inverted telescopic field of view, and the direction of travel of a celestial object across it, as seen by an observer in the northern hemisphere looking due south or – if turned through 180° (the relative positions remain unchanged) – by an observer in the southern hemisphere looking due north. The position angle scale is shown round the outside.

It is convenient to use the drift of a celestial object as a reference. Owing to the Earth's spin, the Sun, Moon, planets and stars all appear to move through the field of view of a stationary telescope from east (following, or f) to west (preceding, or p). Having used the drift of objects through the field of view to establish the p and f points, the observer may determine the north and south points by remembering 'PSFN' (or 'poisonous snakes feel nice') as the clockwise order of the four directions in the field. The field of view is often divided into four quadrants: north–following, south–following, south–preceding and north–preceding. Accurate *position angle* measurements of one object with respect to another use a 0–360° scale (north 0°, east or following 90°, south 180°, and west or preceding 270°).

Figure 4 shows the approximate orientation of the field of view of an inverting telescope, in either the northern or the southern hemisphere.

Angular distances on the celestial sphere

The distance from thumb to little finger of an outstretched hand at arm's length is about 20°. The following approximate separations between pairs of stars may also be found useful in determining distances on the celestial sphere; others can easily be measured from the star charts. The separations are measured along a great circle passing through the two stars.

$\frac{1}{2}°$ = the angular diameter of the Sun or Moon
$1\frac{1}{4}°$ = δ to ε Orionis, or β to λ Crucis
$2°$ = α to γ Aquilae, or α to δ Scorpii
$2\frac{1}{2}°$ = α to β Aquilae
$4°$ = α to β Canis Minoris, or α to β Crucis
$5°$ = α to β Ursae Majoris, or α to β Centauri

The total area of the celestial sphere is 41 253 square degrees.

ASTRONOMICAL INSTRUMENTS

Binoculars

Binoculars are almost indispensable, and make an ideal first instrument for the newcomer to astronomy, being far more effective than a small, cheap telescope. They need not (in fact should not) be large or high-powered, or the benefits of extreme portability and general ease of use will be lost.

Binoculars have particular combinations of magnification and aperture, and these are given in the form, for example, 8 × 30, which indicates a magnification of ×8 and an aperture of 30 mm. For astronomical work the larger the aperture the better, although beyond a certain size – about 70 mm – binoculars become rather cumbersome for a hand-held instrument. The 8 × 40 and 10 × 50 specifications are popular, but the purchaser is strongly advised to beware of cheap binoculars, allegedly for astronomical use, with excessive magnifications of ×20 or more.

Any good-quality binoculars, even the smallest, will reveal far more stars than are visible with the unaided eye, as well as the brighter star clusters, nebulae and galaxies plotted on the star charts. Their advantages of wide field of view and erect image, which allow easy reference to the naked-eye view and to the charts, simplify the initial location of objects even when a telescope is being used. Some large objects, such as the Pleiades star cluster or rich gatherings of stars in the Milky Way, may be more impressive in binoculars than through any telescope. For some branches of amateur astronomy, variable-star observation and comet-hunting in particular, binoculars of the appropriate size may be the preferred instrument.

A pair of binoculars cannot be used effectively if unsupported: resting the instrument itself or the observer's elbows on a rigid base is necessary to reduce the 'dancing' effect caused by the observer's heartbeat and inevitable muscular tremor.

Binoculars may be used for:

(a) general viewing of the constellations, star fields and the Milky Way
(b) acting as an adjunct to the main telescope, to identify the general location of an object before bringing the finder to bear on it
(c) locating planets or bright stars in twilight, when their precise location in the sky is uncertain
(d) observing the brighter variable stars
(e) observing any large-scale sky feature, such as the zodiacal light, aurorae, a bright comet or even meteor trains
(f) following artificial satellites.

Field glasses or opera glasses are often found in second-hand or antique shops. Unfortunately their very simple optical design offers a prohibitively small field of view, and they cannot be recommended for astronomical use.

ASTRONOMICAL TELESCOPES

These are of three main types: refracting, reflecting and catadioptric, each with its own advantages, but for all three types the effectiveness is determined largely by the *aperture* – the clear diameter of the lens or mirror which receives and focuses light from the object being observed. Bigger apertures bring greater *light-gathering power* and higher *resolution*. For general astronomical purposes, any good-quality telescope of between 75 and 100 mm aperture will permit interesting and useful observational work in a number of fields, while pleasing views of many objects may be obtained with smaller telescopes or even binoculars.

Light-gathering power or 'light-grasp'. The larger the aperture, the greater the amount of light received and focused by the telescope. As light-grasp theoretically increases in proportion to the square of the aperture, a telescope of 75 mm aperture (henceforth referred to as a 75 mm telescope) has twice the light-grasp of a 50 mm telescope, while a 100 mm has nearly twice the light-grasp of a 75 mm.

A telescope's aperture helps to determine the faintest detectable stars (the *limiting magnitude*). The values in Table 10 were calculated from the formula

$$m = 2.7 + 5 \log D$$

where D is the telescope aperture in millimetres. This formula was derived from observational tests on faint stars in the Pleiades with a wide range of apertures. Factors such as atmospheric conditions and the observer's skill influence the limiting magnitude to such an extent that the calculated values must be regarded as very approximate.

Resolution. Although all night-time stars appear as immeasurably small points of light, their image at the focus of a lens or mirror has a finite diameter, which corresponds to an angular diameter on the celestial sphere of $116/D$ arcsec (D being the aperture in millimetres). This is the so-called *Dawes' limit*. Stars separated in the sky by less than this angular distance cannot be clearly resolved, or shown separated, no matter how high a magnification is used. Hence every telescope has a *resolving limit* determined by its aperture alone. Table 10 gives Dawes' limit for various apertures.

Similarly, the amount of detail visible on the Moon and planets is in theory determined by aperture alone, although this limit is less easy to define because of the extended nature and low contrast of planetary markings.

The refractor

The refractor essentially consists of two lenses: a large one of long focal length called the *object glass* or *objective*, which forms at its focus an image of the star or other object (Figure 5(a)), and a small lens of much shorter focal length, known as the *eyepiece* or *ocular*. The eyepiece, in effect,

Table 10. Limiting magnitude and Dawes' limit. Approximate values are given for the faintest star visible and the separation of the closest pair of objects distinguishable for telescopes of various apertures.

Clear aperture		50	60	75	100	112.5	125	150	200	250	300
	(mm)	50	60	75	100	112.5	125	150	200	250	300
	(in.)	2.0	2.4	3.0	4.0	4.5	5.0	6.0	8.0	10.0	12.0
Limiting magnitude Faintest star visible	(mag.)	11.2	11.6	12.1	12.7	13.0	13.2	13.6	14.2	14.7	15.1
Dawes' limit Closest stars resolvable	(arcsec)	2.3	1.9	1.5	1.2	1.0	0.9	0.8	0.6	0.5	0.4

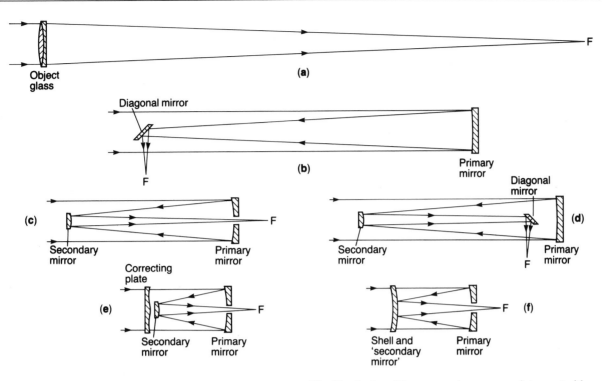

Figure 5. Different types of telescope. For telescopes of similar aperture, the path of light-rays from a celestial object is shown through (a) a refractor, (b) a Newtonian, (c) a Cassegrain, (d) a Cassegrain–coudé, (e) a Schmidt–Cassegrain and (f) a Maksutov–Cassegrain, to the focus F.

enables the observer to obtain a close-up view of the image formed by the object glass.

The objective is composed of two or more lenses or *elements*, which combine to minimize the amount of false colour in the image that would be produced by a single lens. The quality of an objective is largely determined by how well it overcomes this *chromatic aberration*. The usual two-element *achromat* inevitably shows a faint bluish halo around bright stars and at the edge of the Moon. This *secondary spectrum* can be reduced by making the lenses from glass with unusual characteristics, such as fluorite, or by adding more lens elements, but both alternatives are expensive.

The *focal ratio* of an object glass (the focal length divided by the aperture) is usually about 10 (written *f*/10) or slightly longer in order to help minimize secondary spectrum; therefore even a refractor of modest aperture is bulky, and instruments of more than 100 mm aperture can hardly be considered portable.

The reflector

In this form of telescope a concave mirror (the *main* or *primary mirror*) takes the place of the refractor's objective lens. This mirror is held in a cell at the lower end of the telescope tube, and the light rays from the object pass down the tube to be reflected back to a focus at the upper end. What happens then depends on the design of the telescope.

The Newtonian. The converging rays are intercepted by a small flat mirror (known as the *flat* or *diagonal*) inclined at 45° to the main mirror, which reflects the light to the side of the tube (Figure 5(b)) where the eyepiece is situated. This form is most convenient for small and medium-sized reflectors (up to an aperture of perhaps 400 mm), since their tubes are much shorter than the tubes of refractors of the same aperture (focal ratios usually between *f*/5 and *f*/8). Thus the eyepiece is usually at a convenient height for making observations.

The Cassegrain. After being reflected by the main mirror, the rays are sent back down the tube by a small convex mirror (the *secondary*), either passing through a hole in the primary mirror (Figure 5 (c)) or being reflected out through the side of the tube by a Newtonian-type diagonal (Figure 5(d)). The classical Cassegrain effectively compresses a long focal length, typically *f*/20, into a short tube and is – or can be – a very compact instrument. Today there are few classical Cassegrains on the market, and most telescopes now made to the Cassegrain design are of the catadioptric type (see below).

Telescope mirrors are optically worked and coated on their front surfaces, so that unlike everyday mirrors (which are coated on the back) the light does not pass through the glass at all. This permits the use of opaque materials such as low-expansion glass of the type used for ovenware, or even ceramics, to minimize the effect of temperature change on the delicate optical surface.

The reflective coating is usually of aluminium, deposited by vaporization under vacuum. A clear overcoating, usually of silicon monoxide, is often applied on top of the aluminium to protect the surface and increase its lifetime.

Overcoatings have also been developed to protect very delicate silver coatings, which were once the norm but were abandoned in favour of the more durable aluminium. Silver coatings reflect about 93% of visible light, aluminium about 89%. Without a protective layer, however, silver quickly tarnishes and requires replacing, often in six months or less. Special multilayer coatings can reflect nearly 100% of visible light, but rarely would a telescope intended for visual work warrant the expense of such a coating.

Catadioptric telescopes

These are instruments which use both refraction and reflection to form the image. The two forms of most interest to the amateur are Cassegrain-type designs which use a primary mirror with a spherical curvature, rather than the parabolic curvature that is normal in reflectors. A spherical mirror is much easier to manufacture than a parabolic one, but its images suffer from the defect of *spherical aberration*.

In the *Schmidt* system (Figure 5(e)) a thin, specially figured, almost flat lens is placed at the top of the tube. This lens corrects the aberration of the primary mirror and carries the convex secondary mirror at its centre.

In the *Maksutov* system (Figure 5(f)) the corrective lens is a sharply curved 'shell' of glass. In many designs the centre of the inner (convex) surface is aluminized to give the effect of a secondary mirror.

Both these telescopes have the advantage of combining a short tube, typically less than twice the aperture, with an effective focal ratio of between $f/10$ and $f/15$. They therefore offer the chance of owning a truly portable instrument with an aperture of up to 300 mm or so.

Eyepieces and magnification

An eyepiece acts as a magnifying glass, but whereas the latter is usually a single lens that is convex on both sides, a telescope eyepiece may contain two or more lenses of various types. The lens nearest the eye is the *eye lens*; the one furthest from it the *field lens*.

A good eyepiece should:

(a) correct for chromatic aberration
(b) correct for spherical aberration
(c) have a 'flat' field – in other words, images should be in focus both at the centre and at the edge of the field of view
(d) have a large field of view, with at least reasonable definition near the margins
(e) be free from 'haunting', or ghost images of bright objects.

The performance of an eyepiece is as important as that of the other optical elements in the telescope. A given eyepiece may not produce equally good results on all telescopes. Factors (a) and (b) above depend crucially on the focal ratio of the object glass or mirror; the simpler and cheaper types of eyepiece may work perfectly when used

with an $f/15$ refractor, but their inherent aberrations will be all too evident at the focus of an $f/5$ Newtonian.

Eye relief. An eyepiece forms an image of the objective or primary mirror known as the *exit pupil*, and the distance between the outer surface of the eyepiece and this image is called the eye relief. Since the pupil of the observer's eye needs to be brought to the plane of the exit pupil if the full field of view of the eyepiece is to be seen, large eye relief is essential if spectacles need to be worn.

Field of view. If the telescope is aimed at the bright daylight sky, with the eye at the exit pupil, a circular disk of light is seen. The apparent angular diameter of this disk is the *apparent field of view* of the eyepiece. Its value, for different designs, can range from about 25° to 80°. Dividing the apparent field of view by the magnification of the eyepiece gives the *real field of view*.

Inverted image. An astronomical telescope, whether reflector or refractor, gives an inverted image. Binoculars and terrestrial telescopes contain extra lenses or prisms to restore the orientation, but these are omitted from astronomical telescopes in the interests of maximum light transmission and image quality. Some catadioptric telescopes incorporate an 'erect-image' system to allow them to be used on terrestrial objects.

Types of eyepiece and their uses. Eyepiece types once thought to be complex and costly have now become common and comparatively cheap. Furthermore, new varieties have become available in response to the popularity of certain telescope designs such as short-focus reflectors and long-focus but compact catadioptrics.

In general the simpler and cheaper designs are perfectly acceptable for instruments of large f-number, or as long as quite a small field of view is acceptable to the observer. But with low f-numbers, or where a wide field of view free from distortion is needed, the requirements become more demanding.

Eyepiece barrels can be either $1\frac{1}{4}$ in. (31.7 mm) push-fit, $1\frac{1}{4}$ in. threaded (16 threads per inch – RAS standard thread, now obsolescent) or 24.5 mm push-fit sizes, with 2 in. (50 mm) push-fit for ultra-wide-field eyepieces. Focal lengths are normally in the range 4–40 mm, while apparent fields of view vary from 30° to 50° for standard eyepieces, and from 60° to over 80° for wide-field eyepieces. Various types of eyepiece are shown in Figure 6.

Huygenian. The commonest type for small refractors. Has a somewhat curved field of view, i.e. the field edge may require slight refocusing. Unsuitable for f-numbers below 10, which rules out most reflectors. The *Huygenian–Mittenzwey*, of slightly different design, has a wider field of view.

Ramsden. A flatter but narrower field of view than the Huygenian, with the drawback that the field lens can be in

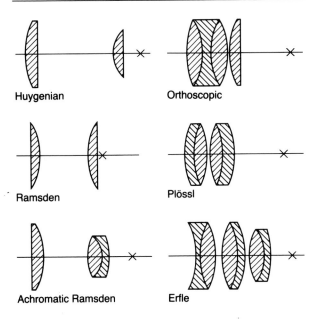

Figure 6. The more common types of eyepiece. The Huygenian and Ramsden both consist of two plano-convex lenses. In the achromatic Ramsden one of these is replaced by an achromatic doublet. The orthoscopic eyepiece contains a cemented triple achromat. The Plössl is made up of two achromats. The form of Erfle shown here contains three doublets, but in other forms one or two of these can be replaced by a single-element lens. In each case the position of the exit pupil is marked by a cross.

focus, revealing any dust on it. Suffers from ghost images, but is usable on instruments of up to $f/6$.

Kellner. Very widely used eyepiece for binoculars, as it has a fairly wide and flat field and large eye relief. Virtually all eyepieces described as Kellners are in fact *achromatic Ramsdens*. It is a versatile and popular design which gives excellent results at $f/8$ and is usable down to $f/4$, though with some aberrations at the field edges.

Orthoscopic. Noted for its fairly wide, distortion-free field and large eye relief. It is a good standard eyepiece, suitable for most types of telescope and available in a wide range of focal lengths.

Plössl. Can give wider and flatter fields than orthoscopics, and preferred by many observers. The name is used for several types of eyepiece of slightly differing design. Because of its good reputation some manufacturers have also applied the name to quite different designs.

Erfle. The standard low-power, wide-field eyepiece, with a field of view of around 60° and a focal length of 20 mm or longer. The *König* is a variant of the Erfle, usually with shorter focal length.

Other wide-field eyepieces. There are now a number of special ultra-wide-field eyepieces, some with apparent fields of 80° and more, such as the *Nagler*, suitable only for focal lengths less than 20 mm. In addition to offering 'picture-window' views through a telescope, such eyepieces

are especially useful with telescopes that are not equipped with a drive system: the wider field requires the telescope to be moved less often to keep an object in view. While these eyepieces are generally very well made, with multilayer coatings to maximize the light transmitted through their many elements, they also tend to be quite expensive.

Magnification. The magnifying power of a telescope is determined by the ratio of the focal length of its objective lens or primary mirror to that of the eyepiece. For example, a refractor or Newtonian having a focal length of 1500 mm used with an eyepiece of 20 mm focal length will give a magnification or power of 1500/20 = 75 diameters, usually written ×75. Therefore the magnification provided by any eyepiece is not unique, but depends on the focal length of the telescope with which it is used.

High magnification, although it can show more detail than low magnification, has its drawbacks:

(a) the field of view is smaller

(b) the effects of bad seeing are more pronounced

(c) any tremors in the tube, or faults in the drive, become more noticeable.

In addition, low magnification reveals more detail in extensive objects such as comets or large nebulae by concentrating their light. A range of magnifications is therefore necessary for general work, and a minimum of three different powers should be available:

(a) *low power*, about 0.3 to 0.4 times the telescope aperture in millimetres (×25 to ×30 for a 75 mm telescope) for showing the greatest possible area of sky

(b) *medium power*, about 1.0 to 1.2D (×75 to ×100 for a 75 mm telescope) for general views

(c) *high power*, about 2.0 to 2.5D (×150 to ×200 for a 75 mm telescope) for studying objects such as close double stars, or planetary detail.

For larger instruments the powers may be scaled down: a satisfactory low power on a 300 mm telescope would be about ×75 (0.25D). Powers greater than about ×400 are rarely beneficial because the slight atmospheric tremors that prevail even on the best of nights then begin to affect the image. Very high magnifications also tend to reduce the contrast of lunar and planetary markings, although they can improve the visibility of close double stars.

The Barlow lens is a small concave lens that diverges rather than converges light rays passing through it; it should be achromatic. When placed before the eyepiece it has the effect of increasing the effective focal length of the telescope by a selected factor, usually ×2. Since the magnification of an eyepiece is directly proportional to the effective focal length of the telescope, a Barlow lens doubles the range of magnifications obtainable with a set of eyepieces. It also enables high powers to be obtained without the need to use eyepieces of very short focal length and correspondingly small eye relief.

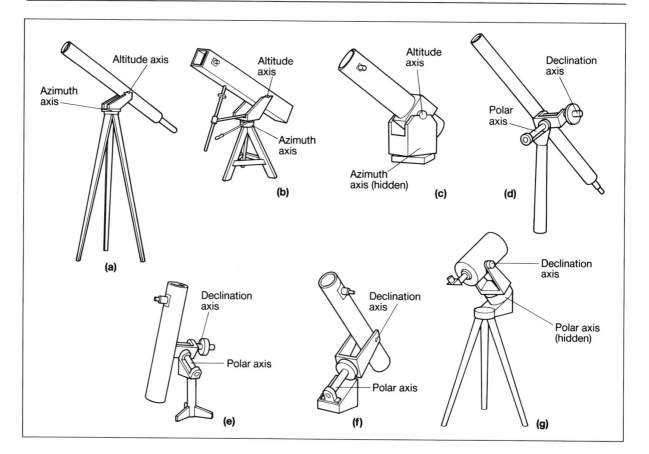

Figure 7. Different types of telescope mounting. (a) A simple altazimuth mounting for a small refractor, (b) a 'traditional' fork-type altazimuth mounting for a Newtonian, (c) a Dobsonian altazimuth mounting for a Newtonian, (d) a German equatorial mounting for a refractor (or Cassegrain-type telescope), (e) a German equatorial mounting for a Newtonian, (f) a fork equatorial mounting for a Newtonian and (g) a fork equatorial mounting for a catadioptric telescope.

Telescope mountings

However high a telescope's optical quality may be, the instrument will not perform as it should unless it is properly mounted. A good mounting must:

(a) prevent the tube from shaking – the image should not vibrate when the eye is brought to the eyepiece or when the focusing knob is turned

(b) allow smooth and responsive control, whether in moving the telescope to seek an object and bring it to the centre of the field, or in keeping it there as the Earth turns

(c) allow the telescope to be pointed anywhere in the sky, or at least to within a few degrees of the horizon.

Types of mounting. Mountings can be divided into two main types: *altazimuth* and *equatorial* (Figure 7).

In the altazimuth type the telescope is linked to two axes at right angles to each other, one permitting motion in

altitude (vertically) and the other in azimuth (horizontally). Traditionally the altazimuth has been associated with small, cheap 'beginner's telescopes', but its mechanical simplicity has led to its recent adoption not only as a popular mounting for more advanced amateurs' telescopes, but also for the new generation of large professional instruments. However, continual adjustment is necessary in both altitude and azimuth in order to follow a celestial object as the Earth spins. The *Dobsonian* mounting is a variation on the altazimuth design. In recent years it has become very popular for large-aperture, short-focus reflectors.

The equatorial mounting simplifies matters by having a *polar axis* aligned with the Earth's axis. By driving the instrument around this single axis once a day, in a direction opposite to the Earth's spin, the telescope tube remains pointing at a given star, as shown in Figure 8. Initial pointing is done by moving the telescope in RA, using the polar axis, and in declination, using the *declination axis*. An electric motor usually supplies the drive for the polar axis.

Refractors, reflectors and catadioptrics have different mounting requirements, so they are considered separately.

Mountings for refractors. Since the eyepiece is at the lower end of the tube, and the tube is long, the mounting needs to be high off the ground. The traditional support for a small refractor is a tall tripod or, for apertures greater than about 100 mm, a permanently fixed column. Of the equatorial mounts, the *German* type has the advantage that it allows

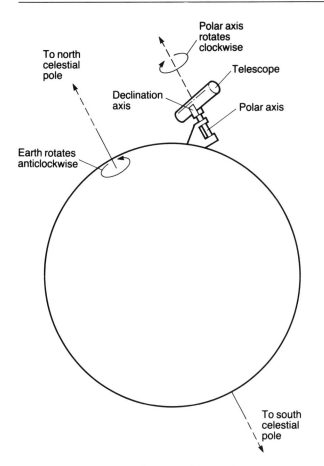

Figure 8. The principle of the equatorial mounting.

the long tube to be pointed towards the region of the celestial pole.

Mountings for reflectors. Since the tube is relatively short, and the eyepiece (in a Newtonian) is near the upper end, a low mounting is most convenient. The Dobsonian altazimuth mounting has the virtues of cheapness and rigidity: the tube is pivoted just above the mirror and swings vertically inside a short, box-like fork which turns horizontally on a base-plate. By using practically frictionless Teflon as a bearing surface for both axes, it is possible to move the tube through small and controlled angles by hand while observing. The success of this simple mounting has led to a new enthusiasm for large-aperture, short-focus Newtonian telescopes, since the low cost of making (or buying) the mounting means that more aperture may be bought for the same total expenditure.

Equatorially mounted Newtonians are usually mounted in the German style on a short pillar; a fork mounting is also suitable. Classical Cassegrains are mounted like refractors.

Mountings for catadioptrics. The tubes of these telescopes are extremely short, so they are usually supplied in a fork mount, which has the advantage of needing no counterweight. The motor drive and short polar axis are concealed

in the base, and the instrument may stand on its own legs or be fitted to a tripod or pillar. Their compactness, and the fact that there is little overhanging weight, makes these instruments extremely steady and a pleasure to use; however, their benefits must be weighed against their drawbacks, which include lower image contrast.

Accessories

There are many accessories available for work in different observational fields. Great advances in the sensitivity and precision of professional instruments have been at least matched by the enterprise of advanced amateurs and commercial suppliers. Some of the more common accessories are described below.

Dew-cap. On damp nights, dew forms on exposed surfaces. The outer lens of an object glass, or the correcting lens of a catadioptric telescope, is particularly vulnerable, and must be protected by a dew-cap. This is a cylinder of non-conductive material projecting, ideally, a distance of two to three times the telescope's aperture in front of the lens. A simple tube rolled from thin black card has a minimal effect on the balance of the telescope, and is easily renewed as required.

Filters. Colour filters are sometimes used in lunar and planetary work. Since most astronomical objects are relatively dim and weakly coloured (even the Moon, which appears blinding in a telescope, is pale by daytime standards), the eye relies mainly on the non-colour-sensitive rods of the retina for its information. However, if a coloured object is observed through a filter of its own tint, it should appear brighter than if viewed through a filter of the opposite colour (e.g. a green filter for a red object).

Small pieces of flexible photographic filter may be mounted in separate cardboard holders or in a rotating wheel. The spectral characteristics of six Kodak Wratten filters that are widely used are illustrated in Figure 9.

Special filters which transmit an extremely narrow range of wavelengths can be used to suppress the effect of artificial light. The so-called *nebula filters*, which transmit only the waveband in which nebulae shine most brightly, effectively darken the sky background and enhance the visibility of nebulae.

Filters for observing the Sun require special care as sunlight concentrated at the eyepiece of even the smallest telescope can cause permanent eye injury. Solar filters should cover the objective of the telescope to reduce the Sun's energy before it enters the optical system. Filters that attach only to the eyepiece should not be used since the intense sunlight at this point is strong enough to shatter glass filters.

The best solar filters are made by depositing a layer of metal, usually aluminium, onto optical-quality glass or sheets of thin, optically uniform plastic such as Mylar. Coloured plastic or 'smoked' glass should never be used.

Even if such material reduces the sunlight to the point where it will not dazzle the eye, harmful infrared energy can still pass through the material. Although there are many filters on the market, rarely is it necessary to have a 'full-aperture' solar filter. Because sunlight heats the air and makes it turbulent, it is generally not possible to see features smaller than 1 arcsec on the Sun's surface. Features this small can be resolved with telescopes of about 125 mm aperture. Many observers with larger instruments therefore 'stop' their telescopes down by using a solar filter 125–150 mm in diameter.

Finders. A good finder may be considered essential for even the smallest astronomical telescope, particularly to an observer locating objects with reference to nearby stars.

The finder serves its purpose if it permits the naked-eye view of the region to be rapidly reconciled with what is seen in the main telescope.

Therefore a finder must have a wide field of view (and hence low magnification) which will take in at least one convenient naked-eye star to act as a guide to the field being sought. A magnification of ×5, with a suitable eyepiece, will give an adequate 10° field, and an aperture of 30–40 mm will reveal sufficient stars to allow the object (or the part of sky in which the object lies) to be brought into a low-power view with the main instrument. Whether the finder should give an upright or an inverted image is a matter of individual preference. Large instruments, and those used regularly for variable-star work, may have a second and more powerful finder to bridge the gap between the two apertures.

Selecting a Telescope

Refractors

Advantages
Excellent definition and image contrast since there is no central obstruction in the optical path
The optics hold their alignment well
There are no reflecting surfaces requiring maintenance
Simple eyepieces work well

Disadvantages
The bulkiest telescope for its aperture
Difficult to mount rigidly
Only the smallest apertures are portable
All but the costliest objective lenses suffer from false colour
Usually not suitable for photography without filters to reduce secondary spectrum
Per unit of aperture, object glasses cost more than reflecting or catadioptric optical systems
The eyepiece can reach awkward viewing positions

If *critical definition* of planetary detail or close double stars is desired, then aperture for aperture a refractor is best. However, for the same price can be bought a Newtonian of about double the aperture of a refractor.

Newtonian reflectors

Advantages
Per unit of aperture, Newtonians are the cheapest optical system
The eyepiece is usually in a convenient viewing position
Equally suitable for photographic and visual use
Fairly compact, and therefore do not require a tall tripod or pillar
Can readily be obtained in apertures far larger than those of other systems

Disadvantages
Sensitive to optical alignment, which in any case is less permanent than with a refractor
The aluminized surfaces gradually deteriorate
The diagonal mirror and its support diffract light and reduce image contrast, as well as blocking some of the light reaching the primary mirror

If *aperture* is the major consideration (i.e. if the aim is the observation of variable stars or deep-sky objects to the faintest possible limit), then a Newtonian will be the choice. A small Newtonian is the ideal instrument for the beginner.

Catadioptrics (Cassegrain-type)

Advantages
Extremely compact and therefore highly portable
The whole sky can be observed from a comfortable sitting position
Keen competition between firms promotes quality for the price
The reflective coatings are well protected in the enclosed tube
Equally suitable for photographic and visual use

Disadvantages
Lower image contrast, as the relatively large secondary obstruction causes more light scattering than occurs in other systems
With low powers, the large secondary obstruction produces a 'blind spot' near the centre of the field

If *portability* and general convenience are required, the compact catadioptric systems have much to recommend them.

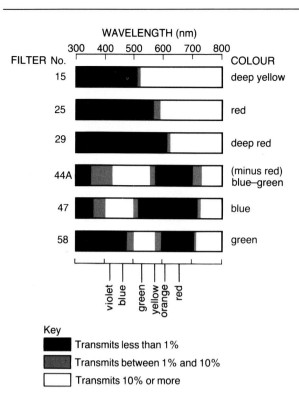

Figure 9. Colour filters for astronomical use. The charts show the wavelengths absorbed and transmitted by six Kodak Wratten filters commonly used for observations. All these filters transmit infrared. Filters W29 and W47 are dense, and are best suited to apertures over 200 mm.

The direction of the finder must be adjustable. Cross-hairs inside the eyepiece serve to indicate the centre of the field of view in the main telescope.

Guide telescopes. Instruments used for photography requiring exposures of more than a few seconds are often provided with a high-power auxiliary telescope of smaller aperture. By keeping a nearby guide star accurately centred on cross-hairs in the eyepiece, any residual tracking errors may be compensated. Another method is to guide on a star imaged by the main telescope, using an eyepiece set to one side of the film-holder.

Micrometers. In astronomy, a micrometer is used to measure the angular distance between two objects, either at the telescope itself or on a photograph. The *filar micrometer*, in which two fine webs can be moved a measured distance apart, is the traditional instrument for measuring the separation of double stars, but many other types suitable for amateur construction have been devised. In the *double-image* type a movable divided lens or glass plate permits the image of two stars to be superimposed, the amount of motion required to do so indicating the separation.

The *object-grating* or *diffraction* micrometer has the advantage of being simple to make, if not to use. A grating of several spaced parallel strips in front of the telescope produces a set of spurious images around each star; by manipulating the grating to create a symmetrical star

pattern, the separation (and position angles) of the stars may be determined.

In addition to measuring double stars, some amateurs have been successful in measuring, to professional standards, the positions of minor planets and comets on photographs with home-made equipment.

Photometers. Devices for determining the brightness of a star at the telescope can be divided into *visual* and *photoelectric* kinds. Most visual photometry depends on the equalization principle: the observer has to judge when the star appears equal in brightness to a comparison star. This may be achieved either by using a real comparison star, and dimming one or the other by artificial means such as interposing a wedge of tinted glass; or by using an artificial comparison star projected into the field of view from a suitable instrument, and adjusting its brightness.

In photoelectric photometry a light-sensitive device is used to record the star's brightness. To calibrate the system, measures of other stars of known magnitude are taken. Photoelectric photometry is more accurate than visual methods, but the associated equipment is more expensive and complex.

Star diagonals. Observing objects within about 30° of the zenith with a refractor or Cassegrain-type telescope will cause neck-strain unless a suitable observing chair is available. A star diagonal contains a plane mirror or a totally reflecting prism and produces a more comfortable observing angle, although at the cost of some loss of light and reversal of the image.

TESTS, ADJUSTMENTS AND MAINTENANCE OF THE TELESCOPE

Optical quality

A reflecting telescope whose optical surfaces nowhere depart from the ideal by more than 1/20th of the wavelength of light should give almost perfect definition.

The tolerance of an objective lens is less strict, but harder to define, because with two or more elements there are more surfaces to consider. However, manufacturers' claims about optical quality should be treated with caution. Without facilities for making a proper laboratory test, the only satisfactory way of judging the optical quality of a telescope is by its actual performance on a celestial object.

Chromatic aberration. To test for the achromatism of a refractor, observe the bright limb of the Moon or the planet Venus when it is well above the horizon and against a fairly dark sky, using a medium power. A faint blue–violet halo is acceptable, but green or any other colour is not. The test should be repeated with other eyepieces to ensure that what is observed is not an artifact of the particular eyepiece used.

Spherical aberration means that rays refracted or reflected by different zones of the objective lens or primary mirror do not share a common focus. It is best studied by observing the image of a third-magnitude star under high power, with the eyepiece alternately pushed and pulled a few milli-metres inside and outside the position of best focus. The star's image, expanded into a small disk, should appear identical on either side of focus, with no rays or flares extending from its edge. In a Newtonian or Cassegrain-type telescope there will be a round spot at the centre represent-ing the outline of the diagonal or secondary mirror. The secondary spectrum of a refractor will produce a greenish-yellow fringe outside the focus, and a reddish fringe inside the focus.

This test has the advantage over studying the quality of a focused star image or trying to resolve double stars at the limit of resolution (Table 10), in that seeing effects are minimal. On many nights a star viewed with high power is a small 'boiling' blur several times larger than it would be in calm air. However, the disadvantage is that slight differ-ences in the appearance of the disks have little or no effect on the performance – in other words, it may be misleadingly sensitive until the observer has gained some experience of testing different telescopes.

Magnification and field size

The magnification of a particular eyepiece may be calcu-lated by dividing its focal length into the focal length of the telescope. However, its focal length may not be marked or may be incorrect, or the focal length of the telescope itself (particularly if it is a Cassegrain) may not be accurately known. It is possible to measure the focal length of a Newtonian or a refractor by focusing an image of the Moon onto a piece of semi-transparent paper stretched over the mouth of the draw-tube, and to measure the distance to the object glass or (via the flat) to the primary mirror.

To find the magnification directly, focus the telescope on a star or a remote terrestrial object, and then point it at an illuminated surface such as a white wall, or even a sheet of card (but *not* the daylight sky, whose brilliance will produce an erroneous result). Holding a magnifying glass, focus on the exit pupil, which will be seen as a sharp-edged circle of light, either at or a little way behind the eyepiece. The diameter of this circle divided into the aperture of the telescope gives the magnification. A metal scale marked in half-millimetres or a vernier calliper held in the plane of the exit pupil will give the diameter (and hence the magnifica-tion) to within a few percent.

To find the diameter of the field of view set the telescope so that a star near the celestial equator, such as Delta (δ) Orionis or Zeta (ζ) Virginis, may pass through the centre of the field. Measure in minutes and seconds how long it takes to pass across the field of the stationary telescope, and multiply by 15 to derive the field diameter in minutes and seconds of arc.

Optical adjustment

If the optical components are not properly aligned, or *collimated*, the image quality will suffer. Some instruments,

particularly small refractors and catadioptric telescopes, are – in theory at least – permanently adjusted by the manufacturer, and must be returned to them should any mishap occur. Larger refractors, and all reflecting tele-scopes, should have provision for collimating the optics. The object glass of a refracting telescope is much less sensitive to misalignment than is the primary mirror of a Newtonian.

Refractors should have three sets of push–pull screws link-ing the objective cell to the tube. If the image appears flared to one side, or if the defocused image is elongated rather than circular, adjust the pair of screws nearest the axis of the defect. By trial and error the asymmetry should dis-appear. If it does not, then the object glass is defective or has not been properly adjusted in its cell, and should be examined by an expert.

Newtonian telescopes have to be adjusted in several stages, and having an assistant can be helpful. It is best done in daylight, with the tube pointing at the sky; an eyepiece is not used until final testing on a star. For a totally misaligned instrument (Figure 10(a)), the procedure is as follows:

(a) The diagonal should be central in the tube, except in a very-short-focus reflector where the centre of the di-agonal should be offset a small distance away from the eyepiece. The arm or set of vanes ('spider') on which it is mounted should be adjustable for the purpose.

(b) The diagonal should be on the axis of the draw-tube. Again, there should be provision for moving the diago-nal along the axis of the main tube. To ensure that the eye is central in the draw-tube, fit a disk with a central viewing hole at the end of the draw-tube, which should be racked out to its fullest extent. With the diagonal holder correctly positioned, the view down the draw-tube should be as in Figure 10(b).

(c) The reflection of the primary mirror must be made central in the outline of the diagonal, as in Figure 10(c). The adjusting screws at the back of the diagonal holder are used for this purpose.

(d) The optical axis of the primary mirror must pass through the centre of the diagonal. This will have been achieved when the black outline of the diagonal is centred on the bright reflected image of the primary mirror. This dark spot is always most distant from the primary-mirror adjusting screw that should be turned inwards: in Figure 10(c) the screw nearest the position marked by the arrow must be turned inwards to bring the outline of the diagonal to the centre, as in Figure 10(d).

Final collimation (using the primary mirror's adjusting screws) must await a star test, when very slight adjustment should be all that is necessary to produce a perfectly sym-metrical image, both in and out of focus. After adjustment (c), the image of the primary in the diagonal of a short-focus Newtonian (*f*/6 or less) should be displaced slightly down the tube rather than being perfectly concentric, since the

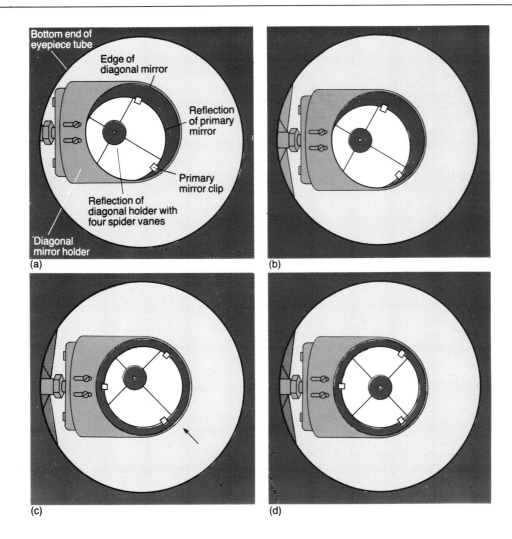

Figure 10. Collimation of a Newtonian telescope. (a) The view down the empty draw-tube – everything is misaligned. (b) The diagonal holder has been correctly positioned, with the outer edge of the diagonal centred on the edge of the draw-tube. (c) The image of the primary mirror has been centred on the edge of the diagonal. (d) The reflection of the diagonal has been centred on the image of the primary mirror. *Source*: Alan M. MacRobert, *Sky & Telescope*, Vol. 75, p. 260 (1988).

converging cone of light from the primary is wider where it strikes the lower part of the diagonal.

Cassegrain telescopes are adjusted in the same manner and sequence as for Newtonians, with the difference that the image of the primary in the secondary mirror must always be perfectly symmetrical.

A perfect star image. When the air is steady and the instrument carefully adjusted and focused, the image of a fairly bright star will appear under high magnification as a minute disk – almost a point of light – surrounded by two or three bright concentric rings. It is impossible to portray the extreme delicacy of these *diffraction rings* as they appear on the best observing nights. True diffraction rings are more likely to be observed in refractors than reflectors, partly because the refractor's longer focal ratio brings the rings into prominence, but mainly because the diagonal or secondary mirror of a reflector produces spurious and brighter diffraction rings of its own.

Setting up an equatorial telescope

The fundamental requirements of an equatorial mounting are that

(a) the polar and declination axes are at right angles
(b) the axis of the telescope tube is at right angles to the declination axis
(c) the polar axis is parallel to the Earth's axis.

Points (a) and (b) are, or should be, the responsibility of the manufacturer. Here it is assumed that just the polar axis remains to be aligned.

The procedure can be divided into alignment in azimuth and alignment in altitude. In practice fine adjustments to one are likely to affect the other, so that alternate and increasingly fine tuning is needed.

Initial rough adjustment in azimuth (i.e. in the north–south direction) may have to be done before the mounting is set up at the observing site to ensure that final precise setting is within the range of the adjusting screws. Sufficiently accurate methods include observation of the Pole Star (for observers in the northern hemisphere), observation of the Sun at local noon (allowing for the equation of time) and using a surveyor's compass (allowing for the current magnetic variation). Having defined the meridian by these or other methods, set the declination axis horizontal, and twist the mounting in azimuth until the telescope tube can be aligned north–south by rotating it in declination alone.

Once this is done, the polar axis can be set approximately in altitude by measuring the angle it makes with the horizontal, which should be equal to the observer's latitude. An adjustable protractor or a home-made wedge can be used in conjunction with a spirit-level to obtain an accuracy of a degree or so, which is sufficient for initial purposes.

Fine adjustment for a permanent mounting may have to be spread over more than one night. Some recommended methods assume that the Pole Star is observable, which it is not south of the equator; others require accurate right ascension and declination circles. However, satisfactory adjustment can be obtained by using a high magnification to observe the north–south drift, if any, of stars in different parts of the sky as they are tracked east to west by turning the polar axis.

The principle behind the method is as follows. If the azimuth of the polar axis is too far *west* of the pole, then a star crossing the meridian appears to drift *north* (and vice versa). If the altitude of the polar axis is too *high*, then a star due *east* (ideally with an hour angle of 270° and an altitude of about 40°) will appear to drift *north*, while one to the *west* (hour angle 90°) will appear to drift *south* (and vice versa if the altitude of the polar axis is too low).

The observations must be made with the highest possible magnification, using an eyepiece equipped with cross-hairs. Defocusing the star slightly allows the hairs to be projected as black lines on its disk, and any errors of symmetry caused by drifting are readily apparent. By trial and error the drift can be reduced, if not to zero, then at least to an acceptable value.

For routine visual work, satisfactory accuracy will have been achieved when the object remains at the centre of the field for the duration of the observation. If the mounting includes circles of sufficient precision for finding faint objects, then the pointers must be calibrated using stars of known RA and declination.

The work most demanding of accurate polar alignment is long-exposure photography of deep-sky objects.

Portable equatorials, if always used at the same observing site, may be positioned each time fairly accurately if location points are set into the ground to take the tripod legs. Alternatively, a sighting telescope may be designed to fit onto the polar axis, so that the position of the celestial pole is centred on the cross-hairs. The telescope itself could also be used for this purpose, provided (a) it can be accurately set at a declination of 90°, and (b) the optical axis of the telescope is then truly parallel to the polar axis. Some telescope mountings come equipped with special built-in sighting telescopes for making quick and accurate polar alignment.

Care and maintenance

Before bringing a portable telescope indoors after a night's observing, cover the object glass or mirror with the cover provided for the purpose, or the optical surface will become dewed in the warmer air. In any case, an instrument should not be stored in a warm room since thermal currents will be set up in the tube when it is taken outside into the cold air. Ideally, the telescope should already be at the outside air temperature before observing is begun, so a garage or secure shaded garden shed is a suitable place for storage. If a telescope is housed in an observatory, the structure should be opened up as soon as the temperature begins to fall in the evening to allow both the inside of the building and the telescope to achieve thermal equilibrium.

Cleaning lenses. It is inadvisable to take an eyepiece or objective lens to pieces without expert advice. Only the exposed surfaces should be cleaned; these are of course the most likely to become dirty.

Although scattered specks of dust have little noticeable effect on the image, they can cause permanent marks if rubbed; therefore they must be carefully removed with a soft lens brush. The lens may then be gently wiped with a piece of damp cotton-wool (absorbent cotton). Care must be taken not to make the surface wet, as moisture may penetrate the lens mount. If available, pure (industrial) alcohol is excellent; common methylated spirit (denatured alcohol) contains oils which can leave smears. A really dirty lens may be cleaned with a strong domestic detergent, although industrial detergent, which is free from oily additives, is preferable.

Never press hard on the glass, and use a clean area of the swab for each stroke until the surface appears generally clean. Wipe with gentle lifting strokes in one direction so as to bring the dirt clear of the glass.

Some eyepieces such as the Plössl and Erfle have an outer component of flint glass. Being softer than crown glass, such surfaces need to be treated with particular care to minimize abrasion.

Old objective lenses may be stained between the elements, and the outer surfaces, particularly that of the inner (flint) lens, may have developed permanent dull patches. Such a lens should be sent away for professional treatment.

Cleaning mirrors. All the mirrors in a reflecting telescope should be closely covered when not in use, and never allowed to become dewed. Small reflectors often have no provision for protection, apart from perhaps a cap over the mouth of the tube; it is then well worth making lightweight covers (plain cardboard is better than nothing) to protect the mirror surfaces from the air.

Mirrors should be removed from their cells every six months and washed in warm water with detergent, and any adhering dust particles carefully swabbed off with a cotton-wool pad. Even if the coatings seem to have thinned so much that a light bulb can be seen shining through them, this need not mean that reflectivity has dropped by more than a few percent. A more important defect is a general dulling of the coating, which reduces the contrast and hence the visibility of faint detail.

ASTROPHOTOGRAPHY

Choice of camera

A conventional single-lens reflex (SLR) camera is very convenient for astrophotography. But many modern cameras, which have autoexposure only, no B setting and electronic shutters, are unsuitable.

The ideal SLR camera for astrophotography would have:

(a) manual shutter speed control
(b) a B shutter speed, which together with a locking cable release allows the shutter to be kept open for any length of time
(c) a wide range of other shutter speeds, especially those of several seconds' duration
(d) a mirror which can be locked in the 'up' position so as to prevent undue vibration when beginning an exposure
(e) easily replaceable viewing screens, with the availability of a clear screen with a single reticle for focusing by parallax (see below)
(f) a viewing screen magnifier, ideally one which replaces the normal pentaprism viewing system, for more accurate focusing
(g) a mechanical shutter, rather than an electronic one which drains the battery during a long exposure (some electronic shutters will operate on B setting without the battery, however)
(h) light weight, to reduce balance problems when the camera is on the telescope.

Choice of film

Films are usually categorized by their *speed* (sensitivity to light); whether they are black-and-white or colour; and whether they are *negative*, for making prints, or *reversal films*, which produce transparencies.

The speeds defined by the International Standards Organization (ISO) are identical with the older ones of the American Standards Association (ASA) and Deutsche Industrie Norm (DIN). Older cameras are still calibrated in ASA and DIN speeds. A standard film for everyday photography may have a speed of ISO 100/21°, usually simply called ISO 100; one with double the sensitivity has an ISO speed of twice this figure. In general, faster films have lower contrast and are more grainy than slower ones. A slow film may be ISO 25; a very fast one, at ISO 3200, is 128 times faster and will therefore record stars over five magnitudes fainter in a short exposure.

Graininess is often undesirable, particularly where it masks fine detail, so the choice of film is often a compromise between exposure time and image quality.

(a) Black-and-white film has the advantage of being easy to process and print at home. There is a wide range of films, including many with special characteristics such as narrow spectral sensitivity. Virtually all black-and-white films are negative films.
(b) Colour print film is very widely available, but with comparatively few different emulsions. Home processing is more complex than with black-and-white film, and commercially made machine prints are often unsatisfactory for astronomical subjects. Many negatives will not be printed by automatic machines as there appears to be nothing on them.
(c) Colour transparency film offers a wide variety of emulsions, and can usually be processed by the user, though there are fewer commercial laboratories than for colour print film, particularly outside large towns. It has the advantages that the colour rendering is not subject to variations in print quality and, since no prints are needed, costs are lower. A greater brightness range can be shown on a transparency than on a print.

In general, use slow, contrasty, fine-grain films where detail is important, such as in planetary photography. Fast films are more suited to constellation photography and nova patrols, and where maximum sensitivity is needed in short exposures, such as for aurorae and meteors. For deep-sky work it is generally better to use a slow or medium-speed film, and to expose for longer, than to use fast films (unless the object is very faint).

Focal length and image scale

Astrophotography gets more difficult as the focal length increases. Every type of lens has its uses: short focal lengths, such as the standard 50 mm camera lens, give small image scales and a wide field of view ($28° \times 41°$) on 35 mm film, ideal for meteor, aurora or constellation photography. Planetary detail, however, requires the large image scale provided by a telescope.

The image scale depends solely on the focal length, the formula being

$$\theta = 57.3/F$$

where θ is the image scale in degrees per millimetre and F is the focal length in millimetres. So for a 50 mm focal-length lens the Moon's image will be on average less than 0.5 mm across, while with a 500 mm telephoto lens it will be 4.4 mm across and the field of view is then 2°.8 × 4°.1, which is appropriate for extended star clusters and associations.

The brightness of the image, however, depends on both focal length and lens diameter – that is, on the focal ratio. This applies to extended objects only; for stars, which are points of light, the image brightness depends solely on the lens diameter.

A photograph of a nebula taken with a focal ratio of *f*/2.5 will show the same amount of nebulosity whether the optical system is a standard camera lens or a large telescope. What changes, however, is the image scale and the faintest star that can be recorded with a given exposure time and film.

Using ordinary cameras

In the simplest form of astrophotography, a firmly mounted camera is focused on infinity. An exposure time of a few seconds with a standard lens at full aperture (say *f*/2) and everyday film (say ISO 100) will show a number of stars in the night sky. The faintest stars in the image will be tiny points of light which are hard to see. Photographs taken at twilight or in moonlight can show foreground details, adding pictorial value.

Increasing the exposure time beyond a few seconds results in trailed star images because of the rotation of the Earth. Slight trailing makes the faint images easier to see, but it soon becomes obvious. Long exposures, in which the images are considerably trailed, can produce interesting and attractive pictures, especially in colour, as the star colours are clearly visible.

The exposure time that gives noticeable trailing varies with the focal length of the lens and the declination of the object. Table 11 provides a useful guide.

With fast films, camera apertures of *f*/2.8 or faster and the exposure times given in Table 11, it is possible to photograph stars fainter than naked-eye visibility. (It is, incidentally, usually worth stopping down the camera lens by at least one stop from full aperture, e.g. *f*/2.8 rather than *f*/2.0, to improve the image quality.) To record fainter objects requires longer exposure times, and for this some sort of driven mounting is needed.

Driven camera mounts

One popular method is to mount the camera piggyback on a driven, equatorially mounted telescope. The mounting's motor or its slow motions can track the stars sufficiently accurately to give crisp pictures with exposures of several minutes using short focal-length lenses.

An alternative is to use a system which is calculated to give the correct drive rate. Suitable devices include portable battery- or clockwork-driven equatorial camera platforms, and the hand-operated Scotch mount, so named by its inventor G. Y. Haig, and also called a screw drive or

barndoor mount. In its simplest form the Scotch mount consists of two hinged boards, with the hinge aligned on the celestial pole, as shown in Figure 11. Turning a screw threaded through one of the boards at a controlled rate separates them so that a camera mounted on the top board tracks the stars. Haig's original design uses a screw of pitch 1 mm at a distance of 229 mm from the hinge. Turning this screw once a minute in synchronism with the second hand of a watch gives the correct rate.

The system works well for exposures up to 15 minutes with 50 mm lenses, but the drive errors increase with time because the screw is straight and not the arc of a circle, and for longer exposures more elaborate systems are needed. But the basic Scotch mount has the advantage of being simple, cheap and easily made.

Polar alignment

All equatorial camera platforms must be aligned on the celestial pole. This is made easier by adding a sighting device or small telescope, parallel to the polar axis, which can then be pointed at the true position of the pole with the help of one of the polar region maps (Figure 3 on pages 60 and 61). Since there is no bright star exactly at either pole, there is likely to be an alignment error. The maximum polar alignment error allowable with a particular focal length of lens, for similar tolerances to trailing as given in Table 11, is given by the formula

$$394°/Ft$$

where F is the focal length in millimetres and t is the exposure time in minutes.

If the mount is aligned on Polaris or Sigma (σ) Octantis (both about 1° from their respective poles) rather than the true pole, then the maximum exposure time t_{max} (in

Table 11. Star trailing tolerances. Exposure times, in seconds, at which star trailing becomes noticeable for various focal lengths and declinations.

Focal length (mm)	Declination of object			
	0°	40°	60°	80°
20	25	33	50	144
24	21	27	41	120
28	19	23	36	103
35	14	19	29	82
50	10	13	20	58
85	6	8	12	34
100	5	7	10	30
135	4	5	7	21
200	2.5	3	5	14
300	1.7	2.1	3	10
400	1.2	1.6	2.5	7
500	1.0	1.3	2.0	6
750	0.7	0.9	1.3	4
1000	0.5	0.7	1.0	3
1500	0.3	0.4	0.7	1.9
2000	0.2	0.3	0.5	1.4

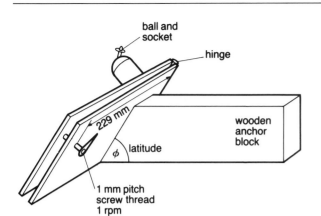

Figure 11. The Scotch mount. The dimension shown is for a screw of pitch 1 mm and a rotation of 1 rpm, but can be adapted for other values. The design can be modified for any latitude, and the massive anchor block is not needed if a tripod bush can be fitted.

minutes) without noticeable image distortion can be approximated as

$$t_{max} = 400/F$$

For a 50 mm lens, therefore, exposures of up to 8 minutes can be made before alignment errors become noticeable.

No matter how accurate the polar alignment, however, neither the Scotch mount nor electrically driven camera platforms will give very good results with long focal lengths or long exposure times. For these, more elaborate systems and some form of guiding are necessary.

Guided exposures

For focal lengths longer than about 200 mm, the driving rate should be monitored through an eyepiece, and fine guiding corrections made as necessary. There are several ways of correcting the drive rate of a camera platform or telescope, including:

(a) Varying the rate of a synchronous electric motor by altering the a.c. frequency supplied to it, by means of a variable-frequency oscillator (VFO). This method is suitable for units driven from a domestic electricity supply, though it is possible to get *inverters* which provide a.c. voltage from batteries.

(b) Varying the stepping rate of a stepper motor. These run on low d.c. voltages, and associated electronics will be necessary to provide a string of pulses whose rate can be varied. Because this system can be run from batteries, it is ideal for portable telescopes.

(c) With a worm-and-wheel drive, turning the whole worm and motor slightly, independently of the drive rate.

(d) Using a tangent arm on the declination axis whose position can be adjusted by turning a screw, or alternatively a worm and wheel. Declination corrections should be minor; if they keep having to be made during an exposure it means that the polar axis is misaligned.

(e) Moving the camera or film holder alone, while allowing the telescope to drive uncorrected.

However the drive rate is corrected, it must be possible to monitor the drive by viewing a star through the main telescope, or through its finder or guide telescope using an eyepiece with cross-wires (a reticle), preferably illuminated. Such eyepieces are available commercially, and generally have focal lengths of about 12 mm or 18 mm.

Guiding arrangements

If the main instrument is used for guiding, the guide star must be outside the camera's field of view, off the optical axis. At the same time it must be close enough to the axis for it to be focused to an acceptable point. The usual method is to insert a small prism into the optical path just to one side of the frame area. This is a very convenient method, and add-on guiders complete with illuminated reticle eyepieces are available commercially. Another advantage is that as the guide eyepiece is close to the camera, there is little risk of movement between the two. A drawback, however, is that it can be hard to find a sufficiently bright guide star at the right distance from the object being photographed.

The main alternative method is to use a separate guide telescope. Ideally this should be on adjustable mountings so that it is possible to guide either on the object being photographed, if it is suitable, or on a guide star anywhere in the vicinity. The drawbacks of this method are that it is more cumbersome since it requires a separate telescope, with the risk of some flexure in the fixings between the guide eyepiece and the camera's focal plane. The advantages are that the guide star can be chosen, and that the system can be adapted to photograph comets.

Many comets are so diffuse that it is difficult to guide on them. They move relative to the stars, and for exposures of more than a few minutes this can give trailing of the comet's image. The solution is to use a guide eyepiece which can be shifted slightly by a micrometer screw thread. The comet's motion is calculated beforehand from its ephemeris, and the eyepiece is moved in the opposite direction and at the same rate by shifting it a predetermined distance every minute or so; the guide star is then recentred. This results in trailed stars but a sharp comet image. The steps should be fine enough to produce straight rather than jagged trails.

Photography through a telescope

Although a camera lens can be pointed through the eyepiece of a telescope, with both focused on infinity, it is more usual to remove the lens of the camera and attach the camera body to the eyepiece mount of the telescope. Adapters to suit most lens mounts and eyepiece fittings are available commercially. To use the full field of the instrument, no eyepiece is used. There must be enough focusing range within the limits of the normal eyepiece position to allow for the thickness of the camera body – about 50 mm. Many Newtonians intended for visual work do not have this range, so it will be necessary either to move the entire secondary and focusing assembly nearer the mirror, or to move the mirror up the tube.

To increase the effective focal length, and hence the image scale, such as for planetary photography, use an eyepiece or Barlow lens to project the image; extension tubes may be needed. Pictures can be taken in this way even if there is not enough focusing range for direct photography.

The effective focal length is obtained by first calculating the magnification M of the image given by the eyepiece. This depends on the distance of the eyepiece in front of the film, d, and on its focal length F:

$$M = (d/F) - 1$$

Measure d from the film plane, shown on most cameras by the symbol $\ominus$, to the estimated location of the field stop in the eyepiece. (If a Barlow lens is used rather than an eyepiece, note that its quoted magnification applies only when it is used visually with an eyepiece, and its power when used to project an image into a camera will be different.) The effective focal length is now the telescope's original focal length multiplied by M.

To increase the field of view, giving a smaller image scale, use a *telecompressor* (rich-field adapter) – an achromatic positive lens inside the focus position. These are available commercially, mainly for use with Schmidt–Cassegrain telescopes which otherwise are rather slow, with a comparatively small field of view. The image quality at the field edges may, however, be poor when using a telecompressor and there is bound to be *vignetting*, with the image dimmer at the edges.

Focusing methods

It is essential to have some means of checking the focus from time to time. With long focal lengths or fast lenses the zone of sharp focus is only a small fraction of a millimetre deep, and temperature changes during a session can easily defocus an instrument. Suitable focusing methods include a ground glass screen, a parallax focusing screen, a knife-edge and a Ronchi grating.

To focus by parallax requires a clear screen with a reticle or mark on it. With a magnifier, the eye is moved from side to side until the reticle and the image move together. A knife-edge focuser works in the same way on a star image as the same test for telescope mirrors does with an artificial star. It uses a knife-edge at the focal plane of the camera, exactly where the film emulsion will be. It must be possible to look through the back of the camera, so for an SLR the back must be opened before loading the film. Point the telescope at a moderately bright star and move the eye from side to side. The objective should be filled with the star's light, which is cut off instantly right across the objective by the knife-edge only when it is exactly in the focal plane. If it is slightly in front of or behind the focus position, its shadow will be visible moving one way or the other. Those who are more familiar with the Ronchi mirror test can use a Ronchi grating instead of the knife-edge.

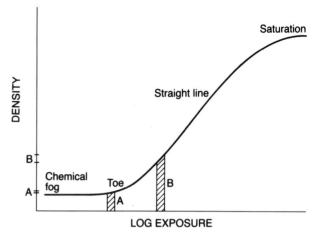

Figure 12. A typical characteristic curve for an emulsion. A small exposure increase at A, on the toe of the curve, produces less density on the film than a similar increase at B, on the straight-line part.

Emulsion characteristics

The technical specifications of an emulsion for astrophotography are its characteristic curve, spectral sensitivity, resolving power, graininess and reciprocity failure characteristics.

An emulsion's *characteristic curve* reveals how the film responds to varying exposures to white light. It is a graph of photographic density, the degree of darkening of the developed emulsion against exposure time. A typical characteristic curve (Figure 12) has a *toe*, where light produces little response. The curve then rises more steeply, following a more-or-less straight line. At the long-exposure end the emulsion saturates at a maximum density.

There is an unavoidable *chemical fog* level, providing a minimum background density to the emulsion, even in the absence of any exposure to light. A faint object produces a small increase in density over this fog level. On the toe, a small exposure increase produces a rather small density increase, but on the straight-line part, where the *contrast* is higher, the response to the same small exposure is greater. This is why it is better to go for exposures with a certain sky background level – to get onto the straight-line, higher-contrast part of the curve and so make faint objects more detectable.

Different emulsions have different characteristic curves. An overall shift to the left means that the emulsion is basically faster. In general, the faster emulsions have lower contrast.

Each emulsion has a recommended development time, chosen by the manufacturer to give pleasing results for everyday photography. But astronomers are often interested in getting the best performance out of the film, so it is common practice to give more development (*push-processing*) or to use a more active developer than is recommended. Increasing the development gives greater contrast, but also raises the chemical fog level. In some cases it can mean that a given exposure produces more response than on an inherently faster film developed normally, i.e. the film's speed seems to have increased.

Colour emulsions have three sensitive layers, responding to red, green and blue light, so they have three characteristic curves rather than one. Each layer may respond differently to push-processing, resulting in a *colour cast*. Reversal film curves are a mirror image of negative ones, so a small exposure increase gives a decrease in the density.

The *spectral sensitivity* curve of a film shows its response to light of different colours. It is usually different from the colour response of the eye, in that the dark-adapted eye is most sensitive to yellow–green light, while film may be most sensitive to blue or red light, with maybe several peaks in its sensitivity distribution. This is why the colours of emission nebulae on film are almost invariably different to the colours seen by a visual observer.

A film's *resolving power* is its ability to reveal fine detail. It is measured by photographing a test object, then studying the images to determine the finest detail that is resolved. The contrast of the test object has a bearing on the resolving power: if a stark black-and-white chart with a contrast ratio of 1000 : 1 corresponds to resolving a double star, then one of contrast 1.6 : 1 is representative of fine planetary detail. Resolving power is quoted in lines per millimetre (more accurately, the separation of line pairs). High resolving power for a low-contrast test object is around 100 lines/mm, typical of a slow film, while a fast film might have a value of 40 lines/mm.

Any photographic image, when examined closely, will show a grainy structure, caused by clumping of the tiny grains that form the image. The subjective impression of this structure is called the *graininess*, or often just the *grain*, of the film. Manufacturers often quote only a subjective term such as 'fine grain'. It is rare for them to admit to any emulsion having 'coarse grain'.

Reciprocity failure. In everyday photography, doubling the exposure time (say from 1/250 second to 1/125 second) gives twice the effect on the film. This is the reciprocity law. But at low light levels this no longer happens: the reciprocity law breaks down, and the emulsion is said to suffer from reciprocity failure. In practice this means that after a certain time a doubling of the exposure time produces only a slight improvement in the faintest magnitude recorded.

There are several ways of overcoming reciprocity failure. One is to cool the emulsion to as low as −80°C. Cold cameras are available commercially, but they are inevitably more difficult to use than conventional cameras.

Baking the emulsion was once a popular technique. The process drives off the water and oxygen which desensitize the emulsion, and creates more locations where the development process can start, so increasing the chance that an incoming photon will be recorded. A typical baking time is 8 hours at 65°C. Baking is most successful for black-and-white emulsions without much red sensitivity.

Today, however, the most popular process is *gas hypersensitization*, often simply called *hypering*, which originally meant baking the film in a hydrogen atmosphere. This has a

similar reducing effect to straight baking. Hydrogen is a dangerous gas, however, so many people prefer to use *forming gas*, which is nitrogen with a small percentage of hydrogen. It works almost as well, and is much safer. Forming gas is not always readily available in small quantities, but some emulsions are available commercially hypered, though with a rather short shelf life.

Different commercial emulsions suffer from reciprocity failure to different extents, which can give rise to apparent anomalies. This is why a rather slow film such as Kodak Technical Pan Film (also known as 2415) can give better results than the super-fast films of ISO 1000 and more now being produced, though only with a much longer exposure time.

Finally, Kodak supply *spectroscopic emulsions* for professional use. These are designed to have little reciprocity failure, and are mostly available in plate formats to special order only, and at enormous cost.

Other ways of improving performance. *Pre-flashing* the film is one way to get somewhat better results from it, particularly if the skies are so dark that the sky background remains unexposed. The technique is to give an overall pre-exposure so that any additional photons from true astronomical objects can readily have an effect. The pre-exposure time should be between 1/100 and 1 second.

Another, quite different way to improve the chances of recording faint objects is to superimpose several weak exposures. This normally works only with negative films. For example, to get an image of a planet dense enough for printing might require a 2 second exposure. Four exposures, each of 0.5 second exposure time on pre-flashed film, would yield one rather dense image, but with less graininess because there are more, overlapping, grains forming the image. In addition, the shorter exposure times should give better resolution of detail in poor seeing.

There are other ways of bringing out the most from a negative image. Some images have an enormous brightness range which cannot be shown in a single print. To reduce this range, a slightly defocused positive copy of low contrast and density is made, and sandwiched together with the original to make a print. Areas that were previously of low density will now be denser, so compressing the overall range.

Alternatively, copying an original onto high-contrast film using diffuse illumination makes faint deep-sky objects more visible, though brighter objects will saturate the film. Sandwiching several such copies from separate originals reinforces any faint objects just at the limit of detectability on the individual exposures.

Photography through filters

Differential reciprocity failure between the layers of colour film can give rise to colour shifts at long exposure times. One way round this is to make separate exposures on black-and-white film through red, green and blue filters which, together with the film's colour sensitivity, cover the visible spectrum. The final image is produced by combining the three separate exposures, through the appropriate colour printing filters, in the darkroom.

Light pollution rejection (LPR) filters are designed to block strong emission lines from the mercury or sodium lamps commonly used for streetlights, while transmitting strong emission lines of astrophysical interest. They are very effective for photographing emission nebulae. LPR filters are expensive, and a cheaper alternative is a red filter such as a Wratten 25 or 29, used in conjunction with a red-sensitive film. This combination records emission nebulae particularly well, in addition to stars, and reduces light pollution. In badly light-polluted areas the deeper red Wratten 29 filter, a long exposure time and a fast film are needed, and the method can give excellent results.

Summary of techniques

A suitable instrument, film and trial exposure time are given below for each subject. The exposure time is only a guide, and in poor conditions a much longer exposure may be needed. For instruments with a lower f-number give less exposure, and vice versa.

Sun. Prime focus on medium-sized refractors or catadioptrics, $f/10$ to $f/15$; full-aperture Mylar filter; slow film, 1/30 second. Same conditions for partial eclipses. *Total eclipses:* long telephoto lens, e.g. 500 mm $f/8$. No filter during totality. Slow film; give exposures from 1/250 to 1 second.

Moon. *Whole disk:* prime focus with focal length longer than 750 mm. Slow or medium film. Exposures depend strongly on phase. For $f/8$ expose as follows: *full*, 1/125 second; *quarter*, 1/30 second; *crescent*, ⅛ second. *Total eclipses:* telephoto lens, fast film, 10 seconds. *Surface details:* use eyepiece projection to give $f/40$ or more. Medium to fast film; 1 second.

Planets. As large a telescope as possible; focal length 1500 mm or longer. Use eyepiece projection to give $f/40$ or more. *Venus:* slow film; ⅛ second. *Mercury, Mars:* medium-speed film, ¼ second. *Jupiter:* medium-speed film, ½ second. *Saturn:* medium to fast film, 1 second.

Minor and outer planets. Photograph as stars.

Zodiacal light. Wide-angle, fast camera lens; very fast film; 1 to 5 minutes driven or undriven.

Aurora. Standard or wide-angle camera lens, $f/2$, fast film, 5 to 15 seconds.

Meteors. Standard camera lens, $f/2$, fast film, 5 minutes driven or undriven.

Constellations. Camera lens, one stop less than full aperture; slow to very fast; 10 seconds to 30 minutes depending on film and sky brightness. Driven exposures give star images; undriven, star trails.

Stars and star clusters. Guided exposures using large apertures at prime focus or with eyepiece projection. Medium to fast film; 1 to 15 minutes.

Comets. As for stars, but guided on comet's motion. Comets with long tails require shorter focal lengths, such as 300 mm $f/4$, preferably on large format film.

Deep-sky objects. Large objects, such as the Orion Nebula, can be photographed with a telephoto lens and fast film, e.g. 200 mm $f/4$, 5 minutes. For better results, and for most galaxies, use large aperture, fast f-number, at prime focus with slow to medium film, preferably hypered, for 15 minutes.

IV

THE SOLAR SYSTEM

THE SUN

The Sun is a rather ordinary yellow dwarf star. But because it is over a quarter of a million times closer than its nearest stellar neighbour, we can study it in much greater detail than any other star, even with small instruments. It is blindingly brilliant, so special precautions have to be taken while observing it. *Never look at the Sun directly through any optical instrument. Even staring at the Sun with the naked eye for any length of time can cause damage.* The safest technique is to project the Sun's image onto a card, as described in the section Observing the Sun (p. 84).

Physical data

Mass: 1.99×10^{30} kg ($= 3.33 \times 10^5$ Earth masses)
Diameter: 1.392×10^6 km
Volume: 1.41×10^{27} m^3 ($= 1.30 \times 10^6$ Earth volumes)
Mean density: 1.41×10^3 kg m^{-3}
Surface gravity: 273.87 m s^{-2} ($= 27.94$ Earth gravity)
Escape velocity: 6.18×10^5 m s^{-1}
Total radiation emitted: 3.83×10^{26} W
Mean distance from Earth: 1.496×10^{11} m
Inclination of axis to perpendicular to plane of ecliptic: $7°.25$
Sidereal period of axial rotation (at latitude 17°): 25.38 d
Spectral type: G2V
Absolute visual magnitude: 4.83
Apparent visual magnitude: −26.7
Effective temperature: 5770 K

The Sun's place in the Galaxy

Our Galaxy (the Milky Way) contains about 10^{11} stars and has a flattened, spiral structure roughly 25 kiloparsecs in diameter. The Sun is located about 8 kiloparsecs from the centre, and just a few parsecs north of the galactic plane. The stars in the solar neighbourhood are, on average, revolving around the centre of the Galaxy with a velocity of about 250 km s^{-1} and make a complete revolution in approximately 200 million years. In addition, the Sun moves with respect to the nearby stars with a velocity of around 19.5 km s^{-1} in the direction of a point on the borders

of the constellations Hercules and Lyra, near the bright star Vega. This point is known as the *solar apex*, and its approximate coordinates are RA 18h, dec. +30°.

The structure of the Sun

The interior. Gravitational forces create enormous temperatures (about 15×10^6 K) and pressures (3×10^{11} atmospheres) at the centre of the Sun. Under these conditions, nuclear reactions occur which turn hydrogen nuclei into helium nuclei, releasing a large amount of energy in the process. It is this energy which has kept the Sun shining for perhaps 4.5×10^9 years, and will continue to power it for a similar time to come.

The high-energy radiation produced in the centre gradually diffuses outwards, taking perhaps 10 million years to reach the surface, in a long series of absorption and re-emission processes. Eventually, about three-quarters of the way from the centre to the surface, convection takes over, conveying heat to the *photosphere* (the visible surface) largely through rising columns of hot gas. The gas cools at the surface, and is carried down again to be reheated. Since hot gas emits more light than cool gas, the pattern of convective cells can be seen at the surface as *granulation*. Each granule is about 1500 km across.

The surface and above. The average temperature of the photosphere is about 5800 K, and the gas pressure perhaps a tenth of that at the Earth's surface. Under these conditions many of the common atoms are at least partially *ionized* (stripped of some of their electrons), forming a *plasma*. As light passes upwards through the Sun's outer layers, the atoms and ions in those layers absorb radiation at certain wavelengths; measurement of the strength of these *absorption lines* in the solar spectrum tells us the composition of the Sun, at least at the surface. It appears to be about 90% hydrogen and 10% helium (by numbers of atoms), with other constituents making up less than 1%.

For about 500 km above the photosphere the temperature continues to fall gradually. However, for the next 1500 km a gentle rise sets in, and the temperature reaches 10 000 K at the top of the *chromosphere*, named after the red-coloured rim which can be seen around the Sun at the

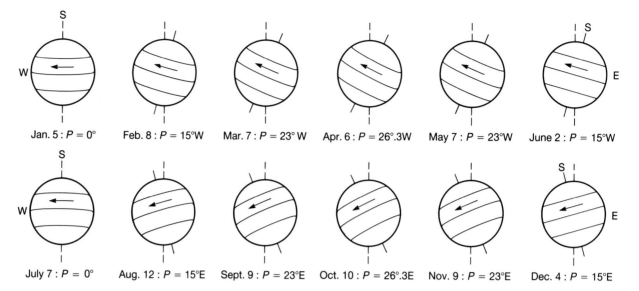

Jan. 5 : $P = 0°$　　Feb. 8 : $P = 15°W$　　Mar. 7 : $P = 23° W$　　Apr. 6 : $P = 26°.3W$　　May 7 : $P = 23°W$　　June 2 : $P = 15°W$

July 7 : $P = 0°$　　Aug. 12 : $P = 15°E$　　Sept. 9 : $P = 23°E$　　Oct. 10 : $P = 26°.3E$　　Nov. 9 : $P = 23°E$　　Dec. 4 : $P = 15°E$

Figure 13. The apparent motion of sunspots across the Sun's disk at various times of the year. The dashed vertical line is the line of the hour circle. The diagram shows apparent motion as viewed in an inverting telescope from the northern hemisphere; for use in the southern hemisphere the diagram should be inverted.

time of a total solar eclipse. The colour of the chromosphere is caused by the emission of red light from hydrogen. The spectrum of the chromosphere can be obtained during the few seconds at the beginning and end of a total eclipse when the chromosphere flashes out as the brighter photosphere is covered. This so-called *flash spectrum* consists of a number of bright lines, many of which coincide in wavelength with those seen in absorption in the photosphere.

Above the chromosphere the temperature rises very sharply to over 500 000 K through a zone only a few hundred kilometres thick called the *transition region*; it is best observed in the far ultraviolet part of the spectrum using instruments carried by rockets and satellites. Above the transition region is the *corona*, a vast envelope of tenuous gas reaching far out from the Sun, which can be seen as a pearly halo of light at the time of a total eclipse. Its shape varies with the sunspot cycle (see below), being more uniform and symmetrical at maximum and exhibiting a much more irregular structure at times of low activity, when it shows long equatorial streamers and polar tufts and plumes. The coronal temperature is between one and two million kelvin and, with the extremely low densities prevailing, highly ionized atoms can be found, e.g. iron with up to 15 of its 26 electrons stripped away.

The corona is continually being replenished by material from below while losing material into interplanetary space at the rate of about three million tonnes per second in what is called the *solar wind*, which gusts with speeds of a few hundred kilometres per second. This flow appears to be strongest from *coronal holes*, extensive areas of the corona lower in density and temperature than their surroundings, where the magnetic field flows directly out from the Sun.

Surface features

The complex interplay of convection, radiation and magnetic fields produces a number of different surface features.

Sunspots. Throughout history, when the Sun has been observed rising or setting through a mist, dark patches have been reported periodically on its surface. These sunspots are actually regions lower in temperature than the surrounding area which thus appear dark by contrast. The *umbra* is the darker central part, with a temperature of about 4500 K, while the *penumbra*, which surrounds it, is only a few hundred degrees cooler than the photosphere. The penumbra of a well-developed sunspot is always larger in area than the umbra. Sunspots vary in size from small *pores*, about the size of granules, which can only be seen clearly in high-resolution photographs taken under conditions of good seeing, up to large groups covering several billion square kilometres.

The usual unit for estimating areas of sunspots is a millionth of the visible disk, which corresponds to an area of about 3 million square kilometres. For a spot to be visible to the naked eye, its area must be greater than about 500 millionths; a very large group may cover several thousand millionths.

The Scottish astronomer Alexander Wilson noted in 1774 that sunspots appear to be depressions in the solar surface; the effect is most pronounced at the limb where the part of the penumbra closer to the limb becomes broader and the umbra is displaced away from the centre of the spot. The explanation of this so-called *Wilson effect* is that the gas in and above the sunspot is cooler and less dense than at the normal surface, so that we can see deeper into the photosphere in the region of the umbra. This gives the impression that the umbra is depressed.

Sunspots never appear near the poles, and are generally confined between latitudes 35° north and south, although they are seldom found right on the equator. Most individual sunspots last for a few days, although large ones and groups

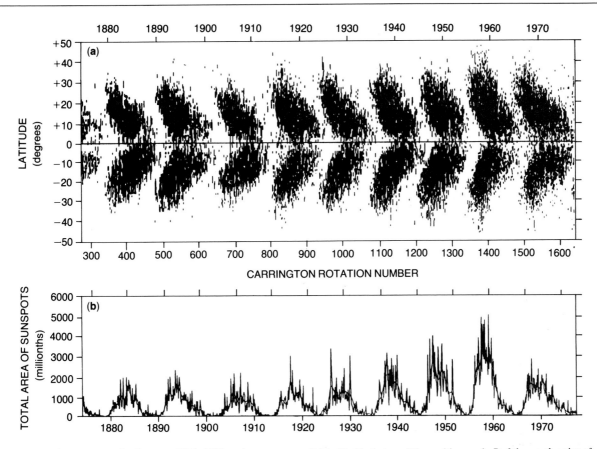

Figure 14. (a) Solar butterfly diagram, 1874–1976, and (b) corresponding plot of area covered by sunspots. This figure represents the results gathered by the Greenwich Photoheliographic Programme using data from Greenwich/Herstmonceux, Cape Town, Kodaikanal (India), Mount Wilson and Debrecen (Hungary) Observatories.

can persist for several weeks. The daily motion of spots across the disk from east to west demonstrates the rotation of the Sun, which is faster at the equator than it is at the poles. The synodic period (i.e. as viewed from the Earth as it revolves around the Sun) is 27.275 d at a latitude of 17° (sometimes referred to as the mean synodic period). For other latitudes ϕ the synodic period P, in days, is given by

$$P \simeq 26.75 + 5.7 \sin^2 \phi$$

The corresponding sidereal period for latitude 17° is 25.38 d, which is adopted as the mean rotation period of the Sun. Each rotation of the Sun is identified by a number in a series called *Carrington rotations* started by the English astronomer R. C. Carrington. Rotation No. 1 began on 1853 November 9.

The Sun's axis of rotation is inclined at 7°.25, and the Earth's axis of rotation at 23°.5, to the vertical to the plane of the ecliptic; hence the direction of the Sun's axis as viewed from the Earth changes throughout the year. In consequence, the apparent motion of sunspots in transit across the disk changes with the seasons as illustrated in Figure 13. To determine the true latitude and longitude of a spot at a particular time the observer needs to know the

Table 12. Variation of the position angle P of the north point of the Sun's disk during the year.

Date	P	Date	P
Jan. 5, July 7	0°	July 7, Jan. 5	0°
Jan. 16, June 26	5°W	July 18, Dec. 26	5°E
Jan. 27, June 15	10°W	July 30, Dec. 16	10°E
Feb. 8, June 2	15°W	Aug. 12, Dec. 4	15°E
Feb. 23, May 18	20°W	Aug. 28, Nov. 20	20°E
Mar. 7, May 7	23°W	Sept. 9, Nov. 9	23°E
Mar. 18, Apr. 25	25°W	Sept. 21, Oct. 29	25°E
Apr. 6	26°.3W	Oct. 10	26°.3E

Table 13. Variation of the heliographic latitude B_0 of the centre of the Sun's disk during the year.

Date	B_0	Date	B_0
Dec. 7, June 6	0°	June 6, Dec. 7	0°
Dec. 16, May 29	1°S	June 14, Nov. 30	1°N
Dec. 23, May 20	2°S	June 23, Nov. 21	2°N
Jan. 1, May 11	3°S	July 2, Nov. 13	3°N
Jan. 10, May 2	4°S	July 11, Nov. 4	4°N
Jan. 20, Apr. 21	5°S	July 21, Oct. 25	5°N
Feb. 1, Apr. 10	6°S	Aug. 3, Oct. 12	6°N
Feb. 19, Mar. 21	7°S	Aug. 23, Sept. 22	7°N
Mar. 5	7°.2S	Sept. 8	7°.2N

position angle of the Sun's axis and the heliographic latitude of the apparent centre of the Sun's disk; these data are given in Tables 12 and 13 (see also Observing sunspots, p. 85).

The solar cycle. Observations carried out over more than three centuries have shown that the number of sunspots rises and falls with an average period of 11.1 years, although the actual figure can vary between about 8 and 16 years. Activity can vary appreciably from one cycle to another. The rise to maximum is normally more rapid than the decline, taking about 4.5 years. At sunspot minimum no spots may be seen for weeks on end, while large spots occur most frequently around maximum. At the beginning of a cycle spots tend to occur at the higher latitudes, both north and south, but as the cycle develops they are to be found progressively nearer the equator. This effect (known as *Spörer's law*) is shown beautifully by the *butterfly diagram*, first plotted in 1904 by E. W. Maunder of the Royal Observatory, Greenwich, in which the number and latitude of spots is shown as a function of time. Figure 14(a) shows all the data collected during the 103 years of the Greenwich Photoheliographic Programme until its termination in 1976. The corresponding sunspot areas are plotted in Figure 14(b), which shows that different cycles are far from identical.

Although an 11-year periodicity is evident in sunspot activity, studies of magnetic fields on the Sun have shown that the true cycle of activity is actually twice as long, i.e. 22 years. Sunspots, particularly those in groups, are regions of intense magnetic activity and the magnetic polarities of the spots reverse in each successive 11-year cycle. For example, if in the northern hemisphere of the Sun the preceding spot of a pair has a north magnetic polarity, then the following spot has a south magnetic polarity; in the southern hemisphere the polarities of the preceding and following spots are the other way round. This pattern of polarities persists in each hemisphere throughout a given cycle, but when the spots of the next cycle start to appear at high latitudes they have the opposite magnetic polarities to those of the previous cycle.

The strong, localized magnetic fields on the Sun hold the key to the existence of sunspots, for they seem to constrain the movement of hot gas and prevent the convection of heat locally, thereby keeping the area affected by the magnetic fields cooler than the rest of the photosphere.

Sunspot numbers. For objectively recording sunspot activity, the Wolf (or Zurich) Relative Sunspot Number may be used; it is named after Rudolf Wolf of Zurich Observatory who introduced the system in the 19th century. It takes into account sunspot groups as well as individual spots. If g is the number of spot groups, f the total number of spots and k a factor depending on the instrument used and the observer, then the Wolf number R is given by

$$R = k(10g + f)$$

For telescopes about 100 mm in aperture, k may be taken to be equal to 1. Hence, if an observer notes 3 sunspot groups and 11 individual spots on a given day, then the sunspot number for that day is $30 + 11 = 41$. The Wolf numbers are usually averaged for a year, and have ranged from 0 at minimum to nearly 200 at high maxima.

Mean daily frequency (MDF). This is a measure of the average number of *active areas* on the Sun over a given period, usually one month. Active areas include the bright patches called faculae as well as sunspots. Any group of sunspots or faculae more than 10° in longitude or latitude from another may be classed as one active area. For example, if during one month 9 active areas are seen on 13 days of observation, then the mean daily frequency for that month is $9/13 = 0.69$.

Other surface features

Faculae are streaky bright patches generally found close to sunspots, and best seen near the edge of the disk since they contrast well with the darkened limb. They are often the precursors of sunspots and may also be found after the disappearance of spots, although they can also be seen at high latitudes. *Plages* or *flocculi* are clouds of hot gas in the upper chromosphere related to faculae, and best seen in the light emitted by ionized calcium.

Prominences are jets of gas which rise above the chromosphere and are shaped by magnetic fields, often forming arcs. They are clearly seen above the limb during solar eclipses. Prominences appear to be relatively cool, dense clouds of gas which can exist in the corona for many hours, steadily pouring material back into the photosphere. Prominences, along with *sprays*, *surges* and *loops*, are more common on an active Sun at times of sunspot maxima, although long-lasting *quiescent prominences* display their curtain-like form at other times. When seen in projection against the Sun's bright disk, they are sometimes termed *filaments*.

Spicules are jets of gas with a spiky, fiery appearance that last for a few minutes. They are found in the lower chromosphere, particularly at the edge of granulation patterns, where they line up.

Flares are another short-lived phenomenon of the Sun's active regions. A sudden release of energy accelerates charged particles in the plasma, which proceeds to emit radiation across the whole spectrum – from X-rays to radio waves. Particles are ejected from the Sun and travel out through the Solar System, sometimes causing disturbances in the Earth's ionosphere, including aurorae, a day or so later.

Observing the Sun

It is extremely dangerous to attempt to observe the Sun unless proper precautions are taken. If they are not, blindness may well be the penalty. Although special filters are available that cover the full aperture of the telescope, by far the safest method is to support a smooth, white card 30 cm behind the

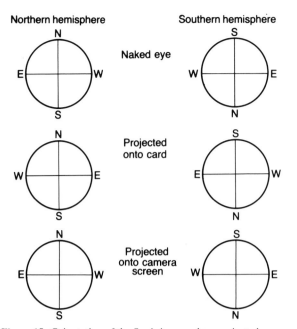

Northern hemisphere		Southern hemisphere
Naked eye		
Projected onto card		
Projected onto camera screen		

Figure 15. Orientation of the Sun's image when projected.

eyepiece of the telescope and to focus the image of the Sun projected onto it. To avoid looking at the Sun while pointing the telescope, use the shadow of the telescope cast on the card as a guide. The cardinal points are shown in Figure 15 for two different methods of projection.

The image of the Sun will appear noticeably darker towards the edges, an effect known as *limb darkening*. When we look at the centre of the disk we are looking deeper into the photosphere, where the temperature is higher, compared with what we see when looking at the edge. Faculae are most noticeable against the limb-darkened regions.

Observing sunspots. In studying the motion of sunspots across the disk, the inclination of the Sun's axis must be accounted for because the apparent path of sunspots varies with the time of year (Figure 13). They move in straight lines only around June 6 and December 7, when the Earth lies in the plane of the Sun's equator. From January to May, sunspots follow a curved path to the north because the south pole of the Sun is then tilted towards the Earth. From July to November, sunspots curve towards the south because the Sun's north pole is leaning towards us. The paths of sunspots across the disk show the greatest curvature near March 7 and September 9, when the south and north poles respectively are tilted towards us at their maximum of $7°.25$.

The *Astronomical Almanac* and the *Handbook* of the British Astronomical Association give the following information necessary for determining the true heliographic coordinates of a point on the disk:

P, the position angle of the northern end of the Sun's axis
B_0, the heliographic latitude of the centre of the disk
L_0, the heliographic longitude of the centre of the disk.

THE MOON

The Moon is the Earth's natural satellite, orbiting at a mean distance of 384 400 km; its diameter is 3476 km, only 29% smaller than that of the planet Mercury (for other data see Table 19 on p. 99). Although the Moon appears bright at night its surface rocks are in fact very dark, reflecting less than 10% on average of the light falling on them. The Moon has essentially no atmosphere or magnetic field, although the magnetization of its surface rocks indicates that a strong magnetic field existed early in its geological history. Our knowledge of the Moon has come from Earth-based observations, from spacecraft pictures and data, and from experiments set up on the lunar surface and samples brought back for analysis, mainly by the Apollo astronauts, but also by unmanned Soviet spacecraft.

The motions of the Moon

The orbital motions of the Moon and Earth, together with their axial rotations, have several effects on the observation of lunar surface features.

Rotational phenomena. The Moon and Earth orbit around their common centre of mass, or *barycentre*, with a period of 27.321 66 d (a sidereal month). Because the Earth is 81.3 times more massive than the Moon, this centre of mass lies within the body of the Earth itself, about 1700 km below its surface. The Moon rotates on its axis in the same length of time as it takes to make one orbit of the centre of mass; this is described as a *captured* or *synchronous* rotation, and is a consequence of tidal friction. The result is that the Moon presents the same face to the Earth, although with slight irregularities caused by libration (see below).

Phases. As the Moon orbits the Earth we see varying amounts of its illuminated hemisphere, producing the familiar cycle of phases: new moon (when all of the illuminated side faces away from the Earth), crescent, half moon, gibbous and full moon, followed by the same sequence in reverse order. One cycle of phases (e.g. from one new moon to the next) is called a *lunation* or a synodic month. It has a mean length of 29.530 59 d, longer than a sidereal month because the Earth moves in its own orbit around the Sun during that time, so the Moon has to travel further to reach the same relative position as at the start of the month. The actual value of the synodic month can vary from about $29\frac{1}{4}$ to $29\frac{3}{4}$ days, largely because of the varying speed of the Earth in its elliptical orbit.

A considerable amount of light is reflected from the Earth onto the Moon's surface, and at the crescent phase near new moon this makes the Moon's night side faintly visible. This effect is called *earthshine*, and the appearance it produces is known popularly as 'the old moon in the new moon's arms'.

Libration. Although the Moon keeps essentially the same hemisphere turned towards the Earth, the alignment is not perfect. There are two 'rocking' motions, called *libration in*

Continued on p. 94

EAST

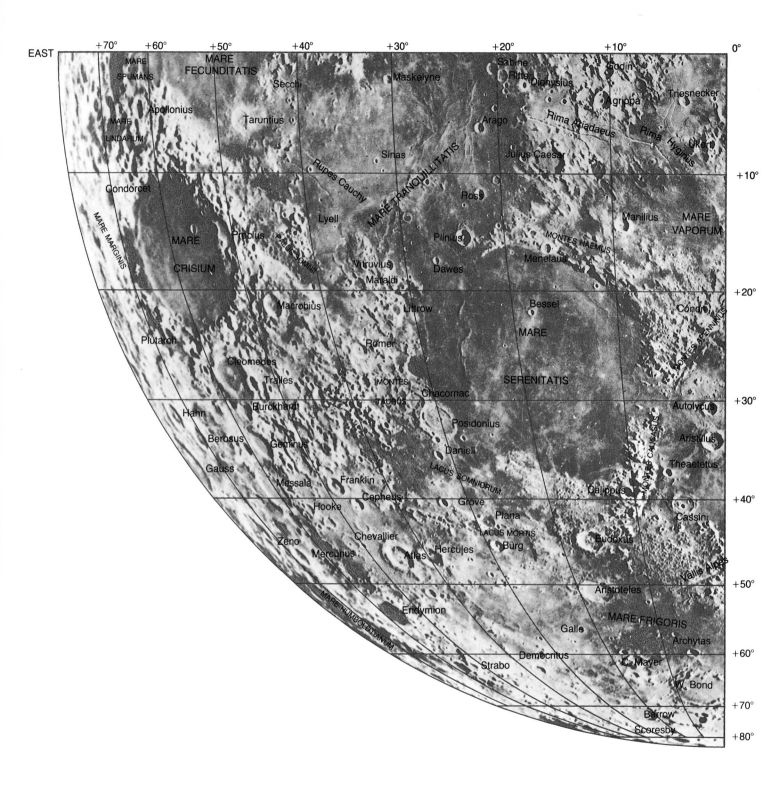

| +70° | +60° | +50° | +40° | +30° | +20° | +10° | 0° |

MARE SPUMANS
MARE FECUNDITATIS
Secchi
Maskelyne
Sabine
Ritter
Dionysius
Godin
Triesnecker
Apollonius
Taruntius
Arago
Rima Ariadaeus
Agrippa
MARE UNDARUM
Sinas
Julius Caesar
Rima Hyginus
Ukert

+10°

Condorcet
Rupes Cauchy
MARE TRANQUILLITATIS
Ross
Manilius
MARE VAPORUM
Proclus
Lyell
MARE MARGINIS
MARE CRISIUM
PALUS SOMNII
Plinius
MONTES HAEMUS
Vitruvius
Dawes
Menelaus
Maraldi

+20°

Macrobius
Littrow
Bessel
Condon
Plutarch
Römer
MARE
MONTES APENNINUS
Cleomedes
MONTES TAURUS
SERENITATIS
Autolycus
Tralles
Chacornac
Aristillus
Burckhardt
Posidonius
Theaetetus

+30°

Hahn
Geminus
Daniell
MONTES CAUCASUS
Berosus
LACUS SOMNIORUM
Calippus
Gauss
Messala
Franklin
Grove
Cassini
Cepheus
Plana
Autolycus

+40°

Hooke
Chevallier
LACUS MORTIS
Eudoxus
Vallis Alpes
Zeno
Atlas
Hercules
Bürg
Mercurius
Aristoteles

+50°

MARE HUMBOLDTIANUM
Endymion
MARE FRIGORIS
Galle
Archytas
Democritus
C. Mayer
Strabo
W. Bond

+60°

Barrow
Scoresby

+70°
+80°

NORTH

Figure 16 (pages 86 to 93). Map of the Moon divided into four quadrants: (a) Quadrant I (NE), (b) Quadrant II (NW), (c) Quadrant III (SW) and (d) Quadrant IV (SE), with a grid of selenographic coordinates and names of major features. South is at the top, as it appears in an inverting telescope. The accompanying lists give the longitude and latitude of each named crater to the nearest degree, and its diameter in kilometres. Since many craters are highly irregular in shape, these diameters are only approximate. Other named features are also listed.

(a) *Quadrant I*: north-east

Crater	Longitude	Latitude	Diameter (km)	Crater	Longitude	Latitude	Diameter (km)
Agrippa	10 E	4 N	46	Plutarch	79 E	24 N	68
Apollonius	61 E	4 N	52	Posidonius	30 E	32 N	100
Arago	21 E	6 N	26	Proclus	47 E	16 N	28
Archytas	5 E	59 N	32	Ritter	19 E	2 N	31
Aristillus	1 E	34 N	55	Römer	36 E	25 N	40
Aristoteles	17 E	50 N	89	Ross	22 E	12 N	26
Atlas	44 E	46 N	87	Sabine	20 E	1 N	30
Autolycus	1 E	31 N	40	Scoresby	14 E	78 N	56
Barrow	8 E	72 N	93	Secchi	43 E	2 N	25
Berosus	70 E	33 N	74	Sinas	31 E	9 N	12
Bessel	18 E	22 N	16	Strabo	54 E	62 N	55
W. Bond	4 E	65 N	158	Taruntius	46 E	5 N	56
Burckhardt	56 E	31 N	57	Theaetetus	6 E	37 N	25
Bürg	28 E	45 N	40	Tralles	53 E	28 N	43
Calippus	11 E	39 N	31	Triesnecker	4 E	4 N	24
Cassini	4 E	40 N	56	Ukert	1 E	8 N	24
Cepheus	45 E	41 N	40	Vitruvius	31 E	17 N	28
Chacornac	32 E	30 N	51	Zeno	72 E	45 N	65
Chevallier	51 E	45 N	52				
Cleomedes	56 E	27 N	126	**Other features**			
Condorcet	70 E	12 N	74				
Conon	2 E	22 N	22	Lacus Mortis			
Daniell	31 E	35 N	27	Lacus Somniorum			
Dawes	26 E	17 N	18				
Democritus	35 E	62 N	39	Mare Crisium			
Dionysius	17 E	3 N	18	Mare Fecunditatis			
Endymion	56 E	54 N	125	Mare Frigoris			
Eudoxus	16 E	44 N	70	Mare Humboldtianum			
Franklin	47 E	39 N	56	Mare Marginis			
Galle	22 E	56 N	21	Mare Serenitatis			
Gauss	79 E	36 N	181	Mare Spumans			
Geminus	57 E	34 N	86	Mare Tranquillitatis			
Godin	10 E	2 N	35	Mare Undarum			
Grove	33 E	40 N	27	Mare Vaporum			
Hahn	74 E	31 N	84				
Hercules	39 E	47 N	67	Montes Apenninus			
Hooke	55 E	41 N	37	Montes Caucasus			
Julius Caesar	15 E	9 N	90	Montes Haemus			
Littrow	31 E	21 N	31				
Lyell	41 E	14 N	32	Palus Putredinis			
Macrobius	46 E	21 N	64	Palus Somnii			
Manilius	9 E	14 N	39				
Maraldi	35 E	19 N	40	Rima Ariadaeus			
Maskelyne	30 E	2 N	24	Rima Hyginus			
C. Mayer	17 E	63 N	38				
Menelaus	16 E	16 N	27	Rupes Cauchy			
Mercurius	65 E	46 N	68				
Messala	60 E	39 N	124	Sinus Medii			
Plana	28 E	42 N	44				
Plinius	24 E	15 N	42	Vallis Alpes			

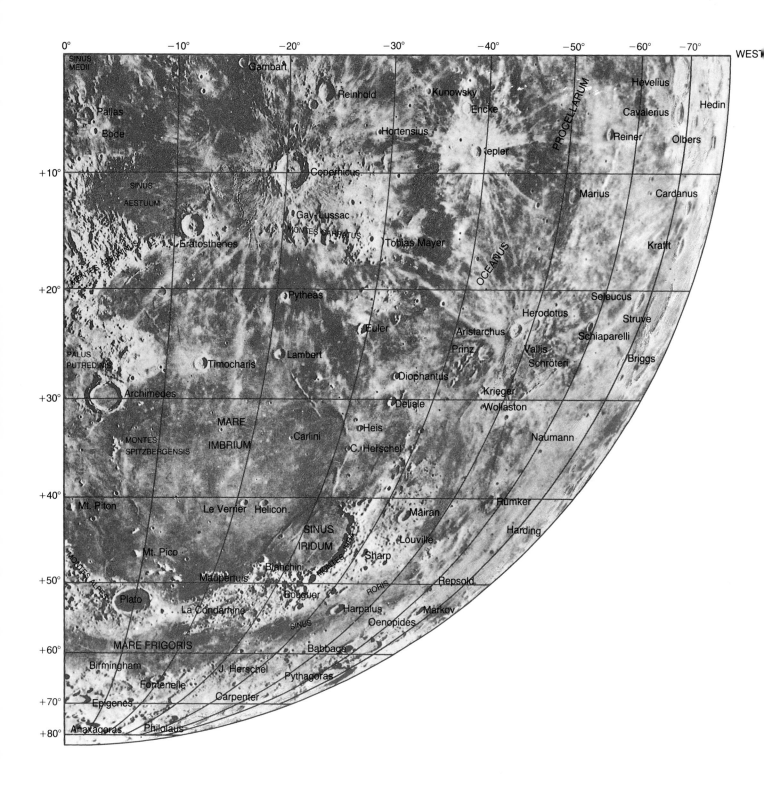

0°　−10°　−20°　−30°　−40°　−50°　−60°　−70°　WEST

SINUS MEDII

Gambart

Pallas

Bode

Reinhold

Kunowsky

Encke

Hortensius

Kepler

PROCELLARUM

Hevelius

Cavalerius

Reiner

Hedin

Olbers

+10°

SINUS AESTUUM

Copernicus

Gay-Lussac

MONTES CARPATUS

Eratosthenes

MONTES APENNINUS

Tobias Mayer

OCEANUS

Marius

Cardanus

Krafft

+20°

Pytheas

Euler

Herodotus

Aristarchus

Prinz

Vallis Schröteri

Seleucus

Struve

Schiaparelli

Briggs

PALUS PUTREDINIS

Lambert

Timocharis

Diophantus

Krieger

Wollaston

+30°

Archimedes

Delisle

Naumann

MARE IMBRIUM

Carlini

Heis

C. Herschel

MONTES SPITZBERGENSIS

+40°

Mt. Piton

Le Verrier

Helicon

Mairan

Rümker

Harding

Mt. Pico

SINUS IRIDUM

Louville

Sharp

Repsold

MONTES JURA

Bianchini

+50°

Maupertuis

Bouguer

RORIS

Harpalus

Markov

La Condamine

Oenopides

SINUS

Plato

MONTES ALPES

Babbage

+60°

MARE FRIGORIS

Birmingham

J. Herschel

Pythagoras

Fontenelle

Carpenter

+70°

Epigenes

Anaxagoras

Philolaus

+80°

NORTH

(b) *Quadrant II*: north-west

Crater	Longitude	Latitude	Diameter (km)	Crater	Longitude	Latitude	Diameter (km)
Anaxagoras	10 W	74 N	52	Oenopides	64 W	57 N	69
Archimedes	4 W	30 N	83	Olbers	76 W	7 N	71
Aristarchus	47 W	24 N	40	Pallas	1 W	6 N	50
Babbage	57 W	60 N	144	Philolaus	32 W	72 N	71
Bianchini	34 W	49 N	40	Plato	9 W	51 N	100
Birmingham	11 W	64 N	98	Prinz	44 W	26 N	52
Bode	2 W	7 N	19	Pythagoras	62 W	63 N	128
Bouguer	36 W	52 N	23	Pytheas	21 W	20 N	20
Briggs	69 W	26 N	39	Reiner	55 W	7 N	30
Cardanus	72 W	13 N	50	Reinhold	23 W	3 N	48
Carlini	24 W	34 N	11	Repsold	77 W	51 N	107
Carpenter	51 W	70 N	58	Schiaparelli	59 W	23 N	24
Cavalerius	67 W	5 N	60	Seleucus	67 W	21 N	43
Copernicus	20 W	10 N	93	Sharp	40 W	46 N	40
Delisle	35 W	30 N	25	Struve	77 W	23 N	183
Diophantus	34 W	28 N	18	Timocharis	13 W	27 N	34
Encke	37 W	5 N	29	Tobias Mayer	29 W	16 N	33
Epigenes	5 W	67 N	55	Wollaston	47 W	31 N	10
Eratosthenes	11 W	14 N	58				
Euler	29 W	23 N	28				
Fontenelle	18 W	63 N	38	**Other features**			
Gambart	15 W	1 N	26				
Gay-Lussac	21 W	14 N	26	Mare Frigoris			
Harding	72 W	43 N	23	Mare Imbrium			
Harpalus	43 W	53 N	40				
Hedin	76 W	3 N	143	Montes Alpes			
Heis	32 W	32 N	14	Montes Apenninus			
Helicon	23 W	40 N	25	Montes Carpatus			
Herodotus	50 W	23 N	35	Montes Jura			
C. Herschel	31 W	34 N	13	Montes Spitzbergensis			
J. Herschel	41 W	62 N	156				
Hevelius	68 W	2 N	118	Oceanus Procellarum			
Hortensius	28 W	6 N	15				
Kepler	38 W	8 N	31	Palus Putredinis			
Krafft	73 W	17 N	51				
Krieger	45 W	29 N	22	Pico			
Kunowsky	32 W	3 N	18	Piton			
La Condamine	28 W	53 N	37				
Lambert	21 W	26 N	30	Rümker			
Le Verrier	21 W	40 N	21				
Louville	46 W	44 N	36	Sinus Aestuum			
Mairan	43 W	42 N	41	Sinus Iridum			
Marius	51 W	12 N	41	Sinus Medii			
Markov	63 W	53 N	41	Sinus Roris			
Maupertuis	27 W	50 N	46				
Naumann	62 W	35 N	10	Vallis Schröteri			

SOUTH

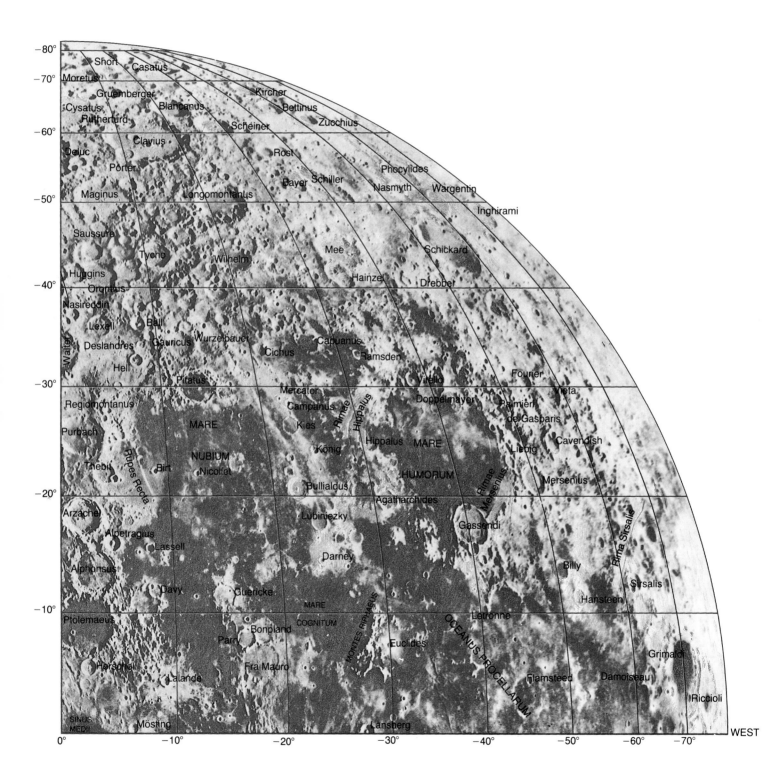

-80°
-70°
-60°
-50°
-40°
-30°
-20°
-10°

Short
Casatus
Moretus
Gruemberger
Kircher
Cysatus
Blancanus
Bettinus
Rutherford
Scheiner
Zuochius
Deluc
Clavius
Rost
Porter
Phocylides
Maginus
Bayer Schiller
Nasmyth
Wargentin
Longomontanus
Inghirami

Saussure
Tycho
Mee
Schickard
Huggins
Wilhelm
Orontius
Hainzel
Drebbel
Nasireddin
Lexell
Ball
Deslandres
Gauricus
Wurzelbauer
Capuanus
Hell
Cichus
Pitatus
Ramsden
Regiomontanus
Mercator
Vitello
Fourier
Purbach
Campanus
Doppelmayer
Vieta
Thebit
Kies
Hippalus
Palmieri
de Gasparis
MARE
König
Hippalus
Cavendish
Birt
NUBIUM
MARE
Liebig
Nicollet
HUMORUM
Mersenius
Arzachel
Bullialdus
Agatharchides
Alpetragius
Lubiniezky
Gassendi
Lassell
Darney
Billy
Alphonsus
Hansteen
Davy
Guericke
Sirsalis
Ptolemaeus
MARE
Latronne
Bonpland
COGNITUM
Parry
Euclides
Grimaldi
Herschel
Fra Mauro
Flamsteed
Damoiseau
Lalande
Riccioli
SINUS
MEDII
Mösting
Lansberg

Walter
Rupes Recta
Rimae
Hippalus
Rimae
Mersenius
Rima Sirsalis
MONTES RIPHAEUS
OCEANUS PROCELLARIUM

0° -10° -20° -30° -40° -50° -60° -70°

WEST

(c) *Quadrant III*: south-west

Crater	Longitude	Latitude	Diameter (km)	Crater	Longitude	Latitude	Diameter (km)
Agatharchides	31 W	20 S	49	Maginus	6 W	50 S	163
Alpetragius	4 W	16 S	40	Mee	35 W	44 S	132
Alphonsus	3 W	13 S	118	Mercator	26 W	29 S	47
Arzachel	2 W	18 S	104	Mersenius	49 W	21 S	82
Ball	8 W	36 S	40	Moretus	5 W	71 S	114
Bayer	35 W	52 S	47	Mösting	6 W	1 S	26
Bettinus	45 W	63 S	71	Nasireddin	0 W	41 S	51
Billy	50 W	14 S	46	Nasmyth	56 W	50 S	77
Birt	8 W	22 S	17	Nicollet	12 W	22 S	15
Blancanus	22 W	64 S	105	Orontius	4 W	40 S	110
Bonpland	17 W	8 S	60	Palmieri	47 W	29 S	40
Bullialdus	22 W	21 S	59	Parry	15 W	8 S	46
Campanus	28 W	28 S	48	Phocylides	57 W	53 S	114
Capuanus	27 W	34 S	60	Pitatus	13 W	30 S	105
Casatus	30 W	73 S	110	Porter	10 W	56 S	52
Cavendish	54 W	25 S	56	Ptolemaeus	2 W	9 S	153
Cichus	21 W	33 S	40	Purbach	2 W	26 S	118
Clavius	14 W	58 S	225	Ramsden	32 W	33 S	24
Cysatus	6 W	66 S	49	Regiomontanus	1 W	28 S	118
Damoiseau	61 W	5 S	36	Riccioli	74 W	3 S	152
Darney	23 W	15 S	15	Rost	34 W	56 S	49
Davy	8 W	12 S	35	Rutherfurd	12 W	61 S	50
de Gasparis	51 W	26 S	32	Saussure	4 W	43 S	56
Deluc	3 W	55 S	47	Scheiner	27 W	60 S	110
Deslandres	5 W	32 S	235	Schickard	55 W	44 S	227
Doppelmayer	41 W	28 S	64	Schiller	40 W	52 S	125
Drebbel	49 W	41 S	30	Short	7 W	75 S	71
Euclides	29 W	7 S	13	Sirsalis	60 W	12 S	44
Flamsteed	44 W	4 S	21	Thebit	4 W	22 S	55
Fourier	53 W	30 S	51	Tycho	11 W	43 S	84
Fra Mauro	17 W	6 S	94	Vieta	56 W	29 S	87
Gassendi	40 W	17 S	110	Vitello	38 W	30 S	45
Gauricus	13 W	34 S	80	Wargentin	60 W	50 S	84
Grimaldi	68 W	5 S	220	Wilhelm	21 W	43 S	107
Gruemberger	10 W	67 S	94	Wurzelbauer	16 W	34 S	82
Guericke	14 W	11 S	60	Zucchius	50 W	61 S	64
Hainzel	34 W	41 S	70				
Hansteen	52 W	11 S	45	**Other features**			
Hell	8 W	32 S	33				
Herschel	2 W	6 S	41	Mare Cognitum			
Hippalus	30 W	25 S	58	Mare Humorum			
Huggins	1 W	41 S	63	Mare Nubium			
Inghirami	68 W	47 S	90				
Kies	23 W	26 S	44	Montes Riphaeus			
Kircher	45 W	67 S	72				
König	25 W	24 S	22	Oceanus Procellarum			
Lalande	9 W	4 S	24				
Lansberg	27 W	0 S	40	Rimae Hippalus			
Lassell	8 W	15 S	23	Rimae Mersenius			
Letronne	42 W	11 S	120	Rima Sirsalis			
Lexell	4 W	36 S	63				
Liebig	48 W	24 S	38	Rupes Recta (Straight Wall)			
Longomontanus	22 W	49 S	145				
Lubiniezky	24 W	18 S	44	Sinus Medii			

SOUTH

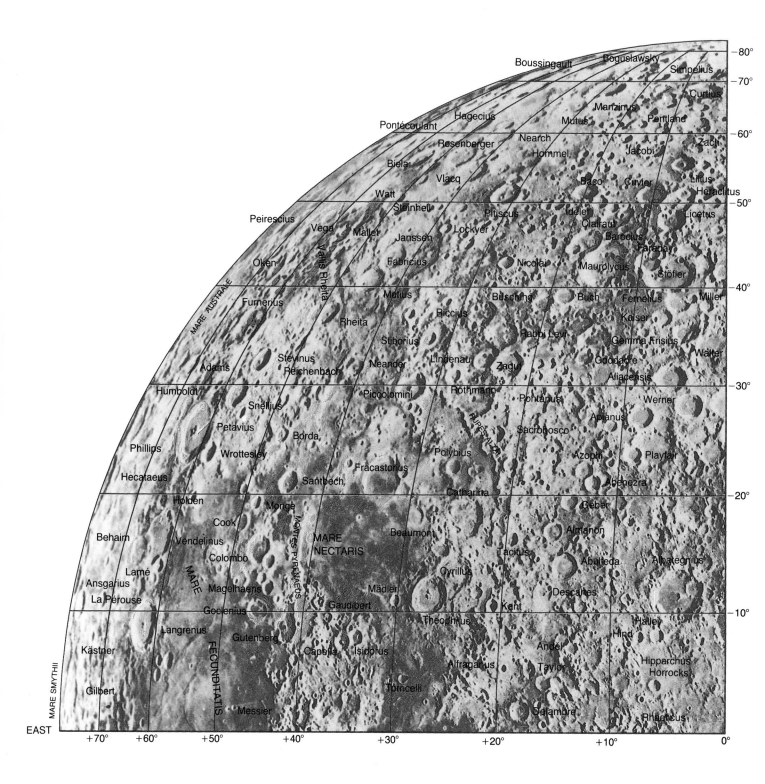

−80°
−70°
−60°
−50°
−40°
−30°
−20°
−10°

Boussingault
Boguslawsky
Simpelius
Curtius
Manzinus
Pentland
Mutus
Zach
Hagecius
Pontécoulant
Nearch
Jacobi
Rosenberger
Hommel
Biela
Baco
Cuvier
Lilius
Vlacq
Heraclitus
Watt
Steinheil
Pitiscus
Ideler
Licetus
Peirescius
Clairaut
Vega
Lockyer
Barocius
Mäller
Faraday
Oken
Janssen
Nicolai
Maurolycus
Stöfler
Fabricius
Metius
Büsching
Buch
Fernelius
Miller
Furnerius
Riccius
Kaiser
Rheita
Rabbi Levi
Gemma Frisius
Stiborius
Goodacre
Walter
Stevinus
Neander
Lindenau
Zagut
Adams
Reichenbach
Aliacensis
Humboldt
Piccolomini
Rothmann
Werner
Snellius
Pontanus
Apianus
Petavius
Borda
Sacrobosco
Phillips
Polybius
Azophi
Playfair
Wrottesley
Fracastorius
Abenezra
Hecataeus
Santbech
Catharina
Holden
Monge
Geber
Behaim
Cook
Beaumont
Almanon
Vendelinus
Tacitus
Abulfeda
Albategnius
Lamé
Colombo
MARE
Cyrillus
Descartes
Ansgarius
Magelhaens
NECTARIS
Kant
La Pérouse
Mädler
Halley
Goclenius
Theophilus
Hind
Kästner
Langrenus
Gaudibert
Andël
Hipparchus
Gutenberg
Capella
Isidorus
Alfraganus
Taylor
Horrocks
Gilbert
Messier
Torricelli
Delambre
Rhaeticus

MARE AUSTRALE
Vallis Rheita
RUPES ALTAI
MONTES PYRENAEUS
MARE
FECUNDITATIS
MARE SMYTHII

EAST
+70° +60° +50° +40° +30° +20° +10° 0°

(d) *Quadrant IV*: south-east

Crater	Longitude	Latitude	Diameter (km)	Crater	Longitude	Latitude	Diameter (km)
Abenezra	12 E	21 S	42	Mädler	30 E	11 S	28
Abulfeda	14 E	14 S	62	Magelhaens	44 E	12 S	38
Adams	68 E	32 S	66	Mallet	54 E	45 S	58
Albategnius	4 E	11 S	136	Manzinus	27 E	68 S	98
Alfraganus	19 E	5 S	21	Maurolycus	14 E	42 S	114
Aliacensis	5 E	31 S	80	Messier	48 E	2 S	10
Almanon	15 E	17 S	49	Metius	43 E	41 S	88
Anděl	12 E	10 S	34	Miller	1 E	39 S	61
Ansgarius	79 E	13 S	94	Monge	48 E	19 S	37
Apianus	8 E	27 S	66	Mutus	30 E	64 S	78
Azophi	13 E	22 S	48	Nasireddin	0 E	41 S	51
Baco	19 E	51 S	70	Neander	40 E	31 S	52
Barocius	17 E	45 S	82	Nearch	39 E	58 S	75
Beaumont	29 E	18 S	53	Nicolai	26 E	42 S	42
Behaim	80 E	17 S	56	Oken	76 E	44 S	72
Biela	51 E	55 S	76	Peirescius	68 E	47 S	62
Boguslawsky	43 E	73 S	97	Pentland	12 E	65 S	56
Borda	47 E	25 S	44	Petavius	61 E	25 S	177
Boussingault	55 E	70 S	130	Phillips	76 E	27 S	100
Buch	18 E	39 S	54	Piccolomini	32 E	30 S	89
Büsching	20 E	38 S	52	Pitiscus	31 E	50 S	82
Capella	35 E	8 S	45	Playfair	8 E	23 S	48
Catharina	23 E	18 S	97	Polybius	25 E	22 S	42
Clairaut	14 E	48 S	75	Pontanus	14 E	29 S	54
Colombo	46 E	15 S	78	Pontécoulant	66 E	58 S	91
Cook	49 E	17 S	47	Rabbi Levi	24 E	35 S	81
Curtius	5 E	67 S	95	Reichenbach	48 E	30 S	71
Cuvier	10 E	50 S	75	Rhaeticus	5 E	0 S	46
Cyrillus	24 E	13 S	93	Rheita	47 E	37 S	70
Delambre	18 E	2 S	53	Riccius	26 E	37 S	70
Descartes	16 E	12 S	48	Rosenberger	43 E	55 S	96
Fabricius	42 E	43 S	78	Rothmann	28 E	31 S	43
Faraday	9 E	42 S	69	Sacrobosco	17 E	24 S	96
Fernelius	5 E	38 S	70	Santbech	44 E	21 S	64
Fracastorius	33 E	21 S	124	Simpelius	15 E	73 S	70
Furnerius	60 E	36 S	125	Snellius	56 E	29 S	83
Gaudibert	38 E	11 S	28	Steinheil	46 E	49 S	67
Geber	14 E	19 S	46	Stevinus	54 E	33 S	74
Gemma Frisius	13 E	34 S	88	Stiborius	32 E	35 S	43
Gilbert	76 E	3 S	107	Stöfler	6 E	41 S	137
Goclenius	45 E	10 S	60	Tacitus	19 E	16 S	40
Goodacre	14 E	33 S	46	Taylor	17 E	5 S	38
Gutenberg	41 E	9 S	71	Theophilus	26 E	11 S	100
Hagecius	47 E	60 S	76	Torricelli	28 E	5 S	20
Halley	6 E	8 S	36	Vega	63 E	45 S	76
Hecataeus	79 E	22 S	125	Vendelinus	62 E	16 S	147
Heraclitus	6 E	49 S	90	Vlacq	39 E	53 S	89
Hind	7 E	8 S	29	Walter	1 E	33 S	135
Hipparchus	5 E	5 S	150	Watt	49 E	50 S	66
Holden	62 E	19 S	47	Werner	3 E	28 S	70
Hommel	33 E	55 S	125	Wrottesley	57 E	24 S	57
Horrocks	6 E	4 S	31	Zach	5 E	61 S	71
Humboldt	80 E	27 S	204	Zagut	22 E	32 S	84
Ideler	22 E	49 S	39				
Isidorus	33 E	8 S	39				
Jacobi	11 E	57 S	68	**Other features**			
Janssen	42 E	45 S	190				
Kaiser	7 E	36 S	53	Mare Australe			
Kant	20 E	11 S	32	Mare Fecunditatis			
Kästner	79 E	7 S	120	Mare Nectaris			
Lamé	64 E	15 S	84	Mare Smythii			
Langrenus	61 E	9 S	133				
La Pérouse	77 E	11 S	78	Montes Pyrenaeus			
Licetus	7 E	47 S	75				
Lilius	6 E	55 S	61	Rupes Altai			
Lindenau	25 E	32 S	53				
Lockyer	37 E	46 S	34	Vallis Rheita			

longitude and *libration in latitude*, which together allow us to see a total of about 59% of the Moon's surface (although only 50% at any one time, of course). Libration in longitude is due to the slight ellipticity of the Moon's orbit. This causes the speed at which the Moon appears to move around the Earth to vary; however, the speed of rotation of the Moon on its axis is constant. The net result is that the Moon appears to rotate back and forth around its axis by about ±7°.5 east and west. Libration in latitude occurs because the Moon's equator is inclined to its orbital plane by about ±6°.5. Tables showing the amount of libration at a given time are published in yearly almanacs.

Surface features

The lunar maps (Figure 16 on pages 86 to 93) show the part of the Moon visible from the Earth. The maps are presented with south at the top; this is the orientation as seen by a northern hemisphere observer in a standard, inverting astronomical telescope. West is then shown to the right, following the modern International Astronomical Union definition of west on the Moon (by the earlier convention, west on the Moon corresponded to west in the sky as seen from the Earth, i.e. towards the western horizon).

Most major surface features are named after famous people, particularly astronomers and other scientists, a practice begun by the Italian astronomer Giovanni Riccioli in 1651. Small features are labelled by the name of a nearby large feature, followed by one or more letters, although individual names have been given to certain small features of particular interest.

Maria. These are the darker and smoother parts of the surface. They were so named by early observers who thought that they were expanses of water (*maria* is Latin for 'seas'; singular *mare*). Some of the maria fill lowland basins that are nearly circular (e.g. Mare Crisium or Mare Imbrium), whereas others are quite irregular in outline (e.g. Mare Frigoris). The dark, relatively smooth material appears in most cases to be basaltic lava that erupted from the Moon's deep interior mainly between 4000 million and 3000 million years ago. The maria form the 'Man in the Moon' pattern visible to the naked eye on the Moon's near side. The lunar far side has been surveyed by spacecraft; it contains no large mare areas, but craters and bright highlands abound.

Craters. These are the most abundant features on the Moon. Craters are roughly circular or hexagonal in outline, with a central depression surrounded by raised walls. Numerous craters can be seen through even a low-power pair of binoculars. The largest craters have diameters of many hundreds of kilometres, while the smallest are too small to be visible in even the largest telescopes. Small craters are commonly bowl-shaped, while large craters have flat floors. Where craters overlap, it is almost always the smaller crater that is superimposed on the larger one.

Large craters often have a mountain or group of mountains at their centre, while the largest craters have an even more complex interior structure, consisting of concentric rings of mountains. There appears to be no basic difference – other than size – between the largest craters and the circular mare basins.

There has been much controversy over the origin of lunar craters. Currently, most researchers accept that most of the craters were formed by the impact of meteoroids and small asteroids striking the lunar surface at speeds in excess of $10 \, \text{km s}^{-1}$. However, many craters show evidence of later modification by volcanic activity or by forces of tension or compression at the surface. A few craters are almost certainly of volcanic origin; some of these are found at the heads of sinuous rilles or on domes (see below). Generally they are less than 10 km in diameter, have subdued rims, are often elongated in shape and tend to appear in chains.

Highlands. The brighter parts of the lunar surface are systematically higher and rougher than the mare surfaces, and are known to be generally older. Many of the Apollo rock samples from the bright areas are more than 4000 million years old. The highland topography is dominated by large and small craters in various stages of preservation, and the most prominent mountain ranges often form the rims of the circular mare basins.

Rays. These systems of bright streaks radiate across the lunar surface for up to 1000 km from young, prominent craters such as Tycho and Copernicus. They dominate the appearance of the full moon but are scarcely visible under low illumination. Rays are apparently splash patterns from impact craters, and consist either of deposits of material ejected from the main crater or of small secondary impact craters that have churned up the pre-existing surface.

Rilles and faults. There is a variety of well-defined elongated valleys on the lunar surface to which the word 'rille' is applied. Some are sites where part of the lunar surface has subsided between two nearly parallel faults or fractures – these are called *linear rilles*. In places the fractures are curved, being controlled by the stresses around some large central structure such as a circular mare basin, producing what are known as *arcuate rilles*. Faults sometimes occur as individual features, the most famous being the Straight Wall (also known as Rupes Recta) in Mare Nubium, traceable for at least 120 km. It is actually a scarp about 250 m high. The shadow cast by the fault causes the Straight Wall to show as a dark line before full moon; after full moon the face of the fault scarp shows as a bright line.

Perhaps the most striking lunar valleys are the *sinuous rilles*, meandering valleys up to several hundred kilometres long which usually originate in a rimless crater-like structure at their high end, and become shallower and narrower as they wind their way downhill. These are volcanic features, caused either by fast-moving lava flows or by the collapse of roofs over underground lava channels, as occurs on the Earth. In 1971 the Apollo 15 astronauts David Scott and James Irwin drove to the edge of Hadley Rille at the foot of the lunar Apennines and took photographs of the stratification revealed in the valley walls.

Domes. These are low, rounded hills with slopes of only a few degrees, often with a small crater at their summit. They tend to occur in groups, generally in areas that have been volcanically active. Their distinctive shape suggests that they formed from lava that was more viscous (stickier) than the surrounding surface, perhaps with an unusual composition.

Changes on the surface. The ages of the rocks returned by the Apollo missions imply that almost all of the Moon's volcanic activity took place more than 3000 million years ago. Also, the present rate of formation of craters by meteoroid impact is so low that changes are unnoticeable, even through the largest telescopes. Old reports of small permanent changes are now discredited, but more intriguing are the reports of temporary appearances of coloured patches on the surface or occasional obscurations of normally distinct features. These events, known as *transient lunar phenomena* (TLPs), appear in particular areas, notably the craters Aristarchus, Gassendi and Alphonsus. Whether these events are real, perhaps some kind of gas release from the lunar interior, or whether they are an artifact of unusual observing conditions is still debatable.

Observing the Moon

The appearance of a lunar surface feature changes greatly according to the direction from which sunlight falls upon it. The illumination varies over the course of each lunation as the Sun rises, culminates and sets over a given feature. Changes in appearance are the most dramatic when the feature is near the terminator, since shadows are then at their longest and slight changes in relief are easily picked out; it is like observing a road surface at night by the light from a car's headlights.

Libration produces small variations in illumination and viewing geometry from one lunation to the next; these changes are most noticeable for features near the limb and can amount to as much as 20°. The net effect is that a great deal of information can be deduced about the topography of an area by observing it systematically over many lunations around local sunrise and sunset.

By contrast, virtually no topographic detail is discernible near full moon because there are no shadows. However, this is the time to observe albedo differences on the surface, which generally indicate variations in surface structure and composition. Lunar rays are the most obvious high-albedo features, but there are more subtle albedo differences across the dark surfaces of maria. A crater which is prominent near the terminator may appear to vanish close to full moon if its walls and floor are of similar surface structure and composition. Only craters which are young and bright (e.g. Aristarchus or Kepler), or older craters substantially filled with mare lavas to give dark floors (e.g. Grimaldi or Plato), are readily identifiable under all illuminations.

Position of the terminator. It is useful to quote the position of the terminator at the time of an observation. Yearly almanacs list the longitude of the morning terminator on the Moon, known as the Sun's selenographic colongitude, symbol S. If libration is ignored, the selenographic colongitude is 270° at new moon, 0° at first quarter, 90° at full moon and 180° at last quarter. The selenographic colongitude increases by about 0°.5 per hour, and by 12°.2 per day.

Repetition of the same phase. The mean lunation lasts just over $29\frac{1}{2}$ days, but the length of a given lunation can range between $29\frac{1}{4}$ and $29\frac{3}{4}$ days. Hence the same phase of illumination near the same time of night recurs after two lunations (59 d), $1\frac{1}{2}$ hours later in the evening on average; then again after four lunations and 3 hours later in the evening, and so on up to 15 lunations (442 d 23 h) when the phase recurs 1 hour earlier in the evening.

The mean interval from one lunar perigee to the next, known as the mean anomalistic month, is 27.554 55 d, and recurs at the same phase after 14 lunations, or about $1\frac{1}{4}$ months later in the following year, so that optimum conditions gradually disappear for a time.

Objects near the limb. Features near the limb are best placed for observation when a suitable viewing phase coincides with a favourable libration that brings them as far as possible onto the visible disk. Limb features are nearest the centre of the disk when their position angle (measured from the Moon's north pole) added to the position angle of the Moon's axis is closest to the position angle of maximum libration as tabulated, for example, in the *Handbook* of the British Astronomical Association.

Position angle of the Moon's axis. This oscillates some 25° each side of the hour circle over the course of a month, the extremes occurring as the Moon crosses the celestial equator, i.e. when the Moon's RA is 0h or 12h. The position angle is zero when the Moon is around RA 6h and 18h. The

Table 14. The most favourable times for observing the Moon at the principal phases.

	Thin crescent (3–4 days)	First quarter	Full moon	Last quarter	Thin crescent (25–26 days)
N hemisphere	End of April	March	December	September	End of July
S hemisphere	End of October	September	June	March	End of January

position angle of the Moon's axis of rotation is tabulated for each day in the *Astronomical Almanac*.

Best altitude conditions. For any given phase, the Moon is highest in the sky (and therefore visible for longer under better seeing conditions) at one time of the year only. Table 14 indicates the most favourable times for observing the principal phases from the northern and southern hemispheres.

THE PLANETS AND THEIR SATELLITES

Nine major planets orbit the Sun, and all but Mercury and Venus have at least one natural satellite. In addition there are a great many minor planets, commonly known as asteroids, plus countless comets and smaller pieces of orbiting debris.

The four inner planets, Mercury, Venus, Earth and Mars, are relatively small, rocky bodies that are collectively termed the *terrestrial planets*. Jupiter, Saturn, Uranus and Neptune are often known as the *gas giants* because of their composition and size. Pluto, wandering at the edge of the Solar System, is in many ways unlike any of the other planets.

Mercury and Venus are also known as the *inferior planets*, because their orbits are closer to the Sun than that of the Earth. Likewise the planets from Mars outwards are known as the *superior planets*, since their orbits are outside the orbit of the Earth.

The orbits of all the planets are elliptical, some more so than others. The ellipticity of Pluto's orbit is so great that it actually crosses that of Neptune. The distances of the planets from the Sun are often expressed in terms of the Earth's distance, the astronomical unit.

Astronomical unit (AU), the average distance of the Earth from the Sun, is the basic unit of length in the Solar System, and is also the base-line for measurements of the parallax of stars. As defined by the International Astronomical Union, the astronomical unit is 149 597 870 km. The term *unit distance* is sometimes used to refer to a distance of 1 AU. The *light time for unit distance* is the time taken for a beam of light to cover 1 AU; it is almost exactly 499 seconds (8.3 minutes). Another important quantity in measuring the scale of the Solar System is the *solar parallax*, which is the angle subtended by the Earth's equatorial radius as seen from a distance of 1 AU. As defined by the International Astronomical Union, the solar parallax is 8.794 148 seconds of arc.

Planetary orbits

The planets, and indeed all orbiting bodies, obey the three *laws of planetary motion* established by the German mathematician Johannes Kepler between 1609 and 1618:

1. The orbit of each planet around the Sun is an ellipse, with the Sun at one focus.
2. Each planet moves along its orbit so that the radius vector (the line joining the planet and the Sun) sweeps out equal areas in equal times; this means that the closer the planet is to the Sun, the faster it moves.
3. The square of the orbital period of each planet in years equals the cube of its mean distance from the Sun in astronomical units.

In the elliptical planetary orbit shown in Figure 17, the line AB across its greatest diameter is the major axis, and the line DE across its smallest diameter is the minor axis; they are at right angles to each other, and meet at the centre of the ellipse, C. AC or BC is the semi-major axis; this is the mean distance of the planet from the Sun. S is the focus of the ellipse at which the Sun lies; F is the empty focus, where nothing lies. P is a planet moving along its orbit. The line PS is the radius vector.

The eccentricity of an ellipse is given by dividing the distance SF by AB. For most planets the eccentricity is very small, being 0.017 for the Earth, and 0.007 for Venus, the lowest of all. Only Mercury (0.206) and Pluto (0.25) have orbits that depart appreciably from circles.

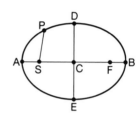

Figure 17. An elliptical planetary orbit.

Perihelion and aphelion. The planet reaches its closest point to the Sun at A in Figure 17. This is termed *perihelion*. The planet is farthest from the Sun at B, known as *aphelion*. The *perihelion distance* (symbol q) and *aphelion distance* (symbol Q) are the distances between the Sun and the planet on these occasions. For an orbit around the Earth, the closest and farthest points are called *perigee* and *apogee*, respectively. For an orbit around Jupiter the corresponding points are termed *perijove* and *apojove*; similar terms are used for other planets.

Orbital elements. An orbit is described by six quantities, known as *elements*. They are the semi-major axis a, the eccentricity e, the inclination i, the longitude of the ascending node Ω, the longitude of perihelion ϖ, and the time of perihelion passage T or the longitude of the orbiting body L at some other time. For double stars the orbital period P is also given. The semi-major axis and the eccentricity define the size and shape of the orbit, the inclination and the longitude of the ascending node together define the plane of the orbit, and the longitude of perihelion defines the orientation of the orbit. (Sometimes the argument of perihelion, ω, is given; this is added to the longitude of the ascending node to find the longitude of perihelion.)

For orbits that are subject to perturbations, elements are given for a specific time; these are called *osculating elements*, and they allow the position of the orbiting object to be calculated for times close to the epoch of osculation.

Aspects of the planets. As seen from the Earth, the planets reach certain positions relative to the Sun that are known as *aspects*. For the superior planets, the two most significant aspects are opposition and conjunction (Figure 18).

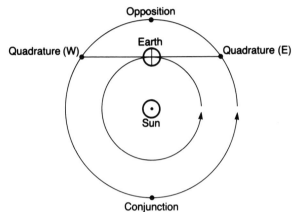

Figure 18. Aspects of the orbit of a superior planet.

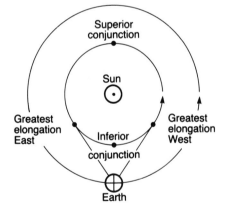

Figure 19. Aspects of the orbit of an inferior planet.

At *opposition* a planet is opposite the Sun in the sky, i.e. its celestial longitude and the Sun's differ by 180°. At opposition a planet is visible all night, and lies on the meridian at midnight. Opposition is the best time to observe the superior planets, since they are then at their closest to the Earth. As seen through a telescope, the apparent size of a planet which has a markedly elliptical orbit, such as Mars, varies considerably depending on whether opposition occurs near the time of the planet's perihelion or aphelion. Perihelic oppositions of Mars are the best times for observation.

At *conjunction*, a planet has the same celestial longitude as the Sun and so lies on the far side of the Sun as seen from the Earth. The planet is then obscured by the Sun's glare. When a planet or the Moon is in line with the Sun, at either opposition or conjunction, it is said to be at *syzygy*; the Moon at syzygy is either new or full.

An additional, less important aspect of the superior planets is *quadrature*, when the angle between the planet and the Sun is 90°. At quadrature, the superior planets can show a slight phase effect; the phase is most noticeable for Mars, which appears distinctly gibbous around this time.

The inferior planets, Mercury and Venus, cannot come to opposition or quadrature, but they have two types of conjunction: *inferior conjunction*, when they lie between the Earth and Sun, and *superior conjunction*, when they lie on the far side of the Sun (Figure 19). The widest angular separation of Mercury and Venus from the Sun is known as *greatest elongation*: either greatest elongation west (in the morning sky) or greatest elongation east (in the evening sky).

Planetary motions

The planets orbit the Sun from west to east, known as *direct motion*. This is the usual direction of motion in the Solar System, although some comets orbit the Sun in the opposite direction, known as *retrograde* motion. Some of the moons of the outer planets also have retrograde orbits.

Around the time of opposition, a superior planet can appear to move temporarily retrograde as the Earth, with its faster orbital motion, catches the planet up and overtakes it. The planet seems to perform a backwards loop in the sky. The points where the planet is changing from direct motion to retrograde motion and back again are called the *stationary points*.

Orbital periods. A planet's orbital period is usually measured relative to the background stars on the celestial sphere; this is known as its *sidereal period*, and can be thought of as the planet's 'year'. The planet's orbital period as seen from the Earth is called its *synodic period*; this is the time taken for the planet to return to a specific aspect, such as conjunction or opposition. The synodic period differs from the sidereal period because the Earth is itself moving in orbit around the Sun. For a moon, the synodic period is the time between successive conjunctions or oppositions as seen from its parent planet.

Visibility of the planets

Of the planets in the Solar System, only Mercury, Venus, Mars, Jupiter and Saturn are naked-eye objects – indeed, they were the only planets known to ancient astronomers. Uranus, which can reach mag. 5.5, is just visible to the naked eye, provided one knows where to look; it is easily found with binoculars. The minor planet Vesta can also be seen with the naked eye when at its best (mag. 5.2), and is well within the reach of binoculars, as are some other minor planets. Neptune, at mag. 8, is a binocular object, but Pluto, at mag. 14, needs a large telescope to be seen at all.

Continued on p. 100

Table 15. Observational data for the planets.

Planet	Angular equatorial diameter					Mean visual magnitude[a]
	at unit distance (1 AU) "	at min. distance "	at max. distance "	at mean greatest elongation "	at mean opposition distance "	
Mercury	6.7	13.0	4.5	7.8	—	0.0
Venus	16.7	65.4	9.6	25.2	—	−4.4
Mars	9.4	25.7	3.5	—	17.9	−2.0
Jupiter	196.9	50.0	30.4	—	46.8	−2.7
Saturn	165.5	20.7	14.9	—	19.4	+0.7[b]
Uranus	70.0	4.1	3.3	—	3.9	+5.5
Neptune	67.0	2.3	2.1	—	2.3	+7.8
Pluto	3.1	—	—	—	0.1	+14.0

[a] Greatest elongation for Mercury and Venus, mean opposition distance for Mars to Pluto.
[b] With rings closed; −0.2 with rings open.

Table 16. Planetary orbital data.

Planet	Mean distance from Sun (AU)	Mean distance from Sun (10⁶ km)	Min. distance from Sun (AU)	Max. distance from Sun (AU)	Eccentricity	Inclination to ecliptic (degrees)
Mercury	0.387	57.9	0.308	0.467	0.206	7.0
Venus	0.723	108.2	0.718	0.728	0.007	3.4
Earth	1.000	149.6	0.983	1.017	0.017	0.0
Mars	1.524	227.9	1.381	1.666	0.093	1.9
Jupiter	5.203	778.3	4.951	5.455	0.048	1.3
Saturn	9.539	1427.0	9.009	10.069	0.056	2.5
Uranus	19.182	2869.6	18.275	20.089	0.047	0.8
Neptune	30.058	4496.6	29.800	30.317	0.009	1.8
Pluto	39.44	5900.1	29.58	49.3	0.25	17.1

Table 17. Planetary periods and motions.

Planet	Sidereal period	Mean synodic period (d)	Mean orbital velocity (km s⁻¹)	Sidereal mean daily motion (degrees)	Sidereal period of axial rotation	Inclination of equator to orbit (degrees)
Mercury	87.969 d	115.88	47.87	4.092	58.65 d	0.0
Venus	224.701 d	583.92	35.02	1.602	243.01 d (R)	177.34
Earth	365.256 d	—	29.79	0.986	23.934 h	23.45
Mars	686.980 d	779.94	24.13	0.524	24.623 h	25.19
Jupiter	11.862 y	398.88	13.06	0.083	9.842 h	3.13
Saturn	29.457 y	378.09	9.65	0.033	10.233 h	26.72
Uranus	84.010 y	369.66	6.80	0.012	17.24 h (R)	97.86
Neptune	164.793 y	367.49	5.43	0.006	16.1 h	29.56
Pluto	248.5 y	366.73	4.74	0.004	6.39 d (R)	117.56

R = retrograde. The rotation period given for Jupiter is at its equator (System I). The rotation period for Uranus is that of its magnetic field.

Table 18. Physical data for the planets.

Planet	Equatorial diameter[a] (km)	Mass (Earth=1)	Volume (Earth=1)	Mean density (10³ kg m⁻³)	Oblateness	Surface gravity (Earth=1)	Escape velocity (km s⁻¹)	Geometrical albedo	Colour index B−V
Mercury	4878	0.06	0.06	5.43	0	0.377	4.25	0.11	0.93
Venus	12104	0.82	0.86	5.24	0	0.902	10.36	0.65	0.82
Earth	12756	1.00	1.00	5.52	0.0034	1.000	11.18	0.37	—
Mars	6787	0.11	0.15	3.94	0.0052	0.379	5.02	0.15	1.36
Jupiter	142800	317.83	1323	1.33	0.065	2.69	59.6	0.52	0.83
Saturn	120000	95.16	752	0.70	0.108	1.19	35.6	0.47	1.04
Uranus	50800	14.50	64	1.30	0.030	0.93	21.1	0.51	0.56
Neptune	48600	17.20	54	1.76	0.026	1.22	24.6	0.41	0.41
Pluto	2300	0.002	0.01	c. 2	0	0.03	c. 1	c. 0.3	0.80

[a]Polar diameters: Earth 12 714 km, Mars 6752 km, Jupiter 133 500 km, Saturn 107 100 km, Uranus 49 300 km, Neptune 47 300 km.

Table 19. Planetary satellites.

Planet and satellite		Mean distance from centre of primary (10^3 km)	(planetary radii)	Orbital period (d)	Inclination[a] (degrees)	Eccentricity[b]	Diameter (km)	Reciprocal mass (planet=1)	Density (10^3 kg m^{-3})	Geometric albedo	Mean opposition magnitude
Earth											
	Moon	384.4	60.27	27.3217	5.15	0.055	3476	81.30	3.34	0.12	−12.7
Mars											
I	Phobos	9.38	2.76	0.319	1.0	0.015	27×21.6×18.8		2.2	0.06	11.3
II	Deimos	23.46	6.91	1.262	0.9−2.7	0.001	15×12.2×11.0		1.7	0.07	12.4
Jupiter											
XVI	Metis	128	1.79	0.295	0	0	40			0.05	17.5
XV	Adrastea	129	1.81	0.298	0	0	25×20×15			0.05	19.1
V	Amalthea	181.3	2.54	0.498	0.4	0.003	270×166×150			0.05	14.1
XIV	Thebe	221.9	3.11	0.675	0.8	0.015	110×90			0.05	15.6
I	Io	421.6	5.9	1.769	0.04	0.004	3630	21400	3.57	0.61	5.0
II	Europa	670.9	9.4	3.551	0.47	0.009	3138	39700	2.97	0.64	5.3
III	Ganymede	1070	15.0	7.155	0.21	0.002	5262	12800	1.94	0.42	4.6
IV	Callisto	1883	26.4	16.689	0.51	0.007	4800	17700	1.86	0.20	5.7
XIII	Leda	11094	155.4	238.72	26.1	0.148	16				20.2
VI	Himalia	11480	160.8	250.56	27.6	0.158	186			0.03	14.8
X	Lysithea	11720	164.2	259.22	29.0	0.107	36				18.4
VII	Elara	11737	164.4	259.65	24.8	0.207	76			0.03	16.8
XII	Ananke	21200	296.9	631 (R)	147	0.17	30				18.9
XI	Carme	22600	316.5	692 (R)	164	0.21	40				18.0
VIII	Pasiphae	23500	329.1	735 (R)	145	0.38	50				17.0
IX	Sinope	23700	331.9	758 (R)	153	0.28	36				18.3
Saturn											
XV	Atlas	137.67	2.29	0.602	0.3	0.000	40×20			0.9	18
XVI	Prometheus	139.35	2.32	0.613	0.0	0.003	140×100×80			0.6	16
XVII	Pandora	141.70	2.36	0.629	0.0	0.004	110×90×70			0.9	16
XI	Epimetheus	151.42	2.52	0.694	0.34	0.009	140×120×100			0.8	15
X	Janus	151.47	2.52	0.695	0.14	0.007	220×200×160			0.8	14
I	Mimas	185.52	3.09	0.942	1.53	0.020	392	12500000	1.17	0.5	12.9
II	Enceladus	238.02	3.97	1.370	0.00	0.005	500	7700000	1.24	1.0	11.7
III	Tethys	294.66	4.91	1.888	1.86	0.000	1060	770000	1.26	0.9	10.2
XIII	Telesto	294.66	4.91	1.888	0	0	34×28×26			0.5	18.5
XIV	Calypso	294.66	4.91	1.888	0	0	34×22×22			0.6	18.7
IV	Dione	377.40	6.29	2.737	0.02	0.002	1120	540000	1.44	0.7	10.4
XII	Helene	377.40	6.29	2.737	0.0	0.005	36×32×30			0.7	18
V	Rhea	527.04	8.78	4.518	0.35	0.001	1530	230000	1.33	0.7	9.7
VI	Titan	1221.8	20.36	15.945	0.33	0.029	5150[c]	4200	1.88	0.21	8.3
VII	Hyperion	1481.1	24.69	21.277	0.43	0.104	410×260×220	33000000		0.3	14.2
VIII	Iapetus	3561.3	59.36	79.330	14.72	0.028	1460	300000	1.21	0.05−0.5	10.2−11.9
IX	Phoebe	12952	215.9	550.48 (R)	177	0.163	220			0.06	16.5
Uranus											
VI	Cordelia	49.77	1.96	0.335		0.0	50				
VII	Ophelia	53.79	2.12	0.376		0.01	50				
VIII	Bianca	59.17	2.33	0.435		0.0	50				
IX	Cressida	61.78	2.43	0.464		0.0	60				
X	Desdemona	62.68	2.47	0.474		0.0	60				
XI	Juliet	64.35	2.53	0.493		0.0	80				
XII	Portia	66.09	2.60	0.513		0.0	80				
XIII	Rosalind	69.94	2.75	0.558		0.0	60				
XIV	Belinda	75.26	2.96	0.624		0.0	50				
XV	Puck	86.01	3.39	0.762		0.0	170				
V	Miranda	129.39	5.09	1.413	4.2	0.003	480	500000	1.26	0.27	16.3
I	Ariel	191.02	7.52	2.520	0.3	0.003	1158	55500	1.65	0.34	14.2
II	Umbriel	266.30	10.48	4.144	0.36	0.005	1172	83300	1.44	0.18	14.8
III	Titania	435.91	17.16	8.706	0.14	0.002	1580	14700	1.59	0.27	13.7
IV	Oberon	583.52	22.97	13.463	0.10	0.001	1524	14500	1.50	0.24	13.9
Neptune											
I	Triton	354.29	14.58	5.877 (R)	159.0	0.0	2700	770		0.4	13.5
II	Nereid	5511	226.8	360.2	27.6	0.75	300	5000000			18.7
Pluto											
	Charon	19.13	12.75	6.387	94	0	1200	4.5	c. 2	0.3	16.8

[a] Orbital inclinations are relative to the planet's equator, except for the Moon and Phoebe, which are relative to the ecliptic. The Moon's inclination relative to the Earth's equator ranges from 18°.28 to 28°.58.

[b] The orbital elements of the outer satellites, particularly the eccentricities, are subject to considerable perturbations.

[c] Diameter of solid body; diameter at cloud top is 5550 km.

R=retrograde.

Brightness. The magnitudes of the planets are measured on the same magnitude scale as the stars. The magnitude of a planet can vary widely, depending on its distance from both the Earth and the Sun, and also – for an inferior planet – on its phase. Table 15 gives the magnitudes of the superior planets when at mean opposition distance; the actual values can vary somewhat depending on whether the planet and the Earth are near perihelion or aphelion at the time of opposition (for example, Mars at its best can outshine Jupiter). The brightness of Saturn is strongly affected by the orientation of its rings; when they are tilted towards us at their maximum angle the planet appears over twice as bright as it does when the rings are presented edge-on.

The values given for the inferior planets, Mercury and Venus, are the magnitudes at mean greatest elongation; these are affected by the actual distances of the planets from the Sun at the time. At greatest elongation Mercury and Venus are seen exactly half-illuminated, but this is not the time when they are at their brightest. Mercury attains its maximum magnitude around the time of superior conjunction, when its fully illuminated side is turned towards us; however, this is of only theoretical interest since at these times Mercury is almost impossible to see, being obscured by the Sun's glare.

Venus, on the other hand, is impossible to miss at greatest brilliancy, when it outshines all objects except the Moon and the Sun. This happens between the times of inferior conjunction and greatest elongation, when the planet shows a crescent phase. On these occasions Venus is nearer the Earth than it is at greatest elongation, which more than compensates for its reduced phase. The contrasting behaviour of Mercury and Venus in this respect is accounted for by their very different visible surfaces: bare rock for Mercury, highly reflective cloud for Venus.

Both Mercury and Venus go through a complete cycle of phases from new (at inferior conjunction) to full (at superior conjunction) and back again as they orbit the Sun. The superior planets do not show such a cycle of phases; at most

Table 20. Planetary ring systems.

Planet and ring	Mean distance from centre of planet (10^3 km)	(planetary radii)	Geometric albedo
Jupiter			
Halo	100–122	1.4–1.71	
Main ring	122–129	1.71–1.81	0.05
Gossamer ring	129–215	1.81–3	
Saturn			
D ring	67.0–74.4	1.12–1.24	
C ring	74.4–91.9	1.24–1.53	
B ring	91.9–117.4	1.53–1.96	
A ring	121.9–136.6	2.03–2.28	0.2–0.6
F ring	140.3	2.34	
G ring	170.0	2.83	
E ring	180–480	3–8	
Uranus			
Rings	41.9–51.1	1.65–2.0	0.04

they can appear slightly gibbous around the time of quadrature. The effect is most noticeable with Mars, which can show a phase as pronounced as 84% at quadrature.

The planets are always to be found close to the ecliptic. Hence any bright 'star' near the ecliptic that does not appear on the maps in this Atlas will be a planet (although it could, just possibly, be a nova or a supernova). The co-ordinates of the planets for any particular night can be found from an almanac, and can then be plotted on the appropriate charts in this Atlas.

The data in the accompanying tables are taken from the *Astronomical Almanac* and the *Handbook* of the British Astronomical Association.

MERCURY

Mercury is the innermost planet, and the least conspicuous of those visible to the naked eye. It is only 40% greater in diameter than our Moon. Mercury orbits the Sun in 88 d and spins on its axis in 58.7 d, exactly two-thirds of its orbital period.

As seen from the Earth, Mercury's apparent movement consists of a periodic oscillation of small amplitude from one side of the Sun to the other, so that it is always close to the Sun, preceding or following it by no more than $2\frac{1}{4}$ hours. It can be glimpsed without a telescope, near the horizon in the twilight at dusk or dawn. Owing to the high eccentricity of its orbit, the elongation east or west of the Sun varies considerably, ranging from 17° 50′ at perihelion to a maximum of 27° 50′ at aphelion. Mercury's actual distance from the Sun ranges from 46 million kilometres at perihelion to 70 million kilometres at aphelion.

From north temperate latitudes Mercury is best observed as an evening star in the spring (eastern elongation) and as a morning star in the autumn (western elongation). For observers at south temperate latitudes the planet is seen at its best as an evening star in the autumn (eastern elongation) and as a morning star in the spring (western elongation). Unfortunately Mercury is near perihelion during its most favourable elongations for northern observers; elongations near aphelion occur when the planet is south of the celestial equator, so observers in the southern hemisphere have the best opportunity to study the planet.

Normally, Mercury is a naked-eye object only near greatest elongation. The planet usually appears about ten days before greatest eastern elongation, disappearing six to seven days later as it recedes into the glare of the Sun. The same intervals, in reverse order, apply to western elongation. In the tropics, where the ecliptic is almost overhead and twilight is of brief duration, Mercury is regularly seen without optical aid. But in higher latitudes it is more fugitive, because the inclination of the ecliptic to the horizon is so acute that even at greatest elongation it is difficult for anyone in a built-up area to spot it.

To find Mercury requires a clear sky when the planet is near its greatest elongation, and a flat, unobstructed horizon. The best method is to sweep the area with binoculars.

Once located, Mercury will then become a relatively easy naked-eye object, scintillating like a bright star – for which it might be mistaken – at a low altitude about half an hour immediately after sunset or before sunrise.

Movements of Mercury

The Earth is moving in the same direction as Mercury, though less rapidly, and the two planets return to the same relative position after 116 days. This is the mean synodic period of Mercury (the interval between successive inferior conjunctions). In one terrestrial year there are six elongations – three in the evening and three in the morning – half of which occur when Mercury is south of the Sun in declination.

Starting at greatest elongation east, Mercury is well seen after sunset. It drops back towards the Sun and reaches inferior conjunction when its phase is new and it cannot be seen. Mercury then moves away from the Sun into the morning sky until it reaches greatest elongation west. The interval from greatest elongation east via inferior conjunction to greatest elongation west is about 44 days. After the morning apparition Mercury turns back towards the Sun, swings behind it and sweeps through superior conjunction, when it is directly opposite the Earth, at full phase, but lost in the glare from the Sun. It then reappears in the evening sky and returns to greatest elongation east. The interval from greatest elongation west to greatest elongation east, through superior conjunction, is about 72 days.

At full phase Mercury subtends an apparent angular diameter of around 4.8 arcsec. This increases to as much as 13.0 arcsec at inferior conjunction but, as already mentioned, Mercury cannot be seen at these positions. At greatest elongation, when half the illuminated hemisphere is turned towards the Earth, it subtends about 8.0 arcsec. Mercury's magnitude at greatest elongation varies from −0.7 to +0.7, a result of its changing distance from the Earth and variations in the phase.

Transits of Mercury

If its orbit were exactly in the plane of the ecliptic, Mercury would *transit* (pass in front of) the Sun once in each synodic revolution. But since its orbit is inclined 7° to the ecliptic, the planet usually passes above or below the Sun as seen from the Earth. A transit occurs only when Mercury is near one of its nodes at inferior conjunction. The ascending node corresponds to the position of the Earth on November 10, the descending node to the position on May 8. If inferior conjunction falls near one of these dates, Mercury will be seen as a tiny black spot moving slowly across the face of the Sun.

November transits are more common, repeating at intervals of 7, 13 and 46 years, according to circumstances. May transits recur at intervals of 13 and 46 years. The last transit was on 1986 November 12; the next five will be on 1993 November 6, 1999 November 15, 2003 May 7, 2006 November 8, and 2016 May 9. The length of the chord traversed by the planet in its passage across the Sun's disk determines the duration of a transit, which can last for up to 9 hours.

Observing Mercury

Mercury is best observed by telescope in daylight, since when it is visible to the naked eye it will be close to the horizon, and viewed under unsatisfactory conditions. But locating the planet in full daylight is fraught with difficulty and the would-be observer must adopt the most stringent safety precautions so as not to meet the blinding glare of the Sun. Daylight observation should be undertaken only if the observer has access to a well-adjusted equatorial fitted with accurate setting circles. Even then success is not guaranteed, chiefly because of the ever-present glare of the Sun and the bad seeing in daylight hours.

While experienced observers using apertures as small as 115 mm have been able to identify the principal surface features, including bright spots which may have been the bright ray systems photographed by the US probe Mariner 10, the general experience is one of frustration and disappointment. The poor conditions under which the planet is observed and its small size are usually blamed, but the real reason is that small apertures are quite incapable of resolving the soft smudges that mottle the surface of the planet. Although observers with exceptionally good eyesight have achieved some remarkable results with small telescopes, for most observers an aperture of at least 300 mm is necessary for serious study. Given a good instrument and a reasonable observing site, Mercury can be a challenging and rewarding subject.

The surface of Mercury

Mariner 10 photographed about a third of Mercury's surface. This lunar-like terrain is heavily cratered, with one huge impact basin 1300 km across, and there are extensive scarps which suggest that the planet contracted during its formation. The surface temperature can vary from −170 °C at night to over 400 °C in the daytime.

VENUS

Venus, the brightest of the planets, is the second in order from the Sun, and somewhat easier to observe than Mercury. It is often visible in full daylight, and when at its greatest brilliancy it will cast a distinct shadow under clear, dark skies away from artificial lights.

Of all the planets Venus is most like the Earth in size, with a diameter of 12 100 km, 95% of the Earth's diameter. It can come closer to the Earth than can any other planet, to within 40 million kilometres, yet we can see nothing of its surface because the planet is permanently covered with cloud.

Venus spins on its axis in a retrograde direction in 243 d, longer than its sidereal period of 224.7 d.

Movements of Venus

Inferior conjunctions of Venus occur at intervals of 584 d; greatest elongations occur about 72 days before and after inferior conjunction, when the planet is 45° to 47° from the Sun. The interval between eastern and western elongations is thus a little over 20 weeks, and that between western and eastern elongations is about 63 weeks.

At superior conjunction, when the planet shows full phase, the apparent diameter is only about 10 arcsec; at inferior conjunction it is over 60 arcsec. At elongation, when the phase is 50%, the apparent diameter is about 25 arcsec. Maximum brightness occurs about 36 days from inferior conjunction – that is, about five weeks after greatest elongation east and five weeks before greatest elongation west. Venus is then the brightest object in the sky, after the Sun and Moon, reaching a magnitude of up to −4.7.

Maximum brightness occurs about every eight years, when the planet reaches perihelion at the end of December. At such times it is south of the equator and is best seen as a morning star in the southern hemisphere. The most favourable time for observers in the northern hemisphere is when Venus reaches perihelion in mid-March; although the planet is then rather fainter than at a December perihelion, it is much higher in the sky.

The phases of Venus are visible in any small telescope or good binoculars. There are even reports of the crescent being seen with the naked eye. But in general the phase is all there is to see.

Observing Venus

Venus, like Mercury, is probably best observed in daylight, although excellent views can be obtained in bright twilight. Neither planet can be regarded as a good object to observe. Venus shows a much larger disk, but the telescope reveals only a thick cloud blanket with no distinctive features.

All that is visible is a brilliant, yellowish disk with a faint pattern of markings. The markings originate in the upper level of the cloud deck, about 65 km above the surface. They are prominent in the ultraviolet and show variations, often over the course of a few hours; some spots, however, last for many days. From detailed studies of Y-shaped dark markings centred on the equator it has been found that the upper clouds rotate in a retrograde direction around the planet every 4 days or so. A careful drawing should be made of all markings seen. It is usual to draw Venus with a diameter of 50 mm.

From time to time areas of the planet appear to brighten; any bright patches seen should be accurately recorded. The most contrasty and prominent markings often appear at the horns of the crescent (the *cusps*). These generally take the form of bright patches known as *cusp caps*, surrounded by dark collars or bands. The cusp caps and dark collars show systematic fluctuations in size and brightness, both short- and long-term.

The terminator of Venus is often irregular in shape. Sometimes part of the terminator appears to be flat rather than curved at both crescent and gibbous phases, while near *dichotomy* (50% phase) the northern half of the terminator may appear concave, the southern half convex. Such effects may arise from cloud features near the terminator.

It has long been known that the observed phase of Venus differs from that predicted. This is known as *Schröter's effect*, after the German astronomer Johann Schröter, who described it in the 1790s. In particular it has been found that the calculated date of dichotomy does not agree with the date on which Venus is seen to have a straight terminator. Dichotomy at evening elongation is normally earlier than predicted, while morning dichotomy is later. The cause is unknown. Some authorities attribute it to observational error, others to atmospheric effects.

Another phenomenon to look out for is the *ashen light*, in which the unilluminated (night) side of the planet seems to glow with a feeble luminosity. This is usually seen when Venus is a fairly narrow crescent, near inferior conjunction. It is difficult not to be subjective in observing this appearance, for the eye tends to connect the two cusps, giving the impression that the entire disk can be seen when in fact it cannot. The most useful observations are those made with an occulting bar in the telescope field, so that the illuminated crescent is hidden.

Colour filters are often used in the observation of Venus. Such observations are of value only if carried out on a carefully controlled basis, with a telescope of large aperture, and are the province of the experienced observer.

Transits of Venus

These are very rare, and occur when inferior conjunction is within a few days of June 7 (descending node) or December 8 (ascending node). Five synodic periods of Venus total almost 8 years, so transits take place in pairs 8 years apart. Such pairs occur at intervals of 105.5 and 121.5 years alternately; the last pair took place in 1874 and 1882. The next pair of June transits will occur on 2004 June 7 and 2012 June 5, and the next December pair in 2117 and 2125.

A transit of Venus is interesting and impressive. Accurate timing of the instants of ingress and egress of the planet can be made. The times required are those of first contact (ingress of preceding limb of planet), second contact (ingress of following limb), third contact (egress of preceding limb) and fourth contact (egress of following limb). Timing may be difficult, since the silhouetted disk of Venus is significantly smaller than the true disk as sunlight is refracted through the planet's atmosphere. This causes a *black drop* to link the silhouetted following limb of the planet with the Sun's limb for a few seconds following apparent second contact; a similar effect may be seen a few seconds before third contact.

The atmosphere of Venus is often seen as a bright ring of light surrounding the black disk of the planet during the transit, extending beyond the Sun's limb between first and second contacts and between third and fourth contacts. This is also a result of the refraction of sunlight in the planet's atmosphere.

The surface of Venus

Soviet lander probes have returned images direct from the surface of Venus, and US and Soviet orbiters have mapped the surface by radar to reveal a world of vast plains, slashed by a deep chasm, scarred by extensive cratering, and dominated by two major uplands which tower prodigiously in one place to 11 km above the average level of the surface.

The surface temperature is over 400°C, and the atmospheric pressure is 90 times greater than on Earth at sea level. The atmosphere is chiefly composed of carbon dioxide, which creates a greenhouse effect, while the dazzling clouds contain large quantities of corrosive sulphuric acid.

MARS

Mars is not an easy object to observe telescopically. Unlike the Moon, Jupiter and Saturn, the planet's small angular diameter makes it disappointing to the beginner. Even at its very best, when at perihelic opposition, the apparent diameter of Mars is only half that of Jupiter. However, observations may be made for several months either side of opposition, the exact duration of observability being governed by the experience of the observer and the size of telescope used.

The interval between oppositions of Mars is longer than for any other planet: 780 d, or a little under 26 months. Thus oppositions occur on average every other year. The distance of the planet at opposition varies between 101 million kilometres for aphelic oppositions, which occur around February, and 56 million kilometres for perihelic oppositions, which occur around August. The apparent diameter of the Martian disk at the most favourable perihelic oppositions is 25 arcsec, whereas at aphelic oppositions it is just under 14 arcsec. At conjunction the apparent diameter is less than 4 arcsec.

When close to opposition the planet is a bright naked-eye object; at perihelic opposition Mars reaches a magnitude of −2.8, similar to Jupiter at its best, and even at aphelic opposition the magnitude is −1.0. Mars appears strongly orange in colour, because its surface rocks contain large amounts of iron oxide.

Extremely favourable oppositions of Mars occur at intervals of 15 and 17 years, the last being 1988 September 28 and the next 2003 August 27. Mars can show a phase which is most pronounced near quadrature, when 84% of the disk is illuminated.

Mars has two tiny satellites, Phobos and Deimos. Both are faint, magnitudes 10.5 and 11.5 at best, and they never stray far from the overwhelming glare of their parent planet. To see them in a moderate aperture, Mars must be placed outside the field of view or be hidden by an occulting bar. Both satellites are irregular in shape, and spacecraft observations have shown that they appear to be captured asteroids.

The thin atmosphere of Mars is composed of about 95% carbon dioxide, 2% nitrogen and 1–2% argon, with a pressure of about 6 millibars at the surface, similar to the pressure of the Earth's atmosphere at an altitude of 30 km. Surface temperatures range from about 0°C down to −125°C. No organic molecules or other traces of life have been discovered.

Observing Mars

At perihelic opposition the south pole of Mars is tilted towards the Sun so that features in the southern hemisphere of the planet are more favourably presented for observation than are those in the north. At aphelic opposition the situation is reversed, the north pole then being tilted towards the Sun.

Bright and dark markings are visible on the orange surface of Mars, as are one or both of the white polar caps. Under favourable circumstances some markings may be visible in telescopes as small as 60 mm, but for serious study of the planet larger instruments are preferable, such as a 200 mm reflector.

The system of nomenclature for the bright and dark areas, using names from terrestrial geography and mythology, was devised in the 19th century by the Italian astronomer Giovanni Schiaparelli. Since then numerous observers have added to his work, culminating in the official chart of Mars published by the International Astronomical Union in 1957, which shows 128 named features. However, these features are simply differences in albedo and do not always coincide with the real topographic features, the craters, mountains and valleys photographed by spacecraft. The US Geological Survey has prepared new charts showing the topographical surface features of Mars. Albedo charts like the one shown in Figure 20 show south at the top, which is the normal telescopic view, but the topographic maps place north at the top.

The exploration of Mars by spacecraft has meant that Mars is no longer the province of the telescopic observer. However, amateur astronomers continue to contribute to our knowledge of Mars because the surface and atmosphere of the planet undergo continual change.

Changes in surface markings. The broad configuration of the albedo markings on Mars has remained more or less the same during the time that the planet has been under telescopic observation, but numerous small-scale changes occur from one opposition to the next. Certain features such as the dusky Pandorae Fretum and Hellespontus appear to darken during the Martian spring to become quite prominent during the summer, fading again in winter. Several other features such as Syrtis Major and Solis Lacus have undergone subtle long-term changes over the years. These changes on Mars are thought to be due to surface dust being blown from place to place, uncovering some areas of rock and obscuring others.

White clouds and hazes. Although only traces of water vapour are detectable in the thin Martian atmosphere, temperatures are so low that saturation frequently occurs

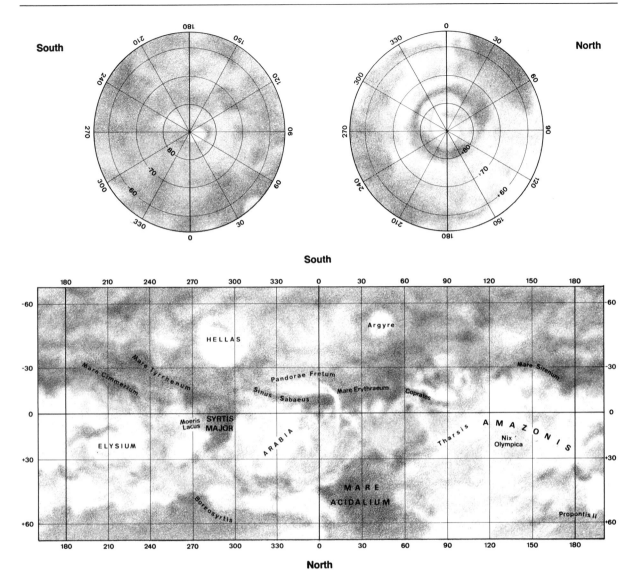

and clouds of volatiles such as water and carbon dioxide ice are quite common. These are particularly noticeable near the polar caps, which may appear enlarged as a result. The general haziness that is commonly seen near the morning or evening terminator is a result of low-level mists and thin layers of surface frost. White clouds often form over the giant volcano Olympus Mons and the other volcanoes on the Tharsis Ridge, particularly on Martian spring and summer afternoons. Cloud also frequently forms in the large impact basins such as Hellas.

Dust storms. Sometimes called yellow clouds because of their colour, small dust storms of limited extent and duration may become visible as they obscure some familiar dark marking, revealing their nature by their movement or by the reappearance of the marking over the course of a few days. During perihelic oppositions when Mars is closest to

the Sun, and therefore temperatures are highest, much larger and more spectacular dust storms may occur. Such major storms broke out after opposition in 1909, 1924 and 1956; in 1971 an extremely large storm occurred, spreading over the whole planet. It appears that these global dust storms originate in the southern hemisphere. It is important to document the times and positions of the storms as they spread, which can sometimes happen quite rapidly over a few days.

Polar caps. Often the most prominent changes visible on Mars are the seasonal growth and shrinking of the polar caps throughout a Martian year. As autumn arrives in one hemisphere the cap expands under a veil known as the *polar hood*, which consists of clouds of carbon dioxide and water crystals; this hood persists throughout the winter. With the onset of spring the mantle of clouds disperses to reveal a

Figure 20 (opposite). Albedo map of Mars, showing the planet's average appearance through telescopes over several oppositions. The positions of the features are based on photographs from the Mariner and Viking space probes. The principal markings on Mars are listed below with their areographic longitude and latitude in degrees; these coordinates are only approximate since many markings are irregular and ill-defined.

Feature	Longitude	Latitude	Feature	Longitude	Latitude
Aeolis	200	5 S	Mare Erythraeum	40	25 S
Aeria	310	10 N	Mare Hadriacum	270	45 S
Aetheria	230	45 N	Mare Serpentis	315	30 S
Amazonis	140	10 N	Mare Sirenum	155	30 S
Amenthes	255	5 N	Mare Tyrrhenum	240	30 S
Aonius Sinus	105	45 S	Margaritifer Sinus	17	5 S
Arabia	330	30 N	Memnonia	150	15 S
Araxes	130	25 S	Meroe	285	35 N
Arcadia	100	50 N	Moab	350	20 N
Argyre	42	51 S	Moeris Lacus	270	8 N
Arnon	330	48 N	Nectar	70	20 S
Aurorae Sinus	50	10 S	Nepenthes	250	15 N
Ausonia	250	45 S	Nereidum Fretum	55	40 S
Baltia	80	65 N	Niliacus Lacus	30	30 N
Boreosyrtis	275	50 N	Nilokeras	55	30 N
Callirrhoe	345	58 N	Nilosyrtis	285	40 N
Candor	73	3 N	Nix Olympica	133	18 N
Casius	260	40 N	Noachis	0	45 S
Cebrenia	210	45 N	Olympia	200	80 N
Cecropia	315	65 N	Ophir	65	10 S
Ceraunius	100	35 N	Ortygia	350	65 N
Cerberus	215	13 N	Oxia Palus	17	8 N
Chalce	15	50 S	Oxus	15	30 N
Chersonesus	280	60 S	Panchaïa	200	65 N
Chryse	25	10 N	Pandorae Fretum	350	25 S
Chrysokeras	100	55 S	Phaethontis	140	45 S
Claritas	97	20 S	Phison	320	15 N
Coprates	65	13 S	Phoenicis Lacus	100	10 S
Cyclopia	225	5 S	Phrixi Regio	65	30 S
Cydonia	350	50 N	Pierius	315	58 N
Deltoton Sinus	310	10 S	Promethei Sinus	280	65 S
Deucalionis Regio	345	15 S	Propontis I	180	40 N
Diacria	180	45 N	Propontis II	180	60 N
Dioscuria	315	50 N	Pyrrhae Regio	30	15 S
Edom	345	3 S	Scandia	150	65 N
Electris	190	45 S	Sinaï	75	15 S
Elysium	210	20 N	Sinus Meridiani	0	5 S
Eridania	210	45 S	Sinus Sabaeus	340	10 S
Eurotas	150	60 N	Sithonius Lacus	240	55 N
Euxinus Lacus	155	40 N	Solis Lacus	80	20 S
Gehon	0	20 N	Stymphalius Lacus	210	55 N
Hellas	294	44 S	Styx	195	20 N
Hellespontica Depressio	340	60 S	Syria	90	12 S
Hellespontus	340	50 S	Syrtis Major	290	10 N
Hephaestus	245	20 N	Tanaïs	70	50 N
Hesperia	225	20 S	Tempe	70	35 N
Hyperboreus Lacus	50	75 N	Tharsis	100	5 N
Iapygia	290	15 S	Thaumasia	80	30 S
Icaria	115	35 S	Thyle I	155	70 S
Isidis Regio	265	20 N	Thyle II	210	70 S
Ismenius Lacus	330	40 N	Thymiamata	13	5 N
Jamuna	45	5 S	Tithonius Lacus	85	5 S
Juventae Fons	63	5 S	Tractus Albus	90	15 N
Lemuria	200	75 N	Trivium Charontis	195	13 N
Libya	265	0	Uchronia	240	70 N
Lunae Lacus	70	15 N	Umbra	290	50 N
Maeotis Palus	125	63 N	Utopia	255	50 N
Mare Acidalium	30	45 N	Vulcani Pelagus	25	32 S
Mare Australe	40	65 S	Xanthe	45	10 N
Mare Boreum	60	60 N	Yaonis Regio	325	45 S
Mare Chronium	225	58 S	Zephyria	190	5 S
Mare Cimmerium	210	20 S			

brilliant white cap that shrinks rapidly as summer approaches, but never quite disappears, always leaving a small residual cap. The shrinking cap is bordered by a conspicuous dark collar. Dark rifts may appear in the cap, such as the Rima Tenuis in the north polar cap. In addition, detached portions of the caps may appear, such as Novus Mons in the south polar cap. The seasonal caps are composed of carbon dioxide ice that sublimes into the atmosphere rather than melts, whereas the residual cap, in the northern hemisphere at least, is composed of water ice. Mars is at perihelion during summer in the southern hemisphere, and the residual south polar cap shrinks to less than half the size of the northern one. Variations in weather patterns mean that the seasonal changes are never quite the same from year to year, and differences should be recorded.

Methods of observing. For any serious study of Mars, regular observations must be made throughout an apparition. Only in this way can the observer become familiar with the planet and thus recognize changes such as clouds or dust storms. For many years, drawings were the only practical means by which the amateur could record Martian detail, but the recent development of high-resolution photographic films such as Kodak TP 2415 has made it possible for amateurs to take high-quality photographs of Mars through telescopes of 250 mm and above.

For most amateurs, though, the usual method of recording detail is to make a drawing of the disk on a blank 50 mm in diameter. Sketch in the main details and then make a note of the time (UT) before entering the finer features. The longitude of the central meridian should be added, obtainable from tables in publications such as the *Handbook* of the British Astronomical Association or the *Astronomical Almanac*. It is also worth estimating the relative intensity of the visible features on a scale of 0 for the bright polar caps to 10 for the black of the night sky.

Colour filters can be useful for emphasizing particular features on Mars. The established range of filters is the Kodak Wratten series (see Figure 9, p. 71). The 15 yellow and 25 red filters will enhance the visibility of the dark markings and assist in the recognition of yellow clouds. The 44A blue, 47 violet and 58 green filters will aid the detection of white clouds and surface frosts by making them appear brighter than in white light, but through these filters the contrast of the dark markings is much subdued. Usually the dark areas are very difficult to see through the 47 filter, but on rare occasions they can be seen quite well. Such occasions are known as 'blue clearings', and their cause is unknown. Filter observations should be made only under conditions of good seeing and with telescopes of suitable size. The 47 filter, for example, is too dense for use with small telescopes.

The surface of Mars

From space missions we know that most of the southern hemisphere of Mars consists of impact-cratered highlands, whereas the northern hemisphere tends to be smoother and one to two kilometres lower. The albedo markings seen through telescopes do not always coincide with topographical features – the dark Syrtis Major, for instance, corresponds to an unremarkable slope at the edge of higher ground. Some bright areas, such as Hellas and Argyre, are deep impact basins (the bottom of Hellas is the lowest area on the planet, more than 4 km deep) whereas the bright markings Elysium and Nix Olympica (corresponding to the volcanic structure Olympus Mons) are areas of high volcanoes. Part of the Valles Marineris, a giant rift valley 4 km deep and 4000 km long, is visible from Earth as the dark streak Coprates.

JUPITER

Jupiter is the most rewarding planet for amateur astronomers to observe. As well as being physically the largest planet, with an equatorial diameter of 142 800 km, for most of the time it is also the one with the largest disk size – always more than 30 arcsec in diameter, and ranging from 44 to 50 arcsec at opposition.

Its mean synodic period is 399 d (just over 13 months), so that oppositions occur about one month later each year. Jupiter's distance from Earth varies from about 670 million kilometres at aphelic oppositions to 590 million kilometres at perihelic oppositions, which occur about every 12 years, in September or October. The opposition magnitude ranges between −2.3 and −2.9. Apart from one or two months either side of conjunction, Jupiter can be observed for most of the year.

The planet's visible surface is the top of a deep and cloudy atmosphere that consists mainly of hydrogen and helium, with substantial amounts of ammonia, methane and simple hydrocarbons. The clouds are believed to consist largely of ammonia crystals, ammonium hydrosulphide and water ice. The cloud layers are marked by dark belts and bright zones that run parallel to lines of latitude.

A 75 mm telescope will reveal some irregularities and spots in the clouds, and a 150 mm telescope will show enough detail to permit useful observations. The spots move visibly within 10 minutes, carried around by the planet's rapid rotation; the period is just under 10 hours. Even the smallest telescopes or binoculars will show the planet's disk and its four main moons as they orbit the planet. Since the axis of rotation of Jupiter is inclined at only 3°, the polar regions are never well seen.

Jupiter is visibly flattened under its rapid rotation, the ratio of the polar to the equatorial diameter being 15 : 16; the rotation is also responsible for drawing out the clouds into the distinctive pattern of zones and belts. Most atmospheric motions are channeled along lines of latitude, so that the atmosphere is dominated by winds blowing east or west at different latitudes.

Infrared observations have revealed variations in temperature across the planet's disk, representing different altitudes. The highest and coldest features are the white and orange ones – i.e. the zones and the Great Red Spot. Lower

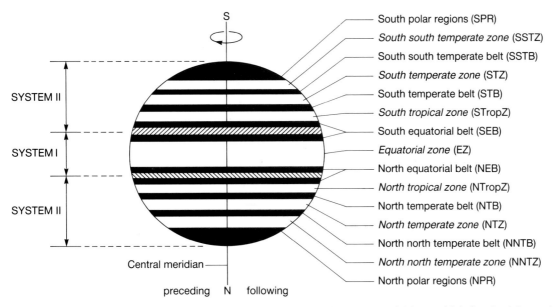

Figure 21. The nomenclature for belts and zones on Jupiter and Saturn. The features, shown here schematically, are subject to considerable change. On Saturn the SSTZ, SSTB, NNTB and NNTZ are rarely seen.

and warmer are the brown belts, and deepest and warmest of all are the dark bluish-grey patches on the North Equatorial Belt's south edge. The planet must have a hot interior as it emits twice as much heat as it receives from the Sun.

Since Jupiter's outer layers are gaseous, the planet does not rotate as a solid body. A fast-moving jet-stream embraces the equatorial region, while at higher latitudes the visible features move more slowly, so two distinct systems of longitude are used when analysing observations. System I of longitude applies to the region about 10° either side of the equator, from the middle of the North Equatorial Belt to the middle of the South Equatorial Belt; its adopted period is 9h 50m 30.003s (878°.90 per day). System II applies to the rest of the planet and has an adopted period of 9h 55m 40.632s (870°.27 per day), very close to the average for the Great Red Spot. Radio astronomers have defined System III of longitude, with a period of 9h 55m 29.711s; this is the rotation period of the planet's magnetic field, which is thought to correspond to the solid core of the planet.

Features of Jupiter

Long-term changes in the intensity, colour or structure of particular belts or zones of Jupiter occur over a number of years. There are large, long-lived features such as the Great Red Spot whose appearance and motion evolve over decades. There is also plenty of activity on time-scales from days to months, some of it spectacular. Many of these phenomena seem to fall into regular patterns over several years, which are replaced by new patterns over several decades. Consistent observations of these phenomena

provide the raw material from which the physicist can begin to deduce the nature of the planet's subsurface layers and the processes at work in them.

Belts and zones. Figure 21 shows the names of the standard belts and zones. They are usually abbreviated by their initial letters, except that 'Tropical' is abbreviated as 'Trop' to avoid confusion with 'Temperate'. Although the belts always revert to this pattern, year-to-year variations are common. Often a belt may be double, in which case the components are labelled (N) for north and (S) for south, as in SEB(N) and SEB(S). The space between them, in this example, is referred to as the SEBZ. (Suffixes, as in SEB_n and SEB_s, have also been used to denote belt components, but the British Astronomical Association now reserves these to denote belt edges.) Sometimes there is a narrow belt within one of the standard zones, termed a 'band', such as the STZB in the STZ. Sometimes a belt may be missing, replaced by white material; this is particularly likely to happen to the NTB, the SEB and sections of the STB. Sometimes there is a substantial colour change; belts can range from slate-grey to reddish-brown, and some zones (particularly the Equatorial Zone) can temporarily adopt colours such as yellow or ochre.

The observer will see many types of feature associated with the belts and zones. They are generally referred to as 'spots', but a variety of more descriptive names are also used: dark 'projections' and bright 'bays' on the edges of belts; white 'ovals' in zones or on the edges of belts; 'barges' (very dark bars, particularly on the NEB_n edge); and 'festoons' (long, curving, dark streaks). Some of the most prominent are described below.

Although most of these features move with currents having rotation periods that differ little from System I or II, outbreaks of spots are occasionally seen which move eastwards or westwards at much greater speeds, of several degrees of longitude per day relative to System II. These speeds define the 'jet-streams'. Amateur records of these outbreaks from before encounters with space probes indicate that jet-streams occur at fixed latitudes on the edges of the standard belts, and the results obtained by space probes have confirmed that there is actually a regular, permanent pattern of jet-streams. They blow in the preceding direction (prograding, decreasing System II longitude) at the equatorward edge of each belt and in the following direction (retrograding, increasing longitude) at the poleward edge of each belt. Only a few of them have ever become observable from Earth, but when they do they produce some of the most impressive events to be seen on the planet, such as the revivals of the SEB (see below).

The following are some of the most conspicuous features and events that may be seen.

The Great Red Spot. This, the most famous feature on the planet, was probably observed by Cassini in 1665, although continuous records of it go back only as far as 1831. It is a huge oval marking which spans the STropZ and indents the SEB south edge. It lies within a great bay in the SEB_s edge, called the *Red Spot Hollow*, and the Hollow is always visible even when the Spot itself is not. The Spot first attracted widespread attention in 1878, when it darkened and developed a vivid brick-red colour; an equally impressive coloration lasted from 1969 to 1975. At other times, the Spot often has a pale fawn or grey colour, or it may be replaced by a white oval within a thin dark ring, or it may even disappear entirely. It appears that the oval structure is permanent, but the colour within it is variable.

The Great Red Spot drifts slowly and irregularly in longitude, and over the past century has performed about three circuits of the planet back and forth. Thus it cannot be attached to any fixed point in the interior of the planet. In the 1960s, professional photography revealed that it was circulating anticlockwise with a period of 6 to 12 days, vividly confirmed by the Voyager probes in 1979. The Spot thus appears to roll like a ball-bearing between the jet-streams on the SEB_s and STB_n. It is now believed that the Great Red Spot is a giant, self-sustaining anticyclonic disturbance in the atmosphere.

White ovals on the STB. These ovals are similar to the Great Red Spot, both in their position with respect to a belt and in their internal circulation. In recent years there have been three of them, called FA, BC and DE, which came into being around 1940 by the subdivision of the STZ into three long sectors. These sectors contracted rapidly to form the three ovals. They have continued to contract slowly, and to move slowly north into the STB; in time they may disappear.

South Tropical Disturbance. A South Tropical Disturbance is a grey barrier across the STZ, lasting for months or years and having a slow drift in decreasing System II longitude. The greatest such Disturbance on record appeared in 1901 as a small dark spot, and expanded greatly in longitude before it finally faded away in 1939. It repeatedly interacted

with the Great Red Spot as it passed it. The Disturbance also gave rise to a remarkable circulating current in which retrograding spots on the SEB_s jet-stream, approaching the concave preceding end of the Disturbance, were diverted around it so as to end up on the STB_n jet-stream, travelling back the way they had come.

Since 1939 at least six shorter-lived phenomena of the same type have been seen, usually starting at the preceding end of the Great Red Spot.

SEB Revival. This is the most spectacular phenomenon to be seen on Jupiter, and recurs at intervals of between 3 and 30 years. The scene is set by the disappearance of the SEB(S) component and the intensification of the Great Red Spot. The Revival begins with a small dark streak across the whitened SEB latitudes. From this focus, many dark and bright spots are poured out, some retrograding on the SEB_s jet-stream and others prograding on the SEB_n (equatorial) jet-stream. A scene of violent activity develops, the Great Red Spot fades, and eventually the SEB is reconstituted.

Projections and plumes on the NEB south edge. Some of these are usually present, and are among the most conspicuous features on the planet. Often they are associated with white spots; a common structure is the 'plume', consisting of a dark projection streaming into an equatorial festoon with a bright white spot at its base. All these features generally move with System I and last for months, but more rapid motions and changes are sometimes observed.

Observing Jupiter

The most important kind of observations that amateurs can make are those aimed at determining the longitudes of spots. To learn about the various phenomena associated with spots, it is necessary to identify individual spots and the currents in which they are moving; and because the spots can change and move rapidly, this can be done only by precise measurements of longitude. (Measurements of latitude are less important, and can be left to specialist observers; latitude can be described relative to the belts, and changes are small.)

Longitude is easy to measure, requiring no more than an accurate clock or watch, and of course a telescope of adequate size – at least a 100 mm refractor or 150 mm reflector. A spot's longitude is measured as the planet's rotation carries it across the *central meridian*, an imaginary line of longitude running down the exact centre of the planet's disk, perpendicular to the belts. The observer simply notes the time, to the nearest minute, at which the spot is judged to be on the central meridian. This is the transit time, and can be judged to within a minute or two (1 minute corresponds to $0°.6$ of longitude.)

The observer should record the transit time along with a description of the feature observed. It is often helpful to sketch the planet or the feature so that the description can be checked in case of doubt. As for all planetary observations, the telescope and the seeing should also be recorded. After the observing session the observer can use published ephemerides to convert the transit times into longitudes: System I for equatorial features (SEB$_n$, EZ, NEB$_s$) and System II for features in other latitudes.

When a sufficient number of transits have been recorded, the results can be plotted on a graph of longitude against time to reveal the motions of the spots. For example, several transits over several weeks will show clearly that the motion of the STB white ovals differs from that of the Great Red Spot by about 0°.4 a day.

Disk drawings are valuable, though less important than transit measurements. Their main value is to record the detailed appearance and location of spots that were transited, to record the existence of spots whose transits were missed, and to provide a record of the changing aspects of the belts and zones. The observer may make sketches of the whole disk or of a particular region. Observations over several hours may conveniently be recorded on a 'strip-map', which is added to continuously as the planet rotates, so as to produce a cylindrical-projection map of the planet.

Complete disk drawings are best made on printed blanks of the flattened disk of the planet; the standard has an equatorial diameter of 64 mm. The observer should look at the planet carefully before starting a drawing, and begin with a quick outline sketch that locates the main features. The details can then be filled in. It is important to record the latitudes, widths and intensities of the belts and zones as faithfully as possible, although for clarity it is advisable to exaggerate the contrast of the markings.

Estimates of the intensities and colours of the belts and zones can also be useful. The intensity of a feature is estimated by allocating it a number on a scale that runs from 0 (brightest) to 10 (black sky). Because they are subjective estimates, they are worth while only if done systematically and repeatedly, so that any changes on the planet can be demonstrated from the accumulated observations of an individual. Colour estimates are usually simple descriptions, and the observer should be familiar with the spurious causes of colour on the disk. (In particular the 'traffic-lights effect' – fringing with red and blue–green as a result of atmospheric refraction – can apply to each zone as well as to the whole disk.)

Jupiter's comparatively low surface brightness and contrast make it difficult to photograph, but film is now available which is sufficiently fast and fine-grained to allow experienced photographers to obtain detailed images, provided the seeing is good. Photographs through red and blue filters can also give useful information on the colours of features. When printing photographs of Jupiter with a view to measuring longitudes and latitudes, it is as well to produce a few examples with the limb overexposed, because the limb is heavily darkened and therefore difficult to define on ordinary photographs.

The satellites of Jupiter

Jupiter has sixteen known satellites, of which four are of mag. 5 to 6 while the others are no brighter than mag. 14.

The four great moons discovered by Galileo – Io, Europa, Ganymede and Callisto – would be visible to the naked eye but for the glare of the planet; they can, however, be seen in binoculars. Because they orbit very close to the equatorial plane of Jupiter, which we see almost edge-on, they usually appear strung out in a line, and they repeatedly pass in front of and behind the planet's disk. A small telescope will show the *transits* of the satellites and their shadows across the face of Jupiter, their *eclipses* by Jupiter's shadow, and their *occultations* by the planet's disk. The four satellites look different when in transit across the planet: Io invisible or a faint grey, and Europa usually invisible, but Ganymede and Callisto very dark. Every six years, during a period of a few months when the Earth passes through the plane of the satellites, they can be seen to eclipse and occult each other in *mutual phenomena*. All the phenomena of the satellites are predicted in ephemerides. Amateurs' timings of these phenomena can be useful in refining the orbits of Jupiter's satellites.

Sometimes two of the inner three Galilean satellites undergo the same phenomenon (e.g. transit) on the same evening, while the third undergoes a different phenomenon (e.g. eclipse or occultation). Such occasions exemplify a mathematical relationship between the orbits, such that the mean planetary longitude of Io, minus three times the longitude of Europa, plus twice the longitude of Ganymede, is always equal to 180°. Thus they can never become lined up on one side of the planet. On rare occasions, all four of Jupiter's main moons may simultaneously be invisible, being either in front of the planet's disk (in transit), behind it (occulted) or in eclipse. Table 21 gives the occasions until the middle of the 21st century on which Jupiter is predicted to appear without its four brightest satellites.

Surface markings on the Galilean satellites are barely visible, even through large telescopes. However, space

Table 21. Disappearances of Jupiter's four brightest satellites.

Date	Begins	Ends
	(UT)	
1990 June 15	22h 47m	24h 19m
1991 Jan. 2	20h 42m	21h 53m
1997 Aug. 27	21h 37m	21h 52m
2001 Nov. 8	16h 26m	16h 42m
2008 May 22	3h 50m	4h 08m
2009 Sept. 3	4h 43m	6h 29m
2019 Nov. 9	12h 16m	12h 53m
2020 May 28	11h 15m	13h 11m
2021 Aug. 15	15h 39m	15h 45m
2033 July 28	3h 06m	4h 59m
2038 May 22	9h 08m	10h 47m
2038 Dec. 9	8h 18m	10h 34m
2049 Oct. 15	3h 44m	3h 59m
2050 May 28	17h 21m	18h 32m

Source: Jean Meeus, *Journal of the British Astronomical Association*, Vol. 98, p. 35 (1987).

probes have revealed extraordinary variety in their surfaces. Io displays continuous volcanic activity, due to the tidal forces induced by the coupled motions of the satellites; the effects of this activity can also be detected by professional Earth-based photometry. Europa has a smooth icy surface covered by a maze of linear markings. Ganymede and Callisto have heavily cratered ice surfaces.

The other satellites fall into three groups of four, and are too faint for most amateur observers. One group, orbiting closer to the planet than Io, includes the 270×150 km satellite Amalthea, plus three others which are less than 110 km across; these three small moons are visible only to spacecraft, as is the tenuous dusty ring which coincides with the innermost satellite orbit. The other two groups of satellites include only one sizeable one (Himalia, 186 km in diameter, mag. 15); all the others are mag. 17 or fainter. They orbit very far from the planet, in highly inclined and perturbed orbits, and are believed to be captured asteroids.

SATURN

Saturn, the second-largest planet (equatorial diameter 120 000 km), is much further from us than Jupiter and its disk appears less than half Jupiter's size in the telescope. Saturn's distance at opposition varies from 1197 million kilometres at perihelion to about 1654 million kilometres at aphelion. The apparent equatorial diameter of Saturn at opposition ranges from 18.4 arcsec at aphelion (June opposition) to 20.7 arcsec at perihelion (December opposition).

Saturn's mean synodic period is 378 d, so that oppositions occur about a fortnight later each year. The planet is observable at some time of the night for nine or ten months every year. However, oppositions vary tremendously in suitability for observation from a particular location, depending on the planet's declination. Oppositions in December or January are the most favourable for observers in the northern hemisphere, but least favourable for observers in the southern hemisphere, because Saturn is then well north of the celestial equator. For oppositions in June or July the situation is reversed, since the planet is then well south of the celestial equator. During one orbit of Saturn around the Sun, which takes 29.5 years, it is therefore usual for an observer at one station to experience relatively favourable apparitions for about 14 years, followed by an equal period of unfavourable apparitions.

The polar diameter of Saturn is about 10% less than the equatorial diameter, the greatest oblateness of any planet in the Solar System. The marked oblateness is connected with the planet's low density, which is less than that of water.

Features of Saturn

Saturn is similar to Jupiter in that it has dark belts and bright zones, and the same nomenclature is adopted as for Jupiter (see Figure 21). Spots may be seen on the belts and in the zones from time to time, but they are usually short-lived, which is why our knowledge of rotation periods for various latitudes is less accurate than for Jupiter. The rotation is found to be 10h 14m at the equator, and longer for higher latitudes. There is no sudden change of rotation period as with System I and System II of Jupiter, merely a gradual lengthening of rotation period towards the poles; one spot seen in 1960 showed a rotation period of about 10h 40m at latitude 60° N.

Hydrogen is the main atmospheric component, with methane, ammonia, phosphine, acetylene and ethane also present. The Voyager probes revealed an extensive haze some 70 km thick that affects the visibility of the belts and zones. Wind velocities in the equatorial region are the highest found for any planet. Like Jupiter, Saturn emits more energy than it receives from the Sun; its effective temperature is 96.5 K, nearly 20 K higher than would be expected if it did not give out heat of its own.

Saturn's rings

The ring system that encircles Saturn's equator can be seen through a small telescope with a magnification of ×50 or so, but larger apertures and magnifications are required to reveal the details of the three major rings: A (the outer), B (the brightest) and C (the inner). The ring system shows itself at various angles, from edge-on to 29.2°, due to a combination of the axial tilt of Saturn, 26.7°, and the 2.5° inclination of Saturn's orbit to the orbit of the Earth. On average, the rings take about 7¼ years to go from fully open to edge-on. The large brightness variation of the planet at opposition, from mag. 0.8 to mag. −0.3, is mainly a result of the varying presentation of the ring system.

Twice in the course of Saturn's orbit round the Sun, at intervals of 13¾ and 15¾ years alternately, the Earth passes through the plane of the rings (the intervals are unequal because of the eccentricity of Saturn's orbit). On each occasion the Earth can pass through the ring plane up to three times, as on 1995 May 22 (north to south), 1995 August 11 (south to north) and 1996 February 12 (north to south). Subsequent dates of the Earth's passage through the ring plane are given in Table 22. When edge-on, the rings are often invisible in small telescopes as they are only a few kilometres thick at the most. But they can present a truly magnificent sight when tilted towards us by a degree or so; the satellites then appear like brightly lit droplets on a spider's web.

All too rarely do the rings pass in front of a bright star, although such an event was observed in 1917 and revealed much detail in ring A. Before the arrival of the two US Voyager space probes at Saturn in 1980 and 1981, such events were a major source of information on ring structure. Within ring A is a division known as *Encke's division* (discovered by Johann Encke), the reality of which was once in dispute but which was shown to be real by the Voyagers. Separating rings A and B is *Cassini's division* (discovered by Giovanni Cassini) which, in good seeing, can be observed with a 75 mm telescope if the rings are fairly well open. This conspicuous division, 3500 km wide, is not totally empty but contains numerous threadlike ringlets. Ring C is the faintest ring normally visible from the Earth. Yet another ring, D, observable from the Earth with large telescopes and under excellent seeing conditions, is found between the inner part of ring C and the planet's globe. The Voyager probes revealed at least three rings outside ring A: in order of increasing distance from Saturn, rings F, G and E.

The rings are not solid but are composed of myriads of tiny particles; the 'divisions' mark thinly populated zones in the rings. Many divisions have been seen and have been shown to occur at specific distances from the planet where ring particles would be drawn away by the regularly repeated gravitational pull of some of the planet's satellites, similar to the Kirkwood gaps in the asteroid belt.

Observing Saturn

All amateur observers can play a part in determining the longitudes of surface features. As with Jupiter, a spot's longitude is determined by accurately recording the time at which it transits the central meridian, the imaginary line which bisects the visible disk perpendicular to the belts. With practice an observer can achieve an accuracy of a minute or two. Longitude tables are available which give the longitude of the central meridian at 0h UT daily. System I (analogous to that on Jupiter) covers the whole of the two equatorial belts and the Equatorial Zone, and has a rotation period of 10h 14m 13s (844° per day). System II, which applies to the rest of the planet, has a period of 10h 38m 25s (812° per day), although there is a gradual lengthening of the rotation period towards the poles.

Re-observation of a given region is possible at the 5th, 7th, 12th and 14th rotations, when a given longitude will be in the same position on the disk within about 3 hours of the time of the initial observation. It is important to ensure that

Table 22. Passages of the Earth through the plane of Saturn's rings in the 21st century.

Date	Direction
2009 Sept. 4	South to north
2025 Mar. 23	North to south
2038 Oct. 15	South to north
2039 Apr. 1	North to south
2039 July 9	South to north
2054 May 5	North to south
2054 Aug. 31	South to north
2055 Feb. 1	North to south
2068 Aug. 25	South to north
2084 Mar. 14	North to south
2097 Oct. 5	South to north
2098 Apr. 26	North to south
2098 June 18	South to north

Source: Richard E. Schmidt, *Sky & Telescope*, Vol. 58, p. 500 (1979).

features timed crossing the central meridian are fully identified in the observing log, for this will greatly increase the value of the observations when they come to be compared and collated with those of other observers.

Disk drawings are important, although less so than the determination of longitudes by the transit method. Drawings provide a record of the changing appearance of the surface of the planet throughout each apparition.

As the apparent shape of Saturn is constantly changing with the changing tilt of the ring system, it is not possible to use a single standard blank. The appropriate outline, depending on the value of B (the Saturnicentric latitude of the Earth relative to the ring plane), is usually traced from a set of standard outlines (obtainable from national observing groups). All observations should be fully documented: the date, time (UT) of the observation, instrument, power used and seeing conditions are all essential to the permanent record. Detailed notes of all important features should be added to the record at the time of observation.

Another useful kind of observation, provided it is carried out systematically and regularly, is the estimation of the relative intensity of various parts of the globe and rings. This is done by assessing the intensities on a numerical scale. European astronomers use the convention that 1 is the brightness of ring B (the bright reference) and 10 the absolute blackness of a deep shadow or dark background sky. The scale adopted in the U.S.A. runs the opposite way, from 8 as the brightest (ring B) to 0 for the background sky. Fractions of $\frac{1}{2}$ may be used to denote intermediate intensities, but intensities quoted to a tenth are quite meaningless.

Colour filters are often used; recommended are Wratten 25 (red) and Wratten 44A (blue), or Wratten 47 (blue) for larger apertures (around 300 mm). Different intensities in red, blue and 'white' light can indicate colour tints, and the belts and zones may appear to be of different widths. A curious effect known as the bicoloured aspect of the rings has been noted, in which one side of the rings, when viewed through a given filter, appears to have a different intensity from that of the opposite side. The effect, when present, is usually seen in ring A and is revealed by comparing the brightness of the two ring arms first through a red filter and then through a blue filter. Sometimes a difference is noticed with one filter alone. The reality of this effect has been confirmed photographically.

The satellites of Saturn

There are ten major satellites, the largest of which is Titan (mag. 8.3 at opposition). A number of smaller satellites, not visible from Earth, were found by the Voyager probes. Most satellites orbit close to the plane of the planet's equator, but Iapetus has a more inclined orbit and Phoebe's orbit is retrograde. They all display variations in brightness, the greatest variation being shown by Iapetus which is about two magnitudes brighter at western elongation than at eastern elongation. Iapetus was shown by the Voyagers to have one hemisphere of bright reflective material, and the other dark.

Titan shows variations in both brightness and colour: it may appear white, yellowish, pink or even red. This is because Titan has an atmosphere of nitrogen in which various organic compounds have been found. It has a surface temperature of 93 K, some 7 K above the equivalent black-body value, so a small greenhouse effect seems to be operating.

The high tilt of the planet's equatorial plane means that satellite phenomena cannot be observed all the time, as is possible with Jupiter, but only during four or five apparitions centred on each passage of the Earth through the ring plane. In each sidereal revolution of the planet there are thus two periods of about ten years when no satellite phenomena can be observed.

Only when the rings are edge-on or the ring angle is very small are the satellites occulted or eclipsed. Titan appears as a dark body against the globe of Saturn when in transit, appearing almost as dark as its shadow, a phenomenon visible in small telescopes. It is interesting to plot the movements of the satellites, but little can be done in the way of useful observation save for estimating their magnitudes; this is difficult to do reliably without photometric equipment, partly because of the glare from Saturn itself. The timing of satellite phenomena which occur at certain apparitions is very useful.

URANUS, NEPTUNE AND PLUTO

Uranus

At mag. +5.5 Uranus is just visible to the naked eye, but it is far from conspicuous. Good binoculars and small telescopes show a tiny, blue–green disk of somewhat fuzzy appearance, with an apparent angular diameter of about 4 arcsec at best.

Visually its most striking feature is its very blandness. A lightish band flanked by narrow dusky belts has been reported, as have large-scale brightenings near the limb. But much of this detail is at the limits of vision, and is suspect.

Uranus is so remote that its apparent brightness varies by only about 20% from opposition to conjunction, and there is no perceptible difference in its general appearance at opposition and quadrature. However, variations in brightness attributable to changes in the planet's atmosphere have been detected, and can be monitored with binoculars by using the methods of the variable star observer. More precise measurements are possible by photoelectric photometry.

Unlike the other planets, Uranus spins on its side – that is, its axis of rotation is almost in the plane of its orbit. The pole of counterclockwise rotation, which, in contrast to the Earth, is the south pole, is tilted 98° with respect to the planet's counterclockwise orbit around the Sun. Uranus is therefore seen in a unique series of orientations: pole-on, on its side, or somewhere in between.

Five moons of Uranus are visible from the Earth, but they require large telescopes to be seen. They all move in virtually circular orbits in the planet's equatorial plane, so whatever event brought about the current axial tilt of Uranus did not disrupt the satellite system.

Neptune

Neptune is an eighth-magnitude object, visible in a small telescope or binoculars. Its apparent angular diameter is about 2.3 arcsec and, like Uranus, it shows a blue–green disk in telescopes of moderate aperture. No detail can be seen except in very powerful instruments, which reveal traces of belts, similar to those of the other major planets, bordering a bright equatorial zone. Changes in brightness are suspected to occur as the planet rotates, but there is uncertainty over the amplitude of variation. In addition, Neptune's brightness has been found to vary with solar activity, becoming fainter at solar maximum, presumably as a result of changes in the planet's atmosphere caused by solar radiation.

In dealing with an object so remote, small instruments are unhelpful, and the average observer can expect to achieve little more than to plot the path of the planet. Coordinates can be extracted from annual ephemerides, and a finder chart sketched from existing maps of the region. Alternatively, the special charts published in the annual *Handbook* of the British Astronomical Association may be used.

Two satellites of Neptune are visible from Earth. Triton (mag. 13) is the innermost satellite. Its motion is retrograde, and its orbit is inclined by 20° to the planet's equator. Nereid is small, very faint and revolves in an extremely eccentric orbit. Its faintness (mag. 18.7) puts it beyond the reach of all but the most powerful of instruments.

Pluto

At visual magnitude 14.5 and photographic magnitude 15.4, Pluto requires a telescope of aperture at least 250 mm in order to be seen. It will, of course, register on photographic film provided the exposure is long enough, but a good star chart is necessary if it is to be identified.

Pluto is the smallest by far of the major planets, with a diameter of 2250 km – smaller than our own Moon. Its orbital eccentricity is greater, and its inclination higher, than for any other major planet. It is also unusual in that it comes inside the orbit of Neptune when it is near perihelion, as is the case from 1979 to 1999.

A satellite, Charon, was discovered in 1978. Charon's maximum separation from Pluto is just 0.8 arcsec and so it can be viewed only under very good seeing conditions, and then only as an elongation of the image of Pluto itself. Charon orbits the planet in 6.39 d at a distance of 19 000 km. Its diameter is just over half that of Pluto, which makes it by far the largest satellite relative to its primary in the Solar System. This is the only planet–satellite pair with both synchronous rotation and synchronous revolution.

MINOR PLANETS

These bodies, often called asteroids, are small worlds orbiting the Sun. Even (1) Ceres, the largest of them, is less than 1000 km in diameter, and only about a dozen are more than 250 km across. One of the largest is (4) Vesta, which has a high albedo and is sometimes faintly visible to the naked eye.

The total number of minor planets is very great; there are probably over 100 000 larger than 1 km. Most of them keep to a broad region of the Solar System between the orbits of Mars and Jupiter known as the *asteroid belt*.

The most interesting minor planets are those that do not orbit within the main belt. For example, (433) Eros, discovered by Witt in 1898, may approach the Earth to within 24 million kilometres, as it did in 1975. Like most other minor planets it is irregular in shape, with a longer diameter of about 30 km. Other minor planets have been known to approach even more closely: Hermes, with an estimated diameter of only 1.5 km, passed the Earth in 1937 at a distance of only 750 000 km.

More than 50 minor planets are now known to cross the Earth's orbit. One, (3200) Phaethon, passes closer to the Sun (within 0.14 AU) than any other known object except for the occasional comet. There may be a fair number of objects whose orbits lie entirely outside that of Jupiter, such as (2060) Chiron. Two groups of minor planets travelling essentially in the orbit of Jupiter, but constrained to remain near the *Lagrangian points* 60° ahead of and behind Jupiter itself, are named after the heroes of the Trojan war: the first Trojan asteroid discovered, (588) Achilles, was found in 1906. Other minor planets, notably (279) Thule and the Hilda-type objects in the outer part of the main belt, have revolution periods that are exact fractions – $\frac{3}{4}$ and $\frac{2}{3}$ – of Jupiter's orbital period. Generally, however, there are obvious holes (the *Kirkwood gaps*) in the distribution of minor planets at exact fractions of Jupiter's period ($\frac{1}{2}$, $\frac{1}{3}$, $\frac{3}{5}$, etc.), which otherwise extends fairly uniformly from about 2.0 to 3.3 AU from the Sun.

The irregular shape and rough surfaces of minor planets are evident in the detectable variation of reflected sunlight as seen from the Earth. This variation, caused mainly by rotation, is usually repeated after several hours. Thus rotation periods are found to be mostly between 5 and 8 hours, although a few minor planets have rotation periods in excess of 24 hours. Spectrophotometry in which a minor planet is observed at selected regions of the spectrum by the

Table 23. The first five minor planets discovered.

Number and name	Year of discovery	Sidereal period (y)	Mean distance from Sun (AU)	Orbital inclination (degrees)	Diameter (km)	Visual magnitude at brightest
(1) Ceres	1801	4.60	2.77	10.6	1000	6.7
(2) Pallas	1802	4.62	2.77	34.8	540	6.7
(3) Juno	1804	4.36	2.67	13.0	250	7.4
(4) Vesta	1807	3.63	2.36	7.1	530	5.2
(5) Astraea	1845	4.13	2.57	5.4	180	8.8

Table 24. Some interesting minor planets.

Number and name	Year first recorded	Sidereal period (y)	Distance from Sun (AU) Maximum	Minimum	Inclination (degrees)	Eccentricity	Approximate diameter (km)
1937 UB Hermes	1937	1.47?	1.90?	0.68?	4.1?	0.47?	1.5?
(24) Themis	1853	5.53	3.55	2.71	0.8	0.13	249
(132) Aethra	1873	4.22	3.62	1.61	25.1	0.38	50?
(153) Hilda	1875	7.92	4.54	3.41	7.8	0.14	119?
(158) Koronis	1876	4.86	3.02	2.72	1.0	0.05	38
(221) Eos	1882	5.23	3.31	2.72	10.9	0.10	98
(279) Thule	1888	8.8	4.32	4.22	2.3	0.01	72?
(433) Eros	1898	1.76	1.81	1.13	10.8	0.22	20
(434) Hungaria	1898	2.71	2.09	1.80	22.5	0.07	11.6
(588) Achilles	1906	11.8	5.95	4.40	10.3	0.15	70?
(944) Hidalgo	1920	14.1	9.68	2.02	42.4	0.66	29?
(1221) Amor	1932	2.67	2.75	1.09	11.9	0.44	5?
(1566) Icarus	1949	1.12	1.97	0.19	23.0	0.83	1.5
(1862) Apollo	1932	1.78	2.30	0.65	6.3	0.56	2.5
(2060) Chiron	1895	50.7	18.8	8.48	6.9	0.38	320?
(2062) Aten	1976	0.95	1.14	0.79	18.9	0.18	0.9?
(2101) Adonis	1936	2.57	3.31	0.44	1.4	0.76	1.5?
(3200) Phaethon	1983	1.43	2.40	0.14	22.0	0.89	5?

use of filters yields much additional information on albedo, surface constitution and diameter, although this area of research is still developing.

Minor planets have been classified according to spectra and albedo. About 75% of them are of *C-type*, with albedo as low as 4%, perhaps containing a fair amount of carbonaceous material. Another 15%, of *S-type*, have moderate albedo (average 14%), and more likely contain silicaceous material. Metals are also present, and in some instances may result in very high albedos: for example 48% for (44) Nysa. Until spacecraft flybys take place, we can speculate that minor planets probably look very similar to Phobos and Deimos, the moons of Mars.

It is believed that most minor planets are debris left over from the early days of the Solar System, the nearby presence of Jupiter having prevented the formation of a larger planet in the region. Subsequent evolution has been influenced by further collisional break-up. Some evidence for this idea is provided by the existence of groups of minor planets (the *Hirayama families*) with rather similar orbits and possibly also similar composition. The three principal families are associated with (221) Eos, (158) Koronis and (24) Themis.

Terminology and naming

For the past century almost all minor planets have been discovered photographically, as their images trail in relation to the stars during a time exposure. Search programmes at professional observatories now account for the vast majority of newly found minor planets. On receipt of astrometric observations, the International Astronomical Union's Minor Planet Center (located at the Smithsonian Astrophysical Observatory, Cambridge, Massachusetts) assigns provisional designations.

Until the late nineteenth century and the introduction of photography, consecutive numbers and names were given to all new objects, even before orbits could be computed for later identification. Nowadays official numbers are not assigned to minor planets until reliable orbits have been computed, which is usually after the object has been well observed in at least three different years. Once the objects have been numbered, they can be named by their discoverers. As of mid-1989, there were more than 4000 numbered minor planets; up to 200 objects are newly numbered each year.

The provisional designation system relates to the time of discovery; thus 1976 DE is the fifth minor planet (E) discovered in the second half of February (D) in 1976. (Before 1925 different letter systems were used, and the older designations have been replaced by designations such as A899 AA, A907 BA and A924 GA.) Many of these 'new' objects are actually repeat observations of previously discovered minor planets, and it is a challenging problem to identify observations of the same object in different years. It is estimated that more than 15 000 individual minor planets have been noted on photographs.

Numbered minor planets are referred to by their number (often given in parentheses, as here) and name, e.g. (439) Ohio, (1677) Tycho Brahe and (3869) Norton. Nowadays names are submitted by discoverers to the Minor Planet Center for approval by a committee, and new numbers and names are published in the *Minor Planet Circulars*, which also contain astrometric observations, orbits and ephemerides.

Observing minor planets

With a small telescope or even binoculars, it is a simple job to pick up the brighter minor planets – those above mag. 8.5. The positions are given in an ephemeris, published for example in the BAA *Handbook* or by the Association of Lunar and Planetary Observers.

Identification is largely a matter of finding the correct star field and spotting the interloper. Fainter minor planets can be confirmed by demonstrating their motion; this is done by drawing the stars in the field and comparing this record with the view in the telescope a couple of hours later, when a minor planet will be seen to have moved. Once identified, the minor planet can be followed nightly against the background stars.

Relatively simple observations can prove interesting and instructive. The brightness of a minor planet may be estimated by making a comparison with stars of known magnitude, in the same way as for variable stars. Minor planets change in brightness as they spin on their axis, and for several of them this can be observed visually: (216) Kleopatra varies by 1 magnitude, for example, and (433) Eros by up to 1.5 magnitudes.

Even if the brightness does not appear to change over the course of one night, it will do over the course of an opposition, increasing as the Earth approaches and decreasing as the Earth draws away. A plot of a minor planet's brightness against time can reveal whether its orbit is near-circular (if the graph is symmetric) or eccentric (if the graph is asymmetric).

Brightness estimates can be adjusted to the standard distance of 1 AU from the Sun and from the Earth, and to 0° phase angle (100% phase) to give values of 'absolute magnitude'. From an analysis of the change in absolute magnitude with phase angle it is possible to derive the albedo, diameter and several other important physical properties. The accuracy of these results will be improved if several observers pool their observations.

Accurate position measurements obtained by photometric astrometry are used to refine the orbital elements, and are published in the *Minor Planet Circulars*. Photoelectric photometry is used by some amateurs to produce accurate light curves of minor planets.

COMETS

About 800 comets have been observed sufficiently well for their orbits to be calculated. Four-fifths of these are long-period comets, taking hundreds, thousands or even millions of years to orbit the Sun. Many of them are 'new' comets approaching the Sun for the first time from a region known as the *Oort comet cloud* that surrounds the Sun at a distance of about 20 000 to 100 000 AU. 'Old' comets are those that have been perturbed by the major planets, principally Jupiter and Saturn, on numerous previous trips to the inner Solar System so that their orbits are now much smaller than originally. A small minority, such as Comet Bowell 1982 I (which passed very close to Jupiter in late 1980), are ejected permanently from the Solar System.

Periodic comets, also known as *short-period comets*, are those with orbital periods of less than 200 years (a somewhat arbitrary division). A typical short-period comet has a period of from 5 to 9 years. Most are too faint for observation with small telescopes, but some can be observed occasionally with binoculars. Of the 150 or so known short-period comets only Halley's Comet consistently attains naked-eye brightness. However, even a very bright comet may escape detection if it approaches us from the direction of the Sun. As most comets have highly elongated orbits (i.e. high orbital eccentricity), they are observable with small telescopes only during a small portion of their orbit near perihelion.

The number of known comets is increasing all the time. As many as two dozen comets may be seen each year, of which perhaps half are new discoveries while the rest are known comets returning. About one-third of discoveries are made by amateur astronomers.

A new comet is generally seen first as a faint, small, misty object, superficially rather like a nebula (with or without central condensation) but with definite individual motion. At the heart of a comet is a tiny irregular *nucleus* a few kilometres across that consists of frozen ices and dust particles. As the comet approaches the inner Solar System the ices sublime and some of the dust grains are released, creating an atmosphere of gas and dust particles that we observe as the comet's fuzzy head or *coma*. The higher density of particles near the nucleus gives rise to a brighter central condensation that obscures the nucleus from view. Sometimes this condensation is star-like in appearance, and is referred to as the *nuclear condensation* or *false nucleus*.

Many comets have both dust and gas tails formed by the vaporization of snow or ice in the nucleus; the gas tail always points away from the Sun. The gas tail is formed when ions in the coma are accelerated by the solar wind along lines of magnetic force. The dust tail is caused by the pressure of sunlight on dust grains. When radiation meets small particles with a diameter about one-third the wavelength of the incident radiation, the resulting pressure is up to 20 or 30 times greater than the gravitational attraction of the Sun. Hence the dust particles are pushed out into orbits of their own, which lag behind the motion of the comet so that the dust tail spreads out into a fan shape.

The comet's loss of material into the coma and tail increases as it nears the Sun, and decreases again on receding from the Sun. The release and behaviour of this material varies from comet to comet and thus makes the prediction of cometary brightness very tricky. An often-used equation for total visual magnitude (m_1) of the coma is known as the *power-law formula*. While it has some value in giving an idea of how a comet's brightness will progress (and so is used extensively in published ephemerides), it is usually applicable over only a small fraction of the comet's orbit. This formula is

$$m_1 = H + 5 \log \Delta + 2.5n \log r$$

where n is the power-law exponent, and Δ and r are the comet's geocentric and heliocentric distances in astronomical units. For newly discovered comets, n is usually assumed to be 4 for the purpose of calculating ephemerides; for so-called *nuclear magnitudes* it is usually assumed that $n = 2$. H in the formula is the 'absolute magnitude' of the comet, which would be its brightness if it were exactly 1 AU from both the Sun and the Earth.

Comets are named after their discoverer (or occasionally the observatories or artificial satellites that discovered them, or in a few cases the people who computed their orbits, such as Halley, Encke or Crommelin); a maximum of three names per comet is allowed. Periodic comets are usually abbreviated with the prefix P, as in P/Halley or P/Pons–Brooks. The orbit of a comet seen at only one perihelion passage is necessarily uncertain; some short-period comets previously seen more than once are now considered lost, perhaps because of the object's physical disintegration. One, P/Biela, was seen in two parts at its last two observed returns (in 1846 and 1852).

Other comets have been observed to split. At least the principal components may survive; it is possible that some of the more unusual minor planets are defunct cometary nuclei that have ceased to be active, probably due to the build-up of a thick crust. Much of the dust in a comet is released and eventually spreads all the way around the comet's orbit. When the Earth intersects this dust, a meteor shower is observed. The Geminids, one of the most persistent showers and appearing each December, are known to be associated with the object classified as minor planet (3200) Phaethon.

In addition to the permanent name, newly discovered comets (and also most short-period comets that are recovered as a result of calculations) are given a provisional designation consisting of the year and a letter (a, b, etc.) indicating the order of recovery or discovery within that year (e.g. comets 1982a, 1982b, etc.; if more than 26 comets are found in a given year, as first happened in 1987, the sequence continues after comet 1987z with comet $1987a_1$, comet $1987b_1$, etc.). Subsequently, when the comet's orbit has been determined reasonably accurately, it is assigned a definitive roman numeral which denotes its order of perihelion passage during the year (e.g. comets 1982 I, 1982 II, etc.). Thus, when P/Halley was recovered in 1982 October, it was designated comet 1982i, but in early 1988 it was redesignated comet 1986 III (the third comet known to have passed perihelion in 1986). Some comets with small orbital eccentricities, such as P/Schwassmann–Wachmann 1 (Schwassmann and Wachmann together discovered three short-period comets) and P/Smirnova–Chernykh, are

Table 25. Orbital elements of some comets. The orbital elements of a comet, especially the period, can change considerably over the course of time as a result of planetary perturbations.

Comet	Orbital period (y)	Inclination (degrees)	Perihelion distance (AU)	Eccentricity	Associated meteor shower(s)
P/Encke	3.3	12	0.34	0.85	Taurids
P/Grigg-Skjellerup	5.1	21	0.99	0.99	
P/Machholz	5.2	60	0.13	0.96	
P/Wild 2	6.2	3	1.49	0.56	
P/Kopff	6.4	5	1.58	0.54	
P/Giacobini–Zinner	6.6	32	1.03	0.71	October Draconids
P/Biela[a]	6.6	13	0.86	0.76	Andromedids
P/Whipple	8.5	10	3.08	0.26	
P/Schwassmann–Wachmann 1	15.0	10	5.45	0.10	
P/Hartley–IRAS	21.5	96	1.28	0.83	
P/Halley	76	162	0.59	0.97	η Aquarids, Orionids
P/Swift–Tuttle[b]	120?	114	0.96	0.96	Perseids
P/Wilk	187	26	0.62	0.98	
Metcalf 1919 V		46	1.12	1.00	*o* Draconids
Ikeya 1964 VIII	391	172	0.82	0.98	η Geminids
Ikeya–Seki 1965 VIII[c]	880	142	0.008	1.00	
Bennett 1970 II		90	0.54	1.00	
Kohoutek 1973 XII		14	0.14	1.00	
Bennett 1974 XV[d]		135	0.86	1.00	
Schuster 1975 II		112	6.88	1.00	
West 1976 VI		43	0.20	1.00	
Bowell 1982 I		2	3.36	1.06	
IRAS–Araki–Alcock 1983 VII[e]		73	0.99	0.99	

[a] Lost.   [b] Believed lost.
[c] Member of the Kreutz sungrazing group, which consists of many comets that are apparently parts of what was once a much larger object.
[d] Disappeared (disintegrated?) just before perihelion.
[e] Passed 0.03 AU from Earth on 1983 May 11.

observable around their entire orbits and are no longer assigned provisional letter designations.

The orbit of a comet is conveniently defined by the time of perihelion passage (T), perihelion distance (q), eccentricity (e), and three angles which define the orientation of the orbit on the sky: the argument of perihelion, (ω), the longitude of the ascending node (Ω) and the orbital inclination (i). The main orbital elements of some comets are given in Table 25. Since the orbit is continually being perturbed by the gravitational attractions of the planets, it is also necessary to state the epoch to which these orbital elements apply. In addition, the jet-like release of material from the nucleus results in 'non-gravitational forces' that have to be taken into account in making accurate predictions of a comet's return.

Observing comets

The three main fields of observing activity are seeking new comets; measuring the positions of known comets (astrometry); and studying the physical structure and characteristics of comets, either visually, photographically or with electronic devices. The areas where amateur astronomers can contribute most to the study of comets are in comet seeking, astrometry, estimating the brightness of comets and recording details of physical structure.

For comet seeking a large-aperture instrument and low magnification are preferable. A good choice of visual instrument is a large pair of binoculars of 100 mm to 150 mm aperture and a magnification of ×20 to ×30. Most visual comet discoveries are made when the comet is within 100° of the Sun, either in the eastern sky before dawn or in the western sky after dusk, because comets do not usually brighten above 10th or 11th magnitude until they are relatively close to the Sun.

Visual seekers should have a careful sweeping routine in which adjacent sweeps overlap slightly and in which the setting or rising regions are accounted for. If an unknown nebulous object is found the comet hunter should consult one or more detailed star charts and cometary ephemerides to see if the object can be identified as a galaxy or nebula, or as a known comet. A faint close grouping of stars can often be mistaken for a diffuse object; one should also be mindful of ghost images. To check a possible visual discovery, different eyepieces (and preferably also different instruments) should be used to look at the object; in photographic observing, images on two or more photographs should be obtained. A comet will normally betray its nature by motion over a period of an hour or two. Possible discoveries should be reported to the nearest national observatory or national observing organization (for addresses see the Appendix), who will forward appropriate information to the

Central Bureau for Astronomical Telegrams, Smithsonian Astrophysical Observatory, 60 Garden Street, Cambridge, Massachusetts 02138, U.S.A., for possible further verification and official announcement of the discovery.

When reporting a discovery, the following information must be given: dates and times (UT) of observations; observing location and equipment used; full name and address (and preferably also telephone number) of discoverer; the object's appearance (including brightness, and amount of condensation, diffuseness and tail, if applicable), and measured positions (with equinox stated) at the times provided.

Photographing comets can yield useful results, such as depicting the changing tail structure in a bright comet. Astrometry is an area in which amateurs have long contributed useful information, particularly on newly discovered comets which are in need of preliminary orbit computations. For astrometry, a telescope or purpose-built camera with focal length of 600 mm or more is needed, and for results to be useful the measurement should be made to an accuracy of 2–3 arcsec. A machine for measuring the photographic image is also needed, as is a good star catalogue. Results for newly discovered comets should be rapidly communicated to the Central Bureau for Astronomical Telegrams.

Visual observations of cometary structure are best made at the telescope with a drawing pencil on white paper. Care should be taken to reproduce accurately the relative sizes and intensities of any structure that is visible. Two directions, for example north and east, should also be carefully indicated on the drawing, together with a small scale-bar giving the scale in minutes of arc.

The total brightness of the coma can be useful – though difficult to measure, because the visual brightness varies tremendously with atmospheric conditions and with even small changes in aperture and magnification. The total brightness of the coma is usually measured by defocusing comparison stars and comparing them with the comet. The three most common methods are as follows:

(a) The *Bobrovnikoff method*, whereby the comet and comparison stars are defocused by the same amount, until the stars' sizes approximately equal the size of the defocused comet. The estimate is then made directly by comparing the known brightnesses of the comparison stars with that of the defocused comet. This method should be used only for comets with intense condensations, i.e. generally the brighter objects, where the apparent coma is usually very small.

(b) The *in-out* or *Sidgwick method*, whereby the memorized image of the in-focus comet is compared with equal-sized, defocused images of comparison stars. There are problems with this method when the coma size is large and the comet has a bright condensation.

(c) A method developed by C. S. Morris in which the comet is defocused just enough to give it an approximately uniform surface brightness. This image is

memorized and compared with comparison stars which are defocused to this same size (note that the stars must be placed further out of focus than the comet to obtain equal image sizes).

In each case at least three different comparison stars should be used. It is also essential to record the instrument (including aperture, type, *f*/ratio, and magnification) used for the magnitude estimate, as well as the apparent coma diameter and the degree of condensation (usually estimated by giving it a number on a scale of 0, totally diffuse, to 9, completely stellar).

METEORS

A meteor, known popularly as a *shooting star* or *falling star*, is caused when a particle of interplanetary dust (a *meteoroid*) enters the Earth's atmosphere at high speed. Collision of the meteoroid with air molecules produces frictional heating, which normally vaporizes the particle completely. The vaporized atoms from the meteoroid collide with more air molecules, and the energy of the collisions strips electrons from the atoms and molecules, a process called ionization. This ionization forms a long train of positively charged ions and negatively charged free electrons behind the meteoroid.

A typical meteor trail occurs at heights of 80 to 100 km above the Earth's surface, and lasts on average for only a fraction of a second, although some can persist for several seconds. During this short time the ions and electrons recombine, giving off light as they do so. It is this brief streak of light that we call a meteor. The dust particles that cause meteors come from comets.

Meteors range in brightness from faint telescopic objects of brief duration to bright fireballs lasting several seconds. About six to ten of them per hour can be seen on any clear, moonless night. These are called *sporadic* meteors, and they enter the atmosphere at random.

At certain times each year the Earth encounters swarms of cometary dust which produce meteor showers. Members of a meteor shower seem to emanate from a particular point on the celestial sphere known as a *radiant*. About ten major showers occur each year, with rates of between about 10 and 100 meteors per hour, plus a large number of showers of feebler activity. Nearly all showers are named after the constellation in which the radiant lies, e.g. the Perseids seem to radiate from Perseus, the Geminids from Gemini.

There are considerable differences from one shower to another. In some the meteors move swiftly, in others they move rather slowly; some have a higher fraction of fireballs than others. Some showers produce a higher proportion of meteors with persistent trains than others.

The intensity of a shower may vary considerably with time. The peak activity of the Quadrantids, for instance, is well defined and lasts only a few hours. On the other hand a shower such as the Orionids has no sharp peak, but its maximum is rather flat, lasting two or three days.

The activity of a particular shower can vary from year to year. Many showers, such as the Perseids and Geminids, show much the same level of activity each year. By contrast, the activity of the Leonids is modest in most years, but at 33-year intervals there can be extraordinary displays with rates of thousands of meteors per hour for short periods. This last happened in 1966, and is predicted to happen again in 1999. The activity of a shower is measured by its *zenithal hourly rate* (ZHR), which is the number of meteors that would be seen by a single observer under a perfectly clear sky with the radiant overhead.

Naked-eye observations

The purpose of visual work is to determine meteor rates and brightness distribution. This is accomplished by watches, normally lasting for one hour, one or more of which are carried out by an observer on a given night.

For each watch the following basic details should be noted: observer's name; correspondence address; observing site, with latitude and longitude; date; time (UT) of start and end of watch to the nearest minute; average stellar limiting magnitude during the watch; and average percentage cloud cover in area of sky being watched.

For each meteor seen during the watch, the observer should note the following details: time (UT) to the nearest minute; meteor brightness to the nearest whole magnitude; whether the meteor was a sporadic, or a member of a shower active on that night; the duration of the associated persistent train, if present, and its behaviour with time; any other details on meteor speed, duration, colour, explosions, etc. Plots of the tracks of meteors are not usually required, except for fireball events or if a radiant position is needed for a suspected new shower.

All observations should be communicated to the meteor section of a national organization (for addresses see the Appendix).

Telescopic observations

For this work one requires a telescope or a pair of binoculars with as wide a field as possible (and therefore a low power). The telescopic observer should supply much the same information as a visual observer. Details of the instrument used, the eyepiece field of view and the celestial coordinates of the centre of the field are required. The observer should also attempt to plot the paths of meteors seen against the field star background. However, telescopic meteor work demands great patience, as the observed meteor rates are usually considerably lower than for the naked-eye observer.

Photographic observations

Ordinary cameras with lenses faster than $f/4.5$ and fast film of ISO 400 and above are suitable for meteor work.

Observers should make timed exposures of about 1 to 10 minutes, depending on their equipment and the observing conditions. The start and end of each exposure should be noted in UT to the nearest 0.1 minute, as should the time, position and nature of any bright meteor thought to have passed through the camera's field of view. Typically, only meteors of magnitude 0 or brighter will be recorded photographically; to increase the number of meteors recorded the observer should use a battery of several cameras rather than just one.

The addition of rotating shutters for velocity measurements, plus cameras at other sites for triangulation, will enable observers to calculate real paths and orbital data for photographed events.

Fireball observations

If an object entering the atmosphere is large enough, it will produce a brilliant fireball with an apparent diameter similar to that of the Sun or the Moon. The object itself may not be completely vaporized before reaching the ground. These surviving rocks, called *meteorites*, are of great importance and it is advantageous to examine them as quickly as possible after the fall. Organizations exist to receive fireball reports so that the fall area can be located quickly. Few major fireballs produce meteorites, but if a sonic boom is heard a meteorite is quite likely to fall.

There is a close similarity between natural fireballs and those produced by the re-entry of artificial satellites, although the latter usually move much more slowly than the natural objects and may take up to a minute to cross the sky.

Because no one can predict the arrival of a fireball, the witnessing of such an event is a matter of luck and reports tend to come from casual observers. Any observer of such an event should contact, as soon as possible, the Smithsonian Institution Scientific Event Alert Network, National Museum of Natural History, Mail Stop 129, Washington, DC 20560, U.S.A. or, if the fireball is seen over the British Isles, the Director, Artificial Satellite Section, BAA (for address see the Appendix). Information on the following is required:

(a) Name and address of observer, observing site, date and time (UT).

(b) Track – if possible, the track through the star background. If this is not possible, then the direction and elevation angle when first seen, when highest in the sky and when last seen. If the object passes virtually overhead, then whether to the left-hand side or right-hand side as the observer faces the direction from which it came.

(c) The magnitude, size, shape and colour, details of tail and presence or absence of dust trail, and fragmentation and extinction.

(d) Sonic effects – estimate of time interval between the passage of the object (known in this case as a *bolide*) and the sonic boom.

Calculation of meteor rates

The observed rates of both shower and sporadic meteors depend on the limiting magnitude, cloud cover and the observer's perception. Moonlight significantly reduces the number of meteors visible, and for five days either side of the full moon only bright meteors will be seen. Shower rates also depend on the elevation of the shower radiant above the horizon – the lower the radiant, the fewer shower meteors will be seen.

The activity of a shower is expressed in terms of its ZHR, which is the number of meteors that would be seen by a single observer if the radiant were at the zenith in a clear sky with a limiting magnitude of 6.5. The *sporadic hourly rate* (SHR) is defined as the hourly rate of sporadic meteors seen by a single observer under clear skies. Hence:

$$ZHR = (N_{sh}/t) \times R \times C_{sh} \times F$$

$$SHR = (N_{sp}/t) \times C_{sp} \times F$$

where N_{sh} and N_{sp} are respectively the number of shower and sporadic meteors seen during the watch, t is the watch duration in hours, R is the correction factor for radiant elevation at mid-watch, C_{sh} and C_{sp} are the correction factors for limiting magnitude for shower and sporadic meteors respectively, and F is the cloud correction factor. The various correction factors are further explained below.

Radiant elevation correction factor (R)

$$R = 1/\sin a$$

where a is the radiant elevation in degrees. This is the simplest formula, though others have been proposed; the higher the elevation, the closer the agreement between the various formulae. The values in Table 26 have been calculated from the above formula. As can be seen, for radiant altitudes lower than 30° the observed rate will be far less than the theoretical ZHR.

Sky limiting magnitude correction factor (C)

$$C = r^{6.5 - LM}$$

where r is the *population index* (the ratio between the true number of meteors in adjacent magnitude classes) and LM is the limiting magnitude. The value for the population index varies among showers, and is usually higher for sporadics than for shower meteors, so no precise figures can be quoted. Observations show that for major showers

values of r between 2.2 and 2.5 are reasonable, while for sporadic meteors a value from 2.5 to 3.0 is usually adopted.

For a perfectly clear sky $LM = 6.5$, and hence the correction factor is 1. The clearer the sky the better, since C is then closer to 1 and relatively insensitive to the value of r. The poorer the sky, the more uncertain are the derived rates.

Cloud correction factor (F)

$$F = 100/(100 - K)$$

where K is the percentage cloud in the area of sky under watch, averaged over the watch period. For a clear sky $F = 1$.

Comments. The above computations are relevant only to the results of a single observer. Correction factors have been derived for two or more observers, but rather than have the uncertainty of yet another correction factor introduced into the computations, observers should keep individual records when observing with others.

A final correction factor, ignored above, is that of contamination of shower rates by sporadic meteors. Since sporadic meteors have random directions, a fraction of them will have paths that align by chance with a shower radiant and will be wrongly recorded as shower members. The effect is small, however, and becomes significant only when considering showers with low rates.

Principal meteor showers

Table 27 gives details of the major night-time streams. The dates for the limits of activity and the peak ZHR should be used as only a rough guide, for the activity of showers can vary with time.

The radiant positions are quoted for the date of maximum activity but, in practice, radiants move slightly from night to night so for other dates the radiant daily motion (where listed in Table 27) should be added or subtracted.

Leap year adjustments cause small variations in the given dates. For example, the best night for Perseid activity in a particular year may be August 11/12 or 12/13. It is always wise to refer to a current handbook or almanac for topical detail of the year's showers, and for other showers that may be particularly active during the year.

Table 26. The radiant elevation correction factor R for various altitudes of the radiant.

Altitude (degrees)	R	Altitude (degrees)	R
5	11.5	35	1.7
10	5.8	40	1.6
15	3.9	45	1.4
20	2.9	50	1.3
25	2.4	65	1.1
30	2.0		

Table 27. Principal meteor showers.

Shower	Dates — Normal limits	Dates — Maximum	Approximate ZHR at maximum	Radiant — Position at maximum (2000.0) RA	Radiant — Position at maximum (2000.0) dec.	Radiant — Daily motion (where known) RA	Radiant — Daily motion (where known) dec.	Notes	Parent comet (where known)
				h m °	°	°	°		
Quadrantids[a]	Jan. 1–6	Jan. 3	60	15 30 (232)	+50			Medium speed; blue	
Corona Australids	Mar. 14–18	Mar. 16	5	16 24 (246)	−48				
Lyrids	Apr. 19–25	Apr. 22	10	18 10 (272)	+32	+1.1	0.0	Swift; brilliant	Thatcher 1861 I
η Aquarids	May 1–10	May 6	35	22 23 (336)	−0i	+0.9	+0.4	Very swift; persistent trains	P/Halley
Ophiuchids	June 17–26	June 20	5	17 23 (261)	−20				
Capricornids	July 10–Aug. 15	July 25	5	21 03 (316)	−15			Yellow; very slow	
δ Aquarids	July 15–Aug. 15	July 29 / Aug. 7	20 / 10	22 39 (340) / 23 07 (347)	−17 / +02	+0.8 / +1.0	+0.18 / +0.2	Double radiant; rather faint meteors	
Piscis Australids	July 15–Aug. 20	July 31	5	22 43 (341)	−30				
α Capricornids	July 15–Aug. 25	Aug. 2	5	20 39 (310)	−10	+0.9	+0.3	Bright yellow; slow	P/Honda–Mrkos–Pajdusaková
ι Aquarids	July 15–Aug. 25	Aug. 6	8	22 15 (334) / 22 07 (332)	−15 / −06	+1.07 / +1.03	+0.18 / +0.13	Double radiant; rather faint meteors	
Perseids	July 23–Aug. 20	Aug. 12	75	03 08 (047)	+58	+1.35	+0.12	Swift; fragmenting; many bright events and trains	P/Swift–Tuttle
Giacobinids	Oct. 6–10	Oct. 8	below 5	17 25 (261)	+57			Only active (if at all) when parent comet is near perihelion	P/Giacobini–Zinner
Orionids	Oct. 16–27	Oct. 22	25	06 27 (097)	+15	+1.23	+0.13	Very swift; with trains	P/Halley
Taurids	Oct. 20–Nov. 30	Nov. 5	10	03 47 (057) / 03 47 (057)	+14 / +22	+0.79 / +0.76	+0.15 / +0.10	Double radiant; very slow; flat maximum	P/Encke
Leonids	Nov. 15–20	Nov. 17	10	10 11 (153)	+22	+0.70	−0.42	Bright with trains; exceptional activity every 33 years	P/Tempel–Tuttle
Geminids	Dec. 7–15	Dec. 13	75	07 31 (113)	+32	+1.1	−0.07	Medium speed; bright; few trains	Minor planet (3200) Phaethon
Ursids	Dec. 17–25	Dec. 22	5	14 27 (217)	+78	+0.88	−0.45	Usually weak	P/Tuttle

[a] Named after the former constellation Quadrans Muralis; the radiant is in Boötes.

ECLIPSES

Solar 'eclipses' are actually occultations of the Sun by the Moon and can occur only at new moon. A solar eclipse can be seen from only a limited area of the Earth's surface. Lunar eclipses occur when the Moon passes into the shadow of the Earth; this can happen only at full moon. They are seen over rather more than half the Earth, wherever the Moon is above the horizon.

Each year at least two solar eclipses occur, and occasionally as many as five. Some years there are no lunar eclipses at all but there can be as many as three, either total or partial (but not counting penumbral eclipses). Solar eclipses outnumber lunar eclipses in the ratio of nearly 5 to 3. Between 2001 and 2100 there are 224 solar eclipses, total and partial.

On average, four eclipses occur each year: two pairs of solar and lunar eclipses, separated by about six months. The maximum number of eclipses in a year is seven: either five solar and two lunar or four solar and three lunar, depending on the precise configuration of the Sun and the Moon. In years with seven eclipses, the solar eclipses are always partial; the lunar eclipses can be total or partial. The last year with seven eclipses was 1982 (when all three lunar eclipses were total). Seven eclipses will occur again in 2094 and 2159, four of the Sun and three of the Moon each time.

Other examples of eclipses are those of satellites when they pass through the shadow of their parent planet, or through the shadow of another satellite; and the 'eclipses' (again, actually occultations) of the components of an eclipsing binary star system.

Predictions of the details of eclipses each year are published in a booklet called *Astronomical Phenomena*.* The *Fifty Year Canon of Solar Eclipses* by Fred Espenak (NASA, 1987; available from Sky Publishing Corp.) gives predictions and maps for solar eclipses from 1986 to 2035, and lists the general characteristics of every solar eclipse from 1901 to 2100. Details of eclipses from 1990 to 2004 are given in Table 28.

Solar eclipses

Solar eclipses may be *total*, *partial* or *annular*, depending on the relative positions and distances apart of the Sun, Moon and Earth at the time. As much as four hours may elapse between first and last contact, but totality may last from an instant, through an average of three or four minutes, to a maximum of $7\frac{1}{2}$ minutes as seen from a point on the equator with the Moon at perigee; the longest eclipse in the next few centuries (Table 29) is that of 2186 July 16, predicted to last 7m 29s.

---

* Obtainable in the U.K. from HMSO Bookshops or from HMSO Publication Centre, PO Box 276, London SW8 5DT; in the U.S.A. from the Superintendent of Documents, US Government Printing Office, Washington, DC 20402.

The width of the Moon's umbra at the Earth can reach 273 km, but is on average less than 160 km. However, the width of the eclipse path can be considerably greater than this if the shadow falls obliquely on the Earth, as it can near the poles. For example, the path of the total eclipse of 2033 March 30, visible from within the Arctic Circle, will have the extraordinary width of 777 km. The zone within which a partial eclipse is seen is at least 3200 km either side of the limit of totality. Total eclipses are rare events for an observer at any one point on the Earth's surface.

An annular eclipse occurs when the Moon is near apogee. At these times it does not appear large enough to cover the Sun completely, and the dark disk of the Moon is surrounded by a bright ring (*annulus*) of sunlight. The maximum shadow width at the Earth during an annular eclipse is 313 km, but again the actual path width can be considerably greater if the shadow falls obliquely – for example nearly 4500 km at the annular eclipse of 2003 May 31. Annularity can be instantaneous (Baily's beads around the entire disk, as on 1966 May 20). It has a maximum of $12\frac{1}{2}$ minutes viewed at the equator with the Moon at apogee, although this theoretical maximum is rarely approached; according to calculations by H. Mucke and J. Meeus the longest annular eclipse between the years 2003 BC and AD 2526 was 12m 26s in AD 150.

Partial eclipses are of little importance, but annular eclipses provide a sensitive way of checking for possible changes in the Sun's diameter. Most important of all are total eclipses, which provide the only opportunity of seeing the Sun's chromosphere, prominences and corona without the need for special instruments. When the Sun is completely hidden the sky becomes dark like deep twilight, and the bright planets and stars can be seen with the naked eye. The Moon appears as an intensely black disk surrounded by the bright inner corona, changing further out into the delicate brush-strokes and plumes of the pearly outer corona. Some red-tinted prominences may be seen.

Baily's beads are sometimes seen for a few seconds at a total eclipse immediately before and after totality, or during a brief annular eclipse, when the thin crescent of the Sun is broken up into a series of bright moving points by mountain peaks along the limb of the Moon, giving the appearance of a string of shining beads. The name derives from the English astronomer Francis Baily, who first described and discussed the beads after the eclipse of 1836. After only a few seconds this display narrows down to just one bead which, together with the appearance of the inner corona around the entire disk, produces the dazzling *diamond ring* effect.

Shadow bands may also occur, shortly before and after totality. They are bands of shadow 100–150 mm wide and up to a metre apart crossing any light-coloured surface, rather like the projection of surface ripples onto the bottom of a bowl of water, and a very clear, transparent sky is needed for them to occur. They are probably caused by irregular refraction of light from the thin crescent Sun in the Earth's atmosphere.

Table 28. Eclipses from 1990 to 2004 (excluding partial and penumbral eclipses of the Moon).

Date	Body eclipsed	Type of eclipse	Maximum duration m:s	Area of visibility
1990 Jan. 26	Sun	Annular	2:03	S New Zealand, Antarctica, South America except NW
Feb. 9	Moon	Total		NW Alaska, Arctic regions, Australasia, Asia, Africa, Europe, Iceland, Greenland
July 22	Sun	Total	2:33	NE Europe, N Greenland, N Asia, Arctic regions, NW North America, Hawaii
1991 Jan. 15–16	Sun	Annular	7:53	E Indonesia, S New Guinea, Australia, New Zealand, part of Antarctica, Polynesia
July 11	Sun	Total	6:53	Hawaii, SW Canada, U.S.A. except extreme NE, Mexico, Central and South America except extreme S
1992 Jan. 4–5	Sun	Annular	11:41	Philippine Islands except NW, extreme E Asia, Japan, Oceania, NE Australia, W North America
June 30	Sun	Total	5:21	South America except NW and extreme S, W and SW Africa, S Madagascar
Dec. 9–10	Moon	Total		Asia except SE, Africa, Europe, Iceland, Greenland, Arctic regions, North America except extreme W, Central America, South America except extreme S
Dec. 23–24	Sun	Partial		NE China, Korea, Japan, extreme SE U.S.S.R., extreme SW Alaska
1993 May 21	Sun	Partial		North America except SE, Arctic regions, Greenland, Iceland, N Scandinavia, NW Asia
June 4	Moon	Total		Extreme S South America, extreme W North America, Pacific Ocean, Antarctica, Australasia, SE Asia
Nov. 13	Sun	Partial		Most of Antarctica
Nov. 29	Moon	Total		Europe, W Africa, Iceland, Greenland, Arctic regions, The Americas, N Asia
1994 May 10	Sun	Annular	6:14	Extreme NE Asia, North and Central America, extreme N South America, West Indies, Arctic regions, Greenland, Iceland, Europe except SE, W Africa
Nov. 3	Sun	Total	4:23	Central and South America, part of Antarctica, S Africa, Madagascar
1995 Apr. 29	Sun	Annular	6:37	Central and South America except extreme S, West Indies, extreme W Africa
Oct. 24	Sun	Total	2:10	Somalia, Arabia, Asia except NE, Japan, Oceania, Australia except S
1996 Apr. 3–4	Moon	Total		W Asia, Africa, Antarctica, Europe, Iceland, Greenland, South America, West Indies, E North America
Apr. 17	Sun	Partial		New Zealand, S Pacific Ocean
Sept. 27	Moon	Total		Extreme W Asia, Africa, Europe, Iceland, Greenland, Arctic regions, Antarctica, The Americas except Alaska
Oct. 12	Sun	Partial		Extreme NE Canada, Greenland, Iceland, Europe, N Africa
1997 Mar. 8–9	Sun	Total	2:50	E Asia, Philippines, Japan, NW North America
Sept. 1–2	Sun	Partial		Australia except extreme N, New Zealand, S Pacific Ocean, part of Antarctica
Sept. 16	Moon	Total		Australasia, Asia except extreme NE, Arctic regions, Antarctica, Africa except extreme W, Europe
1998 Feb. 26	Sun	Total	4:09	E of Hawaii, S and E North America, Central America, N South America, West Indies, extreme S Greenland, extreme W Africa, Portugal
Aug. 21–22	Sun	Annular	3:14	S and SE Asia, Indonesia, Philippines, extreme S Japan, Australasia
1999 Feb. 16	Sun	Annular	0:40	S Africa, Madagascar, Antarctica, Indonesia, S Philippines, Australasia
Aug. 11	Sun	Total	2:23	NE North America, Greenland, Arctic regions, Iceland, Europe, N Africa, Arabia, Asia except E
2000 Jan. 21	Moon	Total		N and NW Asia, W and N Africa, Europe, Iceland, Greenland, Arctic regions, The Americas
Feb. 5	Sun	Partial		Most of Antarctica
July 1	Sun	Partial		SE Pacific Ocean, extreme SW South America
July 16	Moon	Total		Pacific Ocean, extreme SW Alaska, Antarctica, Australasia, SW Asia
July 31	Sun	Partial		Extreme N and NE Asia, Alaska, Canada except SE, Arctic regions, Greenland except S
Dec. 25	Sun	Partial		North America except NW and extreme N, Gulf of Mexico, N Caribbean Sea, extreme S of Greenland
2001 Jan. 9	Moon	Total		Australia except SE, New Guinea, Indonesia, Philippines, Asia, Africa, Europe, Iceland, Greenland, extreme N North America, Arctic regions
June 21	Sun	Total	4:57	E South America, South Atlantic Ocean, Africa except N, Madagascar
Dec. 14	Sun	Annular	3:53	Hawaii, extreme S Alaska, SW Canada, W U.S.A., Mexico, Central America, Caribbean Sea

Table 28 (continued)

Date	Body eclipsed	Type of eclipse	Maximum duration m:s	Area of visibility
2002 June 10–11	Sun	Annular	0:23	SE and extreme NE Asia, Philippines, N Pacific Ocean, North America except N and E
Dec. 4	Sun	Total	2:04	S Africa, Madagascar, Australia except N and E
2003 May 16	Moon	Total		Antarctica, Africa except E, Europe except NE, Iceland, S Greenland, The Americas except NW and extreme N
May 31	Sun	Annular	3:37	Iceland, N Greenland, Arctic regions, N Europe, N Asia, Alaska, N Canada
Nov. 8–9	Moon	Total		Asia except E, Africa, Europe, Iceland, Greenland, Arctic regions, The Americas except SW Alaska
Nov. 23–24	Sun	Total	1:57	Antarctica, S Australasia, extreme S South America
2004 Apr. 19	Sun	Partial		S Africa, S of South Atlantic Ocean
May 4	Moon	Total		Antarctica, Australia, New Guinea, Indonesia, Philippines, Asia except NE, Africa, Europe except extreme N, extreme E South America
Oct. 14	Sun	Partial		E Asia, Hawaii, W Alaska
Oct. 28	Moon	Total		W Asia, Africa except extreme E, Europe, Iceland, Greenland, Arctic regions, The Americas

Source: Planetary and Lunar Coordinates 1984–2000 (HMSO/US Government Printing Office).

Table 29. Forthcoming total solar eclipses lasting longer than 7 minutes.

2150 June 25	7m 14s
2168 July 5	7m 26s
2186 July 16	7m 29s
2204 July 27	7m 22s
2222 Aug. 8	7m 06s
2504 June 14	7m 10s
2522 June 25	7m 13s

Source: H. Mucke and J. Meeus, Canon of Solar Eclipses (Astronomisches Büro, 1973).

Lunar eclipses

Lunar eclipses last much longer than solar ones, up to 4 hours from first to last contact of the umbra, over 6 hours including the penumbral stage. The maximum duration of totality is 1h 47m, as happens on 2000 July 16. There is a noticeable variation from one eclipse to another in the brightness of the eclipsed Moon. Usually the Moon does not vanish completely, as light is refracted onto its surface through the Earth's atmosphere. The eclipsed Moon commonly appears a coppery red colour, but its exact colour and brightness depend on the conditions of cloud, haze and high-altitude dust in the Earth's atmosphere at the time. During a lunar eclipse, a rapid cooling of the lunar surface occurs as the Earth's shadow sweeps across it; detailed measurements have shown that certain so-called 'hot spots' such as the crater Tycho cool less quickly than their surroundings. In a penumbral eclipse the Moon enters only the light outer part of the Earth's shadow (the penumbra), and often no dimming is noticeable to the eye at all.

OCCULTATIONS

An occultation occurs when any object obstructs the view of another, more distant object. Hence a total eclipse of the Sun is strictly an occultation, and eclipsing binary stars are really occulting binaries. Planets and asteroids occult stars, and mutual occultations occur among the satellites of Jupiter. However, the most frequent and readily observed types of occultation are those of stars by the Moon.

Lunar occultations

As it moves in its orbit around the Earth, the Moon regularly occults background stars. Because the Moon has no atmosphere the disappearance and reappearance of a star is instantaneous, so occultations can be timed very accurately by amateurs with only modest equipment. These timings reveal slight changes in the orbit of the Moon and the gradual slowing of the rotation of the Earth due to tidal friction. The motion of the Moon is used in the determination of Terrestrial Dynamical Time (TDT), which gives a smooth measure of time free from the short-term irregular variations in the Earth's rotation. In addition, occultation timings sometimes reveal errors in the accepted positions and proper motions of stars, and a stepwise fading to disappearance rather than an instantaneous vanishing of the star can indicate the existence of previously unrecognized double or multiple stars.

Since the Moon moves through about 1 second of arc in 2 seconds of time, a timing accuracy of only 0.2s is needed to give the Moon's position to 0.1 arcsec, corresponding to about 200 m in the Moon's orbit. Grazing occultations, when the star skims the upper or lower limb of the Moon, are particularly valuable for determining the precise position of the Moon in its orbit.

Observing lunar occultations. A small telescope will permit observation of many occultations of stars of mag. 6.5 and brighter. Disappearances and reappearances are much easier to observe at the dark limb than the bright limb of the Moon, and disappearances are easier to time accurately than reappearances since the star is in view right up until the moment of occultation. The Moon approaches the star in a direction approximately at right angles to the line joining the cusps, or horns, of the Moon. The rate of approach of the Moon to a star is about half a degree (its own apparent diameter) every hour, or the apparent diameter of the crater Copernicus every $1\frac{1}{2}$ minutes.

One simple method of timing occultations requires a good-quality stopwatch, which is started when the star is seen to disappear or reappear and is stopped as soon as possible on a time signal. The telephone time service is very convenient, and short-wave radio time services are available in most parts of the world. The latter system allows occultations occurring in rapid succession to be recorded, and is essential for the observation of grazing occultations when many events may be seen as the star skims the rugged profile of the lunar limb. The usual method is to leave a tape recorder running with the time signals in the background and to call out the disappearances and reappearances as they are seen. Increasing use is being made of lightweight video cameras attached to the telescope with a visual time-display recorded on the tape. Both these methods allow the results to be analysed at leisure with high accuracy. For all occultations, the observer's location and altitude must be accurately established from a map.

The world centre for predictions and subsequent reduction of reports is the International Lunar Occultation Centre (ILOC), Geodesy and Geophysics Division, Hydrographic Department, Tsukiji-5, Chuo-ku, Tokyo 104, Japan. There is also the International Occultation Timing Association (IOTA), 6N 106 White Oak Lane, St Charles, Illinois 60175, U.S.A. Many national astronomical societies coordinate observations among their own members and publish predictions.

Other occultations

Occasionally stars are occulted by asteroids. Predictions of these events are distributed to members by the International Occultation Timing Association, together with the track across the Earth from which the occultation may be seen. The observing technique is similar to that for lunar occultations, except that the occulting body will not usually be visible since the occulted star is normally much brighter than the asteroid. Accurate timing by several observers of the duration of such an occultation yields a cross-section of the asteroid, allowing its size and shape to be derived and its orbit refined.

AURORAE, NOCTILUCENT CLOUDS AND THE ZODIACAL LIGHT

Aurorae

Aurorae are glows in the upper atmosphere of the Earth caused when fast-moving atomic particles (protons and electrons) arrive in the solar wind. Collisions of these particles with atoms and molecules of atmospheric nitrogen and oxygen at heights above 100 km lead to the emission of light, seen as an aurora. Aurorae are most common at times of high sunspot activity, when solar flares inject 'pockets' of energetic particles into the solar wind. Persistent particle streams emitted from coronal holes can also give rise to aurorae (often recurring at 27-day intervals, corresponding to the rotation period of the Sun), but these tend to be less active and extensive than the displays that follow solar flares.

Aurorae are most commonly seen at high latitudes close to the *auroral ovals*, rings of permanent auroral activity 4000 to 5000 km in diameter that surround the Earth's north and south magnetic poles. The arrival of streams of charged particles ejected by solar flares or by coronal holes distorts the Earth's magnetic field and causes the auroral ovals to expand towards the equator. At such times observers at lower latitudes such as those of the British Isles, central North America and Australasia will see auroral displays.

Mid-latitude aurorae, while never exactly the same from one display to the next, do follow a fairly typical pattern. A display may begin as a fairly weak *glow* on the poleward horizon, aptly described by the name *aurora borealis* ('northern dawn') first used in the seventeenth century; the southern hemisphere equivalent is similarly known as *aurora australis*. This glow may remain relatively static or eventually fade away, and simply represents the uppermost parts of a display that is more impressive at higher latitudes.

Under more highly disturbed conditions, the glow may brighten and rise higher into the sky, taking on the form of an *arc* whose lower edge is usually more sharply defined than the upper edge. Folding of an arc produces a ribbon-like *band*. In active displays, vertical *rays* resembling searchlight beams develop along the length of arcs or bands. Rays frequently drift either eastwards or westwards. Sometimes, if a display lies far from the observer, isolated rays extending over the poleward horizon may be the only activity seen.

During extreme disturbances, and rather rarely at temperate latitudes, auroral activity can extend beyond the zenith. In such displays may be seen a *corona*, in which the rays appear to converge on a small area of sky as a result of perspective. Discrete *patches* of auroral light are also seen in some displays, and occasionally they can comprise entire displays.

The brightness of aurorae is rated on a scale from i (the faintest) to iv (the brightest). Aurorae at temperate latitudes range in brightness from weak glows comparable to the Milky Way (brightness i), via moderate displays comparable to moonlit cirrus cloud (brightness ii) to prominent displays comparable to moonlit cumulus cloud (brightness iii). At high latitudes, intense aurorae can cast shadows (brightness iv). Changes in brightness are commonly seen in aurorae. These range from slow *pulsing* over the course of several minutes to extremely rapid *flaming* with a period of seconds. In flaming activity, waves of brightening sweep upwards from the horizon through the aurora, often in the declining phase of a display.

Observing aurorae. Aurorae are diffuse light sources and are therefore best observed with the naked eye. Accurate measurements of the altitude and azimuth of features in a display, made with a simple sighting device (an *alidade*), can be of considerable value in assessing the geographical extent of the aurora at a given time, particularly if several sets of measurements from well-separated observers are available.

Two altitude measurements are of use: the altitude, in degrees, of the highest point on the base of an arc or band (symbol *h*), and the uppermost extent of the display, also in degrees (symbol ↗). An indication of the auroral forms present at the time of observation is useful, along with brightness estimates. Auroral features may be described as *quiet* or *active*. Thus an observer's record of a display might be as follows:

20 00 (UT) Quiet auroral glow, brightness i, ↗10°, 330–020 azimuth
20 25   Active rayed arc, brightness iii, *h*12° ↗40°, 320–040 azimuth

Standard reporting codes recommended by various observing organizations are convenient for providing more concise descriptions of auroral displays.

Photography allows rapid and accurate recording of aurorae. There are few hard-and-fast rules, but the best results seem to be obtained using ISO 400 colour film. Exposures at *f*/2 for 30 to 60 seconds should record weak, static displays, while bright active aurorae should be exposed for only 5 to 10 seconds so as to avoid loss of detail caused by the aurora's motion.

Faint aurorae will normally appear colourless, but more active displays can show pronounced green or red colours. The green colour, which to the naked-eye observer is usually predominant, corresponds to a wavelength of 558 nm; this is caused by excited oxygen atoms, as is the 630 nm red emission. Other colours correspond to emissions from excited nitrogen atoms and molecules. Photographs often enhance auroral greens and reds as a result of the particular colour sensitivities of some emulsions.

Reports of auroral activity are collected by a number of bodies, notably the Aurora Sections of the British Astronomical Association and Royal Astronomical Society of New Zealand, and the Solar Section of the Norwegian Astronomical Society (for addresses see the Appendix).

Noctilucent clouds

Upwelling of cold air from the polar regions of the lower atmosphere during the summer months in each hemisphere carries traces of water vapour to great heights. Condensation of this water vapour, possibly around nuclei provided by meteoric or volcanic debris, produces very tenuous cloud formations, mainly at latitudes of 60° to 80°. The thin sheets of these noctilucent clouds, forming at heights of 80 to 85 km, lie considerably higher in the atmosphere than the cirrus clouds (maximum height 15 km) to which they bear a superficial resemblance. At their great height noctilucent clouds remain sunlit (above the Earth's shadow) long after clouds in the lower atmosphere are in darkness, and are clearly visible against the twilit background of the summer night sky at high temperate latitudes while the Sun is between 6° and 16° below the observer's horizon. Noctilucent clouds can therefore be distinguished by the 'night-shining' nature from which they take their name: clouds in the lower atmosphere are often seen dark in silhouette against noctilucent cloud displays.

Noctilucent clouds often show a distinctive silvery-blue colour, shading off to gold towards the sunward horizon. Like aurorae, noctilucent clouds show a small range of characteristic structures. Displays often consist of regularly spaced *bands* lying roughly parallel to the horizon. Curved forms are described as either *billows* or *whirls*, and interwoven structures have a distinctive herringbone appearance. Featureless background veils are sometimes seen. Displays are usually most extensive in the early evening, fading around midnight when the Sun is furthest below the observer's horizon, or just before dawn.

Since they form not far below the level of aurorae in the atmosphere, noctilucent clouds are believed to be indicative of quiet geomagnetic conditions: sightings are most frequent in the summers around sunspot minima, and it seems that heating of the upper atmosphere by aurorae inhibits noctilucent cloud formation. Observations indicate the existence of a complicated weather system at such altitudes, with winds carrying noctilucent clouds westwards at up to 400 km h^{-1}.

The British Isles, Scandinavia and Canada are well placed for the observation of noctilucent clouds, having long hours of twilight during summer nights and lying reasonably close to the latitudes at which the clouds form. Southern hemisphere land-masses are less favourably placed, though observations can be made from parts of the South Atlantic and Antarctica.

As with aurorae, measurements of the extent in altitude and azimuth of noctilucent cloud displays are useful. It is normally sufficient to take these at intervals of 15 minutes, since noctilucent clouds seldom show very rapid changes. Rough sketches of a display's appearance are of use in conjunction with measurements. Photography of noctilucent clouds is quite straightforward, and attractive results can be obtained with colour film. Typical exposures at *f*/2.8 on ISO 400 film are 2 to 4 seconds.

Reports of noctilucent cloud sightings, and of nights for

which the observer can confidently say that *no* noctilucent cloud was present, are welcomed by the organizations that collect auroral observations.

The zodiacal light

A faint, hazy, conical beam of light, about 15°–20° wide at the base, is sometimes seen in the west after sunset or in the east before sunrise. The main axis of this beam lies approximately along the ecliptic for 90° or more from the horizon, a little south (in southern latitudes, north) of where the Sun is below the horizon. In its brightest parts, it is two or three times as luminous as the Milky Way, but towards its extreme limits it is always exceedingly faint. Its brightness seems to vary from time to time, possibly in response to fluctuations in solar activity. It is brighter when observed within the tropics than in temperate latitudes, partly because the main axis of the cone is more or less at right angles to the horizon, and partly because of the short twilight periods.

From mid-northern latitudes, the zodiacal light is best seen near the vernal equinox in the evening and near the autumnal equinox in the morning (vice versa in the southern hemisphere). Table 30 gives the approximate dates and hours when the ecliptic is most nearly vertical during the short observing season. The position of the foot of the zodiacal light on the horizon for 3 or 4 hours after (or before) the hours mentioned is easily found, as its movement in azimuth westwards may be taken as about 6° per hour over that period; similarly, the decrease per hour in inclination after (or before) greatest verticality is, roughly, 2°.

It is now generally accepted that this light is sunlight that has been scattered by dust particles (micrometeoroids) lying in the plane of the ecliptic and orbiting the Sun. The spectrum of the zodiacal light is essentially the same as that of normal sunlight. The particle sizes lie in the range 1–350 μm, and there is evidence that the zodiacal light is an extension of the F corona (or dust corona) of the Sun.

The Gegenschein.

This phenomenon, also known as the *counterglow*, is a very faint patch of light at or near the antisolar point, i.e. the point on the ecliptic directly opposite the position of the Sun at the time. It is normally elliptical, typically 10° × 20°, although in the tropics it may be seen to extend over 30°. It can normally be seen only on very clear moonless nights, the best times being when the ecliptic is highest above the horizon (December and January for northern observers, June and July for southern observers).

It is thought that the gegenschein is caused by the scattering of sunlight by dust particles orbiting the Sun. The gegenschein is sometimes seen joined to the zodiacal light by a parallel beam of light called the *zodiacal band*.

ARTIFICIAL SATELLITES

An artificial satellite appears as a star-like point of light drifting slowly across the sky, possibly flashing as it tumbles or slowly fading out as it moves into the Earth's shadow and is eclipsed. Many satellites have bright surfaces that reflect sunlight well, so they are easily visible at heights of several hundreds or even thousands of kilometres.

Over 7000 satellites are being tracked in orbit by military radar installations. They include working satellites, dead satellites, discarded rocket stages, fragments from break-ups and many other pieces of space junk. About 10% of all satellites are above the horizon at any moment. Some satellites rival the brightest stars and are clearly visible to the naked eye, while many more can be seen with binoculars. Visual observations by amateurs are of considerable value in following the ever-changing orbits of artificial satellites.

The best time to see satellites is shortly after sunset or before sunrise, when they will be illuminated by the Sun's rays against a dark or fairly dark background. Bright satellites can usually be detected by the time the Sun has dropped 6° below the horizon (civil twilight), but fainter satellites may require the Sun to be 9° or even 12° down before they can be seen.

The satellite will be invisible if it is eclipsed in the Earth's shadow. Eclipses frequently occur while the satellite is crossing the sky. In the pre-dawn sky the situation is reversed, and satellites can often appear high in the sky as they emerge from eclipse.

The speed at which a satellite moves depends on its altitude. The lowest ones, which orbit a few hundred kilometres up, move the quickest (in accordance with Kepler's laws), having periods of about 90 minutes. When passing overhead, these satellites will move at a rate of almost 2° (or four Moon diameters) per second, taking two or three minutes to cross the sky from horizon to horizon, far slower than a meteor. Precise determination of the angular

Table 30. Times, for northern and southern observers, at which the ecliptic is most nearly vertical and the zodiacal light is best observed.

N	Feb. 5	Feb. 12	Feb. 20	Feb. 27	Mar. 7	Mar. 14	Mar. 22
	21.00	20.30	20.00	19.30	19.00	18.30	18.00
S	Aug. 6	Aug. 13	Aug. 21	Aug. 29	Sept. 6	Sept. 13	Sept. 21
N	Sept. 22	Sept. 29	Oct. 7	Oct. 14	Oct. 22	Oct. 30	Nov. 7
	06.00	05.30	05.00	04.30	04.00	03.30	03.00
S	Mar. 23	Mar. 31	Apr. 8	Apr. 15	Apr. 23	Apr. 30	May 8

velocity of an unexpected satellite is of considerable help in identifying it.

Brightness. The brightness of a satellite depends on many factors, including its size and the material of which its surface is made. One that is black or covered in dark solar cells will be fainter than a similar white one. A given satellite will be brighter when nearby (overhead) than when farther away (near the horizon).

As with the Moon, a satellite's brightness varies with phase angle, which is the angle between the Sun and the satellite as seen by the observer. When the phase angle is small (i.e. when the Sun and the satellite are almost in line), most of the sunlit side of the satellite is facing away from the observer and it will appear dark. Conversely, a large phase angle (near 180°) means that the satellite appears nearly fully illuminated and will therefore be much brighter.

Variations in brightness will occur if a satellite is not spherical. Large flat surfaces can cause momentary bright reflections, appearing as sudden flashes in the sky; these can be seen on any clear night.

Orbital changes. A number of forces act on an orbiting satellite, causing its orbit to change. It is well known that air-drag causes a satellite to spiral slowly back to Earth, making its orbit smaller and its period shorter until it finally re-enters the atmosphere and burns up. But other forces are in action, including the gravitational effects of the Earth's equatorial bulge and the pressure of sunlight.

As a result of the changing orientation of the orbit and the movement of the Earth around the Sun, the satellite will not be visible every night, but will have periods of visibility which can range from a few days for low, non-polar satellites to several months for satellites in moderately high-altitude polar orbits with inclinations greater than 90°.

Predictions for artificial satellites are of two types. The first are of a general form, called *equator-crossing* predictions, which give the time and longitude for each south-to-north crossing of the equator; this type of prediction will need further processing to make it applicable to the observer's own site. The second type of prediction, referred to as *look data*, gives the coordinates of the predicted positions in the sky as seen from a particular location on Earth.

Observations. If the predicted positions are marked on the charts in this Atlas, background stars may be selected against which to determine the satellite's position at a given time. This is usually done by timing the passage of the satellite across an imaginary line joining two stars, simultaneously estimating the position of the crossing point. For example, you might estimate that a satellite passed two-fifths of the way between stars A and B. The smaller the

separation between the two stars, the more accurate the estimated position; if the reference stars are several degrees apart the resulting observation will have low accuracy. The observations can be converted into celestial coordinates either by measurement on large-scale charts or by a computer program, using a star catalogue.

Observers of artificial satellites usually prefer binoculars with specifications such as 7×50 or 11×80, or even larger. Some observers have made observations of very high or geostationary satellites through telescopes. For accurate timings a stopwatch is required, as is a source of precise time signals – either the telephone time service or a radio broadcast. Timings are made by starting the watch as the satellite crosses the line between two stars, and stopping it against a time signal. Two timed positions on one transit are preferable to only one.

The times and positions, and possibly an estimate of the brightness of the satellite, are sent to a prediction centre, where they will be combined with data from other observers to produce new orbital elements for future predictions, and to study the perturbations affecting the orbit.

Designations. There are three systems for designating the various objects in orbit. The first is a simple catalogue number assigned in sequence as each new object is detected and tracked in orbit. The second is a name such as Sputnik 1, Apollo 11, Cosmos 1500 or Hubble Space Telescope.

The third system is the international designation, which before 1963 made use of Greek letters but now consists of three parts: the year of launch, the number of the launch in that year and a letter (or letters) indicating the various objects resulting from that launch. Frequently the payload is assigned the letter A, the orbiting rocket stage is labelled B and other items, such as discarded panels, are designated C, D and so on. The letters I and O are omitted to avoid confusion with numbers, so the system provides letters for 24 separate objects. If this is insufficient, e.g. for an explosion in orbit which produces hundreds of objects, double letters are used starting with AA to AZ, followed by BA to BZ, and so on, until ZZ is reached, which allows for up to 600 objects.

Some examples of equivalent designations are given in Table 31.

Table 31. Examples of equivalent designations of objects in orbit.

Catalogue number	Name	International designation
00005	Vanguard 1	1958 β 2
16609	Mir 1	1986–17A
18787	Ariane 1–11 fragment	1986–19UA

V

STARS, NEBULAE AND GALAXIES

THE STARS

CONSTELLATIONS AND NOMENCLATURE

The constellations

A total of 88 constellations, listed in Table 32, cover the entire sky. Nowadays they are regarded as being fixed areas of sky rather than star patterns as originally envisaged by the Greeks, but they remain convenient guides to the location of celestial objects.

The constellations that we know today have grown from a list of 48 published around AD 150 by the Greek astronomer Ptolemy in a book called the *Almagest*. At that time, constellations were regarded as star patterns with no definite boundaries. Many of these star figures, particularly the 12 constellations of the zodiac, were apparently invented by the Babylonians before 2000 BC.

Ptolemy's list remained essentially unchanged until the end of the sixteenth century when two Dutch navigators, Pieter Dirkszoon Keyser and Frederick de Houtman, added 12 new constellations in the south polar region of the sky. A century later seven new constellations were introduced into the northern sky by the Polish astronomer Johannes Hevelius, tucked into gaps between Ptolemy's figures. In the eighteenth century the French astronomer Nicolas Louis de Lacaille placed 14 more constellations in the southern hemisphere, and split up Ptolemy's large and unwieldy Argo Navis, the ship of the Argonauts, into Carina (the keel), Puppis (the poop) and Vela (the sails).

Constellation boundaries. The modern list of 88 constellations was adopted in 1922 by the newly formed International Astronomical Union. Even so, there were still no generally accepted constellation boundaries – charts such as those in the early editions of *Norton's Star Atlas* simply showed dotted lines meandering vaguely between the stars. On behalf of the IAU the Belgian astronomer Eugene Delporte drew up constellation boundaries along arcs of right ascension and declination for the year 1875 (this date was chosen because the American astronomer B. A. Gould

had already devised boundaries for the southern constellations for this epoch). Delporte's boundaries were published in 1930. They are fixed with respect to the stars, but the effect of precession means that they are gradually departing from the lines of right ascension and declination along which they were originally drawn, as can be seen on the charts in this Atlas.

Standard names and abbreviations of the constellations. When the IAU adopted their official list of 88 constellations in 1922, they drew up a list of three-letter abbreviations for each constellation, as given in Table 32. Hence a star such as Alpha (α) Ursae Majoris can for brevity be referred to as α UMa. Note that the genitive case of a constellation's name is used when referring to a star within it (hence Alpha Ursae Majoris means 'alpha of Ursa Major'). The genitive case for each constellation is also given in Table 32.

Star nomenclature

Many of the brightest stars have proper names (Table 33). Some of these names are Greek or Roman in origin, such as Sirius and Spica, but many of them are Arabic, such as Aldebaran. Astronomers use proper names sparingly, preferring instead the system of Greek letters introduced in 1603 by the German astronomer Johann Bayer, and hence known as *Bayer letters*. (See Table 34 for the Greek alphabet.)

Bayer labelled the brightest stars in a constellation with the letters alpha (α), beta (β) and so on, usually (but not always) in order of brightness. Stars are also given numbers, e.g. 61 Cygni, known as *Flamsteed numbers*. These come from a catalogue published in 1725 by the English Astronomer Royal John Flamsteed, in which he listed the stars of each constellation in order of right ascension; however, the Flamsteed numbers were not actually assigned by him but were added later by other astronomers. A star can therefore have several aliases – Betelgeuse is also Alpha (α) Orionis and 58 Orionis, for example. Fainter stars are known by their number in some other catalogue. Variable stars have a nomenclature of their own (see p. 147). Some of the best-known star catalogues are listed in Table 35.

Continued on p. 132

Table 32. The constellations.

Name	Genitive	Abbreviation	Area (square degrees)	Order of size
Andromeda	Andromedae	And	722	19
Antlia	Antliae	Ant	239	62
Apus	Apodis	Aps	206	67
Aquarius	Aquarii	Aqr	980	10
Aquila	Aquilae	Aql	652	22
Ara	Arae	Ara	237	63
Aries	Arietis	Ari	441	39
Auriga	Aurigae	Aur	657	21
Boötes	Boötis	Boo	907	13
Caelum	Caeli	Cae	125	81
Camelopardalis	Camelopardalis	Cam	757	18
Cancer	Cancri	Cnc	506	31
Canes Venatici	Canum Venaticorum	CVn	465	38
Canis Major	Canis Majoris	CMa	380	43
Canis Minor	Canis Minoris	CMi	183	71
Capricornus	Capricorni	Cap	414	40
Carina	Carinae	Car	494	34
Cassiopeia	Cassiopeiae	Cas	598	25
Centaurus	Centauri	Cen	1060	9
Cepheus	Cephei	Cep	588	27
Cetus	Ceti	Cet	1231	4
Chamaeleon	Chamaeleontis	Cha	132	79
Circinus	Circini	Cir	93	85
Columba	Columbae	Col	270	54
Coma Berenices	Comae Berenices	Com	386	42
Corona Australis	Coronae Australis	CrA	128	80
Corona Borealis	Coronae Borealis	CrB	179	73
Corvus	Corvi	Crv	184	70
Crater	Crateris	Crt	282	53
Crux	Crucis	Cru	68	88
Cygnus	Cygni	Cyg	804	16
Delphinus	Delphini	Del	189	69
Dorado	Doradus	Dor	179	72
Draco	Draconis	Dra	1083	8
Equuleus	Equulei	Equ	72	87
Eridanus	Eridani	Eri	1138	6
Fornax	Fornacis	For	398	41
Gemini	Geminorum	Gem	514	30
Grus	Gruis	Gru	366	45
Hercules	Herculis	Her	1225	5
Horologium	Horologii	Hor	249	58
Hydra	Hydrae	Hya	1303	1
Hydrus	Hydri	Hyi	243	61
Indus	Indi	Ind	294	49
Lacerta	Lacertae	Lac	201	68
Leo	Leonis	Leo	947	12
Leo Minor	Leonis Minoris	LMi	232	64
Lepus	Leporis	Lep	290	51
Libra	Librae	Lib	538	29
Lupus	Lupi	Lup	334	46
Lynx	Lyncis	Lyn	545	28
Lyra	Lyrae	Lyr	286	52
Mensa	Mensae	Men	153	75
Microscopium	Microscopii	Mic	210	66
Monoceros	Monocerotis	Mon	482	35
Musca	Muscae	Mus	138	77
Norma	Normae	Nor	165	74
Octans	Octantis	Oct	291	50
Ophiuchus	Ophiuchi	Oph	948	11
Orion	Orionis	Ori	594	26
Pavo	Pavonis	Pav	378	44
Pegasus	Pegasi	Peg	1121	7
Perseus	Persei	Per	615	24
Phoenix	Phoenicis	Phe	469	37
Pictor	Pictoris	Pic	247	59
Pisces	Piscium	Psc	889	14
Piscis Austrinus	Piscis Austrini	PsA	245	60
Puppis	Puppis	Pup	673	20
Pyxis	Pyxidis	Pyx	221	65
Reticulum	Reticuli	Ret	114	82
Sagitta	Sagittae	Sge	80	86
Sagittarius	Sagittarii	Sgr	867	15
Scorpius	Scorpii	Sco	497	33
Sculptor	Sculptoris	Scl	475	36
Scutum	Scuti	Sct	109	84
Serpens	Serpentis	Ser	637	23
Sextans	Sextantis	Sex	314	47
Taurus	Tauri	Tau	797	17
Telescopium	Telescopii	Tel	252	57
Triangulum	Trianguli	Tri	132	78
Triangulum Australe	Trianguli Australis	TrA	110	83
Tucana	Tucanae	Tuc	295	48
Ursa Major	Ursae Majoris	UMa	1280	3
Ursa Minor	Ursae Minoris	UMi	256	56
Vela	Velorum	Vel	500	32
Virgo	Virginis	Vir	1294	2
Volans	Volantis	Vol	141	76
Vulpecula	Vulpeculae	Vul	268	55

Table 33. Proper names of stars. A selection of the most frequently encountered proper names, with the Bayer or Flamsteed designations of the stars to which they apply. Note that some stars have more than one name, for example Alpha (α) Andromedae which is known as either Alpheratz or Sirrah, both derived from Arabic. Alternative spellings of many names may be encountered in different sources.

Name	Designation	Name	Designation	Name	Designation
Acamar	θ Eridani	Celaeno	16 Tauri	Nunki	σ Sagittarii
Achernar	α Eridani	Chara	β Canum Venaticorum	Peacock	α Pavonis
Acrab	β Scorpii	Cor Caroli	α Canum Venaticorum	Phact	α Columbae
Acrux	α Crucis	Cursa	β Eridani	Phecda	γ Ursae Majoris
Acubens	α Cancri	Dabih	β Capricorni	Pherkad	γ Ursae Minoris
Adhara	ϵ Canis Majoris	Deneb	α Cygni	Pleione	28 Tauri
Agena	β Centauri	Deneb Algedi	δ Capricorni	Polaris	α Ursae Minoris
Albireo	β Cygni	Deneb Kaitos	β Ceti	Pollux	β Geminorum
Alcor	80 Ursae Majoris	Denebola	β Leonis	Porrima	γ Virginis
Alcyone	η Tauri	Diphda	β Ceti	Procyon	α Canis Minoris
Aldebaran	α Tauri	Dschubba	δ Scorpii	Propus	η Geminorum
Alderamin	α Cephei	Dubhe	α Ursae Majoris	Pulcherrima	ϵ Boötis
Alfirk	β Cephei	Electra	17 Tauri	Rasalgethi	α Herculis
Algedi	α Capricorni	Elnath	β Tauri	Rasalhague	α Ophiuchi
Algenib	γ Pegasi	Eltanin	γ Draconis	Rastaban	β Draconis
Algieba	γ Leonis	Enif	ϵ Pegasi	Regulus	α Leonis
Algol	β Persei	Errai	γ Cephei	Rigel	β Orionis
Alhena	γ Geminorum	Fomalhaut	α Piscis Austrini	Rigil Kentaurus	α Centauri
Alioth	ϵ Ursae Majoris	Gemma	α Coronae Borealis	Ruchbah	δ Cassiopeiae
Alkaid	η Ursae Majoris	Giedi	α Capricorni	Rukbat	α Sagittarii
Alkalurops	μ Boötis	Girtab	θ Scorpii	Sadachbia	γ Andromedae
Almach	γ Andromedae	Gomeisa	β Canis Minoris	Sadalmelik	α Aquarii
Alnair	α Gruis	Graffias	β Scorpii	Sadalsuud	β Aquarii
Alnasl	γ Sagittarii	Hadar	β Centauri	Sadr	γ Cygni
Alnilam	ϵ Orionis	Hamal	α Arietis	Saiph	κ Orionis
Alnitak	ζ Orionis	Homam	ζ Pegasi	Scheat	β Pegasi
Alphard	α Hydrae	Izar	ϵ Boötis	Seginus	γ Boötis
Alphecca	α Coronae Borealis	Kitalpha	α Equulei	Shaula	λ Scorpii
Alpheratz	α Andromedae	Kochab	β Ursae Minoris	Shedar	α Cassiopeiae
Alrami	α Sagittarii	Kornephoros	β Herculis	Sheliak	β Lyrae
Alrescha	α Piscium	Lesath	υ Scorpii	Sheratan	β Arietis
Alshain	β Aquilae	Maia	20 Tauri	Sirius	α Canis Majoris
Altair	α Aquilae	Markab	α Pegasi	Sirrah	α Andromedae
Alya	θ Serpentis	Megrez	δ Ursae Majoris	Spica	α Virginis
Antares	α Scorpii	Menkalinan	β Aurigae	Tarazed	γ Aquilae
Ankaa	α Phoenicis	Menkar	α Ceti	Taygeta	19 Tauri
Arcturus	α Boötis	Merak	β Ursae Majoris	Thuban	α Draconis
Arkab	β Sagittarii	Merope	23 Tauri	Toliman	α Centauri
Arneb	α Leporis	Mesarthim	γ Arietis	Unukalhai	α Serpentis
Asellus Australis	δ Cancri	Miaplacidus	β Carinae	Vega	α Lyrae
Asellus Borealis	γ Cancri	Mimosa	β Crucis	Vindemiatrix	ϵ Virginis
Asterope	21 Tauri	Mintaka	δ Orionis	Wasat	δ Geminorum
Atlas	27 Tauri	Mira	o Ceti	Wezen	δ Canis Majoris
Atria	α Trianguli Australis	Mirach	β Andromedae	Yed Posterior	ϵ Ophiuchi
Bellatrix	γ Orionis	Mirfak	α Pegasi	Yed Prior	δ Ophiuchi
Benetnasch	η Ursae Majoris	Mirzam	β Canis Majoris	Yildun	δ Ursae Minoris
Betelgeuse	α Orionis	Mizar	ζ Ursae Majoris	Zavijava	β Virginis
Canopus	α Carinae	Mothallah	α Trianguli	Zosma	δ Leonis
Capella	α Aurigae	Muliphein	γ Canis Majoris	Zubenelgenubi	α Librae
Caph	β Cassiopeiae	Naos	ζ Puppis	Zubeneschamali	β Librae
Castor	α Geminorum	Nashira	γ Capricorni		
Cebalrai	β Ophiuchi	Nekkar	β Boötis		

Table 34. The Greek alphabet.

A	α	Alpha	H	η	Eta	N	ν	Nu	T	τ	Tau
B	β	Beta	Θ	θ	Theta	Ξ	ξ	Xi	Y	υ	Upsilon
Γ	γ	Gamma	I	ι	Iota	O	o	Omicron	Φ	ϕ	Phi
Δ	δ	Delta	K	κ	Kappa	Π	π	Pi	X	χ	Chi
E	ϵ	Epsilon	Λ	λ	Lambda	P	ρ	Rho	Ψ	ψ	Psi
Z	ζ	Zeta	M	μ	Mu	Σ	σ	Sigma	Ω	ω	Omega

Table 35. Star atlases and catalogues.

Atlas	Epoch	Author(s)	Date	Coverage[a]	Approximate limiting magnitude	Scale (mm per degree)
Visual						
Norton's 2000.0	2000.0	I. Ridpath *et al.*	1989	w.s.	6.5	3.3
Sky Atlas 2000.0	2000.0	W. Tirion	1981	w.s.	8.0	7.8
SAO Star Atlas	1950.0	Smithsonian Institution	1969	w.s.	9	8.6
AAVSO Variable Star Atlas	1950.0	C. E. Scovil	1980	w.s.	9	15
Uranometria 2000.0	2000.0	W. Tirion *et al.*	1987–88	w.s.	9.5	17
Photographic						
True Visual Magnitude Photographic Star Atlas	1950.0	C. Papadopoulos	1979–80	w.s.	14	30
Atlas Stellarum	1950.0	H. Vehrenberg	1977	w.s.	14	30
Palomar Sky Survey	1950.0	National Geographic Society/ Palomar Observatory	1952	+90° to −27°	20 (red) 21 (blue)	54

Catalogue	Epoch	Author(s)	Date	Coverage[a]	Approximate limiting magnitude	No. of stars listed
Positional and general						
Astronomische Gesellschaft Katalog (AGK3)	1950.0	O. Heckmann and W. Dieckvoss	1975	+90° to −2°	9	183000
Bonner Durchmusterung (BD)	1855.0	F. W. A. Argelander	1859–62[b]	+90° to −2°	9.5	324000
Bonner Durchmusterung (BD) extension	1855.0	E. Schönfeld	1886	−2° to −23°	9.5	133000
Bright Star Catalogue (BS)[c]	1900.0 & 2000.0	D. Hoffleit and C. Jaschek	1982 (4th edn)	w.s.	6.5	9110
Supplement to the Bright Star Catalogue	1900.0 & 2000.0	D. Hoffleit *et al.*	1983	w.s.	7.1	2603
Cape Photographic Durchmusterung (CPD)	1875.0	D. Gill and J. C. Kapteyn	1895–1900	−18° to −90°	10	455000
Catalogue of Stellar Identifications with Selected Data		F. Ochsenbein	1982	w.s.		434000
Catalogue of 3539 Zodiacal Stars (ZC)	1950.0	J. Robertson	1940	z.b.		3539
Cordoba Durchmusterung (CoD or CD)	1875.0	J. M. Thome	1892–1932	−22° to −90°	10	614000
Fourth Fundamental Catalogue (FK4)	1950.0	W. Fricke and A. Kopff	1963	w.s.	7	1135
General Catalogue of 33342 Stars (GC)	1950.0	B. Boss	1937	w.s.	7	33342
Sky Catalogue 2000.0 Vol. 1	2000.0	A. Hirshfeld and R. W. Sinnott	1982	w.s.	8.0	45269
Smithsonian Astrophysical Observatory Star Catalog (SAO)	1950.0	K. L. Haramundanis	1966	w.s.	9	259000
Photometric						
UBV Photoelectric Photometry Catalogue		J. C. Mermilliod	1986	w.s.		87000
Spectroscopic						
Henry Draper Catalogue (HD) and *Henry Draper Extension* (HDE)	1900.0	A. J. Cannon and E. C. Pickering	1918–36	w.s.	9	272000
Michigan Catalogue of Two-Dimensional Spectral Types for the HD stars	1900.0	N. Houk and A. P. Cowley	1975+ (in progress)	w.s.	9	
Double stars						
Fourth Catalog of Orbits of Visual Binary Stars	1900.0	C. E. Worley and W. D. Heintz	1983	w.s.		847
Index Catalogue of Visual Double Stars	1900.0 & 2000.0	C. E. Worley	1977 (2nd edn)	w.s.		70000
New General Catalogue of Double Stars (ADS)	1900.0 & 2000.0	R. G. Aitken	1932	+90° to −30°		17180
Variable stars						
General Catalogue of Variable Stars (GCVS)	1950.0	P. N. Kholopov	1985 (4th edn)	w.s.		28450
New Catalogue of Suspected Variable Stars (NSV)	1950.0	B. V. Kukarkin *et al.*	1982	w.s.		14811

[a] w.s. whole sky; z.b. zodiacal band.   [b] Reprinted 1903.
[c] The star numbers of the *Bright Star Catalogue* (BS) are identical to those of the *Harvard Revised Photometry* (HR).

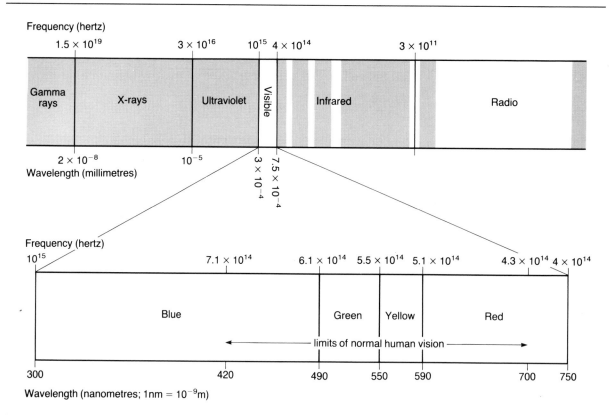

Figure 22. The electromagnetic spectrum. The unshaded regions are 'windows' – wavelength bands to which the full depth of the Earth's atmosphere is transparent.

RADIATION, MAGNITUDE AND LUMINOSITY

Radiation

Virtually all the information we have about most celestial objects comes from analysis of the energy they radiate: radio waves, heat, light, X-rays and gamma rays. These are all forms of *electromagnetic radiation* – energy propagated through space in the form of waves.

The *electromagnetic spectrum* is the complete range of wavelengths of electromagnetic radiation, from the very longest (radio waves) to the very shortest (gamma rays). The radiation is commonly classified somewhat arbitrarily into different ranges of wavelength (or of frequency), as shown in Figure 22. The Earth's atmosphere is opaque to radiation of most wavelengths. Observations in the 'windows' shown in Figure 22, to which the atmosphere is more or less transparent, can be made from ground-based observatories, but radiation from celestial objects at other wavelengths can be studied only from space.

Brightness and magnitude

The apparent brightness of a celestial object is proportional to the amount of radiation from it that is received by the eye (or measuring instrument). Brightnesses are usually expressed on a scale of magnitudes, as explained below. They may be determined accurately by the use of light-sensitive detectors called photoelectric photometers. Separate measures of magnitudes are made in different ranges of wavelength; among these, the V band corresponds quite closely to the response of the human eye. The star charts in this Atlas plot all stars according to their V magnitude.

In Ptolemy's star catalogue (second century AD), which is based on an earlier one by Hipparchus (second century BC), the naked-eye stars were classed into six grades of brightness or *magnitude*. The brightest stars were said to be 1st magnitude; those less bright 2nd magnitude, and so on. The faintest stars that could just be clearly seen with the naked eye were called 6th magnitude. Following the invention of the telescope, the scale was extended for the telescopic stars to magnitudes 7, 8 and so on. An 11th-magnitude star is visible in a 75 mm refractor.

When instrumental methods of measuring the relative brightnesses of stars were developed in the nineteenth century, it was found that two stars differing by one magnitude, as estimated by earlier observers, had a nearly constant brightness ratio of about 2.5, and that an interval of five magnitudes corresponded to a brightness ratio of about 2.5^5, or nearly 100. This discovery led the way to a more precise definition of a continuous scale of magnitude.

Magnitudes are now recorded in tenths, hundredths or even thousandths of a magnitude. Numerically smaller magnitudes continue to denote greater brightness, so that mag. 3.00 is slightly brighter than mag. 3.01, but slightly less bright than mag. 2.99. Some objects are brighter than

Table 36. Ratio of brightness and combined magnitude. For two stars differing in magnitude by a given amount ('Diff.'), the table gives the ratio of their brightnesses and the amount ('Comb.') by which their combined magnitude exceeds that of the brighter star. Thus a double star whose components have magnitudes of 6.00 and 6.50 (Diff. = 0.5) has a combined magnitude of 6.00−0.53 = 5.47. The formulae used are:

Ratio = antilog (0.4 × Diff.)
Comb. = 2.5 × log [1 + antilog (−0.4 × Diff.)]

Diff.	Ratio	Comb.	Diff.	Ratio	Comb.	Diff.	Ratio	Comb.
0.00	1.00	0.75	1.20	3.02	0.31	4.00	39.81	0.03
0.10	1.10	0.70	1.30	3.31	0.29	4.50	63.10	0.02
0.20	1.20	0.66	1.40	3.63	0.26	5.00	100.00	0.01
0.30	1.32	0.61	1.50	3.98	0.24	5.50	158.49	0.01
0.40	1.45	0.57	1.60	4.37	0.22	6.00	251.19	—
0.50	1.58	0.53	1.70	4.79	0.21	6.50	398.11	—
0.60	1.74	0.49	1.80	5.25	0.19	7.00	630.96	—
0.70	1.91	0.46	1.90	5.75	0.17	7.50	1000.00	—
0.80	2.09	0.42	2.00	6.31	0.16	8.00	1585	—
0.90	2.29	0.39	2.50	10.00	0.10	9.00	3981	—
1.00	2.51	0.36	3.00	15.85	0.07	10.00	10000	—
1.10	2.75	0.34	3.50	25.12	0.04	12.50	100000	—

magnitude 1, so for them the scale is extended backwards to zero and then to negative magnitudes, e.g. Sirius (mag. −1.46), Venus (mag. −4.4 at mean greatest elongation), the full moon (mean mag. −12.7), the Sun (mag. −26.7). Where there is no sign, magnitudes are always understood to be positive.

Modern photoelectric magnitudes are always calculated for above the Earth's atmosphere. Even for stars at the zenith the atmosphere absorbs or scatters light of different wavelengths to a degree which varies from time to time and from one place to another. For stars at lower altitudes, atmospheric effects further diminish the brightness and must be allowed for when comparing stars at different altitudes.

Relationships for calculating magnitude differences. The magnitude scale is defined exactly by specifying that two stars having brightnesses in the ratio 1 : 100 have a magnitude difference of precisely 5; and by an agreed list of standard stars which effectively define the zero-point of the scale. If two stars have brightnesses B_1 and B_2, their magnitude difference $m_2 - m_1$ is given by

$$m_2 - m_1 = 2.5 \log (B_1/B_2)$$
$$\text{or} \quad B_1/B_2 = \text{antilog} [0.4(m_2 - m_1)] \simeq 2.512^{m_2 - m_1}$$

The ratios in Table 36 are calculated using this relationship.

Combined magnitude. The combined brightness of two stars (e.g. ones that are so close together that they appear as a single star) is obviously the sum of their individual brightnesses. The combined magnitude m of two stars of magnitudes m_1 and m_2 is given by a more complicated formula:

$$m = m_1 - 2.5 \log\{1 + \text{antilog} [-0.4(m_2 - m_1)]\}$$

Table 36 gives the amounts by which the combined magnitude of two stars is brighter (i.e. numerically less) than that of the brighter component. The combined magnitude of three or more stars can be found by repeated application of the formula. The *integrated* (or *total*) *magnitude* of an extended object such as a galaxy or comet is a measure of the brightness it would have if all its light were condensed to a single, star-like point.

Apparent magnitude. This is the magnitude of a celestial object as directly estimated by the human eye, or determined from a photograph, or measured instrumentally by a photometer, without any correction for the object's distance. It is denoted by the symbol m. In astronomical photometry, measurements of apparent magnitude are made in different wavelength ranges. *Visual magnitudes*, as perceived by the human eye, are denoted by the symbol m_v; *photographic magnitudes*, estimated or measured from photographs, are denoted by m_{pg} if traditional blue-sensitive plates or films are used, and m_{pv} (*photovisual*) if a combination of photographic emulsion and filter is used whose colour response approximates that of the human eye.

For precise work, measurements are made with a photoelectric photometer. Measurements may be made in various wavelength ranges; the most commonly used is the UBV system, U standing for ultraviolet, B for blue and V for visual. The B magnitude approximates to the older m_{pg} scale, and the V magnitude to the older m_v or m_{pv} scale. In some photometers the wavelength range is extended to include red and infrared wavelengths. The effective wavelengths of the U, B and V bands, and the most commonly used infrared bands, are given in Table 37.

Table 37. Effective wavelengths of bands used in photometry. U stands for ultraviolet, B for blue, V for visual and R for red; I to Q are infrared bands.

Band	U	B	V	R	I	J
Effective wavelength (nm)	360	440	550	700	900	1250
Band	H	K	L	M	N	Q
Effective wavelength (μm)	1.62	2.2	3.4	5.0	10.2	19.5

Another important system of photoelectric photometry, introduced by B. Strömgren, uses four filters passing narrower wavelength bands than in the UBV system. These bands are u (ultraviolet), v (violet), b (blue) and y (yellow), and are centred on 350, 410, 470 and 550 nm (nanometres) respectively.

As a general rule, photoelectric magnitudes can be assumed to be correct to within one-hundredth of a magnitude. They have been determined for some 100 000 stars, including almost all those brighter than mag. 6.5. For many fainter stars, visual magnitudes have been determined using visual photometers, which are normally accurate to within a tenth of a magnitude. But for most stars below naked-eye level, the catalogue magnitudes are rough eye estimates made with transit instruments or from photographs, and they may be in error by half a magnitude or more.

Colour index. This is the difference between the magnitudes of a star measured in two different wavelength bands, most commonly B and V, or U and B. The B–V colour index of white stars is close to zero, while for red stars it may be several magnitudes. The B–V colour indices of a few well-known stars are given in Table 38.

Absolute magnitude. Apparent magnitude is no criterion of intrinsic luminosity, as many nearby stars appear far brighter than more luminous ones which are at greater distances. Absolute magnitude is the brightness a star would have if it were a standard distance from us: it is found by calculating what the observed magnitude would be if the star were at a distance of 10 parsecs (about 33 light years), equivalent to a parallax (see p. 137) of 0.1 arcsec. This calculation requires a knowledge of the star's distance. Conversely, if the absolute magnitude can be found by some other means, the distance of the star can be found.

Table 38. Apparent magnitude (m_V), B–V colour index, absolute magnitude (M_V) and spectral class of a few well-known stars.

Star	m_V	Colour index	M_V	Spectral class
Aldebaran (α Tauri)	0.85	+1.54	−0.3	K5
Betelgeuse (α Orionis)	0.50	+1.85	−7.2	M2
Capella (α Aurigae)	0.08	+0.80	+0.4	G6
Rigel (β Orionis)	0.12	−0.03	−8.1	B8

Absolute magnitude is of great importance in stellar research as it enables luminosities to be compared. The Sun's visual absolute magnitude is 4.8; Table 38 gives the apparent and absolute magnitudes of a few well-known stars. The absolute magnitudes of dwarf stars fall off by over a magnitude in each successive spectral type, reaching +15.5 in Proxima Centauri. Those of typical giant stars vary by only two magnitudes (from about +1.1 to −0.8) in the progression from spectral type G to M. The supergiant star Rigel has an absolute magnitude of −8.1, and supernovae at maximum range from about −16.5 to −21. One of the most luminous stars known is S Doradus, at about −9.2, and one of the least luminous is Van Biesbroeck's Star (V1289 Aql), at +18.6.

A star's absolute magnitude M can be calculated from its apparent magnitude m and parallax π in arc seconds, as follows:

$$M = m + 5 + 5 \log \pi$$

Table 39 gives the relationship between distance and magnitude.

Table 39. Distance and magnitude. Increase of distance ('Dist.') for various differences ('Diff.') from 1 to 20 magnitudes, in the absence of interstellar extinction. Thus a mag. 5 star, if it were 100 times further away, would be 10 magnitudes fainter (or mag. 15). The formula used is:

Dist. = antilog (0.2 × Diff.)

Diff.	Dist.	Diff.	Dist.	Diff.	Dist.	Diff.	Dist.
1	1.585	6	15.85	11	158.5	16	1585
2	2.512	7	25.12	12	251.2	17	2512
3	3.981	8	39.81	13	398.1	18	3981
4	6.310	9	63.10	14	631.0	19	6310
5	10.00	10	100.0	15	1000	20	10000

Interstellar extinction and distance modulus. The formula for absolute magnitude given above is strictly correct only in the absence of absorption or scattering of light by interstellar gas and dust. For distant objects a correction needs to be made. If the amount of extinction A can be estimated, the intrinsic apparent magnitude m_0 can be found from $m_0 = m - A$. The *distance modulus* $m - M$ is calculated from

$$m - M = 5 \log(\text{distance in parsecs}) - 5 + A$$

and the corrected distance modulus is then

$$m_0 - M = 5 \log(\text{distance in parsecs}) - 5$$

The amount of extinction suffered by a star's light depends on its location in the Galaxy. It is greatest in the plane of the Milky Way, where it averages about one magnitude per kiloparsec; but in certain regions the extinction can amount to several magnitudes. Extinction diminishes rapidly with distance from the galactic plane. There are formulae that describe statistically the amount of extinction at various galactic latitudes, but to obtain a reliable estimate for a particular star, maps showing interstellar extinction in various directions must be consulted.

Intrinsic colour index. This is obtained by applying corrections for interstellar extinction to the observed colour index. The difference between the observed colour index $(B-V)_{obs}$ and the intrinsic colour index $(B-V)_i$ is called the *colour excess*, denoted by $E(B-V)$. Thus:

$$E(B-V) = (B-V)_{obs} - (B-V)_i = A(B) - A(V)$$

where $A(B)$ and $A(V)$ are the amounts of extinction in the B and V wavelength bands.

Bolometric magnitude. This is a measure of the total radiation received from the star: ultraviolet, light, heat, radio and so on. Measurement may be made by a *bolometer*, a detecting device which produces an output signal that depends on the total incident radiation irrespective of wavelength; but only radiation that penetrates the Earth's atmosphere is registered in this way. An alternative is to make an estimate on the basis of separate measurements taken in the various wavelength bands. The amount of energy received outside the Earth's atmosphere from a star of bolometric magnitude 0.00 is equal to 2.48×10^{-8} watts per square metre.

Bolometric correction (BC). This is the difference between the bolometric magnitude m_{bol} and the apparent visual magnitude (m_v or m_{pv}). Hence the bolometric correction is $BC = m_v - m_{bol}$. The correction is zero for a star with a surface temperature of about 6500 K (i.e. one like the Sun). The bolometric correction is positive for hotter and cooler stars because such stars emit more of their radiation outside the visual range, either in the ultraviolet (hotter stars) or in the infrared (cooler stars). Sometimes, though, the bolometric correction is expressed in the opposite way, $m_{bol} - m_v$, so that it is then negative, not positive.

Polarimetry. Light is a wave motion, the waves being transverse (i.e. the wave oscillations are at right angles to the direction in which the light travels). If the direction of the electric field associated with the radiation remains constant, the radiation is said to be *plane-polarized*. The light from some astronomical sources is partly polarized, and the amount and direction of the polarization can be measured with a photoelectric photometer in conjunction with a polaroid filter. The polarization of starlight can reveal the existence of interstellar dust and strong magnetic fields.

Luminosity

The luminosity of a star is its intrinsic or absolute brightness: it is a measure of the total outflow of radiation from the star. Luminosities may be calculated for any particular wavelength band, or they may be bolometric – covering radiation of all wavelengths. The symbol is L and the unit is the watt. For example the Sun's bolometric luminosity is about 3.8×10^{26} W, which corresponds to radiation

emitted at the surface at $6.2 \times 10^7 \, W \, m^{-2} \, s^{-1}$; it also corresponds to an apparent bolometric magnitude $m_{bol} = -26.79$ and an absolute bolometric magnitude $M_{bol} = +4.76$, slightly brighter than its absolute visual magnitude of $M_V = 4.83$.

The relationship between the luminosity and absolute magnitude of the Sun ($L_\odot$, $M_\odot$) and those of another star (L, M) is given by

$$\log(L/L_\odot) = 0.4(M_\odot - M)$$

Hence if the absolute magnitude of a star can be determined, a rearrangement of the above equation will enable its luminosity to be found. The star Sirius (Alpha (α) Canis Majoris) has an apparent visual magnitude of -1.46, and a parallax of 0.377 arcsec, yielding an absolute visual magnitude of $+1.42$. The bolometric correction for a main-sequence star of spectral class A1, such as Sirius, is -0.62, so its absolute bolometric magnitude is 0.80. Thus Sirius is intrinsically brighter than the Sun by 3.41 magnitudes visually, or 3.96 magnitudes bolometrically. By applying the above relationship we find that the visual luminosity of Sirius is 23 times that of the Sun, and its bolometric luminosity 38 times that of the Sun.

Mass–luminosity relationship. The more massive a star is, the more luminous it is generally found to be. A graph of absolute bolometric magnitude plotted against mass for several stars yields a curve that is represented conveniently by the approximation

$$\log(L/L_\odot) = 3.3 \log(M/M_\odot)$$

This relationship may be used to estimate the mass of single stars, i.e. stars not forming part of a binary or multiple system. It does not apply to white dwarfs, which are underluminous for their mass.

The ratio $M/M_\odot$ varies significantly with spectral class, and also depends on whether the star is a supergiant, giant or dwarf.

DISTANCES, MOTIONS AND PHYSICAL PARAMETERS

The nearest and brightest stars

The 26 nearest stars (including the Sun) are listed in Table 40, and the 26 stars having the greatest visual apparent magnitude in Table 41. For each star the position, apparent and absolute magnitude, spectral classification, estimated parallax and distance are given.

Stellar distances

Light year (l.y.). The light year is a unit of distance frequently used for stars and galaxies. It is the distance covered in one calendar year by a beam of light, which travels at a speed of $299\,792.458 \, km \, s^{-1}$. One light year is 9.46×10^{12} kilometres, equivalent to 63 240 astronomical

Table 40. The nearest stars.

Star	RA 2000.0 h m	Dec. ° ′	Apparent magnitude	Spectral class	Parallax ″	Distance (l.y.)	Absolute magnitude
Sun	—	—	−26.72	G2V	—	—	4.8
Proxima (V645 Cen)	14 29.7	−62 41	11.05 (var.)	M5.5Ve	0.772	4.2	15.5
α Cen A	14 39.6	−60 50	−0.01	G2V	0.750	4.3	4.4
B			1.33	K1V			5.7
Barnard's Star	17 57.8	+04 34	9.54	M3.8V	0.545	6.0	13.2
Wolf 359 (CN Leo)	10 56.5	+07 01	13.53 (var.)	M5.8Ve	0.421	7.7	16.7
BD +36° 2147	11 03.3	+35 58	7.50	M2.1Ve	0.397	8.2	10.5
UV Cet A	01 38.8	−17 57	12.52 (var.)	M5.6Ve	0.387	8.4	15.5
B			13.02 (var.)	M5.6Ve			16.0
Sirius A	06 45.1	−16 43	−1.46	A1Vm	0.377	8.6	1.4
B			8.3	DA			11.2
Ross 154	18 49.8	−23 50	10.45	M3.6Ve	0.345	9.4	13.1
Ross 248	23 41.9	+44 10	12.29	M4.9Ve	0.314	10.4	14.8
ε Eri	03 32.9	−09 28	3.73	K2Ve	0.303	10.8	6.1
Ross 128	11 47.8	+00 48	11.10	M4.1V	0.298	10.9	13.5
61 Cyg A (V1803 Cyg)	21 06.9	+38 45	5.22 (var.)	K3.5Ve	0.294	11.1	7.6
B			6.03	K4.7Ve			8.4
ε Ind	22 03.4	−56 47	4.68	K3Ve	0.291	11.2	7.0
BD +43° 44 A	00 18.5	+44 01	8.08	M1.3Ve	0.290	11.2	10.4
B			11.06	M3.8Ve			13.4
L789-6	22 38.5	−15 19	12.18		0.290	11.2	14.5
Procyon A	07 39.3	+05 13	0.38	F5IV–V	0.285	11.4	2.6
B			10.7	DF			13.0
BD +59° 1915 A	18 43.1	+59 38	8.90	M3.0V	0.282	11.6	11.2
B			9.69	M3.5V			11.9
CoD −36° 15693	23 05.9	−35 51	7.35	M1.3Ve	0.279	11.7	9.6

Source: Alan Batten, *Royal Astronomical Society of Canada Observers' Handbook* (1989).

Table 41. The brightest stars.

Star	Name	RA 2000.0 h m	Dec. ° ′	Apparent magnitude	Spectral class	Parallax ″	Distance (l.y.)	Absolute magnitude
	Sun	—	—	−26.72	G2V	—	—	4.8
α CMa	Sirius	06 45.1	−16 43	−1.46	A1Vm	0.377	8.6	1.4
α Car	Canopus	06 24.0	−52 42	−0.72	A9II	0.028	74	−2.5
α Cen	Rigil Kentaurus	14 39.6	−60 50	−0.27[a]	G2V+K1V	0.750	4.3	4.1[a]
α Boo	Arcturus	14 15.7	+19 11	−0.04	K1.5IIIp	0.097	34	0.2
α Lyr	Vega	18 36.9	+38 47	0.03	A0Va	0.133	25	0.6
α Aur	Capella	05 16.7	+46 00	0.08	G6III+G2III	0.080	41	0.4
β Ori	Rigel	05 14.5	−08 12	0.12	B8Iae	0.013	1400[b]	−8.1
α CMi	Procyon	07 39.3	+05 13	0.38	F5IV–V	0.285	11.4	2.6
α Eri	Achernar	01 37.7	−57 14	0.46	B3Vnp	0.026	69	−1.3
α Ori	Betelgeuse	05 55.2	+07 24	0.50 (var.)	M2Iab	0.005	1400[b]	−7.2
β Cen	Hadar	14 03.8	−60 22	0.61 (var.)	B1III	0.009	320	−4.4
α Cru	Acrux	12 26.6	−63 06	0.76[a]	B0.5IV+B1Vn	0.008	510	−4.6[a]
α Aql	Altair	19 50.8	+08 52	0.77	A7Vn	0.202	16	2.3
α Tau	Aldebaran	04 35.9	+16 31	0.85 (var.)	K5III	0.054	60	−0.3
α Sco	Antares	16 29.4	−26 26	0.96 (var.)	M1.5Iab	0.024	520[c]	−5.2
α Vir	Spica	13 25.2	−11 10	0.98 (var.)	B1V	0.023	220	−3.2
β Gem	Pollux	07 45.3	+28 01	1.14	K0IIIb	0.094	40	0.7
α PsA	Fomalhaut	22 57.6	−29 37	1.16	A3Va	0.149	22	2.0
β Cru	Becrux	12 47.7	−59 41	1.25 (var.)	B0.5III	—	460	−4.7
α Cyg	Deneb	20 41.4	+45 17	1.25	A2Ia	0.000	1500	−7.2
α Leo	Regulus	10 08.4	+11 58	1.35	B7Vn	0.045	69	−0.3
ε CMa	Adhara	06 58.6	−28 58	1.50	B2II	0.001	570	−4.8
α Gem	Castor	07 34.6	+31 53	1.57[a]	A1V+A2V	0.067	49	0.5[a]
γ Cru	Gacrux	12 31.2	−57 07	1.63 (var.)	M3.5III	—	120	−1.2
λ Sco	Shaula	17 33.6	−37 06	1.63 (var.)	B1.5IV	—	330	−3.5

Source: Robert F. Garrison, *Royal Astronomical Society of Canada Observers' Handbook* (1989).

[a] Combined magnitude of double star.   [b] Distance to Orion cluster.   [c]Distance to Scorpius cluster.

Note: Parallaxes and absolute magnitudes of many stars are not well determined. For stars with a parallax smaller than 0″.05, absolute magnitudes and distances have been calculated from the spectral classification and may not be in agreement with the parallax measurement.

Table 42. Distances in parsecs (pc) and light years (l.y.) equivalent to any parallax (π in arcsec). For parallaxes of 0.0001, 0.0002, etc., move the parsec or light year decimal point one place to the right.

π	pc	l.y.	π	pc	l.y.	π	pc	l.y.	π	pc	l.y.	π	pc	l.y.	π	pc	l.y.
0.001	1000	3262.0	0.021	47.62	155.3	0.041	24.39	79.55	0.061	16.39	53.47	0.081	12.35	40.27	0.12	8.33	27.18
0.002	500.0	1631.0	0.022	45.45	148.3	0.042	23.81	77.66	0.062	16.13	52.61	0.082	12.20	39.78	0.14	7.14	23.30
0.003	333.3	1087.0	0.023	43.48	141.8	0.043	23.26	75.85	0.063	15.87	51.77	0.083	12.05	39.30	0.16	6.25	20.39
0.004	250.0	815.4	0.024	41.67	135.9	0.044	22.73	74.13	0.064	15.63	50.96	0.084	11.90	38.83	0.18	5.56	18.12
0.005	200.0	652.3	0.025	40.00	130.5	0.045	22.22	72.48	0.065	15.38	50.18	0.085	11.76	38.37	0.20	5.00	16.31
0.006	166.7	543.6	0.026	38.46	125.4	0.046	21.74	70.90	0.066	15.15	49.42	0.086	11.63	37.93	0.22	4.55	14.83
0.007	142.9	465.9	0.027	37.04	120.8	0.047	21.28	69.40	0.067	14.93	48.68	0.087	11.49	37.49	0.24	4.17	13.59
0.008	125.0	407.7	0.028	35.71	116.5	0.048	20.83	67.95	0.068	14.71	47.96	0.088	11.36	37.06	0.25	4.00	13.05
0.009	111.1	362.4	0.029	34.48	112.5	0.049	20.41	66.56	0.069	14.49	47.27	0.089	11.24	36.65	0.26	3.85	12.54
0.010	100.0	326.2	0.030	33.33	108.7	0.050	20.00	65.23	0.070	14.29	46.59	0.090	11.11	36.24	0.28	3.57	11.65
0.011	90.91	296.5	0.031	32.26	105.2	0.051	19.61	63.95	0.071	14.08	45.94	0.091	10.99	35.84	0.30	3.33	10.87
0.012	83.33	271.8	0.032	31.25	101.9	0.052	19.23	62.72	0.072	13.89	45.30	0.092	10.87	35.45	0.35	2.86	9.319
0.013	76.92	250.9	0.033	30.30	98.84	0.053	18.87	61.54	0.073	13.70	44.68	0.093	10.75	35.07	0.40	2.50	8.154
0.014	71.43	233.0	0.034	29.41	95.93	0.054	18.52	60.40	0.074	13.51	40.08	0.094	10.64	34.70	0.45	2.22	7.248
0.015	66.67	217.4	0.035	28.57	93.19	0.055	18.18	59.30	0.075	13.33	43.49	0.095	10.53	34.33	0.50	2.00	6.523
0.016	62.50	203.9	0.036	27.78	90.60	0.056	17.86	58.24	0.076	13.16	42.92	0.096	10.42	33.98	0.55	1.82	5.930
0.017	58.82	191.9	0.037	27.03	88.15	0.057	17.54	57.22	0.077	12.99	42.36	0.097	10.31	33.62	0.60	1.67	5.436
0.018	55.56	181.2	0.038	26.32	85.83	0.058	17.24	56.23	0.078	12.82	41.82	0.098	10.20	33.28	0.65	1.54	5.018
0.019	52.63	171.7	0.039	25.64	83.63	0.059	16.95	55.28	0.079	12.66	41.29	0.099	10.10	32.95	0.70	1.43	4.659
0.020	50.00	163.1	0.040	25.00	81.54	0.060	16.67	54.36	0.080	12.50	40.77	0.100	10.00	32.62	0.75	1.33	4.349

units or 0.3066 parsecs. The star nearest the Sun, Proxima Centauri, is 4.2 light years away. Smaller units such as the light month, light week, light day, light minute and light second, which are sometimes encountered, are measures of the distances covered by a beam of light in those lengths of time; they are used for instance for distances on the scale of the Solar System. In such units the Moon is about 1.3 light seconds away, and the Sun is 8.3 light minutes away.

Parsec (pc). One parsec is the distance at which a star or other object would have an annual parallax (see below) of 1 second of arc. One parsec is 30.857×10^{12} kilometres, equal to 206 265 astronomical units or 3.2616 light years. No star is known with a parallax this large, the greatest measured parallax being that of Proxima Centauri, 0.772 arcsec, corresponding to a distance of 1.3 parsecs. Commonly used multiples of the parsec are the *kiloparsec* (1000 pc, abbreviated kpc) and *megaparsec* (1 000 000 pc, abbreviated Mpc).

Trigonometric parallax is the angular difference in position of an object when seen from two different places. In Figure 23, which shows a relatively nearby star seen against a background of distant stars, the difference in position of the star when seen by a hypothetical observer located on the Sun and an observer on the Earth at E_1 is called the *instantaneous parallax*. This value can be determined in principle by making observations of the star when the Earth is at E_1 and again six months later when the Earth is at the opposite side of its orbit, at E_2. In practice, during the course of a year the motion of the Earth around the Sun makes the star appear to trace out an ellipse on the celestial

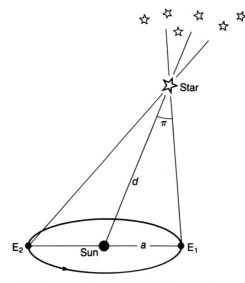

Figure 23. Trigonometric parallax. The distance of a nearby star can be measured by noting its change in position relative to background stars as the Earth moves in its orbit.

sphere. If the star is near the ecliptic, the ellipse will be highly flattened; if the star is near either ecliptic pole it will be almost a circle (the effect of the slight ellipticity of the Earth's orbit can be neglected). The value of the semi-major axis of the ellipse in which the star appears to move is known as the *annual parallax* (π) of the star. This is the maximum displacement of the star from its mean position (as a result of parallax) and corresponds to the configuration where the angle star–Sun–Earth in Figure 23 is 90°. If a is the Sun–Earth distance and d the distance of the star, then if π is expressed in radians, we have $\pi = a/d$. If a is known and π is measured, then d can be obtained.

The value of a is the astronomical unit (AU). In principle this can be measured by means of *planetary parallax*, the difference in the position of the Sun or other object in the Solar System as measured by two observers located at different points on the Earth. The effect of planetary parallax is greatest for an object on the horizon, and it is then known as *horizontal parallax*. The (horizontal) solar parallax is 8.79 arcsec. It is the angle subtended by the equatorial radius of the Earth at the Sun's mean distance of 1 AU, so from a knowledge of the Earth's size we can calculate the size of the astronomical unit. In practice, more accurate methods are used, including determination of the distances of objects in the Solar System by radar.

Parallax depends on distance, the nearest objects having the largest parallaxes. The largest parallax known for an object outside the Solar System is for the star Proxima Centauri, 0.772 arcsec. Most stellar parallaxes are very much smaller than this: only about 1000 stars are known to have parallaxes greater than 0.05 arcsec, and only about 3000 greater than 0.04 arcsec (equivalent to a distance of 25 parsecs).

As a distance-finding method, trigonometric parallax can be employed with Earth-based telescopes only to a range of a few hundred light years at most because of the difficulties of measuring very small angles. However, telescopes in space now offer considerable improvements in parallax measurements. Other forms of parallax can be obtained, several of them utilizing the distance modulus (see p. 134) for stars at large distances. Some of these forms are described below.

Spectroscopic parallax. A good estimate of the true absolute magnitude of many stars can be obtained from an examination of their spectra (see p. 140). This can be compared with the observed apparent magnitude, and, after correction for interstellar extinction, a distance or parallax derived.

Absolute magnitudes can be estimated in other ways for certain types of star. In particular the Cepheid variables (see p. 152) show a well-defined relationship between absolute magnitude and period of light variation (the period–luminosity law), and so measurement of the period provides a value of absolute magnitude for the distance modulus. Because of their great luminosity, Cepheids can be used as 'standard candles' for measurements out to very large distances.

Dynamical parallax. With binary stars (see p. 144) whose orbit is well known, the distance can be estimated by assuming initially that their combined mass is two solar masses (see p. 139), then using Newton's generalization of Kepler's third law, which relates the period of revolution of the pair of stars to the linear dimensions of the orbit. The linear dimensions are compared with the observed angular dimensions of the stars' orbit to give an initial estimate of the distance. As the apparent magnitudes of the components are known, their absolute magnitudes may then be calculated and the mass–luminosity relationship used to improve the estimate of their masses. The sequence of calculations is repeated until the difference between successive mass estimates is sufficiently small. Fortunately an error in the estimated mass of the system does not produce a large error in the value of the dynamical parallax.

Secular parallax. The nearby stars (those within about 100 pc of the Sun) together define a *local standard of rest* relative to which their mean motion is zero. These stars are together revolving around the galactic centre with a velocity of about 250 km s^{-1}, and this motion is at present carrying them towards a point in the constellation Cygnus. Relative to this moving group of nearby stars, the Sun has its own velocity of about 19.5 km s^{-1} towards a point in the constellation Hercules. This motion provides a base-line for parallax measurements that is continually increasing. The average distance of a group of stars can thus be derived from observations of their proper motion (see below).

Stellar motions

The motion of a star relative to the Sun can be considered to consist of two components: a radial component R (*radial velocity*), i.e. motion in the line of sight, and a transverse component T (*transverse velocity*). If both R and T can be determined, then the star's velocity V is obtained from $V = \sqrt{(R^2 + T^2)}$, and the direction θ of its motion relative to the radial direction from the Sun is found from $\tan \theta = T/R$.

Radial velocity can be obtained from the displacement of the lines of a star's spectrum caused by the *Doppler effect*. The velocity is obtained directly, and it is not necessary to know the distance of the star. A positive radial velocity means the star is receding, while a negative value means the star is approaching. Radial velocities in excess of ± 100 km s^{-1} are rarely found in stars; most values lie between -40 and $+40$ km s^{-1}. Periodic variations in radial velocity reveal the orbital motion of spectroscopic binaries (i.e. double stars too close to be separated visually).

Proper motion. The transverse component of stellar motion shows up as a secular change in the position of a star. The observed angular displacement in one year is known as *annual proper motion* and is generally expressed in arc seconds. The largest known value of proper motion (symbol μ) is that of Barnard's Star at 10.3 arcsec per year. To convert proper motion to transverse velocity it is necessary to know the parallax of the star. The transverse velocity V_μ is then given by $V_\mu = 4.74\,\mu/\pi$ km s^{-1}. The proper motion thus obtained, after allowing for parallax, aberration and so on, gives the transverse component of velocity relative to the Sun; to obtain the star's motion relative to the local standard of rest it is necessary to allow for solar motion (see the section on Secular parallax, above). Owing to proper motion the shapes of the constellations are slowly changing, but the effect is imperceptible in a human lifetime.

High-velocity stars. There are a number of stars in the neighbourhood of the Sun whose velocities relative to the Sun are extremely high, greater than $200\,km\,s^{-1}$. The explanation for these apparently high velocities is that most of the stars in the Sun's neighbourhood, and the Sun itself, are moving around the centre of our Galaxy in approximately circular orbits with velocities of the order of $250\,km\,s^{-1}$. The high-velocity stars, however, do not share this circular motion, but usually travel around the galactic centre in eccentric orbits. They are generally members of the galactic halo.

Runaway stars are stars of spectral type O or early B with unusually high space velocities (i.e. velocities relative to the Sun). They are thought to be produced when there is a supernova explosion in a close binary system. Three of the best known are 53 Arietis, AE Aurigae and Mu (μ) Columbae, which diverge from a comparatively small area in the constellation Orion.

Stellar masses

Only for binary stars (see p. 144) can the masses of stars be obtained directly. If the orbital period P in years, the mean angular separation a and the parallax π are known, then the combined mass of the pair can be obtained in terms of solar masses from the formula

$$(M_1 + M_2)/M_\odot = a^3/\pi^3 P^2$$

If the position of the centre of mass can be obtained, then the ratio of the distances of the two stars from the centre of mass will yield the ratio of the masses; the individual masses can then be found.

The masses of stars can be estimated from the mass–luminosity relationship if their absolute magnitudes are known. Stars with masses less than $0.1\,M_\odot$ or greater than $10\,M_\odot$ are rare, but only a few tens of stars have accurately known masses.

Stellar temperatures

It is difficult to assign an unambiguous value to the 'temperature' of a star. Several definitions are used, some of which are listed below.

Effective temperature (T_{eff}). For a star, the effective temperature is the temperature of a *black body* – i.e. a perfect radiator – of the same radius as the star that radiates the same total amount of radiation – i.e. that has the same bolometric luminosity as the star. For the Sun, the effective temperature is the temperature of the photosphere, about $5800\,K$ (kelvin).

Colour temperature (T_c) is the equivalent black-body temperature that fits the slope of the observed energy distribution measured between two wavelengths. It can be related to colour index. If the B–V colour index is denoted by I, then the colour temperature in kelvin is

$$T_c = 7200/(I + 0.64)$$

The value of the colour temperature determined in this way may differ from the effective temperature, as stars do not radiate exactly as black bodies. For the Sun ($I = 0.63$), the colour temperature is $5700\,K$.

The central temperatures of stars are much higher than the surface temperatures: the temperature at the centre of the Sun is thought to be about 15 million kelvin. In the tenuous outer atmosphere of the Sun, the corona, the kinetic temperature (i.e. the temperature corresponding to the velocities of atomic particles) is of the order of two million kelvin.

Stellar diameters

Only a few dozen stars have had their diameters measured directly, as telescopes at ground level do not reveal stellar disks. The first direct measurements of stellar diameters were made by *stellar interferometry*, which is based on applying the principle that there will be interference of light from different parts of an object of finite size. Three major classes of interferometers have been used: the Michelson (phase) interferometer, the Brown–Twiss (intensity) interferometer, and the Labeyrie (speckle) interferometer. These have yielded values for the angular diameters of a few giant stars such as Betelgeuse. For Betelgeuse a value of 0.030 arcsec (variable, since the star pulsates) has been derived by speckle interferometry at a wavelength of $740\,nm$. If a distance of 1400 l.y. is taken, the diameter comes out as $1.9 \times 10^9\,km$, rather greater than the orbit of Jupiter. (Other estimates give a closer distance for Betelgeuse, which would mean that its diameter is correspondingly smaller.)

Where interferometric observations are not possible, diameters can be estimated by observing occultations of stars by the Moon. They can also be calculated for the components of eclipsing binaries, from the observed durations of their eclipses, in conjunction with radial velocity measurements that yield the velocities of the components in their orbits. In general, however, diameters are inferred from a consideration of effective temperature and luminosity, using *Stefan's law*, which states that the flux of radiation from a black body is proportional to the square of its radius and the fourth power of its temperature. Thus if two stars have the same effective temperature, but differing luminosities, then it follows that the radius of the one with the higher luminosity must be greater than that of the other (see the section below on Spectral classification).

Typical stellar diameters range from several hundred million kilometres (supergiants), through 1.4 million kilometres for the Sun, down to a few thousand kilometres for some white dwarfs. Neutron stars (see p. 142) are thought to have diameters of only tens of kilometres.

Stellar densities

Although stellar radii vary enormously, stellar masses do not vary by such large amounts. Consequently there are large variations in stellar densities. The Sun has a mean density of $1.4 \times 10^3\,kg\,m^{-3}$; supergiants may have mean densities of about 10^{-2} kg m^{-3}; white dwarfs have densities in the range 10^8–10^{11} kg m^{-3}; and neutron stars probably have densities of 10^{16}–10^{18} kg m^{-3}.

SPECTRAL CLASSIFICATION

Stars may be classified into various types on the basis of features in their spectra. In the 1860s the Italian astronomer P. A. Secchi made the first attempt to classify the stars by visually observing their spectra, and divided the stars into four groups. Later classifications were based on photographs of spectra and were much more finely divided. The Harvard classification system, first introduced by E. C. Pickering in 1890 and later developed by A. J. Cannon and W. P. Fleming, was the immediate precursor of the system currently in use. The current system is variously called the MKK (after Morgan, Keenan and Kellman), MK (Morgan, Keenan) or Yerkes system.

The MKK system applies two labels to a spectrum. The first, the *spectral class*, correlates closely with a star's temperature; the second, *luminosity class*, is related to the star's intrinsic brightness. Stars are allocated to the spectral and luminosity classes by comparison with standard stars which define the system.

Spectral class

Over 90% of stars can be allocated to one of seven spectral *types*. These are designated by letters inherited from the older Harvard system, and in order of decreasing temperature they are:

O   B   A   F   G   K   M

A traditional mnemonic is 'Oh Be A Fine Girl Kiss Me'. In principle each type is potentially divisible into (at least) ten *classes*. As defined by P. C. Keenan in 1985, there are actually only between four and nine classes in each type, but some astronomers have introduced more. These classes are indicated by a numerical suffix, with some gaps in the numbering; e.g. O5, B9.5. A star of class A5 has a spectrum roughly half-way between spectra of stars of classes A0 and F0.

The criteria used to place a star accurately into its spectral class are exceedingly complex. Nevertheless, the principal features in the spectra of each of the main types, indicated by absorption lines, may be quite simply listed:

O   ionized helium (He II)
B   neutral helium; first appearance of hydrogen
A   hydrogen dominant, plus singly ionized metals
F   hydrogen weaker, ionized calcium (Ca II)
G   Ca II prominent, hydrogen very much weaker; neutral metals
K   neutral metals prominent
M   molecular bands, particularly titanium oxide (TiO).

In addition to the above sequence there are various side-branches and additional codes. Type W (the Wolf–Rayet stars) contains hot stars showing broad, intense emission lines, including He II. Type C (formerly split into types R and N) contains the cool carbon stars, where the TiO bands of type M are replaced by bands of cyanogen, carbon monoxide and molecular carbon (C_2). The spectra of type S stars have bands of zirconium oxide. White dwarf stars comprise type D and, although they are not part of the MKK system, the letters P and Q are sometimes used for, respectively, the emission spectra of planetary nebulae and the peculiar spectra of novae.

For historical reasons the spectra of hot stars (O, B, A) are often referred to as *early-type*, and those of cool stars (K, M, C, S) as *late-type* spectra; stars of types F and G are sometimes called *intermediate-type*.

Luminosity class

Within a given spectral class a bright star will be larger and have more rarefied outer regions than a faint star. Hence, the more luminous a star, the narrower its spectral lines, since pressure is often one of the principal line-broadening mechanisms. Thus, on the basis of the quality of the spectral lines (together with, in some cases, intensity differences), the stars in a given spectral class may be further separated into their luminosity classes. The luminosity class is denoted by a roman numeral between I and V placed after the spectral type, e.g. F2III. The main luminosity classes are:

I   supergiants
II   bright giants
III   giants
IV   subgiants
V   main-sequence dwarfs
VI   subdwarfs
VII   white dwarfs

(see Figure 24). Some classes (in particular the supergiants) are subdivided by using the suffixes a, ab and b. A notation such as III–IV indicates an object intermediate between two classes.

Thus the full MKK classification of a normal star consists of a letter and an arabic numeral to denote the temperature class, and a roman numeral to denote the luminosity class. The full spectral classes of some of the brighter stars are:

δ Ori: O9.5II	β Per: B8V
α CMi: F5IV–V	α CrB: A0IV
β Cas: F2III	Sun: G2V
β Cet: K0III	α Ori: M2Iab

In addition to the standard spectral class notation, lower case letters may be added after the luminosity class to show certain non-standard features in the spectrum. These include:

e   emission lines (f in some O-type stars)
m   metallic lines
n   nebulous lines
p   peculiar spectrum
q   lines with blue-shifted absorption and red-shifted emission, indicating the presence of an expanding shell (P Cygni stars)
v   variable spectrum.

Table 43. Distribution of stars according to spectral type. The table gives the percentage of the stars in the *Bright Star Catalogue* belonging to each of the main spectral types.

O	B	A	F	G	K	M	Others
0.5	19	22	14	13	25	6	0.4

Examples of the use of this notation are:

γ Cas: B0IVnpe   α CMa: A1Vm
P Cyg: B1Iapeq   ζ Pup: O5Iafn

The full system of classification allows 90–95% of all stellar spectra to be dealt with. The remainder are composite spectra of unresolved double or multiple stars, or stars with major individual peculiarities.

Table 43 gives the distribution of stars in the *Bright Star Catalogue* according to their spectral type. Table 44 gives the spectral class, absolute magnitude M_V, bolometric magnitude M_{bol}, effective temperature T_{eff}, mass, diameter, luminosity and mean density for dwarf, giant and supergiant stars. The spectral class, luminosity class and colour index are closely related, and often the B–V colour index may be used in place of spectral class; Table 45 relates the spectral and luminosity classes of stars to their B–V and U–B colour indices.

STELLAR EVOLUTION

The Hertzsprung–Russell (HR) diagram

This diagram is a very convenient way in which to display the relationship between the spectral class (colour index, temperature) and luminosity (absolute magnitude) of stars. Figure 24 is an HR diagram in which the spectral class is plotted along the horizontal axis, with cool stars to the right and hot stars to the left, and the absolute magnitude is plotted vertically. Most stars are found to lie in a band running from top left to bottom right, called the *main sequence*. The remainder – supergiants, giants, white dwarfs and so on – are found in other specific regions. The HR diagram provides a very useful visual aid to the understanding of the evolution of the stars.

Star formation. Stars are thought to condense out of clouds of gas, principally hydrogen clouds, heating up as they

Table 44. Some physical parameters for stars of various luminosity and spectral classes.

Spectral class	M_V	M_{bol}	T_{eff} (K)	Mass	Diameter (relative to the Sun)	Luminosity	Mean density (10^3 kg m^{-3})
Main sequence (V)							
O5	−5.8	−10	40000	40	18	500000	0.01
B0	−4.1	−6.8	28000	18	7.4	20000	0.06
B5	−1.1	−2.6	15500	6.5	3.8	800	0.17
A0	+0.7	+0.1	9900	3.2	2.5	80	0.28
A5	+2.0	+1.7	8500	2.1	1.7	20	0.55
F0	+2.6	+2.6	7400	1.7	1.3	6.3	0.98
F5	+3.4	+3.4	6580	1.3	1.2	2.5	1.07
G0	+4.4	+4.3	6030	1.10	1.05	1.26	1.3
G5	+5.1	+5.0	5520	0.93	0.93	0.79	1.6
K0	+5.9	+5.8	4900	0.78	0.85	0.40	1.8
K5	+7.3	+6.7	4130	0.69	0.74	0.16	2.4
M0	+9.0	+7.8	3480	0.47	0.63	0.063	2.5
M5	+11.8	+9.8	2800	0.21	0.32	0.008	10
M8	+16	—	2400	0.10	0.13	0.0008	63
Giants (III)							
G0	+1.1	+1.1	5600	2.5	6.3	32	0.016
G5	+0.7	+0.5	5000	3.2	10	50	0.004
K0	+0.5	+0.2	4500	4.0	16	80	0.0013
K5	−0.2	−1.0	3800	5.0	25	200	0.0004
M0	−0.4	−1.8	3200	6.3	—	400	0.0001
M5	−0.8	−3	—	—	—	1000	—
Supergiants (I)							
B0	−6.4	−9	30000	50	20	250000	0.008
A0	−6.2	−7	12000	16	40	20000	0.0003
F0	−6	−6.0	7000	12.5	63	8000	0.00006
G0	−6	−5.2	5700	10	100	6300	0.000013
G5	−6	−5.2	4850	12.5	125	6300	0.000006
K0	−5	−5.4	4100	12.5	200	8000	0.000002
K5	−5	−6	3500	16	400	16000	0.0000004
M0	−5	−7	—	16	500	32000	0.0000002

Table 45. Relationship between spectral class and colour index.

Spectral class	Main sequence (V) B–V	Main sequence (V) U–B	Giants (III) B–V	Giants (III) U–B	Supergiants (I) B–V	Supergiants (I) U–B
O5	−0.35	−1.15	—	—	—	—
B0	−0.31	−1.06	—	—	−0.25	−1.2
B5	−0.16	−0.55	—	—	—	—
A0	0.00	−0.02	—	—	0.00	−0.3
A5	+0.13	+0.10	—	—	—	—
F0	+0.27	+0.07	—	—	+0.25	+0.25
F5	+0.42	+0.03	—	—	—	—
G0	+0.58	+0.05	+0.65	+0.3	+0.70	+0.60
G5	+0.70	+0.19	+0.85	+0.53	+1.06	+0.87
K0	+0.89	+0.47	+1.07	+0.90	+1.39	+1.34
K5	+1.18	+1.10	+1.41	+1.5	+1.70	+1.7
M0	+1.45	+1.28	+1.60	+1.8	+1.94	+1.7
M5	+1.63	+1.2	+1.85	+2.3	+2.14	—

Source: C. W. Allen, *Astrophysical Quantities* (Athlone Press, 1973).

contract and so moving from right to left across the HR diagram. When conditions in the central regions of the protostar are suitable, i.e. when the temperature there reaches about ten million kelvin, nuclear reactions can take place in which helium is produced by fusion from hydrogen, with the release of large amounts of energy. At this stage the star reaches a stable state as it joins the main sequence at a position determined principally by its mass. The more massive the star, the greater its luminosity, and the further up will it join the main sequence.

Main-sequence lifetime. A star will spend most of its life-time on the main sequence. Just how long it does spend there is determined by the *Schönberg–Chandrasekhar limit*, which states that the amount of helium in the central core of the star cannot exceed about 12% of the mass of the star. More massive stars consume energy much faster, as shown by the mass–luminosity relationship, so their available hydrogen is consumed more quickly and their main-sequence lifetimes are much shorter. While the Sun is expected to have a main-sequence lifetime of about 10^{10} years, a highly luminous B0 star would probably spend only a few million years on the main sequence.

Red giants. The main-sequence stage is followed by the onset of hydrogen burning in a shell surrounding the core, and the star begins to evolve fairly rapidly away from the main sequence. The surface temperature usually decreases, but the radius of the star increases during this stage of its evolution and so too does the luminosity, and the star becomes a red giant.

The subsequent evolution of a red giant depends on its mass, and may be very complicated with several passages back and forth across the HR diagram. In more massive stars the density and temperature of the core reach a flash-point and a new series of nuclear reactions begins: first the burning of helium into carbon, and later of carbon into heavier elements. Stars of less than about $0.4M_\odot$ will not

have a helium-burning stage, but their evolution is so slow that probably no such star in our Galaxy has had time to complete its main-sequence stage.

Eventually every star must run out of nuclear fuel, at which point it will cease to generate the radiation needed to support its structure. Its centre will certainly contract, although its outer layers may be expelled in the form of a stellar wind (perhaps giving rise to a planetary nebula), or in a more violent process.

White dwarfs. A relatively low-mass star such as the Sun is thought eventually to evolve into a white dwarf, with a density of at least $10^8 \, \text{kg m}^{-3}$. The luminosity is then very low but the surface temperature is high, so these stars are found to the lower left of the HR diagram. There is no energy-producing process operating in white dwarfs, so they will eventually cool down to non-luminous bodies (black dwarfs, not to be confused with black holes).

Neutron stars. It seems that a star more massive than $1.4M_\odot$ cannot become a white dwarf unless it loses sufficient mass in some way to bring it below this limit. A star or stellar remnant of mass greater than $1.4M_\odot$ may collapse to a superdense state in which atoms are broken down and nuclear components combined to form a body composed of neutrons. Such neutron stars, with densities of the order of $10^{18} \, \text{kg m}^{-3}$, have been identified with the *pulsars*, discovered in 1967. The outbursts of some supernovae are thought to be triggered by the collapse of a star's central regions to the neutron star stage.

Black holes. It is possible that very massive objects may enter a state of gravitational collapse where no known physical process can halt the contraction. The body will then contract to within a critical radius known as the *Schwarzschild radius*, at which point its gravitational field becomes so strong that no radiation can escape from it. Such an object is known as a black hole.

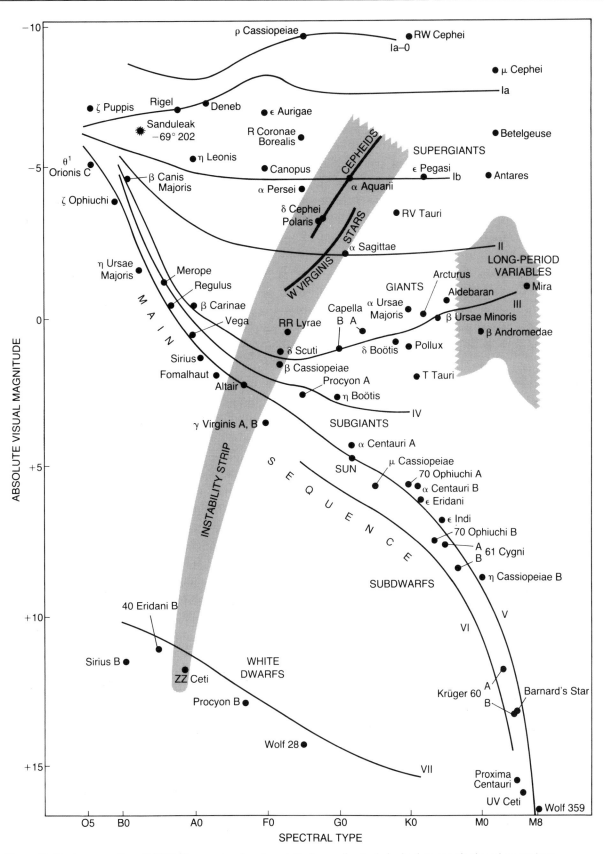

Figure 24. Hertzsprung–Russell (HR) diagram showing stars plotted according to their absolute magnitude and spectral type. Luminosity increases from bottom to top; temperature increases from right to left; colour index increases from left to right. The roman numerals indicate luminosity classes. Many stars are seen to lie on the main sequence; the instability strip is a region in which pulsating variables are found. *Source*: James B. Kaler, *Sky & Telescope*, Vol. 75, p. 482 (1988).

Stellar populations

Stars in the arms of spiral galaxies are, in general, bluer and richer in heavy elements than stars in the galactic nuclei or in elliptical galaxies. The stars in the spiral arms are called *Population I* stars, and are thought to be younger than stars in the nuclei and in elliptical galaxies, which are called *Population II* stars. In our own Galaxy, which is believed to be an ordinary spiral of type Sb/Sc, Population I stars are found in the disk of the Galaxy, while Population II stars are found in the spherical halo, which includes the globular clusters, and towards the galactic centre. The greater proportion of heavy elements in Population I stars is probably a result of their having formed in part from material which had already been processed in earlier generations of stars and returned to the interstellar medium by, for example, stellar winds or supernova explosions.

DOUBLE STARS

Double stars appear to the naked eye as a single point of light, but when viewed through a telescope are found to be two stars. The stars may be connected gravitationally, or may simply happen to lie in nearly the same direction (optical pairs). Triple stars have three, quadruple stars four and multiple stars many components. The brightest star of a multiple is usually designated A, and the companion(s) B, C and so on, as in Sirius A, Sirius B. The fainter star of a pair is sometimes called the *comes* (plural *comites*) or companion.

Binary stars

Binary stars are physically related double stars that orbit around a common centre of gravity. A binary star is said to be a *visual binary* if the components may be resolved in the telescope and their orbital motion can be measured over a period of time. If the relative motion of the components is constant and in a straight line, however, they are probably not a binary but an *optical pair*. A *spectroscopic binary* is one that is detected from the periodic doubling or displacement of lines in its spectrum; an *eclipsing binary* is detected by the periodic variations in its magnitude (see the section on Variable stars, p. 145). A binary star may be simultaneously a visual and a spectroscopic binary, or simultaneously a spectroscopic and an eclipsing binary. The orbital periods range from a fraction of a day to many centuries; visual binaries generally have periods of at least two years, while the other two types generally have much shorter periods.

Even if no relative motion is detectable, the physical association of two stars may be suspected if they appear to be at a similar distance and to have the same radial and transverse motion through space. Often, though, the only indication is that a pair of stars have *common proper motion* (c.p.m.).

Multiple stars may also be connected gravitationally; they are usually found to consist of a close binary pair that moves in a larger orbit with another star, which may also be a close binary. Theta[1] (θ^1) Orionis, known as the Trapezium, contains four bright, well-separated components visible in small telescopes; they are undoubtedly physically connected, but it seems unlikely that they can be moving in stable orbits. Two of the bright components are eclipsing binaries, so the system contains at least six stars, and there are several fainter components which may also be connected. Trapezium-like objects may be thought of as small star clusters. About half the stars in the neighbourhood of the Sun are components of binary or multiple systems.

Observing double stars

Some of the more interesting doubles are indicated in the notes preceding each star chart. The column PA gives the position angle of the companion relative to the brighter component, and the column Dist. gives the separation of the components in arc seconds.

Telescopes of greater aperture are required to separate close doubles. A good telescope of aperture D mm should just enable a pair of stars of sixth magnitude to be distinguished under high power if their separation is $116/D$ arcsec (Dawes' limit; see Table 10 on p. 64). If the components are unequal in brightness, or if they are much brighter or fainter than sixth magnitude, a larger aperture will be needed to separate a given pair than this formula would suggest.

For binary stars whose orbits have been calculated, the notes preceding each star chart give the predicted PA and distance for epoch 2000.0. The BASIC computer program on p. 145 may be used to obtain approximate predictions for other dates. The calculation requires seven orbital elements:

P orbital period (years)
T date of periastron (in decimal form)
a semi-major axis of orbit (arc seconds)
e eccentricity of orbit
i inclination of orbit to plane of sky (degrees)
ω argument of periastron (degrees)
Ω PA of ascending node (degrees)

In a visual binary system, the companion is said to be at *periastron* when its actual distance (as distinct from its apparent distance) from the main star is a minimum, and at *apastron* when it is a maximum. Together a and e define the size and shape in space of the orbit of the companion relative to the brighter component; these may be very different from the size and shape of the apparent orbit projected onto the celestial sphere. Between them i, ω and Ω define the orbit's orientation. The motion of the companion is *direct* when the position angle is increasing, and *retrograde* when it is decreasing; the inclination i is given as between 0° and 90° for direct motion, and between 90° and 180° for retrograde motion.

Many double and multiple stars present an attractive spectacle in the telescope, especially when the components are of contrasting colours. Useful work can be done by making regular measurements of the PA and distance of binary stars with a micrometer. The masses of stars can be directly determined only by the observation of binary stars. Fewer than 200 visual binaries have well-determined orbits; some orbital elements (not all well-determined) are given in Table 46.

VARIABLE STARS

Variable stars are stars whose brightness changes with time. Figure 25 shows some typical graphs of magnitude against time, or *light curves*, for different types of variable star.

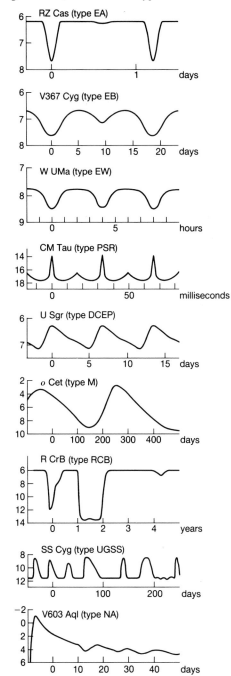

Figure 25. Typical light curves for several types of variable star.

Double Star Program

This BASIC program takes as its input the seven orbital elements for a binary system, and calculates for any specified date the position angle and separation to an accuracy sufficient for observational purposes.

```
10   DEF FN C(W) = 1.745329252E - 2 * W
20   PX = 3.141592654:C = 6.283185307
30   INPUT "Period, P (years)              ";P
40   INPUT "Date of periastron, T          ";T
50   INPUT "Semi-major axis, a             ";A1
60   INPUT "Eccentricity, e                ";S
70   INPUT "Inclination, i                 ";I
80   INPUT "Arg. of periastron, w          ";W
90   INPUT "PA of ascending node           ";L
100  I = FN C(I):L = FN C(L):W = FN C(W)
110  N = C / P
120  INPUT "Date of obs. (year)            ";D
130  MA = N * (D - T)
140  GOSUB 300
150  R = A1 - A1 * S * COS (EA)
160  Y = SIN (NU + W) * COS (I)
170  X = COS (NU + W)
180  Q = ATN (Y / X)
190  IF X < 0 THEN Q = Q + PX: GOTO 210
200  IF Q < 0 THEN Q = Q + C
210  TH = Q + L: IF TH > C THEN TH = TH - C
220  RH = R * X / COS (Q)
230  PRINT "PA = "; INT (TH / FN C(1) * 10 + 0.5) / 10;"deg."
240  PRINT "Sep. = "; INT (RH * 100 + 0.5) / 100;"arcsec"
250  INPUT "New date? (Y/N) ";AN$
260  IF AN$ = "Y" THEN GOTO 120
270  INPUT "New binary? (Y/N) "; AN$
280  IF AN$ = "Y" THEN GOTO 10
290  IF AN$ = "N" THEN END
300  M = MA - C * INT (MA / C):EA = M
310  A = EA - (S * SIN (EA)) - M
320  IF ABS (A) < 1E - 6 THEN GOTO 350
330  A = A / (1 - (S * COS (EA)))
340  EA = EA - A: GOTO 310
350  TU = SQR ((1 + S) / (1 - S)) * TAN (EA / 2)
360  NU = 2 * ATN (TU)
370  RETURN
```

Example. The orbital elements for Xi (ξ) Ursae Majoris are entered, and the program calculates the PA and separation on 2000 Jan. 1 (2000.0) and on 2010 Jul. 1 (2010.5):

Period, P (years)	59.84
Date of periastron, T	1995.01
Semi-major axis, a	2.53
Eccentricity, e	0.414
Inclination, i	122.65
Arg. of periastron, w	127.53
PA of ascending node	101.59
Date of obs. (year)	2000
PA = 272.7 deg.	
Sep. = 1.77 arcsec	
New date? (Y/N) Y	
Date of obs. (year)	2010.5
PA = 204.9 deg.	
Sep. = 1.63 arcsec	

Table 46. Orbital elements of some visual binaries: the orbital period *P*, date of periastron *T*, semi-major axis of orbit *a*, eccentricity of orbit *e*, inclination of orbit to plane of sky *i*, argument of periastron *ω* and PA of ascending node *Ω*.

ADS[a]	Star	RA h m	Dec. 2000.0 ° '	Magnitudes		P (y)	T	a "	e	i °	ω °	Ω °
17175	85 Peg	00 02.2	+27 05	5.8	8.9	26.27	1988.92	0.83	0.38	50.0	94.4	288.6
434	λ Cas	00 31.8	+54 31	5.5	5.8	640	1958.0	0.586	0.0	47.7	0.0	174.4
520	β 395	00 37.3	−24 46	6.3	6.4	25.00	1999.00	0.670	0.22	78.0	142.0	112.0
671	η Cas	00 49.1	+57 49	3.5	7.5	480	1889.6	11.994	0.497	34.76	268.59	278.42
755	36 And	00 55.0	+23 38	6.0	6.4	164.68	1957.15	1.014	0.31	46.45	4.65	171.5
	p Eri	01 39.8	−56 12	5.8	5.8	483.7	1813.49	7.817	0.534	142.82	18.37	13.12
1394	ε Scl	01 45.6	−25 03	5.4	8.6	1192	2076.2	4.652	0.0	180.0	0.0	0.0
1538	Σ 186	01 55.9	+01 51	6.8	6.8	170.3	1893.35	1.05	0.708	73.59	220.72	40.41
1598	48 Cas	02 02.0	+70 54	4.7	6.4	60.44	1964.78	0.653	0.345	22.8	4.5	64.2
1615	α Psc	02 02.0	+02 46	4.2	5.2	933	2098.6	4.0	0.696	120.9	225.4	23.3
1631	10 Ari	02 03.7	+25 56	5.9	7.3	288	1932.2	1.256	0.56	55.0	162.5	25.4
1630	γ² And	02 03.9	+42 20	5.5	6.3	61.1	1952.1	0.296	0.93	111.1	171.15	104.15
1778	o Cet	02 19.3	−02 59	var.	9.5	400	2001.5	0.85	0.66	111.3	106.0	118.5
1860	ι Cas AB	02 29.1	+67 24	4.6	6.9	840.0	1550.0	2.27	0.40	132.0	299.0	6.3
2402	α For	03 12.1	−28 59	4.0	6.6	314	1947.0	4.367	0.76	81.5	42.0	117.7
2616	7 Tau	03 34.4	+24 28	6.6	6.7	600	1911	0.719	0.71	155.2	228.4	5.6
2799	OΣ 65	03 50.3	+25 35	5.8	6.2	62.28	1937.80	0.430	0.62	83.19	349.46	26.08
4241	σ Ori	05 38.7	−02 36	4.0	6.0	170.0	1970.0	0.25	0.07	165.0	299.0	124.5
4263	ζ Ori	05 40.8	−01 57	1.9	4.0	1509	2070.6	2.728	0.07	72.0	47.3	155.5
4841	η Gem	06 14.9	+22 30	var.	8.8	473.7	1819.7	1.08	0.54	142.7	26.2	84.5
5423	α CMa	06 45.1	−16 43	−1.5	8.3	50.09	1994.31	7.500	0.592	136.53	147.27	44.57
5400	12 Lyn AB	06 46.2	+59 27	5.4	6.0	699.0	1740.0	1.66	0.03	180.0	154.84	0.0
5514	14 Lyn	06 53.1	+59 27	5.6	6.8	480.0	1950.0	0.736	0.53	56.4	130.0	58.8
5559	38 Gem	06 54.6	+13 11	4.7	7.7	1943.8	2276.0	8.194	0.15	125.54	128.2	36.75
5983	δ Gem	07 20.1	+21 59	3.5	8.2	1200	1437.0	6.975	0.11	63.28	57.19	18.4
6175	α Gem	07 34.6	+31 53	1.9	2.9	467.0	1958.0	6.805	0.343	114.5	249.5	41.3
6420	9 Pup	07 51.8	−13 54	5.6	6.2	23.18	1985.25	0.58	0.69	77.8	67.7	103.3
6650	ζ Cnc AB	08 12.2	+17 39	5.6	6.0	59.7	1989.7	0.884	0.32	172.0	233.0	58.0
6650	ζ Cnc AB−C	08 12.2	+17 39	5.1	6.2	1150	1960.0	7.96	0.26	144.6	163.9	256.7
6914	β 208	08 39.1	−22 40	5.3	6.7	140	1982.5	1.888	0.25	83.6	287.4	30.7
	I 314	08 39.4	−36 36	6.5	7.6	66.5	1992.2	0.527	0.86	102.0	341.0	55.7
6993	ε Hya	08 46.8	+06 25	3.4	6.8	890.0	1933.0	4.536	0.29	42.0	203.1	55.5
7114	ι UMa	08 59.2	+48 02	3.1	10.2	817.9	1993.90	9.09	0.79	57.8	129.7	4.8
7203	σ² UMa	09 10.4	+67 08	4.8	8.2	1067	1919.7	6.20	0.81	146.2	331.5	99.7
7307	Σ 1338	09 21.0	+38 11	6.8	7.0	389.05	1998.59	1.516	0.291	15.8	258.88	28.13
7390	ω Leo	09 28.5	+09 03	5.9	6.5	118.227	1959.40	0.880	0.557	66.05	302.65	325.69
	ψ Vel	09 30.7	−40 28	4.1	4.6	33.99	1969.74	0.795	0.44	58.5	48.4	287.2
7545	φ UMa	09 52.1	+54 04	5.3	5.4	105.5	1987.7	0.36	0.46	28.0	48.0	118.4
7555	γ Sex	09 52.5	−08 06	5.6	6.1	75.60	1958.10	0.385	0.70	143.3	151.4	36.7
7724	γ Leo	10 20.0	+19 51	2.2	3.5	618.56	1743.32	2.505	0.843	36.37	162.54	143.24
7846	β 411	10 36.1	−26 40	6.7	7.5	210.1	1948.23	0.982	0.80	126.1	35.8	144.8
8119	ξ UMa	11 18.2	+31 32	4.3	4.8	59.84	1995.01	2.530	0.414	122.65	127.53	101.59
8148	ι Leo	11 23.9	+10 32	4.0	6.7	192.0	1948.47	1.92	0.55	130.5	140.0	52.2
8197	OΣ 235	11 32.3	+61 05	5.8	7.1	72.87	1981.50	0.813	0.398	47.7	130.7	81.0
8539	Σ 1639	12 24.4	+25 35	6.8	7.8	678.0	1891.0	1.30	0.946	161.0	334.0	105.7
8573	β 28	12 30.1	−13 24	6.5	8.6	161.53	1943.94	1.385	0.728	18.76	70.82	99.68
	γ Cen	12 41.5	−48 58	2.9	2.9	84.50	1931.22	0.930	0.79	112.9	187.8	2.4
8630	γ Vir	12 41.7	−01 27	3.5	3.5	171.37	1836.433	3.746	0.881	146.05	252.88	31.78
	β Mus	12 46.3	−68 06	3.7	4.0	383.1	1872.29	1.735	0.53	61.3	98.32	161.8
8695	35 Com	12 53.3	+21 14	5.1	7.2	510	1931.0	1.42	0.15	35.0	243.0	230.1
8974	25 CVn	13 37.5	+36 18	5.0	6.9	240.0	1863.95	1.091	0.83	144.02	137.92	67.04
	α Cen	14 39.6	−60 50	0.0	1.3	79.92	1955.56	17.515	0.516	79.24	231.56	204.87
9343	ζ Boo	14 41.1	+13 44	4.5	4.6	123.44	1897.59	0.595	0.957	142.0	1.47	129.99
9413	ξ Boo	14 51.4	+19 06	4.7	6.9	151.505	1909.361	4.904	0.512	140.04	203.92	348.1
9425	OΣ 288	14 53.4	+15 42	6.8	7.5	215.4	1819.3	1.09	0.60	112.5	0.0	4.7
9494	44,i Boo	15 03.8	+47 39	5.3	var.	225.0	1796.0	3.772	0.43	83.9	38.8	57.8
9617	η CrB	15 23.2	+30 17	5.6	5.9	41.623	1975.631	0.907	0.276	59.02	39.91	203.72
	γ Cir	15 23.4	−59 19	5.1	5.5	180.0	2036.0	1.16	0.48	103.0	250.0	250.0
9626	μ² Boo	15 24.5	+37 21	7.0	7.6	260.1	1865.0	1.463	0.59	135.4	338.5	174.9
9701	δ Ser	15 34.8	+10 32	4.2	5.2	3168	1700.0	6.02	0.31	112.6	274.6	166.8
	γ Lup	15 35.1	−41 10	3.5	3.6	147.0	1887.0	0.59	0.49	95.6	301.0	92.8

[a] The ADS number is the number given in the *New General Catalogue of Double Stars*, which covers as far south as −30°.

Table 46 (*continued*)

ADS[a]	Star	RA h m	Dec. 2000.0 ° ′	Magnitudes	P (y)	T	a ″	e	i °	ω °	Ω °
9909	ξ Sco AB	16 04.4	−11 22	4.9	4.9	45.69	1996.83	0.72	0.74	36.9	348.2	201.7
9979	σ CrB	16 14.7	+33 52	5.6	6.6	1000	1828.0	6.599	0.78	33.33	84.35	7.74
10074	α Sco	16 29.4	−26 26	var.	5.4	878	1461	2.90	0.10	90	0.0	93.7
10087	λ Oph	16 30.9	+01 59	4.2	5.3	129.87	1939.54	0.970	0.618	26.8	158.9	52.5
10157	ζ Her	16 41.3	+31 36	2.9	5.5	34.487	1967.80	1.355	0.46	132.9	290.9	229.2
10279	20 Dra	16 56.4	+65 02	7.1	7.3	577.85	1865.09	1.183	0.324	96.85	241.91	68.4
10345	μ Dra	17 05.3	+54 28	5.7	5.7	482.0	1964.0	3.330	0.37	143.4	204.3	267.4
10418	α Her	17 14.6	+14 23	var.	5.4	3600	3635	4.68	0.0	155.8	180.0	119.6
	MlbO 4 AB	17 19.0	−34 59	6.1	7.6	42.09	1975.86	1.82	0.574	128.2	247.5	313.0
	BrsO 13	17 19.1	−46 38	5.5	8.7	2205	1907.76	23.90	0.90	44.9	331.8	137.0
10660	26 Dra	17 35.0	+61 52	5.3	8.0	76.0	1950.40	1.52	0.16	105.7	322.0	152.0
11005	τ Oph	18 03.1	−08 11	5.2	5.9	280.03	1829.0	1.494	0.718	59.32	49.78	63.04
11046	70 Oph	18 05.5	+02 30	4.2	6.0	88.30	1984.30	4.560	0.495	120.8	13.2	301.4
	h 5014	18 06.8	−43 25	5.7	5.7	191.23	1841.68	1.062	0.522	145.18	190.41	49.23
11483	OΣ 358	18 35.9	+16 59	6.8	7.0	292.0	1784.0	1.358	0.48	134.23	19.43	16.63
11635	ε¹ Lyr AB	18 44.3	+39 40	5.0	6.1	1165.6	1152.4	2.78	0.19	138	165.7	29.0
11635	ε² Lyr CD	18 44.4	+39 37	5.2	5.5	585.0	1644.5	2.95	0.49	120.5	88.0	17.4
	γ CrA	19 06.4	−37 04	4.8	5.1	120.42	1998.80	1.907	0.313	149.0	350.0	53.0
12880	δ Cyg	19 45.0	+45 08	2.9	6.3	827.6	1885.8	3.20	0.487	147.0	134.0	98.7
14296	λ Cyg	20 47.4	+36 29	4.9	6.1	391.3	1795.0	0.777	0.45	133.8	298.4	138.6
14360	4 Aqr	20 51.4	−05 38	6.4	7.2	187.0	1896.2	0.855	0.47	68.3	46.9	173.9
14499	ε Equ AB	20 59.1	+04 18	5.8	6.1	101.4	1920.21	0.656	0.702	92.8	339.3	105.2
14636	61 Cyg	21 06.9	+38 45	5.2	6.0	653.3	1676.94	24.31	0.40	55.0	147.0	171.4
14787	τ Cyg	21 14.8	+38 03	3.8	6.4	49.9	1989.5	0.88	0.25	134.2	119	159.7
15270	μ Cyg	21 44.1	+28 45	4.8	6.1	507.5	1962.5	4.278	0.58	76.5	160.0	109.6
15281	κ Peg	21 44.6	+25 39	4.7	5.0	11.558	1990.688	0.255	0.288	108.4	126.9	111.1
15600	ξ Cep	22 03.8	+64 38	4.4	6.5	3800	1750.0	11.5	0.24	109.0	114.0	85.0
15971	ζ Aqr	22 28.8	−00 01	4.3	4.5	856	1957.6	5.055	0.495	131.25	55.12	310.22
16538	π Cep	23 07.9	+75 23	4.6	6.6	150.0	1934.3	0.86	0.60	37.6	99.1	83.0
16666	o Cep	23 18.6	+68 07	4.9	7.1	796.2	2134.38	2.991	0.17	58.2	268.7	37.9
16836	72 Peg	23 34.0	+31 20	5.7	5.8	241.2	1857.45	0.447	0.28	35.6	129.0	123.8

[a] The ADS number is the number given in the *New General Catalogue of Double Stars*, which covers as far south as −30°.

The *amplitude* of a variable star is the difference between its magnitudes at maximum and at minimum. The variations may be periodic, semi-periodic or irregular, with time-scales from a fraction of a second to many centuries. Frequently, other aspects of the star – such as its radial velocity, temperature or spectrum – are also found to be variable.

Nomenclature of variable stars. For the variables in each constellation not already assigned a Bayer letter or roman letter, the German astronomer F. W. A. Argelander set aside the capital roman letters from R to Z. After Z, the double forms RR to RZ, SS to SZ, and so on to ZZ were used, which provided for 54 variable stars in any constellation. As that number proved insufficient, AA to AZ, BB to BZ, and so on were also used, J being omitted, extending the capacity to 334 variables per constellation. The simplest system, by which the variables of each constellation are denoted by the letter V followed by a number, is used from V335, when QZ has been reached. These designations are assigned when the type of variability has been ascertained. A variety of provisional designations are used for unconfirmed variables, of which the most important are the NSV numbers of the *New Catalogue of Suspected Variable Stars*

(Nauka, 1982), e.g. NSV 14811. Novae are now designated in the same way as other variable stars, but until they receive a final designation they are provisionally referred to by constellation, year and (if necessary) number; e.g. Nova And 1986 is now called OS And; Nova Vul 1984 No. 2 is now QU Vul.

Types of variable star

Table 47 lists the *types* currently recognized. They are arranged in six *classes*. Stars in the eruptive, pulsating, cataclysmic and X-ray classes are sometimes called *intrinsic* variables, as the light changes are due to physical changes in the stars themselves; stars in the rotating and eclipsing classes are *extrinsic* variables, as the light changes are a geometrical effect. Some of the more important types are described below.

Extrinsic variables

Eclipsing variables are binary systems for which the observer's line of sight is close to the stars' orbital plane, so that the two stars periodically eclipse each other. The consequent light variations will show two different minima.

Continued on p. 151

Table 47. Types of variable star.

Type	Abbreviation	Amplitude (magnitudes)	Period[a]	Spectrum	Distribution[b] (%)	Notes
Eruptive variables						
FU Ori	FU	6	—	Ae–Ge	0.01	Gradual rise over months to max. lasting many years; also called *fuors*
γ Cas	GCAS	up to 1.5	—	BIII–Ve	0.4	Shell stars; temporary fades
Irregular	I	—	—	—		Poorly studied stars of unknown spectral type
	IA	—	—	O–A		Poorly studied irregular variables of early spectral type
	IB	—	—	F–M		Poorly studied irregular variables of intermediate and late spectral type
Orion	IN, INS	up to several magnitudes	—	—		Young objects in diffuse nebulae; 'S' is added to denote rapid variation
	INA, INSA	—	—	B–A or Ae		Orion variables of early spectral type; occasional abrupt Algol-like fades; example T Ori
	INB, INSB	—	—	F–M, Fe–Me		Orion variables of intermediate or late spectral type; F-type stars may show Algol-like fades; example BH Cep
T Tau	IT	—	—	Fe–Me		Orion variables with intense emission of Fe I at 404.6 and 413.2 nm; example RW Aur
	INT	—	—	Fe–Me		T Tau stars in diffuse nebulae; example T Tau itself
	IS	0.5–1.0	—	—		Rapid irregular variables not in nebulae
	ISA	—	—	B–A or Ae		Rapid irregular variables of early spectral type
	ISB	—	—	F–M, Fe–Me		Rapid irregular variables of intermediate and late spectral type
All types I					5	
R CrB	RCB	1–9	—	Bpe–R	0.1	Cyclic pulsations and irregular deep fades
RS CVn	RS	0.2	—	—	0.05	Close binaries with chromospheric activity
S Dor	SDOR	1–7	—	Bpeq–Fpeq	0.05	High-luminosity stars, usually in diffuse nebulae and with expanding shells
UV Cet	UV	up to 6	—	KVe–MVe	3	Flare stars
	UVN	—	—	Ke–Me	1	Flaring Orion variables; example V389 Ori
Wolf–Rayet	WR	up to 0.1	—	W	0.03	Non-stable mass outflow; example V1042 Cyg
Pulsating variables						
α Cyg	ACYG	0.1	days to weeks	B–AIaeq	0.09	Non-radially pulsating supergiants
β Cep	BCEP	0.01–0.3	0.1–0.6	O8–B6I–V	0.3	Radial or non-radial pulsation
	BCEPS	0.015–0.025	0.02–0.04	B2–B3IV–V		Short-period group of β Cep variables
Cepheids	CEP	up to 2	1–135	F–KIb–II	0.6	Radial pulsation
W Vir	CW	0.3–1.2	0.8–35	—	0.01	Population II Cepheids
	CWA	—	8–35	—	0.4	Long-period W Vir stars; example W Vir itself
	CWB	—	0.8–8	—	0.2	Short-period W Vir stars; example BL Her
δ Cep	DCEP	—	—	—	1	Population I or classical Cepheids
	DCEPS	up to 0.5	up to 7	—	0.2	Short-period group of classical Cepheids; example δ Cep itself
δ Sct	DSCT	0.003–0.9	0.01–0.2	A0–F5III–V	0.3	Radial or non-radial pulsators; Population I
	DSCTC	up to 0.1	—		0.4	Low-amplitude group of δ Sct stars; present in open clusters; example EW Aqr
Irregular	L	—	—	—	3	Slow irregular variables
	LB	—	—	K, M, C, S	6	Slow irregular variables of late spectral type; example CO Cyg
	LC	1	—	K, M, C, S	0.2	Slow irregular supergiant variables of late spectral type; example TZ Cas
Mira	M	2.5–11	80–1000	Me, Ce, Se	21	Long-period variable giants
PV Tel	PVTEL	0.1	0.1 d to 1 y	Bp	0.01	Helium supergiants; example PV Tel
RR Lyr	RR	0.2–2	0.2–1.2	A–F	6	Radial pulsators of Population II; formerly called short-period Cepheids or cluster-type variables
	RRAB	0.5–2	0.3–1.2	—	14	Steep ascending branch on light curves; example RR Lyr itself

[a] In days unless otherwise stated.
[b] The percentages are based on the numbers of each type in the *General Catalogue of Variable Stars*. They do not necessarily reflect the true distribution; for example, brighter stars and stars showing larger variations are more likely to be discovered than fainter or small-amplitude variables.

Table 47 (*continued*)

Type	Abbreviation	Amplitude (magnitudes)	Period[a]	Spectrum	Distribution[b] (%)	Notes
	RRC	up to 0.8	0.2–0.5	—	1	Nearly symmetrical light curves; example SX UMa
RV Tau	RV	up to 4	30–150	F–M	0.3	Radially pulsating supergiants with alternating primary and secondary minima
	RVA	—	—	—	0.09	RV Tau stars with constant mean magnitude; example AC Her
	RVB	—	—	—	0.05	RV Tau stars with mean magnitude varying up to 2 mags in periods of 600–1500 d; example DF Cyg
Semiregular	SR	1–2	20–2000	—	5	Noticeable periodicity, but with irregularities
	SRA	up to 2.5	35–1200	M, C, S	3	Red giants with persistent periodicity; example Z Aqr
	SRB	—	20–2300	M, C, S	3	Red giants with poorly defined periodicity; example RR CrB
	SRC	1	30 d to several years	M, C, S	0.2	Red supergiants; example μ Cep
	SRD	0.1–4	30–1100	F–K	0.3	Giants and supergiants of intermediate spectral types; example SX Her
SX Phe	SXPHE,	up to 0.7	0.04–0.08	A2–F5	0.05	Population II subdwarfs resembling δ Sct stars
ZZ Cet	ZZ	0.001–0.2	30–1500 s	—		Non-radially pulsating white dwarfs
	ZZA	—	—	DA		ZZ Cet stars with only hydrogen absorption lines in spectrum; example ZZ Cet itself
	ZZB	—	—	DB		ZZ Cet stars with only helium absorption lines in spectrum; example V777 Her
	ZZO	—	—	D0		Very hot ZZ Cet stars with He II and C IV absorption lines; example GW Vir
All types ZZ					0.08	

The following suffix may be added (e.g. CEP(B)):

| | B | — | — | — | | Beats caused by two simultaneous pulsation modes |

Rotating variables

Type	Abbreviation	Amplitude (magnitudes)	Period[a]	Spectrum	Distribution[b] (%)	Notes
α^2 CVn	ACV	0.01–0.1	0.5–160	B8p–A7p	0.6	Main-sequence stars with strong magnetic fields and anomalously strong lines of Si, Sr, Cr and rare earth elements
	ACV0	0.01	0.004–0.1	Ap	0.02	α^2 CVn stars with rapid non-radial pulsations; example DO Eri
BY Dra	BY	up to 0.5	up to 120	G–M, Ge–Me	0.1	Rotating dwarfs with starspots and chromospheric activity
Ellipsoidal	ELL	up to 0.1	—	—	0.2	Close binaries with changing visible surface area, but no eclipses; example b Per
FK Com	FKCOM	c. 0.5	up to several days	G–K	0.01	Rapidly rotating giants with non-uniform surface brightness
Pulsars	PSR	up to 0.8	0.001–4 s	—	0.004	Rapidly rotating neutron stars with narrow beams of optical radiation; example CM Tau
	R	0.5–1.0	—	—		Close binaries showing reflection of light of hot component on surface of cool component; brightness varies as system rotates; example KV Vel
SX Ari	SXARI	0.1	1	B0p–B9p	0.06	High-temperature analogues of α^2 CVn variables, sometimes called *helium variables*

Cataclysmic variables (explosive and nova-like)

Type	Abbreviation	Amplitude (magnitudes)	Period[a]	Spectrum	Distribution[b] (%)	Notes
AM Her	AM	up to 5	—	—	0.004	Polars; close binaries containing compact object with strong magnetic field; accretion on magnetic poles gives rise to emission of polarized light
Novae	N	7–19	—	—	0.2	Thermonuclear runaway on white dwarf component of close binary
	NA	—	—	—	0.3	Fast novae, fading by 3 mags in 100 d or less; example GK Per

[a] In days unless otherwise stated.
[b] The percentages are based on the numbers of each type in the *General Catalogue of Variable Stars*. They do not necessarily reflect the true distribution; for example, brighter stars and stars showing larger variations are more likely to be discovered than fainter or small-amplitude variables.

Table 47 (*continued*)

Type	Abbreviation	Amplitude (magnitudes)	Period[a]	Spectrum	Distribution[b] (%)	Notes
	NAB	—	—	—	0.004	Novae of intermediate speed; example V400 Per
	NB	—	—	—	0.1	Slow novae, fading by 3 mags in 150 d or more; example RR Pic
	NC	up to 10	—	—	0.03	Very slow novae, at max. for more than 10 y; often classed with Z And stars; example RR Tel
Nova-like	NL	—	—	—	0.1	Insufficiently studied objects with outbursts like novae, or resembling old novae; example V Sge
	NR	—	10–80 y	—	0.03	Recurrent novae; example T CrB
Supernovae	SN	20+	—	—		Catastrophic explosion of star
	SNI	—	—	—		Type I supernovae: no hydrogen lines; fading at 0.1 mag per day for 20–30 d, then at 0.01 mag per day; example Z Cen
	SNII	—	—	—		Type II supernovae: hydrogen lines present; usually fading at 0.1 mag per day 40–100 d after max.; example SN 1987A
All types SN					0.02	
U Gem	UG	2–9	10 to 1000+	—	0.6	Dwarf novae; pulsed release of gravitational energy from accretion disk around white dwarf component of close binary
SS Cyg	UGSS	2–6	—	—	0.3	Dwarf novae with outbursts lasting several days
SU UMa	UGSU	4–9	—	—	0.08	Dwarf novae with short outbursts like SS Cyg stars, and occasional supermaxima 2 mags brighter and five times longer
Z Cam	UGZ	2–5	10–40	—	0.2	Dwarf novae with cyclic outbursts interrupted by standstills at intermediate magnitudes
Z And	ZAND	up to 4	—	—	0.2	Close binaries consisting of a cool star and a hot one exciting an extended envelope; often called *symbiotic stars*

Eclipsing variables

Type	Abbreviation	Amplitude (magnitudes)	Period[a]	Spectrum	Distribution[b] (%)	Notes
Eclipsing	E	—	—	—	3	Binary stars in which one component periodically passes in front of the other
Algol	EA	—	0.2–10 000+	—	11	Nearly spherical components, with contact times identifiable from light curve
β Lyr	EB	up to 2	over 1	B–A	2	Ellipsoidal components, with continuous change in brightness
W UMa	EW	up to 1	up to 0.8	F–G	2	Components almost in contact; primary and secondary minima nearly equal

The following suffixes may be added (e.g. EA/AR/RS):

Type	Abbreviation	Amplitude (magnitudes)	Period[a]	Spectrum	Distribution[b] (%)	Notes
	AR	—	—	—		Detached system of AR Lac type; both components are subgiants, and neither fills its inner equipotential surface (Roche lobe)
	D	—	—	—		Detached system
	DM	—	—	—		Detached main-sequence system
	DS	—	—	—		Detached system with subgiant component
	DW	—	—	—		Resembles contact systems of W UMa type, but components not in contact
	GS	—	—	—		Giant or supergiant component(s)
	K	—	—	—		Contact system, both components filling their Roche lobes
	KE	—	—	O–A		Contact system of early spectral type
	KW	—	—	F0–K		Contact system of W UMa type; primary is main-sequence star, and secondary lies below and to left of it in HR diagram
	PN	—	—	—		Nucleus of planetary nebula
	RS	—	—	—		RS CVn system; see eruptive variables above

[a] In days unless otherwise stated.
[b] The percentages are based on the numbers of each type in the *General Catalogue of Variable Stars*. They do not necessarily reflect the true distribution; for example, brighter stars and stars showing larger variations are more likely to be discovered than fainter or small-amplitude variables.

Table 47 (*continued*)

Type	Abbreviation	Amplitude (magnitudes)	Period[a]	Spectrum	Distribution[b] (%)	Notes
	SD	—	—	—		Semi-detached system; less massive, subgiant component fills Roche lobe
	WD	—	—	—		White dwarf components
	WR	—	—	—		Wolf–Rayet component(s)
X-ray binaries						
	X	—	—	—		Close binaries containing compact object (white dwarf, neutron star or black hole)
Burster	XB	0.1	—	—		X-ray and optical bursts lasting seconds or minutes; example V801 Ara
	XF	—	—	—		Rapid X-ray and optical fluctuations in fraction of a second; example V1357 Cyg
Irregular	XI	1	—	—		Variations over minutes or hours; example V818 Sco
	XJ	—	—	—		Relativistic jets present; example V1343 Aql
	XND	4–9	—	—		X-ray novae or transients, with a dwarf or subgiant component of spectral type G–M; outbursts lasting up to several months but no envelope ejected; example V616 Mon
	XNG	1–2	—	—		X-ray novae or transients with an early-type giant or supergiant component; example V725 Tau
	XP	up to several magnitudes	1–10	—		X-ray pulsars, with periods of 1 s to 100 m; slower light change caused by rotation of ellipsoidal component; example GP Vel
	XPR	2–3	—	—		X-ray pulsars showing reflection effect – 'normal' component is irradiated by X-rays, and brightness varies as system rotates; example HZ Her
Polars	XPRM	1–5	—	—		X-ray pulsars with strong magnetic field; accretion on magnetic poles gives rise to emission of polarized light; example BL Hyi
	XR, XRM	—	—	—		Resemble types XPR, XPRM, but presumed X-ray pulsar not observed as the X-ray beam is never in the line of sight; example AN UMa
All types X					0.2	
Other types						
	S	—	—	—	0.6	Unstudied stars with rapid light changes
	★	—	—	—	0.2	Unique types of variable not fitting above classification; example VY CMa

[a] In days unless otherwise stated.

[b] The percentages are based on the numbers of each type in the *General Catalogue of Variable Stars*. They do not necessarily reflect the true distribution; for example, brighter stars and stars showing larger variations are more likely to be discovered than fainter or small-amplitude variables.

The deeper minimum, when the star with the greater surface brightness is eclipsed, is called the primary eclipse; the shallower minimum is called the secondary eclipse. If the eclipse is total or annular then the minima may have flat bases. Eclipsing binaries account for nearly a fifth of all known variables. Their periods are subject to slight variation, and useful work can be done in timing the eclipses, either by making visual estimates or, for more accurate results, by photoelectric photometry. They are classified into three types, depending on the shapes of their light curves.

In *Algol-type eclipsing binaries* (type EA), the times when eclipses begin and end can be identified from the light curve, and between consecutive eclipses there is little variation. Algol-type curves may be produced by systems in which the components are sufficiently far apart for them (or at least the one with the higher surface brightness) to retain a normal shape and structure (detached system, Figure 26(a)). The *Roche lobe* is a volume around the star beyond which it cannot expand without losing material in the direction of the other component.

In *Beta Lyrae-type* systems (type EB) the brightness varies continuously, and the times when eclipses begin and end cannot be identified from the light curve. They may be detached systems with ellipsoidal components, or ones in which the component of greater surface brightness fills its

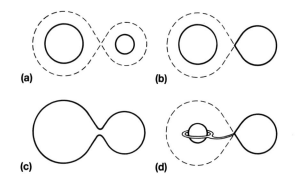

Figure 26. Configurations of interacting binary stars: (a) detached, (b) semi-detached, (c) contact and (d) semi-detached with accretion disk. In each case the dashed line represents a surface of equal gravitational potential in the rotating frame of the binary.

Roche lobe (semi-detached system, Figure 26(b)), and much of the variation is a result of the changing visible area of this star as the system rotates.

In *W Ursae Majoris* systems (type EW) both components almost fill their Roche lobes, or overfill them so that the stars are actually in contact (Figure 26(c)). The light curves resemble those of Beta Lyrae systems, but the periods are generally shorter and the primary and secondary minima are of a similar depth.

Pulsars (type PSR) are normally radio variables, but two – the pulsar in the Crab Nebula and the Vela Pulsar – have also shown periodic light variations. It is believed that a pulsar is a neutron star (see p. 142) which is left behind after a supernova explosion. The variations are caused by the object's rotation combined with a directional form of light emission. The Crab Pulsar (CM Tau) has a period of 0.033 s. The Vela Pulsar (HU Vel) is one of the faintest known variable stars, ranging between B magnitudes 23.2 and 25.2 in a period of 0.089 s.

Intrinsic variables

Two-thirds of the known variable stars are *pulsating variables*. They may pulsate radially, remaining spherical in shape, or non-radially, with the shape deviating periodically from a sphere. *Cepheid variables* are bright, radially pulsating stars whose period and mean magnitude are closely related. They are subdivided into *classical Cepheids* (type DCEP) and *W Virginis stars* (type CW); closely related are the *Beta Cephei* or *Beta Canis Majoris stars* (type BCEP), the *Delta Scuti stars* (type DSCT), the *RR Lyrae stars* (type RR) and the *SX Phoenicis stars* (type SXPHE). The cause of the variations appears to be a self-propagating, periodic ionization and recombination of helium in the star's atmosphere which causes a periodic variation in the opacity. The changing opacity in turn produces a change in the star's radius and temperature, and hence in its luminosity.

Mira stars (type M), or *long period variables*, are late-type giants with periods and amplitudes that are subject to appreciable variation from cycle to cycle, making them objects which amateur observers can usefully study. The *semiregular variables* (type SR) sometimes resemble small-amplitude Mira stars, but the variations are often subject to great irregularity, as in the *irregular variables* (type L) and the *RV Tauri stars* (RV). The periods of these objects are generally not well known, and they merit further study, although their typically small amplitudes and redness make them difficult to observe visually.

Eruptive variables are a very mixed class of stars whose brightness varies because of violent processes and flares taking place in their chromospheres and coronae. They constitute about a tenth of the known variables. The *R Coronae Borealis stars* (type RCB) are carbon-rich stars that are particularly worth monitoring for their sudden fades, which are caused by the ejection of a cloud of soot.

Cataclysmic variables make up only 2% of known variable stars, but they are one of the most important fields of research for the amateur. Most are close binaries in which one component is usually a white dwarf surrounded by an accretion disk formed by matter lost by the other component, which is usually a cool star (Figure 26(d)). They are liable to undergo occasional outbursts. In the *dwarf novae* (type UG) the outbursts are semi-periodic, pulsed releases of gravitational energy from material in the accretion disk. Outbursts in the *novae* (type N) are the result of thermonuclear runaway, the explosive burning of hydrogen to helium on the surface of the white dwarf. It is likely that all novae are *recurrent novae* with very long periods, and that in most cases only one outburst has been observed. Estimates of the frequency of nova outbursts in our Galaxy range from 12 to 100 per year, although only two or three per year are actually seen. The *symbiotic stars* (types NC and ZAND) are also important objects to monitor for possible outbursts, as are the *nova-like variables* (type NL) which may be ex-novae or pre-novae. The outbursts of *supernovae* (type SN) are typically one million times as energetic as those of novae; at maximum they can be as bright as an entire galaxy. *Type I supernovae*, which are less common, may be exploding white dwarfs in close binaries, while *Type II supernovae* are massive stars whose cores undergo a catastrophic collapse after their nuclear fuel has been exhausted.

Table 48 lists the known supernovae and novae in our Galaxy that are believed to have reached mag. 6.5 or brighter. Many novae are not found until they are on the decline, but an estimate of their maximum brightness can be made by comparison with the light curves of other novae; such estimates are distinguished by a question mark in the table. Many so-called 'new stars' were recorded in earlier years. Thus the appearance of a new star in about 150 BC is said to have led Hipparchus to draw up his catalogue of stars, but generally the old records are vague and indefinite, and in some cases undoubtedly refer not to novae but to comets.

Table 48 shows that most bright novae have appeared in the Milky Way regions, within 10° of the galactic equator. They have also been commoner towards the galactic centre

Table 48. Bright galactic novae and supernovae.

Year AD	Nova	Type	Greatest magnitude	Approximate galactic Long. °	Lat. °	RA 2000.0 h m	Dec. ° '
185	Cen	SN	−6	313	0	14 20	−60
1006	Lup	SN	−8	327	+14	15 02.8	−41 57
1054	CM Tau	SN	−6	185	−6	05 34.5	+22 01
1572	B Cas	SNI?	−4.0	120	+1	00 25.3	+64 09
1604	V843 Oph	SNI	−3	5	+7	17 30.6	−21 29
1670	CK Vul	N	2.6	63	+1	19 47.6	+27 19
1783	WY Sge	N	6	53	−1	19 32.7	+17 45
1848	V841 Oph	NB	2?	8	+18	16 59.5	−12 54
1866	T CrB*a*	NR	2.0	42	+48	15 59.5	+25 55
1876	Q Cyg	NA	3.0	90	−8	21 41.7	+42 50
1887	V Per	N	4?	133	−5	02 01.9	+56 44
1890	T Pyx*a*	NR	6.5	257	+10	09 04.7	−32 23
1891	T Aur	NB	4.2	177	−2	05 32.0	+30 27
1895	RS Car	N	5.0?	291	−1	11 08.1	−61 56
1898	V1059 Sgr	NA	2.0?	22	−8	19 01.8	−13 10
1898	RS Oph*a*	NR	4.3	20	+10	17 50.2	−06 43
1899	V606 Aql	NA	5.5?	36	−7	19 20.4	−00 08
1901	GK Per	NA	0.2	151	−10	03 31.2	+43 54
1903	DM Gem	NA	4.8	185	+12	06 44.2	+29 57
1905	V1015 Sgr	NA	6.5?	359	−6	18 09.1	−32 28
1910	OY Ara	NA	5.1?	334	−4	16 40.8	−52 26
1910	DI Lac	NA	4.6	103	−5	22 35.8	+52 43
1912	DN Gem	NA	3.5	184	+15	06 54.9	+32 09
1917	V840 Oph	NA	5.5?	353	+9	16 54.7	−29 38
1918	GI Mon	NA	5.2?	223	+5	07 26.8	−06 41
1918	V603 Aql	NA	−1.1	33	+1	18 48.9	+00 35
1919	HR Lyr	NA	6.5?	60	+12	18 53.4	+29 14
1920	V476 Cyg	NA	2.0	87	+12	19 58.4	+53 37
1925	RR Pic	NB	1.0	272	−26	06 35.6	−62 38
1926	X Cir	NB	6.2?	314	−5	14 43.0	−65 15
1927	EL Aql	NA	6.4	30	−3	18 56.0	−03 19
1927	XX Tau	NA	5.9	187	−12	05 19.4	+16 43
1934	DQ Her	NB	1.3	73	+26	18 07.5	+45 51
1936	V732 Sgr	NA	6.5	3	−1	17 56.1	−27 22
1936	CP Lac	NA	2.1	102	−1	22 15.7	+55 37
1936	V368 Aql	NA	5.0	44	−4	19 26.6	+07 36
1936	V630 Sgr	NA	4.5	358	−7	18 08.8	−34 20
1939	BT Mon	NA	5?	214	−3	06 43.8	−02 01
1942	CP Pup	NA	0.5	253	−1	08 11.8	−35 21
1943	V500 Aql	NA	6.1?	48	−9	19 52.5	+08 29
1948	CT Ser	N	5?	24	+48	15 45.6	+14 23
1950	DK Lac	NA	5.0?	105	−5	22 49.8	+53 17
1956	RW UMi	NB	6	110	+33	16 47.7	+77 02
1960	V446 Her	NA	3.0	45	+5	18 57.4	+13 14
1963	V533 Her	NA	3.0	69	+24	18 14.3	+45 51
1964	QZ Aur	NA	5.0?	174	−1	05 28.7	+33 19
1967	HR Del	NB	3.5	63	−14	20 42.3	+19 10
1968	LV Vul	NA	5.2	63	+1	19 48.0	+27 10
1969	V2572 Sgr	NA	6.5	2	−10	18 31.6	−32 36
1970	FH Ser	NA	4.5	33	+6	18 30.8	+02 37
1974	V3888 Sgr	N	6.5?	9	+5	17 48.7	−18 46
1975	V3964 Sgr	NA	6?	10	+5	17 49.7	−17 23
1975	V1500 Cyg	NA	2.2	90	0	21 11.6	+48 09
1976	V2104 Oph	N	5.3?	38	+16	18 03.4	+11 48
1976	NQ Vul	NA	6.0	55	+1	19 29.2	+20 28
1982	V1370 Aql	N	6	39	−6	19 23.4	+02 29
1984	PW Vul	NA	6.4	61	+5	19 26.1	+27 22
1984	QU Vul	NA	5.6	69	−6	20 26.8	+27 47
1986	V842 Cen	N	4.6	317	+2	14 36.0	−57 38
1986	OS And	N	6.3	106	−12	23 13.0	+47 28

Adapted from: H. W. Duerbeck, *A Reference Catalogue and Atlas of Galactic Novae* (D. Reidel, 1987).

a Recurrent novae with outbursts in the following years: T CrB 1866, 1946; T Pyx 1890, 1902, 1920, 1944, 1966; RS Oph 1898, 1933, 1958, 1967, 1985.

in Sagittarius. Half of those detected have been between galactic longitudes 0° and 90°, in the region from Sagittarius to Cygnus; but it is possible that a similar number have occurred between 270° and 360°, from Vela to Sagittarius, in the less well-observed southern sky. Amateurs have had considerable success in discovering novae, by searching with binoculars and by means of photographic patrols.

X-ray binaries resemble cataclysmic variables, except that the compact object may be not a white dwarf but a neutron star, or even a black hole. Only a few dozen have so far been identified as optically variable objects.

Secular variables are stars that are suspected to have faded or brightened slowly and steadily over a long period of time. No case is certain, but the presence of such a variable in the Pleiades (possibly Pleione) could be the reason why they are sometimes called the Seven Sisters, although there are only six fairly bright naked-eye stars in the cluster.

Observing variable stars

Visual estimates are made by comparing the variable with comparison stars of constant brightness. Special charts are required. These are issued by organizations such as the American Association of Variable Star Observers (AAVSO), or the Variable Star Section of the British Astronomical Association (BAA) or of the Royal Astronomical Society of New Zealand (RASNZ). (For addresses see the Appendix.) At least two comparison stars should be used for each estimate. It is possible to make visual estimates that are accurate to within about 0.1 mag.

A few variables are bright enough to be followed with the naked eye. Binoculars bring many more variables into range, though of course most variables are telescopic objects. Variables with an amplitude of at least 0.4 mag. that reach mag. 6.5 or brighter at maximum are given in the lists of interesting objects preceding the star charts. In addition, known variables with an amplitude of at least 0.1 mag. are indicated with a special symbol on the charts.

For really accurate estimates, photoelectric methods are used. Information is available from International Amateur–Professional Photoelectric Photometry (IAPPP), c/o Dr D. S. Hall, Dyer Observatory, Vanderbilt University, Nashville, Tennessee 37235, U.S.A., as well as from the national organizations mentioned above.

Atmospheric extinction.

If the brightness of a variable star is estimated using comparison stars that are not at about the same altitude as the variable – as is sometimes unavoidable – the result will be in error as the light from the variable and the comparison stars will have traversed different thicknesses of the Earth's atmosphere. The errors can be balanced to some extent by making estimates against comparison stars both above and below the variable. Alternatively, allowance may be made for the difference in extinction between the variable and each comparison star. The approximate figures in Table 49 may be used, unless haze is present.

CLUSTERS, NEBULAE AND GALAXIES

Nomenclature. Brighter star clusters, nebulae and galaxies are often referred to by their number in the catalogue prepared by the French astronomer Charles Messier and published over the period 1771–1784. These so-called *Messier objects* are listed in Table 50 (on pages 156 and 157). The Messier or M numbers are used on the star charts in this Atlas, other objects being identified by their number in J. L. E. Dreyer's *New General Catalogue of Nebulae and Clusters of Stars* published in 1888, or their number in its two supplements, the *Index Catalogue* (1895) and the *Second Index Catalogue* (1908).

Star clusters

Many of the stars that we see are scattered randomly along the spiral arms of our Galaxy, but a great number are concentrated in relatively compact groups called star clusters. They fall into two main categories, *open clusters* and *globular clusters*, each type having its own characteristics.

Open clusters. Over a thousand open star clusters are known. They are often referred to as *galactic clusters*, as they are found in the plane of the Galaxy. As their name suggests, open clusters are loose collections of stars that have no well-defined shape; their diameters are generally no more than a few tens of light years. The numbers of stars in open clusters can vary considerably. For example, the sparse cluster M18 (NGC 6613) in Sagittarius contains only about a dozen members whereas M11 (NGC 6705) in Scutum contains 500 stars or more, making it one of the richest open star clusters known.

A number of open clusters are visible to the unaided eye, notably the Pleiades (M45) in Taurus. As with other open

Table 49. Atmospheric extinction. The dimming of starlight by scattering and absorption increases with the thickness of the Earth's atmosphere through which it passes, i.e. with zenith distance, and must be allowed for when estimating a star's brightness. This table gives values for the approximate extinction in a clear sky by comparison with the value at the zenith.

Zenith distance	47°	58°	64°	69°	71°	73°	75°	77°	79°	80°	82°	84°	86°	88°	89°
Extinction (mag.)	0.1	0.2	0.3	0.4	0.5	0.6	0.7	0.8	0.9	1.0	1.2	1.5	2.0	2.5	3.0
Altitude	43°	32°	26°	21°	19°	17°	15°	13°	11°	10°	8°	6°	4°	2°	1°

star clusters, the Pleiades stars were formed together in the same region of space. Indeed, traces of the original nebula from which the Pleiades were formed can still be seen in the form of wisps of dust and gas surrounding members of the group.

The Pleiades cluster is thought to be about 50 million years old, making it comparatively young. Once a cluster forms, gravitational perturbations from the rest of the Galaxy can slowly break up the group, eventually dispersing the individual stars. However, some dense clusters such as NGC 188 in Cepheus and NGC 6791 in Lyra have remained bound together for 5000 million years or more.

Associations are loose-knit groups of young stars that have recently been born in the spiral arms of the Galaxy. *OB associations* consist of hot, massive stars of spectral types O and B, numbering from 10 to 100, scattered over an area several hundred light years in diameter. OB associations are often centred on an open cluster, as in the case of the Perseus OB1 association which is centred on the double cluster h and Chi (χ) Persei. The Orion Nebula is the centre of a major OB association. The nearest to us is the Sco–Cen association, about 500 light years away, stretching from Scorpius to Crux. *T associations* are similar groups containing faint, low-mass T Tauri stars and hence are much less prominent than OB associations.

Moving clusters. As an open cluster travels through space, its member stars move in paths which are more or less parallel to one another, but because of perspective the paths as seen from the Earth appear to converge on (or diverge from) a particular point in the sky known as the convergent point. This fact provides astronomers with a means of determining the distances of clusters, by finding three values for the individual stars in the moving cluster: their radial velocities towards or away from us (measured from the Doppler shift in their spectra), their proper motions and their angular distances from the convergent point. Once these values are known accurately for as many stars as possible, then the distance to the cluster can be calculated using simple geometry.

Obviously, the closer a star cluster is to us the easier it is to make the required measurements, as motion across the sky is easier to detect for nearby stars than for those at greater distances. The closest rich cluster is the Hyades in Taurus. A great deal of work has been devoted to determining its exact distance by the method described above, and the best current estimate is about 150 light years.

Some moving clusters are much more spread out than the Hyades, for example the Ursa Major moving cluster. This cluster includes five of the stars in the Plough, or Dipper (β, γ, δ, ϵ and ζ Ursae Majoris) and also Sirius. It seems that the Sun is actually passing through the outskirts of this cluster.

Globular clusters. Unlike open clusters, which are found within the spiral arms of the Galaxy, globular clusters are situated mainly in the *galactic halo*, a spherical volume of space surrounding the Galaxy. Most of the 140 or so globular clusters known in our Galaxy are seen to lie in a region close to the galactic centre.

Globular clusters are huge, spherical concentrations of stars, tens to hundreds of light years in diameter. The stars they contain are generally much older than those in open clusters. In a globular cluster the density of stars is high, about one star per cubic light year, sufficient to resist disruption by the tidal forces exerted by the Galaxy. Globulars are among the oldest known objects in the Universe, with ages of 10 000 million years or more.

Some globulars can be seen without optical aid, the best examples being the 4th-magnitude Omega (ω) Centauri and 47 Tucanae, both in the southern hemisphere. Omega Centauri is the brightest globular in the sky, at a distance of around 17 000 light years; it is thought to contain more than a million stars. The brightest example in the northern sky is the 6th-magnitude M13 in Hercules. To the unaided eye, M13 appears as a fuzzy star-like object; a telescope is needed to resolve some of the million stars that comprise it.

Nebulae

Large amounts of gas and dust are present in the Galaxy, consisting mainly of hydrogen. This material is thought to account for around 10% of the total mass of the Galaxy. Less than 1% of the material is dust, which reveals itself through the effect it has on starlight. Light from distant stars which passes through the interstellar dust is dimmed, and also reddened because the extinction of the light is greater for shorter (bluer) wavelengths. Interstellar absorption is most conspicuous along the plane of the Milky Way, where most of the interstellar material is concentrated.

Emission nebulae. Some interstellar matter is concentrated in clouds known as nebulae, of which there are several types. If a nebula is situated close to one or more hot, bright stars, the energy from the stars may cause it to emit light of its own. Ultraviolet radiation from the nearby stars ionizes the hydrogen in these so-called HII regions, which causes the nebula to glow. Many emission nebulae are known, the most famous being the Orion Nebula (M42), visible to the unaided eye as a misty patch of light just to the south of the Belt of Orion. The Orion Nebula lies at a distance of around 1600 light years and has a diameter of about 30 light years. Deep inside this huge gas cloud is the multiple star Theta (θ) Orionis, the four brightest components of which form a conspicuous group called the Trapezium on account of its shape. The energy from the hottest components of the Trapezium causes the gas within the Orion Nebula to shine.

Reflection nebulae contain dust that reflects light from nearby stars. They have a characteristic blue colour, in contrast to the predominantly red glow of emission nebulae. One of the best-known reflection nebulae is that surrounding the stars of the Pleiades.

Dark nebulae appear as dark areas in the sky and contain no stars; in fact they blot out the light from stars behind them.

Continued on p. 158

Table 50. The Messier objects.

M	NGC	RA h m	Dec. 2000.0 ° ′	Constellation	Size[a] ′	Integrated magnitude	Description
1	1952	5 34.5	+22 01	Tau	6×4	c. 8.4	Supernova remnant
2	7089	21 33.5	−0 49	Aqr	13	6.5	Globular cluster
3	5272	13 42.2	+28 23	CVn	16	6.4	Globular cluster
4	6121	16 23.6	−26 32	Sco	26	5.9	Globular cluster
5	5904	15 18.6	+2 05	Ser	17	5.8	Globular cluster
6	6405	17 40.1	−32 13	Sco	15	4.2	Open cluster
7	6475	17 53.9	−34 49	Sco	80	3.3	Open cluster
8	6523	18 03.8	−24 23	Sgr	90×40	c. 5.8	Diffuse nebula
9	6333	17 19.2	−18 31	Oph	9	c. 7.9	Globular cluster
10	6254	16 57.1	−4 06	Oph	15	6.6	Globular cluster
11	6705	18 51.1	−6 16	Sct	14	5.8	Open cluster
12	6218	16 47.2	−1 57	Oph	14	6.6	Globular cluster
13	6205	16 41.7	+36 28	Her	17	5.9	Globular cluster
14	6402	17 37.6	−3 15	Oph	12	7.6	Globular cluster
15	7078	21 30.0	+12 10	Peg	12	6.4	Globular cluster
16	6611	18 18.8	−13 47	Ser	7	6.0	Open cluster
17	6618	18 20.8	−16 11	Sgr	46×37	7	Diffuse nebula
18	6613	18 19.9	−17 08	Sgr	9	6.9	Open cluster
19	6273	17 02.6	−26 16	Oph	14	7.2	Globular cluster
20	6514	18 02.6	−23 02	Sgr	29×27	c. 8.5	Diffuse nebula
21	6531	18 04.6	−22 30	Sgr	13	5.9	Open cluster
22	6656	18 36.4	−23 54	Sgr	24	5.1	Globular cluster
23	6494	17 56.8	−19 01	Sgr	27	5.5	Open cluster
24		18 16.9	−18 29	Sgr	90	c. 4.5	*See notes*
25	IC4725	18 31.6	−19 15	Sgr	32	4.6	Open cluster
26	6694	18 45.2	−9 24	Sct	15	8.0	Open cluster
27	6853	19 59.6	+22 43	Vul	8×4	c. 8.1	Planetary nebula
28	6626	18 24.5	−24 52	Sgr	11	c. 6.9	Globular cluster
29	6913	20 23.9	+38 32	Cyg	7	6.6	Open cluster
30	7099	21 40.4	−23 11	Cap	11	7.5	Globular cluster
31	224	0 42.7	+41 16	And	178×63	3.4	Spiral galaxy
32	221	0 42.7	+40 52	And	8×6	8.2	Elliptical galaxy
33	598	1 33.9	+30 39	Tri	62×39	5.7	Spiral galaxy
34	1039	2 42.0	+42 47	Per	35	5.2	Open cluster
35	2168	6 08.9	+24 20	Gem	28	5.1	Open cluster
36	1960	5 36.1	+34 08	Aur	12	6.0	Open cluster
37	2099	5 52.4	+32 33	Aur	24	5.6	Open cluster
38	1912	5 28.7	+35 50	Aur	21	6.4	Open cluster
39	7092	21 32.2	+48 26	Cyg	32	4.6	Open cluster
40		12 22.4	+58 05	UMa		8	*See notes*
41	2287	6 47.0	−20 44	CMa	38	4.5	Open cluster
42	1976	5 35.4	−5 27	Ori	66×60	4	Diffuse nebula
43	1982	5 35.6	−5 16	Ori	20×15	9	Diffuse nebula
44	2632	8 40.1	+19 59	Cnc	95	3.1	Open cluster
45		3 47.0	+24 07	Tau	110	1.2	Open cluster
46	2437	7 41.8	−14 49	Pup	27	6.1	Open cluster
47	2422	7 36.6	−14 30	Pup	30	4.4	Open cluster
48	2548	8 13.8	−5 48	Hya	54	5.8	Open cluster
49	4472	12 29.8	+8 00	Vir	9×7	8.4	Elliptical galaxy
50	2323	7 03.2	−8 20	Mon	16	5.9	Open cluster
51	5194−5	13 29.9	+47 12	CVn	11×8	8.1	Spiral galaxy
52	7654	23 24.2	+61 35	Cas	13	6.9	Open cluster
53	5024	13 12.9	+18 10	Com	13	7.7	Globular cluster
54	6715	18 55.1	−30 29	Sgr	9	7.7	Globular cluster

[a]The dimensions given are as seen on long-exposure photographs and, for galaxies in particular, are larger than the sizes that will be seen visually.

M1	Crab Nebula	M27	Dumbbell Nebula
M8	Lagoon Nebula; contains a star cluster	M31	Andromeda Galaxy
M11	Wild Duck Cluster	M40	Faint double star Winnecke 4, mags. 9.0 and 9.6
M16	Surrounded by the Eagle Nebula	M42, M43	Orion Nebula
M17	Omega Nebula	M44	Praesepe, the Beehive Cluster
M20	Trifid Nebula	M45	The Pleiades; no NGC or IC number
M24	Star field in Sagittarius, containing the open cluster NGC 6603	M51	Whirlpool Galaxy

Table 50 (*continued*)

M	NGC	RA h m	Dec. 2000.0 ° '	Constellation	Size[a] '	Integrated magnitude	Description
55	6809	19 40.0	−30 58	Sgr	19	7.0	Globular cluster
56	6779	19 16.6	+30 11	Lyr	7	8.2	Globular cluster
57	6720	18 53.6	+33 02	Lyr	1	c. 9.0	Planetary nebula
58	4579	12 37.7	+11 49	Vir	5×4	9.8	Spiral galaxy
59	4621	12 42.0	+11 39	Vir	5×3	9.8	Elliptical galaxy
60	4649	12 43.7	+11 33	Vir	7×6	8.8	Elliptical galaxy
61	4303	12 21.9	+4 28	Vir	6×5	9.7	Spiral galaxy
62	6266	17 01.2	−30 07	Oph	14	6.6	Globular cluster
63	5055	13 15.8	+42 02	CVn	12×8	8.6	Spiral galaxy
64	4826	12 56.7	+21 41	Com	9×5	8.5	Spiral galaxy
65	3623	11 18.9	+13 05	Leo	10×3	9.3	Spiral galaxy
66	3627	11 20.2	+12 59	Leo	9×4	9.0	Spiral galaxy
67	2682	8 50.4	+11 49	Cnc	30	6.9	Open cluster
68	4590	12 39.5	−26 45	Hya	12	8.2	Globular cluster
69	6637	18 31.4	−32 21	Sgr	7	7.7	Globular cluster
70	6681	18 43.2	−32 18	Sgr	8	8.1	Globular cluster
71	6838	19 53.8	+18 47	Sge	7	8.3	Globular cluster
72	6981	20 53.5	−12 32	Aqr	6	9.4	Globular cluster
73	6994	20 58.9	−12 38	Aqr			*See notes*
74	628	1 36.7	+15 47	Psc	10×9	9.2	Spiral galaxy
75	6864	20 06.1	−21 55	Sgr	6	8.6	Globular cluster
76	650–1	1 42.4	+51 34	Per	2×1	c. 11.5	Planetary nebula
77	1068	2 42.7	−0 01	Cet	7×6	8.8	Spiral galaxy
78	2068	5 46.7	+0 03	Ori	8×6	8	Diffuse nebula
79	1904	5 24.5	−24 33	Lep	9	8.0	Globular cluster
80	6093	16 17.0	−22 59	Sco	9	7.2	Globular cluster
81	3031	9 55.6	+69 04	UMa	26×14	6.8	Spiral galaxy
82	3034	9 55.8	+69 41	UMa	11×5	8.4	Irregular galaxy
83	5236	13 37.0	−29 52	Hya	11×10	c. 7.6	Spiral galaxy
84	4374	12 25.1	+12 53	Vir	5×4	9.3	Elliptical galaxy
85	4382	12 25.4	+18 11	Com	7×5	9.2	Elliptical galaxy
86	4406	12 26.2	+12 57	Vir	7×6	9.2	Elliptical galaxy
87	4486	12 30.8	+12 24	Vir	7	8.6	Elliptical galaxy
88	4501	12 32.0	+14 25	Com	7×4	9.5	Spiral galaxy
89	4552	12 35.7	+12 33	Vir	4	9.8	Elliptical galaxy
90	4569	12 36.8	+13 10	Vir	10×5	9.5	Spiral galaxy
91	4548	12 35.4	+14 30	Com	5×4	10.2	Spiral galaxy
92	6341	17 17.1	+43 08	Her	11	6.5	Globular cluster
93	2447	7 44.6	−23 52	Pup	22	c. 6.2	Open cluster
94	4736	12 50.9	+41 07	CVn	11×9	8.1	Spiral galaxy
95	3351	10 44.0	+11 42	Leo	7×5	9.7	Spiral galaxy
96	3368	10 46.8	+11 49	Leo	7×5	9.2	Spiral galaxy
97	3587	11 14.8	+55 01	UMa	3	c. 11.2	Planetary nebula
98	4192	12 13.8	+14 54	Com	10×3	10.1	Spiral galaxy
99	4254	12 18.8	+14 25	Com	5	9.8	Spiral galaxy
100	4321	12 22.9	+15 49	Com	7×6	9.4	Spiral galaxy
101	5457	14 03.2	+54 21	UMa	27×26	7.7	Spiral galaxy
102							*See notes*
103	581	1 33.2	+60 42	Cas	6	c. 7.4	Open cluster
104	4594	12 40.0	−11 37	Vir	9×4	8.3	Spiral galaxy
105	3379	10 47.8	+12 35	Leo	4×4	9.3	Elliptical galaxy
106	4258	12 19.0	+47 18	CVn	18×8	8.3	Spiral galaxy
107	6171	16 32.5	−13 03	Oph	10	8.1	Globular cluster
108	3556	11 11.5	+55 40	UMa	8×2	10.0	Spiral galaxy
109	3992	11 57.6	+53 23	UMa	8×5	9.8	Spiral galaxy
110	205	0 40.4	+41 41	And	17×10	8.0	Elliptical galaxy

Source: A. Hirshfeld and R. W. Sinnott (eds.), *Sky Catalogue 2000.0*, Vol. 2 (Sky Publishing Corp./Cambridge University Press, 1985).

[a]The dimensions given are as seen on long-exposure photographs and, for galaxies in particular, are larger than the sizes that will be seen visually.

M57	Ring Nebula	M97	Owl Nebula
M64	Black Eye Galaxy	M102	Duplicate of M101
M73	Small group of four faint stars	M104	Sombrero Galaxy

They can take on a wide variety of shapes, ranging from the relatively uniform Coalsack in Crux to the long, winding Snake Nebula in Ophiuchus. Depending on their location, dark nebulae resemble either a blank region of sky or a conspicuous dark patch superimposed on a much brighter background. An example of the latter is the famous Horsehead Nebula, south of Zeta (ζ) Orionis, which is seen against the backdrop of the bright nebula IC 434. When first noticed on a photographic plate taken in 1889, the Horsehead was considered to be simply a gap in the bright nebula. The American astronomer E. E. Barnard recognized it for what it really was, and went on to compile a catalogue of dark nebulae; many of these objects are now classified by their Barnard numbers.

Bok globules are small, nearly spherical patches of dark nebulosity, thought to be stars in the very early stages of forming. They are named after Bart J. Bok, the Dutch astronomer who first drew attention to them. Bok globules can be seen against a number of nebulae, notably the Lagoon Nebula (M8) in Sagittarius and the Rosette Nebula (NGC 2237–2244) in Monoceros.

Planetary nebulae, when seen through a telescope, sometimes resemble planetary disks and were so named by Sir William Herschel in 1782. Planetary nebulae result from the ejection by old stars of their outer layers. This discarded material then takes the form of an expanding shell of gas surrounding the star. Because hotter regions of the central star have been exposed, its surface temperature is very high and can reach 100 000 K. Once the material has been ejected the central star begins the collapse into a white dwarf. Planetary nebulae are fairly short-lived, and within a few tens of thousands of years the expanding shell of gas dissipates into surrounding space. Not all planetary nebulae are symmetrical in shape, and there are many which have unusual appearances, including the Dumbbell Nebula (M27) in Vulpecula and the Little Dumbbell Nebula (M76), also known as the Butterfly, in Perseus. Planetary nebulae shine through the same process of ionization that takes place within emission nebulae. Over a thousand planetary nebulae are known, many within the reach of amateur telescopes.

Supernova remnants. Objects like the Crab Nebula (M1) in Taurus and the Veil Nebula (NGC 6960–6992) in Cygnus are the gaseous remnants of stars that have undergone supernova explosions. During these spectacular and destructive events, stars eject most of their material, creating expanding clouds of matter which eventually disperse into space. The two objects mentioned above differ considerably in appearance. The Crab Nebula is seen as a faint, diffuse patch of light and resulted from a supernova which was observed by Chinese astronomers in 1054. The Veil Nebula, on the other hand, is a huge loop of material thought to have been ejected more than 30 000 years ago. The Crab can be glimpsed in small telescopes, but larger instruments are needed to bring out the filaments of gas forming the Veil.

Our Galaxy

The Sun is a member of the Galaxy, a huge, spiral-shaped star system containing at least 100 000 million stars. The Galaxy has three main regions: the *central bulge*, *disk* and *halo*. The densest part of the bulge is known as the *nucleus*. The bulge itself contains old Population II stars together with small amounts of interstellar material, and has a diameter of 20 000 light years and a thickness of 10 000 light years.

In contrast to the central bulge, the disk contains much younger Population I stars, many of them in open clusters. The disk also contains much more interstellar material than the central bulge. The disk is about 100 000 light years in diameter, the Sun being roughly two-thirds of the way from the centre to the edge, and about 3000 light years thick, although this varies somewhat across its width. The stars in the disk travel around the galactic centre in orbits that are more or less circular. Stars and gas closer to the centre orbit more quickly than those further out; the Sun, about 30 000 light years from the centre, takes around 220 million years to complete one orbit.

The halo takes the form of a spherical volume of stars surrounding the central bulge. Most of the stars of the halo are collected into globular clusters, which travel around the galactic centre in elliptical paths. The stars within the halo are very old; like the stars in the central bulge they are Population II objects, poor in heavy elements.

Interstellar extinction restricts the range at which stars can be observed along the plane of the Galaxy. The centre of the Galaxy, located in the direction of the constellation Sagittarius, is not visible optically, but observation at radio and infrared wavelengths has enabled astronomers to probe the galactic centre and to map the overall structure of the Galaxy. The galactic centre has been identified with the strong radio source Sagittarius A. The distribution of hydrogen clouds reveals that the galactic disk has a spiral structure, and that most of the Population I stars and the gas in the galactic disk are grouped into spiral arms radiating from the nucleus. In the arms, new stars are still being born from interstellar clouds.

The *Milky Way* is composed of thousands of millions of stars in the galactic disk, and may be seen as a great ring of faint light, extending right round the celestial sphere and inclined at about 63° to the plane of the ecliptic. It is brightest in Cygnus and Aquila (northern hemisphere) and in Scorpius and Sagittarius (southern hemisphere), and faintest in Monoceros. The Coalsack is the most prominent of the many 'gaps' in the Milky Way, which are dark nebulae close to the galactic plane lying between us and the star clouds beyond.

Lying close to the Galaxy are two dwarf irregular galaxies – the *Large* and *Small Magellanic Clouds*. They are visible in the southern hemisphere as extensive, nebulous naked-eye objects and are, in fact, satellites of the Galaxy itself. The Large Magellanic Cloud is the closest external galaxy, lying at a distance of around 160 000 light years, on the Dorado–Mensa border. The Small Magellanic Cloud lies at a distance of about 200 000 light years in Tucana.

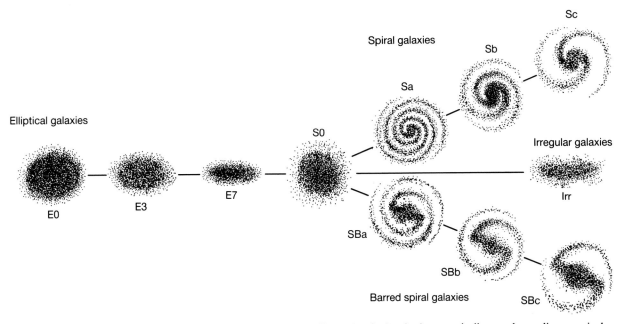

Figure 27. The classification of galaxies. This diagram is sometimes called the 'tuning-fork' diagram; it does not represent an evolutionary sequence.

Galaxies

The Galaxy is by no means unique in the Universe, and within the range of present-day telescopes lie thousands of millions of galaxies beyond our own. The best-known example of an external galaxy is the galaxy in Andromeda (M31), which is visible to the naked eye under good conditions as a faint misty patch of light. The Andromeda Galaxy is larger than our own and also has a spiral structure; it lies at a distance of around 2.2 million light years.

Although both the Milky Way Galaxy and M31 are spirals, not all galaxies have spiral structure. There are several different types of galaxy, classified as shown in Figure 27.

Elliptical galaxies are highly symmetrical systems which possess no spiral or other structure. They are denoted by E and a number from 0 to 7 to indicate the shape, which ranges from spherical (E0) to highly flattened (E7). The E0 type galaxies resemble huge globular clusters. Elliptical galaxies are deficient in interstellar matter, and the most massive ellipticals are considerably more massive than our own Galaxy. Dwarf ellipticals are denoted by the prefix d, and supergiant ellipticals by the prefix c.

Normal spiral galaxies. Like our own, these galaxies have spiral arms containing stars, gas and dust which extend from a central nucleus. They are classified as Sa, Sb or Sc according to the relationship between the nuclear bulge and the spiral arms. An Sa system has a relatively large central bulge and tightly wound spiral arms; Sb systems have more or less equally prominent spiral arms and nuclear regions; Sc galaxies possess small nuclear masses and loose, open spiral arms. S0 galaxies, known as lenticular galaxies, are an intermediate type between elliptical and spiral galaxies.

Barred spiral galaxies are similar to the ordinary spirals, except that the spiral arms emanate from each end of a luminous bar of material which straddles the nucleus. They are classified similarly to the spirals as SBa, SBb or SBc.

Irregular galaxies have no ordered structure and in many ways resemble large star clouds; most are lower in mass than our own Galaxy. They are denoted by I or Irr.

Active galaxies and quasars. A small percentage of galaxies have unusually bright centres, apparently the result of activity around a central, massive black hole. Examples are Seyfert galaxies and BL Lac objects.

Seyfert galaxies, named after the American astronomer Carl Seyfert who discovered them in 1943, are spiral galaxies. The brightest of them, at ninth magnitude, is M77 in Cetus. *BL Lac objects* are named after their prototype, BL Lacertae, which was originally classed as an unusual 15th-magnitude variable star; they are thought to be giant elliptical galaxies.

Quasars, also known as quasi-stellar objects (QSOs), are objects of star-like appearance, each giving out as much energy as hundreds of entire galaxies from a volume of space no bigger than our Solar System. Their red shifts show that they lie far off in the Universe, the most distant of them being beyond the known galaxies. There is now considerable evidence that quasars are the highly active centres of spiral galaxies. They may therefore be thought of as extreme forms of Seyfert galaxies. The brightest quasar is the 13th-magnitude 3C 273 in Virgo.

Clusters of galaxies. Most galaxies belong to clusters, groups of galaxies containing anything from a few to several thousand members. Our own Galaxy is a member of the *Local Group*, a collection of around 30 galaxies including at least two other spirals (M31 and M33), the Magellanic Clouds, and numerous dwarf elliptical and irregular systems (Table 51).

Table 51. The Local Group of galaxies.

Galaxy	RA 2000.0 h m	Dec ° '	Integrated magnitude	Type	Distance (kpc)
Andromeda Galaxy (M31)	0 42.7	+41 16	3.4	Sb	730
Milky Way				Sb/Sc	
Triangulum Galaxy (M33)	1 33.9	+30 39	5.7	Sc	900
Large Magellanic Cloud	5 23.6	−69 45	0.1	Irr	50
IC 10	0 20.4	+59 18	10.3	Irr	1300
Small Magellanic Cloud	0 52.7	−72 50	2.3	Irr	60
NGC 205 (M110)	0 40.4	+41 41	8.0	E6	730
NGC 221 (M32)	0 42.7	+40 52	8.2	E2	730
NGC 6822 (Barnard's Galaxy)	19 44.9	−14 48	9	Irr	520
NGC 185	0 39.0	+48 20	9.2	dE0	730
NGC 147	0 33.2	+48 30	9.3	dE4	730
IC 1613	1 04.8	+2 07	9.3	Irr	740
WLM System	0 02.0	−15 28	10.9	Irr	1600
Leo A (Leo III)	9 59.4	+30 45	12.6	Irr	2300
Fornax Dwarf Galaxy	2 39.9	−34 32	8	dE3	130
IC 5152	22 02.9	−51 17	11	Irr	1500
Pegasus Dwarf Galaxy	23 28.6	+14 45	12.0	Irr	1300
Sculptor Dwarf Galaxy	0 59.9	−33 42	10	dE3	85
Leo I	10 08.4	+12 18	9.8	dE3	230
Andromeda I	0 45.7	+38 00	13.2	dE0	730
Andromeda II	1 16.4	+33 27	13	dE0	730
Andromeda III	0 35.4	+36 31	13	dE2	730
Aquarius Dwarf Galaxy	20 46.9	−12 51		Irr	1500
Sagittarius Dwarf Galaxy	19 30.0	−17 41	15	Irr	1100
Leo II (Leo B)	11 13.5	+22 10	11.5	dE0	230
Ursa Minor Dwarf Galaxy	15 08.8	+67 12	12	dE6	75
Draco Dwarf Galaxy	17 20.2	+57 55	11	dE3	80
LGS 3	1 03.8	+21 53	15	Irr	900
Carina Dwarf Galaxy	6 41.6	−50 58		dE	170

Source: A. Hirshfeld and R. W. Sinnott (eds.), *Sky Catalogue 2000.0*, Vol. 2 (Sky Publishing Corp./Cambridge University Press, 1985).

There are many other clusters of galaxies scattered throughout space, one of the nearest being the Virgo Cluster, about 50 million light years away. Both the Local Group and the Virgo Cluster are members of a much larger grouping known as the Local Supercluster, centred on the Virgo Cluster, and containing many of the other nearby clusters as well as a number of individual galaxies.

The recession of the galaxies. All the galaxies outside the Local Group show red shifts in their spectra, indicating that they are receding from us. Furthermore, the velocity of recession of the galaxies is proportional to their distance, a relationship established in the late 1920s by Edwin Hubble and known as *Hubble's law*. The constant relating the velocity of recession to the distance is *Hubble's constant, H*. Currently accepted values of H range from 50 to 100 km s^{-1} per megaparsec. Hubble's law means that a galaxy's distance from us can be determined from its red shift.

The recession of the galaxies is usually interpreted as a general expansion of the Universe, which leads to several theories of the origin and evolution of the Universe:

The *steady-state theory* assumes that new matter is formed in the space between the receding galaxies and that the Universe is infinite in space and time. The theory was first put forward in the late 1940s; modern research has led to it being rejected.

According to the *Big Bang theory*, the Universe came into being at an instant in time, currently estimated at between 10 000 and 20 000 million years ago. Before then, the entire Universe – not just matter but all of space, time and radiation – was concentrated into an intensely hot, superdense state which the Big Bang explosion flung violently outwards. The present expansion of the Universe is thought to be a result of that event.

The *oscillating Universe* is a variation on the Big Bang theory in which the expansion we see today will eventually cease, and a contraction phase will commence. This process continues so that there is an ongoing cycle of Big Bangs, a continual expansion and contraction of the Universe. There is, however, no evidence that the current expansion of the Universe will cease.

Observing deep-sky objects

Star clusters, nebulae and galaxies present some of the most interesting (and popular) targets for amateur astronomers. Many thousands of these objects are within the grasp of small to medium telescopes, although locating them can often be a problem. One way is to use what is sometimes called the 'drift method', whereby a star with virtually the same declination as the object being sought, but a little west of it, is brought into the field of view. Note how many minutes of arc the object is to the east of the star, then leave the telescope stationary so that the sky drifts across the field of view for the required time until the object appears. This method, as well as calling for some patience, requires a convenient star.

Another method is to use setting circles. However, for portable telescopes this is unsatisfactory: too much time may be spent setting up the telescope mounting and, unless the alignment is more or less precise, the object may still not appear in the field of view.

By far the best method is to 'star-hop' to the object being sought. Wide fields of view are best for this and, once a fairly bright nearby star has been located, the observer can literally 'hop' from one star to another, eventually reaching the target. Once an object has been observed several times, it becomes much easier to locate again without the aid of star charts.

A good finder is essential for observing deep-sky objects, particularly when star-hopping. Before looking for deep-sky objects it is important to get your eyes dark-adapted. Also, clear, moonless nights are greatly preferred. Generally, low magnification coupled with a wide field of view is essential for deep-sky observing since, in many cases, the object being observed is either large or faint – or both.

Open clusters can make good targets for small telescopes, and binoculars can reveal many objects of this type to good effect. Because the stars in open clusters are spread out, a wide field of view is essential. This is even more important when it comes to trying to pick out an open cluster against a bright starry background.

Globular clusters, although containing more stars, are much more compact and generally appear as faint, diffuse objects. A higher magnification can help to bring out the brightest individual stars in the cluster. With globulars, experiment with different magnifications and fields of view.

Some diffuse nebulae, such as the Orion Nebula (M42), can be observed with either high or low magnification, although many are large and faint, contrasting little with the surrounding sky. Averted vision may be useful here. The nebula may reveal itself more readily if the telescope is swept back and forth across the area of sky. Both these techniques can help to enhance the contrast between the nebula and the sky. Higher magnifications may be needed to exclude the glare from nearby bright stars when seeking out certain nebulae. The same general rules apply to galaxies as to nebulae.

Low to medium magnifications can be used with planetary nebulae, which are generally small and relatively distinct. With very low powers certain planetary nebulae can appear distinctly star-like, and can be difficult to identify straight away.

One of the biggest problems facing the deep-sky observer is light pollution. To combat this, special filters (often referred to as *nebula filters*) are available. Different types can be obtained to suit different classes of deep-sky object, and their use can greatly enhance the contrast between the object and the background sky. They do this by effectively blocking certain parts of the spectrum which are light-polluted while at the same time allowing through the light from the nebula.

APPENDIX

UNITS AND NOTATION

The International System of Units (SI) has been established by worldwide agreement as a common standard for all scientific disciplines. Astronomers, however, still work with a mixture of incompatible units, many of them unique to astronomy.

The International Astronomical Union (IAU) is responsible for setting standards within astronomy. At its General Assembly in 1988, the IAU strongly urged that only SI units should be used, together with a few other units recognized for use in astronomy. The units and notation described in this section follow the recommendations of the IAU and the Royal Society, tempered by the conventions of current usage.

The International System of Units

In the SI system there are seven *base units* and two dimensionless *supplementary units*, listed in Table 52.

For every physical quantity there is an SI *derived unit* that can be formed from simple combinations of the base and supplementary units. For example, the SI unit of area is the square metre, written m^2, and the unit of velocity is the metre per second, written either m/s or m s^{-1} (the latter is preferred). A small number of derived units are given special names and symbols. The SI unit of force, for example, is the newton (N), defined as $1\,\mathrm{N} = 1\,\mathrm{kg\,m\,s^{-2}}$.

Any SI unit can be modified by a prefix indicating a decimal multiple of the unit (Table 53). The prefixes may also be attached to certain units which are not part of SI. Examples are $10^{-9}\,\mathrm{m} = 1$ nanometre $= 1\,\mathrm{nm}$; $10^3\,\mathrm{m} = 1$ kilometre $= 1\,\mathrm{km}$; $10^6\,\mathrm{pc} = 1$ megaparsec $= 1\,\mathrm{Mpc}$. Note that although the kilogram is the unit of mass, prefixes are attached to the symbol g (gram) and not to kg (e.g. Mg, not kkg).

Practical units used in astronomy

Few of the SI units are commonly used in astronomy. It is more usual to work with a mixture of units traditional to astronomy and units derived from the obsolescent c.g.s. system (centimetre, gram, second) which preceded SI. Table 54 lists some of the more common named units used in astronomy, and shows how they are related to the corresponding SI units. The magnitude system, for measuring the brightness of stars, is dealt with on pages 132 to 135; the various systems of time used in astronomy are discussed on pages 45 to 58. In complex calculations it is often helpful to reduce all quantities to SI units to lessen the risk of conversion errors. Some conversion factors are given in Table 55.

Table 52. Names and symbols for the SI base and supplementary units.

Physical quantity	Name of unit	Symbol
Base units		
Length	metre	m
Mass	kilogram	kg
Time	second	s
Electric current	ampere	A
Thermodynamic temperature	kelvin	K
Luminous intensity	candela	cd
Amount of substance	mole	mol
Supplementary units		
Plane angle	radian	rad
Solid angle	steradian	sr

Table 53. Prefixes for use with SI units. The multiples enclosed in brackets are no longer recommended.

Multiple	Prefix	Symbol	Multiple	Prefix	Symbol
[10^{-1}	deci-	d]	[10	deca-	da]
[10^{-2}	centi-	c]	[10^2	hecto-	h]
10^{-3}	milli-	m	10^3	kilo-	k
10^{-6}	micro-	μ	10^6	mega-	M
10^{-9}	nano-	n	10^9	giga-	G
10^{-12}	pico-	p	10^{12}	tera-	T
10^{-15}	femto-	f	10^{15}	peta-	P
10^{-18}	atto-	a	10^{18}	exa-	E

Table 54. Named units commonly used in astronomy.

Physical quantity	Name of unit (symbol)[a]	Relation to SI unit[b]	Notes and astronomical usage
Length	metre (m)	(SI unit)	More common to use cm or km
	astronomical unit (AU, au)[c]	$1\,\mathrm{AU} \equiv 1.495\,978\,70 \times 10^{11}\,\mathrm{m}$	Astronomical unit of length;[d] approximately the semi-major axis of the Earth's orbit. Mainly Solar System work
	parsec (pc)	$1\,\mathrm{pc} = 3.0857 \times 10^{16}\,\mathrm{m}$	*Parallax sec*ond (distance at which 1 AU subtends an angle of 1″). Mainly stellar and galactic distances. Also kpc, Mpc, Gpc
	light year (l.y.)[c]	$1\,\mathrm{l.y.} = 9.4605 \times 10^{15}\,\mathrm{m}$	Distance traversed in one year by electromagnetic waves in free space. Mainly popular writing
	solar radius ($R_\odot$)	$1\,R_\odot = 6.960 \times 10^{8}\,\mathrm{m}$	Mainly in astrophysics
	angstrom (Å)	$1\,\text{Å} \equiv 10^{-10}\,\mathrm{m}$	Optical wavelengths, atomic and molecular dimensions. Giving way to the nanometre ($10^{-9}\,\mathrm{m}$). Non-IAU
	micron (μm, μ)	$1\,\mu\mathrm{m} \equiv 10^{-6}\,\mathrm{m}$	Common name for the micrometre. (The non-IAU symbol μ is obsolete)
Time[e]	second (s)	(SI unit)	Also ms, μs, ns
	minute (min, m)	$1\,\mathrm{min} \equiv 60\,\mathrm{s}$	The symbol m can be used where there is no risk of confusion with metre
	hour (h, hr)	$1\,\mathrm{h} \equiv 60\,\mathrm{min} \equiv 3600\,\mathrm{s}$	
	day (d)	$1\,\mathrm{d} \equiv 24\,\mathrm{h} \equiv 86\,400\,\mathrm{s}$	Astronomical unit of time[d]
	year (yr, y, a)	$1\,\mathrm{y} \equiv 365.25\,\mathrm{d}$ $= 3.1558 \times 10^{7}\,\mathrm{s}$	Julian year, unless otherwise specified. The symbol 'a' is recommended but rarely used
Mass	kilogram (kg)	(SI unit)	More common to use gram (g). Prefixes must be attached to g, not kg
	solar mass unit ($M_\odot$)	$1\,M_\odot \equiv 1.9891 \times 10^{30}\,\mathrm{kg}$	Astronomical unit of mass[d]
Thermodynamic temperature	kelvin (K)	(SI unit)	Origin of scale is absolute zero, i.e. $0\,\mathrm{K} \equiv -273.15°\mathrm{C}$. As a unit of temperature difference, it is identical to the degree Celsius
Angle (or 'distance' on the celestial sphere)	radian (rad)	See Table 55 (SI unit)	$1/2\pi$ of a circle. Also mrad
	second of arc (″, arcsec)	$1'' \equiv 4.8481 \times 10^{-6}\,\mathrm{rad}$	
	minute of arc (′, arcmin)	$1' \equiv 60'' = 2.9089 \times 10^{-4}\,\mathrm{rad}$	
	degree (°, deg)	$1° \equiv 60' = 1.7453 \times 10^{-2}\,\mathrm{rad}$	
Solid angle (or 'area' on the celestial sphere)	steradian (sr)	(SI unit)	$1/4\pi$ of a sphere
	square degree (deg²)	$1\,\mathrm{deg}^2 = 3.0462 \times 10^{-4}\,\mathrm{sr}$	
Frequency	hertz (Hz)	$1\,\mathrm{Hz} \equiv 1\,\mathrm{s}^{-1}$ (SI unit)	Formerly known as 'cycle per second', c/s. Also kHz, MHz, GHz
Force	newton (N)	$1\,\mathrm{N} \equiv 1\,\mathrm{kg\,m\,s}^{-2}$ (SI unit)	About the weight of an apple
	dyne (dyn)	$1\,\mathrm{dyn} \equiv 10^{-5}\,\mathrm{N}$	C.g.s. unit, in decline. Non-IAU
Energy	joule (J)	$1\,\mathrm{J} \equiv 1\,\mathrm{N\,m}$ (SI unit)	Not yet common in astronomy
	erg (erg)	$1\,\mathrm{erg} \equiv 10^{-7}\,\mathrm{J}$	C.g.s. unit in widespread use. Non-IAU
	electron-volt (eV)	$1\,\mathrm{eV} = 1.6022 \times 10^{-19}\,\mathrm{J}$	Energies of photons and particles. Also keV, MeV
Power	watt (W)	$1\,\mathrm{W} \equiv 1\,\mathrm{J\,s}^{-1}$ (SI unit)	Also kW, MW
	erg per second (erg s⁻¹)	$1\,\mathrm{erg\,s}^{-1} \equiv 10^{-7}\,\mathrm{W}$	C.g.s. unit in widespread use. Non-IAU
	solar luminosity ($L_\odot$)	$1\,L_\odot = 3.90 \times 10^{26}\,\mathrm{W}$	Bolometric luminosity of the Sun (radiated power over all wavelengths). Astrophysics
Pressure	pascal (Pa)	$1\,\mathrm{Pa} \equiv 1\,\mathrm{N\,m}^{-2}$ (SI unit)	Not yet common in astronomy
	bar (bar)	$1\,\mathrm{bar} \equiv 10^{5}\,\mathrm{Pa}$	Also mbar (or mb). Non-IAU
	atmosphere (atm)	$1\,\mathrm{atm} \equiv 101\,325\,\mathrm{Pa}$	International standard atmosphere. Non-IAU
	torr (Torr)	$1\,\mathrm{Torr} \equiv 1/760\,\mathrm{atm} = 133.32\,\mathrm{Pa}$	Formerly millimetre of mercury (mmHg)
Spectral flux density	jansky (Jy)	$1\,\mathrm{Jy} \equiv 10^{-26}\,\mathrm{W\,m}^{-2}\,\mathrm{Hz}^{-1}$	Radio astronomy. Also mJy
Magnetic flux density	tesla (T)	$1\,\mathrm{T} \equiv 1\,\mathrm{V\,s\,m}^{-2}$ (SI unit)	Not yet common in astronomy
	gauss (G)	$1\,\mathrm{G} \equiv 10^{-4}\,\mathrm{T}$	C.g.s. unit in widespread use. Non-IAU

Units marked 'non-IAU' the IAU recommends should no longer be used in astronomy.

[a] Where more than one symbol is given, they are generally in order of preference.

[b] The identity sign ≡ means 'exactly equal to, by definition'; the equals sign = means 'equal to' (to the accuracy given).

[c] Abbreviation; there is no standard international symbol.

[d] This unit is defined in the IAU (1976) System of Astronomical Constants which was adopted for ephemerides in 1984; see the *Astronomical Almanac* for a full list.

[e] See pages 45–58 for a full discussion of the systems of time used in astronomy.

Table 55. Some conversion factors.

1 inch (in.) ≡ 25.4 mm
1 foot (ft) ≡ 12 in ≡ 0.3048 m
1 yard (yd) ≡ 3 ft ≡ 0.9144 m
1 mile (mi) = 1.6093 km
1 UK nautical mile ≡ 6080 ft = 1.8532 km
1 international nautical mile ≡ 1.852 km
1 mi h^{-1} = 0.477 04 m s^{-1}
1 litre (l) ≡ 10^{-3} m^3
1 ounce (oz) = 28.350 g
1 pound (lb) ≡ 16 oz = 0.453 592 kg
1 ton (ton) ≡ 2240 lb = 1016.0 kg
1 tonne (t) ≡ 1000 kg
1 parsec (pc) = 3.2616 l.y. = 206 265 AU
1 light year (l.y.) = 0.3066 pc = 63 240 AU

Temperature conversions

$T(°C) ≡ T(K) - 273.16 ≡ [T(°F) - 32]/1.8$
$T(°F) ≡ 1.8T(°C) + 32 = 1.8T(K) - 459.67$
$T(K) ≡ T(°C) + 273.16 = T(°F)/1.8 + 255.37$

The sign ≡ means 'exactly equal to, by definition'.

Table 56. Some astronomical constants.

Constant	Symbol and value
Speed of light	$c = 299\,792\,458\,\text{m s}^{-1}$
Gaussian gravitational constant	$k = 0.017\,202\,098\,95$
Constant of gravitation	$G = 6.672 \times 10^{-11}\,\text{N m}^2\,\text{kg}^{-2}$
Astronomical unit	$A = 1.495\,978\,70 \times 10^{11}\,\text{m}$
Light time for unit distance	$\tau_A = 499.004\,782\,\text{s}$
Solar parallax	$\pi_\odot = 8''.794\,148$
Mass of the Sun	$M_\odot = 1.9891 \times 10^{30}\,\text{kg}$
Heliocentric gravitational constant	$GM_\odot = 1.327\,124\,38 \times 10^{20}\,\text{N m}^2\,\text{kg}^{-1}$
Mass of the Earth	$M_\oplus = 3.003\,490 \times 10^{-6}\,M_\odot$
	$= 5.9742 \times 10^{24}\,\text{kg}$
Geocentric gravitational constant	$GM_\oplus = 3.986\,005 \times 10^{14}\,\text{N m}^2\,\text{kg}^{-1}$
Equatorial radius of the Earth	$a_c = 6\,378\,140\,\text{m}$
Flattening factor of the Earth	$f = 0.003\,352\,81 = 1/298.257$
Mass of the Moon	$M_\text{☾} = 0.012\,300\,02\,M_\oplus$
	$= 7.3483 \times 10^{22}\,\text{kg}$

At standard epoch 2000.0

Obliquity of the ecliptic	$\epsilon = 23° 26' 21''.448$
General precession in longitude	$\rho = 50''.290\,966\,\text{yr}^{-1}$
Constant of nutation	$N = 9''.2025$
Constant of aberration	$\kappa = 20''.495\,52$

The units for other astronomical quantities, which may not have special names, can be constructed from appropriate combinations of the units in Table 54. For example, density can be measured in kg m^{-3} (SI), g cm^{-3} (c.g.s.) or $M_\odot$ pc^{-3}; Hubble's constant is conventionally measured in units of km s^{-1} Mpc^{-1}.

Note that the unit symbols are not abbreviations and should not be given full stops: so 5 km, not 5 km. or 5 k.m., and 100 Mpc, not 100 M.p.c. Similarly, the letter s should not be added to the symbol to form a plural: three parsecs is written 3 pc, not 3 pcs.

Writing numbers

Very large or very small numbers are best written in *exponential notation*, i.e. in the form $a \times 10^b$, where a is a number between 1 and 10, and b is an integer (whole number). For example, the mass of the electron is 9.11×10^{-31} kg, the velocity of light 2.998×10^8 m s^{-1}.

Where there are more than four significant figures, digits may be grouped in threes from the decimal point for clarity. Commas should not be used for this purpose as the comma is the symbol for a decimal point in most European countries. For example: 12345.678901 km can be written 12 345.678 901 km, but not 12,345.678901 km.

A leading decimal point should be preceded by a zero for clarity: 0.1234, not .1234.

Errors and uncertainties

Every measurement has an uncertainty, or error, which is often denoted by a ± (plus or minus) sign; for example, a distance of 5.34 ± 0.25 kpc. Care should be taken in the interpretation of the error. Unless stated otherwise, the quantity following the ± is assumed to be a *standard error* (s.e.), such that the probability of the true value being in that range is about 68%. (An earlier convention was to quote a *probable error* (p.e.) such that the probability was 50%.) But it is often not possible to estimate an accurate standard error, and the figure may be just a rough indication of the uncertainty.

ASTRONOMICAL CONSTANTS

In 1976 the IAU adopted a consistent set of constants to be used in astronomical computations. The IAU (1976) System of Astronomical Constants came into effect in 1984. Although values of individual constants will become better known as techniques of measurement improve, astronomers should keep to the IAU (1976) System in the interests of consistency. Table 56 lists a selection of constants derived from the IAU (1976) System. A full list is given every year in the *Astronomical Almanac*.

The constant of gravitation, G, is the least well-determined of the fundamental physical constants, with an uncertainty of 1 part in 6000. It follows that the masses of the Sun and all other astronomical bodies have a similar uncertainty. Fortunately, the product GM can be determined with a much greater precision than either G or M alone, and for this reason the constants $GM_\odot$ and $GM_\oplus$ should be used for computing heliocentric and geocentric orbits. Similarly, the ratio of two masses, e.g. $M_\oplus/M_\odot$, can be measured more accurately than can the individual masses.

SYMBOLS AND ABBREVIATIONS

Abbreviations and symbols used in this book or commonly encountered in the astronomical literature (see also Tables 52, 53 and 54).

a	semi-major axis; altitude
A	azimuth; extinction
ADS	Aitken double star catalogue
b	galactic or heliocentric latitude
B_0	heliographic latitude of the centre of the Sun's disk
BC	bolometric correction
c	speed of light
CM	central meridian
c.p.m.	common proper motion
D	aperture (of a telescope)
dec.	declination
e	eccentricity
ET	Ephemeris Time
f	following
F	focal length
g	acceleration due to gravity
GHA	Greenwich hour angle
GMT	Greenwich Mean Time
GST	Greenwich sidereal time
h	altitude
HR	Hertzsprung–Russell (diagram)
i	inclination
IC	Index Catalogue
JD	Julian date
l	galactic or heliocentric longitude
L_0	heliographic longitude of the centre of the Sun's disk
L	luminosity
LHA	local hour angle
LST	local sidereal time
m	apparent magnitude
m_{bol}	apparent bolometric magnitude
m_{pg}	apparent photographic magnitude
m_{pv}	apparent photovisual magnitude
m_v	apparent visual magnitude
m_V	photometric visual magnitude
M	absolute magnitude; magnification; mass
M	Messier catalogue
MJD	modified Julian date
NGC	New General Catalogue
p	preceding
P	period; position angle
PA	position angle
q	perihelion distance

Q	aphelion distance
r	radius vector (i.e. distance from Sun in AU)
RA	right ascension
t	time
T	time of perihelion passage (in an orbit)
T_c	colour temperature
T_{eff}	effective temperature
TAI	International Atomic Time
TDT	Terrestrial Dynamical Time
UT	Universal Time
UTC	Coordinated Universal Time
z	zenith distance
ZHR	zenithal hourly rate
α	right ascension
β	celestial latitude
δ	declination
Δ	geocentric distance, in AU. When used with a suffix it means a correction, as in ΔT
ϵ	obliquity of the ecliptic
λ	wavelength; longitude
μ	proper motion
ν	frequency
π	parallax
τ	light travel time
ϕ	latitude
ω	argument of perihelion
ϖ	longitude of perihelion
Ω	longitude of the ascending node
♈	first point of Aries (vernal equinox)
♎	first point of Libra (autumnal equinox)
☊	ascending node
☋	descending node
○	full moon
●	new moon
O or ◐	gibbous moon
◐ or ☽	first quarter
◑ or ☾	last quarter
★	star
☉	Sun
⊕ or ♁	Earth
☿	Mercury
♀	Venus
♂	Mars
♃	Jupiter
♄	Saturn
♅ or ♅	Uranus
♆ or ♆	Neptune
♇	Pluto

USEFUL ADDRESSES

Royal Astronomical Society, Burlington House, Piccadilly, London W1V 0NL, U.K.

British Astronomical Association, Burlington House, Piccadilly, London W1V 9AG, U.K.

Junior Astronomical Society, 36 Fairway, Keyworth, Nottingham NG12 5DU, U.K.

Federation of Astronomical Societies, c/o Christine Sheldon, Whitehaven, Maytree Road, Lower Moor, Pershore, Worcestershire WR10 2NY, U.K.

Irish Astronomical Association, The Planetarium, Armagh BT61 9DB, Northern Ireland, U.K.

Astronomisches Büro, Hasenwertgasse 32, 1238 Wien, Austria.

Koninklijt Sterrenkundig Genootschap van Antwerpen, Boerhaavestraat 94 Bus 1, 2008 Antwerpen, Belgium.

Astronomisk Selskab, Observatoriet, Øster Voldgade 3, 1350 København K, Denmark.

Ursa Astronomical Association, Laivanvarustajankatu 3, 00140 Helsinki, Finland.

Société Astronomique de France, 3 rue Beethoven, 75016 Paris, France.

Unione Astrofili Italiani, c/o P. Cinzano, Via Garibaldi 38, 35016 Thiene, Italy.

Nederlandsche Vereniging voor Weer en Sterrenkunde, Bureau 'De Koepel', Sterrenwacht Sonnenborg, Zonnenburg 2, 3512 Utrecht, The Netherlands.

Norsk Astronomisk Selskap, Postboks 677, 4001 Stavanger, Norway.

Svenska Astronomiska Sallskapet, Stockholms Observatorium, 133 00 Saltsjöbaden, Sweden.

Schweizerische Astronomische Gesellschaft, c/o Andreas Tarnutzer, Hirtenhofstrasse 9, 6005 Luzern, Switzerland.

Vereinigung der Sternfreunde, Volkssternwarte, Anzinger Strasse 1, 8000 München 80, F.R. Germany.

Astronomical League, 6235 Omie Circle, Pensacola, FL 32504, U.S.A.

Astronomical Society of the Pacific, 390 Ashton Avenue, San Francisco, CA 94112, U.S.A.

American Astronomical Society, 2000 Florida Avenue NW, Suite 300, Washington, DC 20009, U.S.A.

American Association of Variable Star Observers, 25 Birch Street, Cambridge, MA 02138, U.S.A.

Association of Lunar and Planetary Observers, 8930 Raven Drive, Waco, TX 76712, U.S.A.

Society of Amateur Radio Astronomers, c/o John Weiss, PO Box 2632, Montgomery, AL 36105, U.S.A.

Royal Astronomical Society of Canada, McLaughlin Planetarium, 100 Queens Park, Toronto, Ontario, Canada M5S 2C6.

British Astronomical Association, New South Wales Branch, PO Box 103, Harbord, New South Wales 2096, Australia.

National Association of Planetary Observers, PO Box 2, Riverwood, New South Wales 2210, Australia.

Royal Astronomical Society of New Zealand, PO Box 3181, Wellington, New Zealand.

Astronomical Society of South Africa, South African Astronomical Observatory, PO Box 9, Observatory 7935, South Africa.

Sky Observers Association, 155 Fuk Wing Street, 4th Floor, Room 6, Shamshuipo, Kowloon, Hong Kong.

Oriental Astronomical Association, c/o Yamamoto Observatory, 289 Kamitanakami-Kiryutyo otu, Sigaken 520-21, Japan.

European Space Agency, 8–10 rue Mario Nikis, 75738 Paris, France.

National Aeronautics and Space Administration, NASA Headquarters, Washington, DC 20546, U.S.A.

Magazines

Sky & Telescope, PO Box 9111, Belmont, MA 02178–9111, U.S.A.

Astronomy, 1027 N. Seventh Street, Milwaukee, WI 53233, U.S.A.

Astronomy Now, 193 Uxbridge Road, London W12 9RA, U.K.

Southern Astronomy, PO Box 976, Bondi Junction, Sydney, New South Wales 2022, Australia.

GLOSSARY

aberration a defect in an optical system. There are six main types: in *chromatic aberration*, which occurs in lenses, coloured fringes appear around objects; *spherical aberration* is a blurring of the image caused when the inner and outer parts of a lens or mirror have different focal lengths; in *astigmatism*, the star image is focused into an ellipse or a cross; *coma* produces elongated images towards the edge of the field of view; *curved field* results when the focal plane of a lens or mirror is not flat; *distortion* is caused by a difference in magnification between the centre and edge of the field, bowing straight lines either outwards (*barrel distortion*) or inwards (*pincushion distortion*).

aberration of starlight a slight displacement in the observed position of a star, caused by the motion of the Earth in orbit around the Sun.

absorption lines dark lines crossing a spectrum, caused by absorption of certain wavelengths of light by cooler gas. All stars have absorption lines in their spectra because light leaving their surfaces passes through cooler gas in their outer layers. Absorption lines can also be produced by gas between us and the stars.

achromatic referring to a lens that has been corrected for chromatic aberration. An achromatic lens actually consists of two separate lenses, called *elements*, that together cancel out the worst effects of chromatic aberration.

airglow a faint background light in the night sky given out by gases in the ionosphere. The sky can therefore never be completely dark as seen from the surface of the Earth.

Airy disk the disk into which the image of a star is spread by diffraction in a telescope. The size of the disk limits the resolution of a telescope: the larger the aperture, the smaller the Airy disk. It is named after the seventh English Astronomer Royal, Sir George Airy, who calculated its size in 1834. In a refracting telescope nearly 84% of the light from a star goes into the Airy disk, the remainder forming faint diffraction rings around the Airy disk. In telescopes with central obstructions, such as the secondary mirrors in reflecting telescopes, more of the light is diverted from the Airy disk into the surrounding diffraction rings.

albedo the proportion of incoming light that is reflected by a surface, such as that of a planet or moon. A dark surface has a low albedo, while a light surface has a high albedo. The albedo of a planet usually differs from place to place, so for practical purposes the mean albedo is used. Planets with rocky surfaces such as Mercury and Mars have low albedos, while those covered with cloud, such as Jupiter and Venus, have high albedos. Albedo can be expressed in two ways: *spherical albedo* assumes that the body is a sphere with a diffuse surface reflecting incoming parallel light in all directions; *geometrical albedo* compares the reflectance of the planet with a flat white surface of the same diameter as the planet placed at the same position.

alidade a simple instrument for measuring altitudes of celestial bodies above the horizon. In its most basic form the alidade consists of a sighting device attached to a plumb-line that swings freely from the centre of a protractor or similar scale. The altitude of an object can be found from the angle of the plumb-line against the scale.

almanac a book containing timetables of celestial events and predicted positions of celestial objects, usually issued annually.

almucantar a circle on the celestial sphere parallel to the horizon; it is a line of equal altitude, since all objects on an almucantar at a given time are at the same angle above the horizon.

angular diameter the apparent size of a celestial object, usually expressed in degrees, minutes and seconds of arc.

angular distance the apparent distance between two objects on the celestial sphere, such as two stars, usually expressed in degrees, minutes and seconds of arc.

ansae the parts of Saturn's rings that appear like handles on each side of the planet. Singular *ansa*.

apochromat a lens consisting of three or more elements that gives a greater reduction in chromatic aberration than is possible with a normal achromatic (two-element) lens.

apparition the period of time during which a celestial body is well placed for observation, such as an evening apparition of Venus or the apparition of a periodic comet. The word is not used for bodies such as the Moon which are continually visible.

appulse the apparent close approach between two celestial bodies, such as two planets or a planet and a star.

apsides the points in an orbit at which two bodies are closest together (*periapsis*) and farthest apart (*apoapsis*). The line joining these points is called the *line of apsides*, and is the major axis of the orbit.

arc (measure of) angles on the celestial sphere are measured in degrees, minutes and seconds of arc. The terms *arc minute* and *arc second* are used to distinguish these measures from units of time. There are 60 arc minutes in a degree, and 60 arc seconds in an arc minute.

asterism a grouping of stars in the sky larger than a cluster but smaller than a constellation, e.g. the Plough in Ursa Major.

astrometry the branch of astronomy concerned with the precise measurement of the positions of objects on the celestial sphere.

auroral oval a ring of permanent, quiet auroral activity that surrounds the north and south magnetic poles of the Earth. Normally the ovals are fairly narrow and lie about 2000 km from the geomagnetic poles. Under disturbed conditions, though, particularly following solar flares, the ovals expand towards the equator and become broader, most markedly on the side away from the Sun. It is during these expansions that observers at lower latitudes see aurorae.

barycentre the centre of mass, or balance point, of a pair of bodies such as a double star or a moon and planet, around which the two bodies orbit.

Big Bang the hypothetical event that is presumed to have marked the origin of the Universe as we know it. The Universe has been expanding since the Big Bang, which is estimated to have occurred between 10000 million and 20000 million years ago.

black body a hypothetical object that is both a perfect absorber of radiation falling on it and a perfect emitter of radiation. Black-body radiation is the spectrum of light and other radiation that would be emitted by a black body at a given temperature.

black hole a volume of space in which gravity is so great that nothing can escape, not even light – hence it is truly black. Black holes are thought to be produced when very massive stars collapse at the end of their life.

Bode's law a series of numbers that roughly describes the average distances of the planets from the Sun in astronomical units, out as far as Uranus. Take the numbers 0, 3, 6, 12, etc., doubling at each step. Add 4 to each number and divide by 10. Table 57 gives the results, compared with the

Table 57. Bode's law.

Planet	Distance (AU) Bode's law	Actual
Mercury	0.4	0.39
Venus	0.7	0.72
Earth	1.0	1.0
Mars	1.6	1.5
Ceres	2.8	2.8
Jupiter	5.2	5.2
Saturn	10.0	9.5
Uranus	19.6	19.2
Neptune	38.8	30.1
Pluto	77.2	39.5

actual mean distances of the planets. The 'law' breaks down for Neptune and Pluto. The German astronomer Johann Bode drew attention to the relationship in 1772, although it had already been pointed out by his countryman Johann Titius; for this reason it is sometimes called the Titius–Bode law.

captured rotation rotation such that a body spins on its axis in the same time as it takes to orbit another body, so that it keeps one face permanently turned towards the object it is orbiting. Our Moon has a captured rotation, as do many moons of other planets. Captured rotation is brought about by tidal forces.

central meridian (CM) the imaginary north–south line bisecting the disk of a planet, used as a reference for estimating the longitude of planetary features as the planet rotates. The passage of a feature across the central meridian is called a *central meridian transit*.

collimation the act of lining up the optical components of an instrument, such as the mirrors in a reflecting telescope. In spectroscopes the collimator is a lens used to produce a parallel beam of light.

coma (cometary) the cloud of gas and dust, roughly spherical in shape, that makes up the head of a comet. At the centre of the coma is the comet's nucleus, from which the gas and dust escapes. A comet's coma can be between 10000 and 100000 km in diameter.

coma (optical) a flaring of star images towards the edge of the field of view.

comes the companion of a double star (plural *comites*).

commensurable an expression used of orbital periods (e.g. of two moons) that are in proportion to one another by exact fractions such as one-half, one-third or three-quarters.

continuous spectrum a spectrum that consists of an unbroken rainbow of colours, as distinct from a spectrum crossed by dark absorption lines or one that consists of emission lines.

continuum a continuous spectrum (q.v.).

coronal hole a cooler and less dense part of the Sun's corona, through which the fastest part of the solar wind flows.

cosmic rays atomic particles that are moving through space at close to the speed of light. They are mostly protons (the nuclei of hydrogen atoms), although the nuclei of most elements are present in small numbers, and also electrons. Some low-energy cosmic rays come from flares on the Sun, but higher-energy cosmic rays are believed to come from outside the Solar System, probably from supernovae and their remnants. The highest-energy cosmic rays of all seem to come from distant galaxies and quasars.

cosmology the study of the origin and evolution of the Universe.

coudé focus a focal point in a reflecting telescope in which the light is reflected out of the telescope tube along the polar axis of the mounting to a fixed observing position. The coudé focus has the advantage that it does not move as the telescope turns, and so heavy equipment such as large spectrographs can be mounted there.

cryogenic referring to ultra-low temperatures, as needed to liquefy gases. Cryogenic cooling is used to reduce background noise and hence increase the sensitivity of certain instruments. The liquid gases are kept in an insulated flask known as a *cryostat*.

cusp one of the two 'horns' of the crescent Moon or of a planet in crescent phase.

Cynthian adjective referring to the Moon.

Cytherean adjective referring to Venus.

deep sky that part of space beyond the Solar System. Deep-sky objects include star clusters, nebulae, galaxies, double stars and variable stars.

defect of illumination the apparent width of the unilluminated section of a planet's disk as seen from the Earth, usually expressed in seconds of arc. For example, if a planet has an apparent diameter of 10 arcsec and a phase of 80%, its defect of illumination would be 2 arcsec.

dichotomy the moment when the Moon, Mercury or Venus is exactly half-illuminated as seen from the Earth.

differential rotation the rotation of a body in which different parts spin at different speeds; for example, a gaseous planet or a star spins faster at the equator than at the poles.

diffraction the slight bending of light around the edge of an object; light of long wavelengths is diffracted more than light of short wavelengths. This effect is utilized in a *diffraction grating*, a series of closely spaced lines (usually thousands per centimetre) ruled on a piece of glass or metal, that spreads light out into a spectrum. Diffraction gratings are commonly used in spectroscopes. See also Airy disk.

disk the face of a planet, moon or star as seen from the Earth.

dispersion the spreading out of light into a spectrum, as in a spectrograph. The highest dispersions give the best resolution of features in the spectrum.

diurnal daily.

Doppler effect a change in the wavelength of light caused by the motion of the object emitting the light. If the object is moving towards us the wavelengths are shortened, i.e. moved towards the blue end of the spectrum; this is termed a *blue shift*. If the object is receding its light is lengthened in wavelength, i.e. moved towards the red end of the spectrum; this is termed a *red shift*. The amount of shift is revealed by the position of lines of known wavelength in the object's spectrum.

doublet a two-element lens, designed to reduce chromatic aberration.

dwarf star any star on the main sequence of the Hertzsprung–Russell diagram. The Sun is a dwarf star, but many such stars are actually larger than the Sun. The term is also applied to white dwarfs (q.v.), which are not on the main sequence.

early-type star a hot star of spectral type O, B or A.

eccentricity (*e*) a measure of how non-circular an orbit is. The eccentricity of an ellipse ranges between 0 (a circle) and 1 (a parabola). Eccentricity is calculated by dividing the distance between the two foci of the ellipse by the length of the major axis.

element, optical an optical component, such as a mirror, lens or prism. Usually the term is applied to a lens that makes up part of a more complex lens, e.g. a doublet is a lens with two elements, and a triplet is a three-element lens. The additional elements are introduced to correct the aberrations that are present in a single lens.

elongation the angle between the Sun and a planet, or between a planet and a satellite, as seen from the Earth. Elongation is measured along the ecliptic in degrees west or east of the Sun.

emersion the re-emergence of an object after an eclipse or occultation.

emission lines specific wavelengths of light (or other forms of electromagnetic radiation) given out by atoms of a gas. An *emission spectrum* is a spectrum consisting of bright emission lines, for example as produced by the gas of a nebula. Emission lines can appear as bright lines superimposed on a continuous spectrum if given out by hot gas surrounding a star.

ephemeris a table of the predicted positions of a celestial object such as the Moon, the Sun or a planet. Plural *ephemerides*.

epoch an instant in time, such as the beginning or middle of a year, for which positions of stars, orbital elements and other information are given. Since the coordinates of stars are constantly changing because of precession, star positions are referred to a *standard* or *fundamental epoch*. Currently the standard epoch used by astronomers is 2000 January 1, 12h (also written as 2000.0).

equation in astronomy, either a difference between two values or a correction, as for instance in the *equation of time* (difference between mean and apparent solar time) or a *personal equation* (correction for personal error when measuring or timing something).

escape velocity the speed at which any object, from a rocket to a gas molecule, must move to break away permanently from the gravitational pull of a body. For the Earth, the escape velocity at the surface is $11.2\,\mathrm{km\,s^{-1}}$; for the Moon it is $2.4\,\mathrm{km\,s^{-1}}$.

exit pupil the image that an eyepiece forms of a telescope's objective lens or mirror; the higher the magnification of the eyepiece, the smaller the diameter of the exit pupil. In order to see the telescope's full field of view, the pupil of the eye must be brought up to the exit pupil of the eyepiece.

extinction the dimming of starlight by dust in space or by the Earth's atmosphere. Extinction is greater for blue light than it is for red, causing a reddening of starlight. Atmospheric extinction is least at the zenith, where it amounts to a few tenths of a magnitude under clear skies, and increases towards the horizon (see Table 49, on p. 154).

extrapolation the technique of extending a series of figures in order to estimate an additional value beyond the given range.

field star a star in the same field of view as an object under study, but which lies at a different distance and hence has no connection with it, for example foreground stars in the same field of view as a distant galaxy.

first contact the beginning of an eclipse. At a solar eclipse, it is when the Moon starts to move across the face of the Sun; at a lunar eclipse it is when the Moon enters the Earth's umbra.

focal length the distance between a lens or mirror and the point at which it brings parallel light rays to a focus.

focal plane the flat surface at which a lens or mirror forms an image. Some optical systems, notably the Schmidt telescope, form their images on a curved surface known as the *focal surface*.

focal ratio the focal length of a telescope divided by its aperture. For example, a 150 mm telescope of 1200 mm focal length has a focal ratio of *f*/8.

focus (optical) the point at which light rays are concentrated by a lens or mirror to form an image.

focus (of an ellipse) one of the two points whose position determines the eccentricity of an elliptical orbit; plural *foci* (usually pronounced foe-sigh). The two foci lie on the major axis of the ellipse, either side of its centre; the farther apart they are, the greater the eccentricity of the ellipse. The object being orbited lies at one of the foci; the other focus is empty.

following objects move across the sky from east to west because of the rotation of the Earth, so the more easterly of a pair of stars, for example (or the easterly side of a planet), is said to be following. The term is also used of features moving across the face of a body as it rotates, such as sunspots, or spots on Jupiter. The other side is described as preceding (q.v.).

fourth contact the end of an eclipse. At a solar eclipse it is when the Moon moves completely off the face of the Sun; at a lunar eclipse it is when the Moon leaves the Earth's umbra.

frequency (ν) the number of waves passing a fixed point in a given time, usually one second. Frequency is measured in hertz, and is equal to the speed of the waves divided by their wavelength. Hence the longer the wavelength, the lower the frequency, and the shorter the wavelength, the higher the frequency.

fundamental star a star whose position is determined as precisely as possible, and against which the positions of other stars can be compared. The positions of fundamental stars are published in *fundamental catalogues*.

galactic cluster another name for an open star cluster in our Galaxy, so called because they lie in the spiral arms of the Galaxy rather than in the halo around the Galaxy, where the globular clusters lie.

gamma rays radiation of the shortest wavelengths, 0.01 nanometres and less, shorter even than X-rays.

giant star a star that is swelling up in size as it approaches the end of its life. Giant stars have similar masses to normal stars such as the Sun, but they are larger in diameter and considerably more luminous.

gibbous the phase of the Moon or a planet when it is between half and fully illuminated.

Gould's Belt a band of young, brilliant stars at an angle of between 15° and 20° to the plane of our Galaxy, stretching around the sky from Perseus, Taurus and Orion, via Carina, to Centaurus and Scorpius. Gould's Belt is believed to be a spur on the local spiral arm of our Galaxy.

great circle a circle that divides a sphere into two equal hemispheres. On the celestial sphere, a great circle has the Earth at its centre; examples are the celestial equator, the ecliptic and lines of right ascension. Compare small circle.

green flash an effect caused by atmospheric refraction and absorption in which the last visible segment of the setting Sun turns green, sometimes followed by a green ray like a vertical flame at the instant of setting. The phenomenon lasts for only a few seconds, and is best seen over the sea or a distant horizon when the air is clear (i.e. when there is little reddening of the setting Sun). A similar effect can occasionally be seen as the Sun rises.

greenhouse effect the warming of a planet by the trapping of solar radiation in a planet's atmosphere. The greenhouse effect acts particularly strongly on Venus, raising its temperature to very high levels; it operates to a lesser effect in the atmospheres of other planets.

heavy elements in astronomy, all chemical elements heavier than hydrogen and helium; sometimes termed 'metals'.

heliacal rising the occasion on which a star or planet first appears in the dawn sky, after having been too close to the Sun to be visible.

heliacal setting the last occasion on which a star or planet can be seen in the evening sky before it becomes too close to the Sun to be visible.

immersion the entry of a celestial object into a shadow at an eclipse, or the covering of an object at an occultation.

inclination (*i*) the angle at which an orbit is tilted with respect to a plane of reference. For objects orbiting the Sun the inclination is given relative to the plane of the Earth's orbit; for objects orbiting the Earth, relative to the Earth's equator; and for double stars, relative to the plane of the sky. The axial inclination of a body is the angle at which its axis of rotation is tilted to the perpendicular to the plane of its own orbit.

infrared radiation with wavelengths longer than visible red light but shorter than radio waves, i.e. between about 700 nanometres and 1 millimetre.

interferometer a device in which radio or optical waves collected by two or more apertures are combined to give improved resolution, such as for separating two closely spaced objects.

interpolation the technique of estimating a value intermediate between two of a range of given values, for instance the position of a planet on a date between two dates tabulated in an ephemeris.

inverse-square law the law which states that the energy received from a source falls off with the inverse square of the distance of the source. For example, a star twice as far away as another identical star appears four times fainter, three times away it appears nine times fainter, and so on. Forces, including gravity, obey the same law.

ion an atom or molecule that has lost one or more electrons (a *positive ion*) or has gained one or more electrons (a *negative ion*).

ionization the process by which electrons are added to or removed from an atom or molecule, so turning it into an ion.

irradiation the optical effect in which a bright object seen against a dark background appears larger or brighter than it actually is.

Kirkwood gaps regions of the asteroid belt, corresponding to particular distances from the Sun, where few asteroids are found. The gaps are caused by Jupiter's gravity, which perturbs asteroids out of orbits whose period is an exact fraction of Jupiter's orbital period.

Lagrangian points five places at which small bodies can exist in stable orbits in the plane of two much larger bodies. Three of the points lie on a line joining the two large bodies (one point between the two bodies, and the other two points on either side of them). The two other Lagrangian points lie 60° ahead of and behind one of the larger bodies in its orbit around the other; it is at these places in the orbit of Jupiter that the Trojan asteroids are found. Objects cannot exist permanently at the three other Lagrangian points of Jupiter's orbit because they would be perturbed by the gravitational pulls of the other planets.

late-type star a cool star of spectral type K, M, C or S.

light curve a graph of the changing brightness of an object such as a variable star, or a planet or moon as it rotates.

light, speed of light travels at $299\,792.5\,\mathrm{km\,s^{-1}}$ (often rounded to $300\,000\,\mathrm{km\,s^{-1}}$) in a vacuum; this is the fastest speed in the Universe. All other forms of electromagnetic radiation, from X-rays and gamma rays to radio waves, travel at the same speed.

light-time the time taken for a beam of light to travel from a celestial body to the Earth. The effect must be taken into account when timing the occurrence of events such as eclipses of the moons of Jupiter, whose times of occurrence are affected by the distance between Jupiter and the Earth.

limb the apparent edge of the disk of a celestial body as seen from the Earth; regions near the visible edge of the Moon are called limb regions. The leading limb of an object crossing the sky as the Earth rotates is called the *preceding limb*; the trailing limb is called the *following limb*.

local standard of rest a volume of space extending out to about 100 parsecs from the Sun in which the velocities of all stars relative to the Sun average out to zero.

lunation the time taken by a complete cycle of phases of the Moon, such as from one full moon to the next. A lunation lasts 29.53 days; it is the same as a synodic month.

magnetosphere the extension of the Earth's magnetic field into space. The magnetosphere is like a magnetic bubble around the Earth. The Van Allen radiation belts lie within the magnetosphere. Other bodies with magnetic fields also have magnetospheres. The boundary of the magnetosphere is called the *magnetopause*.

magnification the amount by which an optical instrument makes an object appear larger. For example, if a line appears ten times longer when viewed through a telescope, the telescope is said to magnify ten times. The magnification of a telescope depends on the instrument's focal length and on the focal length of the eyepiece in use; eyepieces of shorter focal length produce higher magnifications on a given telescope. Magnification can be calculated by dividing the focal length of the telescope by the focal length of the eyepiece. A magnification of, say, ten is written in the form ×10.

major axis the longest diameter of an ellipse, passing through the two foci of the ellipse.

mean the average of a series of values.

meteor the streak of light, lasting no more than a second or so, produced when a speck of dust from space (a meteoroid) burns up in the Earth's atmosphere, usually at a height of about 100 km.

meteorite a chunk of rock or iron from space that reaches the surface of the Earth or any other body. Large meteorites can produce craters when they hit the ground. Most meteorites are thought to be chips from asteroids, but some fragile stony meteorites called carbonaceous chondrites may come from the nuclei of comets.

meteoroid any small solid object in space. When a meteoroid enters the Earth's atmosphere at high speed it produces a meteor.

Metonic cycle the period of 19 calendar years (6939.6 days) after which the Moon's phases recur on the same day of the year. There are 235 lunations in a Metonic cycle.

minor axis the shortest diameter of an ellipse, at right angles to the major axis.

mock Sun an effect caused by ice crystals in the Earth's atmosphere, which refract the Sun's light so that two diffuse areas of light occur either side of the Sun, 22° from it. These mock Suns, also known as *parhelia* or *sundogs*, usually appear on the rim of a halo surrounding the Sun.

neutron star a tiny, very dense star composed of neutrons. Neutron stars have diameters of only about 20 km, but contain the mass of up to three Suns; if the neutron star had a mass greater than three Suns, gravity would cause it to collapse still further into a black hole. Neutron stars are believed to be left behind after massive stars explode as supernovae at the end of their life; in the explosion, the protons and electrons of the star's core are squeezed together to form neutrons.

node the point at which an orbit crosses a given plane, such as the plane of the Earth's orbit or the Earth's equator. There are two nodes: the *ascending node* (Ω), when the orbiting body moves from south to north, and the *descending node* ($\mho$) when the body moves from north to south. The *line of nodes* is the straight line joining these two nodes. *Regression of the nodes* is the westward movement of the nodes of an orbit caused by the gravitational pull of other bodies, notably the Sun.

oblateness a measure of the amount by which a rotating object such as a star or planet departs from a perfectly spherical shape. Rotation causes the equatorial regions of a sphere to bulge outwards slightly, so that the sphere appears slightly flattened at the poles; hence oblateness is also known as polar flattening. Oblateness is calculated by taking the difference between the equatorial and polar diameters of the object, and dividing by the equatorial diameter. Saturn has the greatest oblateness of any planet in the Solar System, 0.1.

occulting bar a bar that may be moved into the focal plane of an eyepiece so as to obscure a bright object and allow a nearby faint object to be observed.

paraboloid a surface that is curved like a parabola. Main mirrors in telescopes are usually paraboloids, since a paraboloid is free from spherical aberration.

parhelion a mock Sun (q.v.).

penumbra the lighter, outer part of a sunspot or shadow. From within the penumbra of the Moon's shadow, a partial eclipse of the Sun is visible. When the Moon is within the penumbra of the Earth's shadow it is said to be *penumbrally eclipsed*; but the Earth's penumbral shadow is so faint that in practice a penumbral eclipse is scarcely noticeable.

period the interval between the successive occurrences of a cyclical event, such as the time taken for a body to rotate once on its axis or go once around its orbit, or for a variable star to go through one cycle of brightness variations.

perturbation a slight disturbance of the motion of one body caused by the gravitational pull of other bodies.

phase the proportion of the sunlit side of the Moon or a planet that is visible from Earth. Mercury and Venus go through a complete cycle of phases similar to those of the Moon. The outer planets show phases only from gibbous to full, being most gibbous at quadrature.

phase angle the angle between the Sun, a given object and the observer. When the phase angle is 180° the Sun and the object lie in opposite directions, and the object appears fully illuminated. At a phase angle of 0° the Sun and the object are in line, and the sunlit side of the object is turned away from the observer.

photometry the calculation and measurement of the brightness of an object; a device that does this is called a *photometer*. Photometry is often carried out at several wavelengths to determine the colour of a star or other object under study, in order to determine its temperature and to reveal other information about its nature.

photon the behaviour of light in some situations is best explained by assuming that it is not a wave motion, but a stream of particles. A photon is the name given to such a particle (of light or of other electromagnetic radiation).

planisphere a circular map with a rotating mask that can be turned to show the stars as they appear from a given latitude at any time on any date.

population index (r) in meteor astronomy, a factor that describes how the number of meteors goes up with decreasing brightness. For example, if there are n meteors in the magnitude interval m to $m + 1$, there are rn between magnitudes $m + 1$ and $m + 2$, r^2n between $m + 2$ and $m + 3$, and so on. Over the naked-eye magnitude range, r is roughly constant. The exact value of r depends on the particular shower, but is usually in the range 2.2 to 2.5.

position angle the relative position of one object with respect to another, such as the two components of a double star or the position of a star around the Moon's limb at an occultation. Position angle is measured in degrees from north via east, south and west. On the celestial sphere, east is the direction towards the eastern horizon.

preceding term used to describe the side of a planet that leads in its motion across the sky, or of the leading member of a pair of objects such as stars or sunspots. The preceding side can easily be found by watching objects drift through the field of view of a telescope. Compare following.

primary the larger body of an orbiting pair (e.g. the Earth is the Moon's primary) or the brighter member of a binary star. Compare secondary.

prime focus the point at which the main mirror or objective lens of a telescope brings light to a focus, without the intervention of other optical components.

pulsar a star that, every few seconds or less, gives out a rapid flash of energy at radio and other wavelengths. Pulsars are believed to be rapidly rotating neutron stars (q.v.) that flash each time they spin, like a lighthouse beam.

quasar an object that looks like a star but which emits as much energy as hundreds of normal galaxies. Quasars have high red shifts, and hence must lie far off in the Universe. They are thought to be the bright centres of distant galaxies where matter is falling into a giant central black hole.

radiation belts belts of atomic particles trapped inside the magnetosphere of a planet. See also Van Allen belts.

radio astronomy the study of radio waves emitted naturally by objects in space. Radio waves are the longest-wavelength radiation, with wavelengths greater than 1 millimetre.

radius vector the imaginary line joining an orbiting body and the object it orbits.

red dwarf a star that is much smaller and cooler than the Sun. Red dwarfs have about one-tenth the mass of the Sun, and are about one-tenth its diameter.

red giant a large, cool star perhaps ten or more times the diameter of the Sun, produced when a normal star swells up near the end of its life.

red shift a lengthening in the wavelengths of light from a body, usually caused by the motion of the emitting body away from us (a Doppler shift), although a red shift can also be caused by the presence of strong gravitational fields. The red shift of galaxies is usually regarded as being directly related to their distance from us in the Universe – hence the greater the red shift, the more distant the galaxy.

refraction (atmospheric) the bending of light by the Earth's atmosphere which increases the apparent altitude of an object above the horizon. It ranges from zero at the zenith to approximately half a degree at the horizon.

residual the difference between observed and calculated values, such as of the position of a planet in its orbit.

retrograde motion of a body from east to west, the opposite of the prevailing direction of motion in the Solar System. The term retrograde can apply to either the orbital motion or the direction of spin of a planet or moon.

revolution the movement of one body in orbit around another, or around a centre of mass.

rotation the spin of a body on its own axis.

Saros the length of the cycle of solar and lunar eclipses: the period after which the Sun, the Moon and the nodes of the Moon's orbit return to almost the same relative positions. The Saros lasts 6585.32 days (just over 18 years) and contains 223 lunations.

scintillation twinkling (q.v.).

second contact the moment an eclipse becomes total. At a solar eclipse, it is when the Moon completely covers the face of the Sun; at a lunar eclipse, it is when the Moon becomes fully immersed in the Earth's umbra.

secondary a smaller body that orbits around a larger one (e.g. the Moon is the Earth's secondary) or the fainter member of a binary system. Compare primary.

secondary spectrum the slight colour fringing around an image in an achromatic lens, resulting from the fact that chromatic aberration cannot be completely eliminated, even by a two-element lens.

semi-major axis half the longest diameter of an ellipse. The semi-major axis is the average distance of a body, such as a planet, from the object it is in orbit around, such as the Sun.

setting circles scales marked on the polar and declination axes of an equatorially mounted telescope, by which the telescope can be pointed at an object whose coordinates are known.

sidereal to do with the stars. *Sidereal time* is time based on the rotation of the Earth with respect to the stars rather than with respect to the Sun; the *sidereal period* is the orbital period of a body with reference to a fixed star. Compare synodic.

small circle a circle that does not divide a sphere into two equal hemispheres, unlike a great circle (q.v.). On the celestial sphere, small circles do not have the Earth at their centre – for example, circles of declination (other than the celestial equator) are small circles.

solar wind the tenuous stream of atomic particles from the Sun that flows outwards through the Solar System.

spectral lines narrow lines that cross the spectrum of an object; the lines can be either bright (*emission lines*) or dark (*absorption lines*). Each line in the spectrum corresponds to a particular wavelength at which atoms absorb or emit light.

spectrum, visible the rainbow-like band of colours that is produced when light is split into its constituent wavelengths. Features in the spectrum, such as bright and dark lines, tell astronomers about the composition and motion of gas in the object under study.

spectroscope a device for taking the spectrum of an object. Spectroscopes use a prism or a diffraction grating to split light into a spectrum; usually the spectrum is then recorded by an electronic detector, in which case the device is known as a *spectrograph*. A spectroscope with good spectral resolution is said to have high dispersion; it spreads out the wavelengths of light more than a low-dispersion device, but the spectrum is fainter and requires a longer exposure time to be recorded.

supergiant star a star many times the mass of the Sun that is swelling up as it ages. Supergiants are the largest and brightest stars known. Many, perhaps all of them, eventually explode as supernovae.

synodic with respect to the Earth. For example, the *synodic period* of a planet is the time taken for it to return to the same position in the sky as seen from the Earth, and is hence the time between successive conjunctions or oppositions of a planet. The synodic period of the Moon is the time taken for it to go through one cycle of phases. A body's synodic period differs from its sidereal period as a result of the motion of the Earth in its own orbit around the Sun, because of which the body has to travel further to reach the same position as at the start of the period. Compare sidereal.

telluric to do with the Earth, e.g. telluric lines in a star's spectrum are a result of the passage of the star's light through the Earth's atmosphere.

terminator the dividing line between the illuminated and dark portions of a planet or satellite, particularly the Moon. The terminator is the sunrise or sunset line, the boundary between day and night.

third contact the moment when a total eclipse ends. At a solar eclipse, it is when the Sun starts to reappear from behind the Moon; at a lunar eclipse, it is when the Moon starts to emerge from the Earth's umbra.

topocentric as seen from a point on the surface of the Earth. The *topocentric coordinates* of a nearby body in space, such as the Moon, are slightly different from those that would be measured from the centre of the Earth (geocentric coordinates).

twinkling the flickering of a star's light caused by air currents in the Earth's atmosphere which distort the path of light rays, causing the star to change in apparent brightness and to flash different colours, particularly when close to the horizon. Planets do not twinkle as much as stars, because they are not point sources, but under bad conditions even planets can twinkle, especially when low down. A large amount of twinkling is a sign of bad seeing.

ultraviolet radiation with wavelengths shorter than visible violet light but longer than X-rays, from about 10 to 400 nanometres.

umbra the dark central part of a sunspot or shadow. From within the umbra of the Moon's shadow, a total eclipse of the Sun is visible. The Moon is totally eclipsed when it is completely within the umbra of the Earth's shadow; when it is partly immersed in the Earth's umbra, it is partially eclipsed.

Van Allen belts two doughnut-shaped zones of atomic particles around the Earth. The Van Allen belts consist of electrons and protons trapped inside the Earth's magnetosphere.

wavelength (λ) the distance between a given point on one wave to the same point on the next wave. The wavelength of light is usually measured in either nanometres or angstroms (an angstrom is one-tenth of a nanometre). Wavelength is equal to the speed of the wave divided by its frequency – hence high-frequency waves have a short wavelength, and vice versa.

white dwarf a tiny, hot star that is the end-point in the life of stars like the Sun. A typical white dwarf contains as much mass as the Sun compressed into a ball not much larger than the Earth. They cool with age, so the oldest of them are not actually white. The easiest white dwarf to observe is a member of the triple-star system Omicron-2 (o^2) Eridani.

X-rays radiation with wavelengths shorter than ultraviolet light but longer than gamma rays, between about 0.01 and 10 nanometres.

Zeeman effect the splitting of spectral lines into two or more parts by a magnetic field.

zodiac the band of 12 constellations through which the Sun passes each year: Aries, Taurus, Gemini, Cancer, Leo, Virgo, Libra, Scorpius, Sagittarius, Capricornus, Aquarius and Pisces.

Electromagnetic Spectrum Chart

Introduction

We live in a sea of waves. Not the usual type of water waves that we are used to, but a sea of electromagnetic waves. Some of these waves go through us, others bounce off us, while others pass by us as if we never existed. These waves are partly electric waves and partly magnetic waves. The electric and magnetic waves travel together, mutually regenerating each other, at a speed of 186,000 miles per second in a vacuum.

All electromagnetic waves are produced when an electric charge starts or stops moving. If you wiggle or vibrate an electric charge, you will produce an electromagnetic wave. How fast you wiggle the charge determines the wave's frequency, or number of times a wave wiggles each second; and its wavelength, or the distance between wave crests.

To help you picture waves, you can try the following experiment (at least in your head, if not for real). Attach an elastic string to a wall and pull it taut. If you move your hand up and down really fast, you make waves along the string that are closely spaced (high frequency and short wavelength). You can also wiggle it slowly and make widely spaced waves (low frequency and long wavelength). Electromagnetic waves can be made with fast vibrations and short waves or with slow vibrations and long waves. It depends on how fast the electric charge is wiggled.

The Electromagnetic Spectrum Chart shows the vast range of frequencies and wavelengths of electromagnetic waves that we encounter. Moving outward from the center of the chart is a series of arc-shaped bands which describe the electromagnetic waves.

Wavelength Scale

The innermost band is the wavelength scale. The waves are longest at the left, starting with a whopping 10,000,000,000 centimeters (10^{10}cm, or about ¼ the distance to the moon), and decreasing to a sub-atomic-sized .00000000000001 centimeters (10^{-14}cm) on the right.

Frequency Scales

These scales are directly related to the wavelength scale. Shorter waves are made by charges that vibrate more rapidly, and longer waves by charges vibrating more slowly. The first (white) frequency band gives the rate of vibration in cycles per second or Hertz (Hz). This is simply the number of times that the wave wiggles each second. The second (blue) band shows the frequency in commonly used units. Note that for the higher frequencies, the frequency unit has been changed to an energy unit (electron volts). This is because electromagnetic waves seem to act more like energetic particles than like waves at these frequencies. These particles are called "photons."

How Are They Made?

This band gives a few of the many devices that science and technology provide to produce the various types of electromagnetic waves.

General Name

This wide band breaks the electromagnetic spectrum into broad regions. There are no sharp boundaries between regions, and they blend from one to another.

Specific Name

Each broad category is broken into more specific areas, each with its own designation.

The Electromagnetic Spectrum Chart is produced by the Exploratorium with information provided by Westinghouse Corp. and is available from:

The Exploratorium Store

3601 Lyon Street, San Francisco, CA 94123

Other Interesting Sections of the Chart

Radio and Microwave Usage

The left side of the chart is given over to a display of the uses of the radio and microwave regions of the spectrum. The blue bands indicate the frequencies allocated to the purpose indicated. Note, for instance, that the frequencies allocated to television broadcasting are broken into 3 bands: channel 2 to 6, 7 to 13 (both called "VHF" for "Very High Frequency"), and 14 to 83 (called "UHF" for "Ultra-High Frequency"). Notice also that all of the FM radio stations broadcast at frequencies between channels 6 and 7!

Black Body Curves

Above visible light there are three bands with two bell-shaped curves sitting on top. Whenever a solid body is above absolute zero (zero degrees Kelvin or -273°C), its vibrating molecules give off electromagnetic radiation. The hotter the object, the faster the molecules move, and the waves given off become shorter. The two bell-shaped curves show how much of each frequency is given off by two objects at different temperatures. For example, at 20°C (room temperature), more radiation is given off with a wavelength of 10 microns (infrared) than any other. This is the peak wavelength or "wavelength of the radiation center" (top band). This 20°C body gives off four-hundredths of a watt of radiation for every square centimeter of surface area (bottom band). The surface of the sun is at a temperature of 6000 degrees Kelvin, and its peak wavelength is in visible green light. Our eyes have evolved to use the wavelengths most efficiently produced by the sun. These wavelengths make up the narrow band of electromagnetic radiation called visible light.

Emission Spectra

Above the black body curves is a chart that gives the principal wavelengths of radiation emitted by atoms of various elements in an excited gaseous state. Many thousands of the weaker emission lines are not shown.

Atmospheric Absorption Bands

Above the chart of emission spectra is a band that shows what frequencies of electromagnetic radiation are absorbed by the earth's atmosphere and the process or substance responsible for the absorption. Ozone (O_3) blocks dangerous ultraviolet.

X-Ray and Gamma-Ray Absorption

This graph shows the amount of a substance required to absorb or shield 63% of the incident X-rays and gamma-rays as a function of the wavelength. Notice that as the wavelength becomes shorter, the amount of shielding needed increases.

Conclusion

Whether the frequency is high or low, all electromagnetic waves travel at 186,000 miles per second. Notice that visible light only accounts for a very small range of possible frequencies of electromagnetic radiation. If you picture the range of frequencies in the electromagnetic spectrum as the notes on a piano, visible light would take up slightly less than an octave. (This is because blue light has a frequency that is almost double that of red light, and moving up an octave on a piano doubles the frequency.) The electromagnetic spectrum has such a huge range of frequencies that the piano would have not the normal eight octaves, but a mind-boggling 80 octaves. The Keyboard would be forty-two feet long with the "visible light" notes near octave number 52. This would truly be a grand piano! Explore the rest of the chart and discover what else lies in the vast range of frequencies covered here.

Electromagnetic Spectrum Chart Key

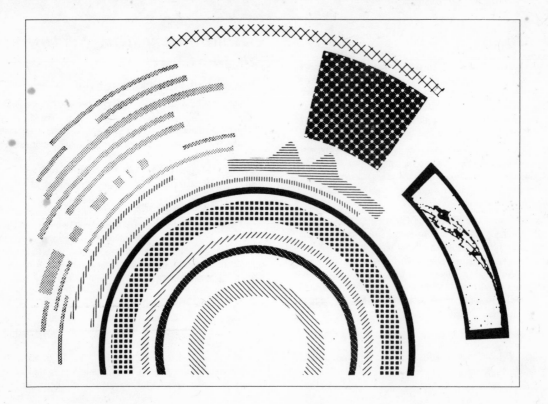

◩	Wavelength scale	▥	Radio & microwave usage
▨	Frequency scale	▤	Black body curves
◪	How are they made?	▦	Radio usage
▦	General name	▦	Emission spectra
■	Specific name	◈	Atmospheric ''windows''

INDEX